ORIGINAL JOURNALS

OF THE

LEWIS AND CLARK EXPEDITION

1804-1806

*WITH FACSIMILES, MAPS, PLANS, VIEWS, PORTRAITS, AND
A BIBLIOGRAPHY*

VOLUME THREE

PART I

*Journals and Orderly Book of Lewis and Clark, from the Shoshoni
Camp on Lemhi River to the Encampment on the Columbia
River near the Mouth of the Umatilla River
August 21, 1805 — October 20, 1805*

THOMAS JEFFERSON

From the original oil painting by Thomas Sully, in the possession
of the American Philosophical Society, Philadelphia

ORIGINAL JOURNALS

OF THE

LEWIS AND CLARK EXPEDITION

1804-1806

PRINTED FROM THE ORIGINAL MANUSCRIPTS
in the Library of the American Philosophical Society and
by direction of its Committee on Historical Documents

TOGETHER WITH

MANUSCRIPT MATERIAL OF LEWIS AND CLARK
from other sources, including Note-Books, Letters, Maps, etc.,
and the Journals of Charles Floyd and Joseph Whitehouse

NOW FOR THE FIRST TIME PUBLISHED IN FULL
AND EXACTLY AS WRITTEN

Edited, with Introduction, Notes, and Index, by

REUBEN GOLD THWAITES, LL.D.

Editor of " The Jesuit Relations and Allied Documents," etc.

VOLUME THREE

PART I

NEW YORK

DODD, MEAD & COMPANY

1905

THE UNIVERSITY PRESS
CAMBRIDGE, U. S. A.

To

THEODORE ROOSEVELT, LL.D.

PRESIDENT OF THE UNITED STATES

Upon the Hundredth Anniversary of the Departure of the
Trans-Mississippi Expedition of Lewis and Clark, this
first publication of the Original Records of
their "Winning of the West" is most
respectfully dedicated

MADISON, WISCONSIN
May 14, 1904

Original Journals of the
Lewis & Clark Expedition

Edited, with Introduction, Notes, and Index by
Reuben Gold Thwaites

As Published in 1904

Volume III, Parts 1 & 2

Vol. III, Parts 1 & 2 Trade Paperback ISBN: 1-58218-654-5
Vol. III, Parts 1 & 2 Hardcover ISBN: 1-58218-663-4

Digital Scanning and Publishing is a leader in the electronic republication of historical books and documents. We publish many of our titles as eBooks, as well as traditional hardcover and trade paper editions. DSI is commited to bringing many traditional and little known books back to life, retaining the look and feel of the original work.

©2001 DSI Digital Reproduction
First DSI Printing: February 2001

Published by DIGITAL SCANNING, INC.
Scituate, MA 02066
www.digitalscanning.com

Original Journals of the Lewis and Clark Expedition
Four Photographs supplied with permission by
Ernst Mayr Library of the Museum of Comparative Zoology
Harvard University, Cambridge, MA 02138
"Snags On the Missouri River" (Vol. 1 part 1)
"Winter Village of the Minatarres" Vol. 1 Part II)
"Fort Mackenzie" (Vol. II Part 1)
"Indians Hunting the Bison" (Vol. III, Part 1)

CONTENTS TO VOL. III

PART I

THE ORIGINAL JOURNALS OF CAPTAINS MERI-
WETHER LEWIS AND WILLIAM CLARK. *The Journals
Proper*

PAGE

CHAPTER XVI. — SEARCHING FOR NAVIGABLE WATERS 3
Lewis's Journal, August 21–26, 1805.
Clark's Journal, August 21–26.

CHAPTER XVII. — DOWN THE LOLO TRAIL 45
Clark's Journal, August 27—October 10, 1805.
Entries by Lewis, September 9, 10, 18–22.

CHAPTER XVIII. — THE RAPIDS OF THE SNAKE AND
COLUMBIA 107
Clark's Journal, October 11–20, 1805.

LIST OF ILLUSTRATIONS

Vol. III — Part I

Thomas Jefferson, from the original oil painting, by Thomas Sully, in the possession of the American Philosophical Society, Philadelphia . . . . *Frontispiece*

PAGE

Indian Utensils and Arms 4

Fish Weir (Lewis, text cut) 7

Indians Hunting the Bison 18

Upper Bitterroot Valley, Montana 56

Map from Clark Field-book, showing Course and Camping places, September 11, 12, 1805 62

Map from Clark Field-book, showing Course and Camping places, September 13–16, 1805 64

Map from Clark Field-book, showing Course and Camping places, September 16–18, 1805 70

Map from Clark Field-book, showing Course and Camping places, September 18–20, 1805 72

Map from Clark Field-book, showing Course and Camping places, September 20–October, 1805 78

Clark's Map showing Kooskooske and Kimooemen rivers (text cut) 102

Map by Clark, interwoven with entry for October 14, 1805 (text cut) 114

Map from Clark Field-book (apparently from a native sketch) locating Indian Tribes, opposite entry for October 15, 1804 116

Columbia River and its waters, showing Indian Fishing Establishments, sketch-map by Clark 118

[ix]

LIST OF ILLUSTRATIONS

PAGE

Map from Clark Field-book, showing Course and Camping places,
October 16–18, 1805 120

Junction of Columbia and Lewis's Rivers, sketch-map by Clark . 130

Map from Clark Field-book, showing Course and Camping place,
October 19, 1805 134

Map from Clark Field-book, showing Course and Camping place,
October 20, 1805 138

Map from Clark Field-book, showing position of Indian lodges,
and places of Encampment for October 20, and the return
journey, April 24, 1806 140

The Original Journals of Captains Meriwether Lewis and William Clark

THE JOURNALS PROPER

The ORIGINAL JOURNALS OF
LEWIS AND CLARK

CHAPTER XVI

SEARCHING FOR NAVIGABLE WATERS

Lewis's Journal, August 21–26, 1805
Clark's Journal, August 21–26

[Lewis :]   *Wednesday August 21ˢᵗ 1805.*

THIS morning was very cold. the ice ¼ of an inch
thick on the water which stood in the vessels exposed
to the air. some wet deerskins that had been spread
on the grass last evening are stiffly frozen. the ink f[r]eizes
in my pen. the bottoms are perfectly covered with frost, insomuch that they appear to be covered with snow. This
morning early I dispatched two hunters to kill some meat if
possible before the Indians arrive; Drewyer I sent with the
horse into the cove for that purpose. The party pursued
their several occupations as yesterday. by evening I had all
the baggage, saddles, and harness completely ready for a
march. after dark, I made the men take the baggage to the
cash and deposit it. I beleve we have been unperceived by
the Indians in this movement. notwithstanding the coldness
of the last night the day has proved excessively warm.
neither of the hunters returned this evening and I was obliged
to issue pork and corn. The mockersons of both sexes are
usually the same and are made of deer Elk or buffaloe skin
dressed without the hair. sometimes in the winter they make
them of buffaloe skin dressed with the hair on and turn the
hair inwards as the Mandans Minetares and most of the nations
do who inhabit the buffaloe country. the mockerson is formed
with one seem on the outer edge of the foot is cut open at the

[3]

instep to admit *the foot and sewed up behind. in this rispect they are the same with the Mandans.* they sometimes ornament their mockersons with various figures wrought with the quills of the Porcupine. some of the dressey young men orniment the tops of their mockersons with the skins of polecats and trale the tail of that animal on the ground at their heels as they walk. the robe of the woman is generally smaller than that of the man but is woarn in the same manner over the sholders. the Chemise is roomy and comes down below the middle of the leg the upper part of this garment is formed much like the shirt of the men except the sholder strap which is never used with the Chemise. in women who give suck, they are left open at the sides nearly as low as the waist, in others, close as high as the sleeve. the sleeve underneath as low as the elbow is open, that part being left very full. the sides tail and upper part of the sleeves are deeply fringed and sometimes ornimented in a similar manner with the shirts of the men with the addi-tion of little patches of red cloth about the tail edged around with beads. the breast is usually ornament[e]d with various figures of party colours rought with the quills of the Porcupine. it is on this part of the garment that they appear to exert their greatest engenuity. a girdle of dressed leather confines the Chemise around the waist. when either the man or the woman wish to disengage their arm from the sleeve they draw it out by means of the opening underneath the arm and throw the sleeve behind the body.[1] the legings of the women reach as high as the knee and are confined with a garter below. the mockerson covers and confins it's lower extremity. they are neither fringed nor ornamented. these legings are made of the skins of the antelope and the Chemise usually of those of the large deer Bighorn and the smallest elk. They seldom wear the beads they possess about their necks; at least I have never seen a grown person of either sex wear them on this part; some [of] their children are seen with them in this way.

---

1 The dresses of the women are a kind of shifts made of the skins of these goats and mountain sheep, which come down to the middle of the leg. Some of them have robes, but others none. Some of the men have shirts, and some are without any. Some also have robes made of beaver and buffaloe skins; but there are few of the former. I saw one made of ground[-]hog skins. — GASS (p. 179).

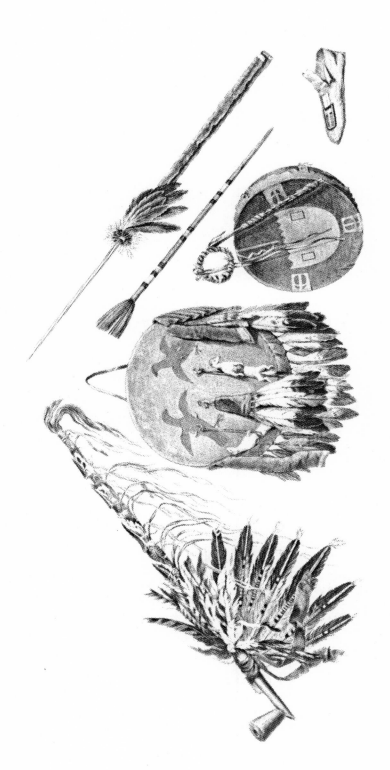

INDIAN UTENSILS AND ARMS

the men and women were [wear] them suspen[ded] from the
ear in little bunches or intermixed with triangular peices of the
shells of the perl oister.   the men also were them attached in
a similar manner to the hare of the fore part of the crown of
the head; to which they sometimes make the addition of the
wings and tails of birds.   the nose in neither sex is pierced nor
do they wear any ornament in it.   they have a variety of small
sea shells of which they form collars woarn indiscriminately by
both sexes.   these as well as the shell of the perl oister they
value very highly and inform us that they obtain them from
their friends and relations who live beyond the barren plain
towards the Ocean in a S. Westerly direction.   these friends
of theirs they say inhabit a good country abounding with Elk,
deer, bear, and Antelope, and possess a much greater number
of horses and mules than they do themselves; or using their
own figure that their horses and mules are as numerous as the
grass of the plains.   the warriors or such as esteem themselves
brave men wear collars made of the claws of the brown bear
which are also esteemed of great value and are preserved with
great care.   these claws are ornamented with beads about the
thick end near which they are peirced through their sides and
strung on a throng of dressed leather and tyed about the neck
commonly with the upper edge of the tallon next the breast or
neck but sometimes are reversed.   it is esteemed by them an act
of equal celebrity the killing one of these bear or an enimy, and
with the means they have of killing this animal it must really
be a serious undertaking.   the sweet sented grass which grows
very abundant on this river is either twisted or plaited and
woarn around the neck in ether sex, but most commonly by
the men.   they have a collar also woarn by either sex.   it [is]
generally round and about the size of a man's finger; formed
of leather or silk-grass twisted or firmly rolled and covered
with the quills of the porcupine of different colours.   the tusks
of the Elk are pierced strung on a throng and woarn as an orniment for the neck, and is most generally woarn by the women
and children.[1]   the men frequently wear the skin of a fox or

---

[1] This custom still prevails among some tribes.   An illustrated article in the
Chicago *Record-Herald* of Aug. 25, 1901, states that the writer visited an Indian

a broad strip of that of the otter around the forehead and head in form of a bando.   they are also fond of the feathers of the tail of the beautifull eagle or callumet bird with which they ornament their own hair and the tails and mains of their horses. also a collar of round bones which look like the joints of a fishes back   The dress of these people is quite as desent and convenient as that of any nation of Indians I ever saw.

This morning early Cap: C. resumed his march ; at the distance of five miles he arrived at some brush lodges of the Shoshones inhabited by about seven families.   here he halted and was very friendly received by these people, who gave himself and party as much boiled salmon as they could eat ; they also gave him several dryed salmon and a considerable quantity of dryed chokecherries.   after smoking with them he visited their fish wear [weir] which was abut 200 y^{ds} distant.   he found the wear extended across four channels of the river which was here divided by three small islands.   three of these channels were narrow, and were stoped by means of trees fallen across, supported by which stakes of willow were driven down sufficiently near each other to prevent the salmon from passing.   about the center of each a cilindric basket of eighteen or 20 feet in length terminating in a conic shape at it's lower extremity, formed of willows, was opposed to a small apperture in the wear with it's mouth up stream to receive the fish.   the main channel of the water was conducted to this basket, which was so narrow at it's lower extremity that the fish when once in could not turn itself about, and were taken out by untying the small ends of the longitudinal willows, which form the hull of the basket.   the wear in the main channel was somewhat differently contrived.   there were two distinct wears formed of poles and willow sticks, quite across the river, at no great distance from each other.   each of these, were furnished with two baskets ; the one wear to take them ascending and the other

village in southern Montana where it was estimated that 20,000 elk-teeth were in the possession of its inhabitants.   On a mother and child were counted 600 of these ornaments, and another woman had the estimated number of 1,500 on her garments. They were highly valued by the Indians, who would seldom part with them.   Three photographs of persons thus adorned were used to illustrate the article ; the negatives are in the possession of L. E. Cavalier, of St. Paul. — ED.

in decending. in constructing these wears, poles were first
tyed together in parcels of three near the smaller extremity;
these were set on end, and spread in a triangular form at the
base, in such manner, that two of the three poles ranged in the
direction of the intended work, and the third down the stream.
two ranges of horizontal poles were next lashed with willow
bark and wythes to the ranging poles, and on these willow
sticks were placed perpendicularly, reaching from the bottom
of the river to about 3 or four feet above it's surface; and
placed so near each other, as not to permit the passage of the
fish, and even so thick in some parts, as with the help of gravel
and stone to give a direction to the water which they wished.
the baskets were the same in form of the others. this is the

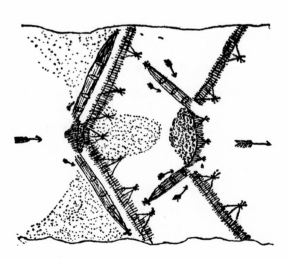

form of the work, and disposition of the baskets. After examining the wears Capᵗ C. returned to the lodges, and shortly
continued his rout and passed the river to the Larᵈ side a little
distance below the wears. he sent Collins with an Indian down

the Lar.ᵈ side of the river to the forks 5 M. in surch of Cruzatte who was left at the upper camp yesterday to purchase a horse and had followed on today and passed them by another road while they were at the lodges and had gone on to the forks. while Cap.ᵗ Clark was at these lodges an Indian brought him a tomehawk which he said he found in the grass near the lodge where I had staid at the upper camp when I was first with his nation. the tommahawk was Drewyer's he missed it in the morning before we had set out and surched for it but it was not to be found I beleive the young fellow stole it, but if he did it is the only article they have pilfered and this was now returned. Cap.ᵗ C. after traveling about 20 miles through the valley with the course of the river nearly N.W. encamped on the Star.ᵈ side in a small bottom under a high Clift of rocks. on his way one of the party killed a very large Salmon in a creek which they passed at the distance of 14 M.ˢ he was joined this evening by Cruzatte and Collins who brought with them five fresh salmon which had been given them by the Indians at the forks. the forks of this river is famous as a gig fishery and is much resorted [to] by the natives. They killed one deer today. The Guide apeared to be a very friendly intelligent old man, Cap.ᵗ C. is much pleased with him.

This day I observed Equal Altitudes of the ☉ with Sextant.

	h	m	s		h	m	s	
A.M.	8.	38.	36.	P.M.	4.	—.	56	Altitude at the time of
".		40.	8.	".		1.	34	observation.
".		42.	45.	".		3.	5.	65°. 57'. 30".

Also observed Meridian Alt.ᵈ of ☉'ˢ L.L. with Octant by the back observation. $\left.\right\}$ 72. —. —. (° ′ ″)

Latitude deduced from this observation. North. 44. 30. 21.7. (° ′ ″)

Mean Latitude of the Forks of Jefferson's river, deduced from three observations of the Meridian Alt.ᵈ of ☉'s L.L. with Octant, and one calculation by means of the hor: ∠ [angle] of the ☉'ˢ center in the P.M. observation for equal Altitudes on the 20.ᵗʰ Instant $\left.\right\}$ N. 44. 35. 28.1 (° ′ ″)

[Clark:]   *August 21ˢᵗ Wednesday 1805*

Frost last night   proceeded on with the Indians I met about
5 miles to there Camp,   I entered a lodge and after smokeing
with all who Came about me I went to see the place those
people take the fish, a wear across the Creek in which there is
Stuk baskets Set in different derections So as to take the fish
either decending or assending   on my return to the Camp
which was 200 'yards only the different lodges (which is only
bushes) brought in to the lodge I was introduced into, Sammon
boiled, and dried Choke Cherᵗ Sufficent for all my party.
one man brought me a *tomahawk* which we expected they had
Stolen from a man of Cap Lewis's party,   this man informed
me he found the tomaᵏ in the grass near the place the man
Slept.   Crossed the River and went over a point of high land
& Struck it again near a Bluff on the right Side ;   the man I
left to get a horse at the upper Camp missed me & went to
the forks which is about five miles below the last Camp.   I
sent one man by the forks with derections to join me to night
with the one now at that place,   those two men joined me at
my Camp on the right Side below the 1ˢᵗ Clift with 5 Sammon
which the Indians gave them at the forks, the place they *gig*
fish at this season.   Their method of takeing fish with a *gig* or
bone is with a long pole,   about a foot from one End is a
Strong String attached to the pole, this String is a little more
than a foot long and is tied to the middle of a bone from 4 to
6 inches long, one end Sharp the other with a whole to fasten
on the end of the pole with a beard [*i. e.,* barb] to the large
end,   the[y] fasten this bone on one end & with the other,
feel for the fish & turn and Strike them So hard that the bone
passes through and Catches on the opposit Side, Slips off the
End of the pole and holds the Center of the bone   Those
Indians are mild in their disposition, appear Sincere in their
friendship, punctial, and decided. kind with what they have,
to spare.   They are excessive pore, nothing but horses   there
Enemies which are noumerous on account of there horses &
Defenceless Situation, have deprived them of tents and all the
Small Conveniances of life.   They have only a few indifferent
Knives, no ax, make use of Elk's horn Sharpened to Sp[l]it

[9]

ther wood, no clothes except a Short Legins & robes of different animals, Beaver, Bear, Buffalow, wolf Panther, Ibex (Sheep), Deer, but most commonly the antilope Skins which they ware loosely about them. Their ornements are Orter Skin d[e]curated with See Shells & the Skins & tales of the white weasel, Sea Shels of different size hung to their Ears hair and breast of their Shirts, beeds of Shells platted Grass, and Small strings of otter Skin dressed, they are fond of our trinkets, and give us those ornements as the most valueable of their possession. The women are held more sacred among them than any nation we have seen and appear to have an equal Shere in all conversation, which is not the Case in any other nation I have seen. their boys & girls are also admited to speak except in Councels, the women doe all the drugery except fishing and takeing care of the horses, which the men ap.ᵗ to take upon themselves. The men ware the hair loose flowing over ther Sholders & face, the women Cut Short, ornements of the back bones of fish Strung, plated grass grains of Corn Strung Feathers and orniments of Birds Claws of the Bear encurcling their necks the most sacred of all the orniments of this nation is the Sea Shells of various Sizes and Shapes and colours, of the bassterd perl kind, which they inform us they get from the Indians to the South on the other Side of a large fork of this river in passing to which they have to pass thro: Sandy & barron open plains without water to which place they can travel in 15 or 20 days. The men who passed by the forks informed me that the S W. fork was double the Size of the one I came down, and I observed that it was a handsom river at my camp I shall in justice to Cap.ᵗ Lewis who was the first white man ever on this fork of the Columbia Call this Louis's [Lewis's] river. one Deer killed this morning, and a Sammon in the last Creek 2½ feet long The Westerley fork of the Columbia River is double the Size of the Easterley fork & below those forks the river is about the Size [of] Jeffersons River near its mouth or 100 yards wide, it is verry rapid & Sholey water Clear, but little timber. This Clift is of a redish brown Colour, the rocks which fall from it is a dark brown flint tinged with that

Colour.   Some Gullies of white Sand Stone and Sand fine &
a[s] white as Snow.   The mountains on each Side are high,
and those on the East ruged & Contain a fiew Scattering pine,
those on the West contain pine on ther tops & high up the
hollows.   The bottoms of this day is wide & rich from some
distance above the place I struck the East fork   they are also
wide on the East   Passed a large Creek which fall[s] in on
the right side 6 miles below the forks   a road passes up this
Creek & to the Missouri.

[Lewis:]   *Thursday August 22ᵈ 1805.*

This morning early I sent a couple of men to complete the
covering of the cash which could not be done well last night
in the dark,   they soon accomplished their work and returned.
late last night Drewyer returned with a fawn he had killed and
a considerable quantity of Indian plunder.   the anecdote with
rispect to the latter is perhaps worthy of relation.   he informed
me that while hunting in the Cove yesterday about 12 OCᵏ he
came suddonly upon an Indian Camp, at which there were a
young man an Old man and a boy and three women, that
they seemed but little supprised at seeing him and he rode up
to them and dismounted turning [his] horse out to graize.
these people had just finished their repast on some roots,   he
entered into conversation with them by signs, and after about
20 minutes one of the women spoke to the others of the
party and they all went immediately and collected their horses
brought them to camp and saddled them   at this moment he
thought he would also set out and continue his hunt, and ac-
corgingly walked to catch his horse at some little distance and
neglected to take up his gun which he left at camp.   the Indians perceiving him at the distance of fifty paces immediately
mounted their horses, the young man took the gun, and the
whole of them left their baggage and laid whip to their horses
directing their course to the pass of the mountains.   finding
himself deprived of his gun he immediately mounted his horse
and pursued; after runing them about 10 miles the horses of

[11]

two of the women nearly gave out and the young fellow with the gun from their frequent crys slackened his pace and being on a very fleet horse road around the women at a little distance   at length Drewer overtook the women and by signs convinced them that he did not wish to hirt them   they then halted and the young fellow approached still nearer, he asked him for his gun but the only part of the answer which he could understand was pahkee which he knew to be the name by which they called their enimies.   watching his opportunity when the fellow was off his guard he suddonly rode along side of him seized his gun and wrest[ed] her out of his hands.   the fellow finding Drewyer too strong for him and discovering that he must yeald the gun had p[r]esents of mind to open the pan and cast the priming before he let the gun escape from his hands; now finding himself devested of the gun he turned his horse about and laid whip leaving the women to follow him as well as they could.   Drewyer now returned to the place they had left their baggage and brought it with him to my camp.   it consisted of several dressed and undressed skins; a couple of bags wove with the fingers of the bark of the silk-grass containing each about a bushel of dryed service burries some ch[ok]echerry cakes and about a bushel of roots of three different kinds dryed and prepared for uce which were foalded in as many parchment hides of buffaloe.   some flint and the instrument of bone for manufactureing the flint into arrow points.   some of this flint was as transparent as the common black glass and much of the same colour, easily broken, and flaked of[f] much like glass leaving a very sharp edge.[1]   one speceis of the roots were fusiform abo[u]t six inches long and about the size of a man's finger at the larger end tapering to a small point.   the radicles larger than in most fusiform roots.   the rind was white and thin. the body or consistence of the root was white mealy and easily reduced by pounding to a substance resembleing flour which

---

1 This " black glass flint " was undoubtedly obsidian, or natural volcanic glass. This is found in various parts of the West, the large and noted Obsidian Cliff in Yellowstone Park being the best known.   The tribes formerly had a quarry there, and the spawls and arrowheads and spear-points thus obtained were bartered from tribe to tribe, as were red pipestone calumets. — O. D. WHEELER.

thickens with boiling water something like flour and is agreeably flavored.   this rout is frequently eaten by the Indians
either green or in it's dryed state without the preparation of
boiling.   another speceis was much mutilated but appeared to
be fibrous; the parts were brittle, hard, of the size of a small
quill, cilindric and as white as snow throughout, except some
small parts of the hard black rind which they had not seperated
in the preperation.   this the Indians with me informed were
always boiled for use.   I made the exp[e]riment, found that
they became perfectly soft by boiling, but had a very bitter
taste, which was naucious to my pallate, and I transfered them
to the Indians who had eat them heartily.   a third speceis
were about the size of a nutmeg, and of an irregularly rounded
form, something like the smallest of the Jarusalem artichoke,
which they also resemble in every other appearance.   they had
become very hard by being dryed,   these I also boiled agreeably to the instruction of the Indians and found them very
agreeable.   they resemble the Jerusalem Artichoke very much
in their flavor and I thought them preferable, however there
is some allowance to be made for the length of time I have
now been without vegitable food to which I was always much
attatched.   these are certainly the best root[s] I have yet seen
in uce among the Indians.   I asked the Indians to shew me
the plant of which these roots formed a part but they informed
me that neither of them grew near this place.[1]   I had set most
of the men at work today to dress the deerskin belonging to
those who had gone on command with Cap! Clark.   at 11.A.M.
Charbono, the Indian Woman, Cameahwait and about 50 men
with a number of women and children arrived.   they encamped near us.   after they had turned out their horses and
arranged their camp I called the Cheifs and warriors together
and addressed them a second time; gave them some further

---

[1] It is not easy to identify these roots fully, as Lewis could describe only the
dried tuber, without seeing the plant.   The first named was probably that of dill
(*Carum*, or *Anethum*), called by the Shoshoni Indians *yampah*.   The third was
probably the wild artichoke (*Helianthus tuberosus*).   Coues thinks that the other is
Lewisia rediviva (Fr. *racine amère*, "bitter root" — giving name to the Bitter
Root Mountains).   See Edward Palmer's "Food Products of the North American
Indians," in *Report* of U. S. Commissioner of Agriculture, 1871, pp. 404–428. — ED.

presents, particularly the second and third Cheifs who it appeared had agreeably to their promise exerted themselves in my favour, having no fresh meat and these poor devils half starved I had previously prepared a good meal for them all of boiled corn and beans which I gave them as soon as the council was over and I had distributed the presents. this was thankfully received by them. the Cheif wished that his nation could live in a country where they could provide such food. I told him that it would not be many years before the whitemen would put it in the power of his nation to live in the country below the mountains where they might cultivate corn beans and squashes. he appeared much pleased with the information. I gave him a few dryed squashes which we had brought from the Mandans he had them boiled and declared them to be the best thing he had ever tasted except sugar, a small lump of which it seems his sister Sah-cah-gar Wea had given him. late in the evening I made the men form a bush drag, and with it in about 2 hours they caught 528 very good fish, most of them large trout. among them I now for the first time saw ten or a douzen of a white speceis of trout. they are of a silvery colour except on the back and head, where they are of a bluish cast. the scales are much larger than the speckled trout, but in their form position of their fins teeth mouth &c they are precisely like them. they are not generally quite as large but equally well flavored.[1] I distributed much the greater portion of the fish among the Indians. I purchased five good horses of them very reasonably, or at least for about the value of six dollars a peice in merchandize. the Indians are very orderly and do not croud about our camp nor attempt to disterb any article they see lying about. they borrow knives kettles &c from the men and always carefully return them. Capt Clark says, " we set out early and passed a small creek at one mile, also the points of four mountains which were high steep and rocky. the mountains are so steep that it is almost incredible to mention that horses had passed them. our road in many places lay over the sharp fragments

1 Probably the common blue-backed salmon of the Columbia (*Oncorhyncus nerka*.) — ED.

of rocks which had fallen from the mountains and lay in
confused heaps for miles together; yet notwithstanding our
horsed[s] traveled barefoot [*i.e.*, unshod] over them as fast as
we could and did not detain us.   passed two bold runing
streams, and arrived at the entrance of a small river where
some Indian families resided.   they had some scaffoalds of
fish and burries exposed to dry.   they were not acquainted
with the circumstance of any whitemen being in their country
and were therefore much allarmed on our approach   several
of the women and children fled in the woods for shelter.   the
guide was behind and the wood thick in which their lodges
were situated   we came on them before they had the least
notice of us.   those who remained offered us every thing they
had, which was but little; they offered us collars of elks tusks
which their children woar, Salmon beries &c   we eat some
of their fish and buries but returned them the other articles
they had offered with a present of some small articles which
seemed to add much to their pacification.   The guide who had
by this time arrived explained to them who we were and our
object in visiting them; but still there were some of the women
and Children inconsoleable, they continued to cry during our
stay, which was about an hour.   a road passes up this river
which my guide informed me led over the mountains to the
Missouri.   from this place I continued my rout along the
steep side of a mountain for about 3 miles and arrived at
the river near a small Island on the lower point of which we
encamped.   in the evening we attempted to gig fish but were
unsuccessfull only obtaining one small salmon.   in the course
of the day we had passed several women and children geather-
ing burries who were very liberal in bestoing us a part of their
collections.   the river is very rapid and shoaly; many rocks
lie in various derections scattered throughout it's bed.   There
are some few small pine scattered through the bottoms, of
which I only saw one which appeared as if it would answer for
a canoe and that was but small.   the tops of the mountains
on the Lar:d side are covered with pine and some also scattered
on the sides of all the mountains.   I saw today a speceis of
woodpecker, which fed on the seeds of the pine.   it's beak

and tail were white, it's wings were black, and every other part of a dark brown.   it was about the size of a robin.[1] ["]

[Clark:]   *August 22ᵈ Thursday 1805.*

We Set out early   passed a Small Creek on the right at 1 mile and the points of four mountains verry Steup high & rockey,   the assent of three was So Steup that it is incredeable to describe   the rocks in maney places loose & Sliped from those mountains and is a Solid bed of rugid loose white and dark brown loose rock for miles.   the Indian horses pass over those Clifts hills beds & rocks as fast as a man, the three horses with me do not detain me any on account of those dificulties,   passed two bold runᵍ Streams on the right and a Small river[2] [*Fishcr. also on the right*] at the mouth of which Several families of Indians were encamped and had Several Scaffolds of fish & buries drying   we allarmed them verry much as they knew nothing of a white man being in their Countrey, and at the time we approached their lodges which was in a thick place of bushes   my guides were behind.   They offered every thing they possessed (which was verry little) to us, Some run off and hid in the bushes   The first offer of theirs were Elks tushes from around their childrens necks, Sammon &c.   my guide attempted [to] passify those people and they Set before me berri[e]s, & fish to eate,[3]   I gave a fiew Small articles to those fritened people which added verry much to their pasification but not entirely as some of the women & Childᵣ Cried dureing my Stay of an hour at this place,   I proceeded on the Side of a verry Steep & rockey

[1] This bird is now known as the American nutcracker (*Picicorvus columbianus*). Here ends Codex F. — ED.

[2] Now the north fork of Salmon River. — ED.

[3] Those of the natives who are detached in small parties appear to live better, and to have a larger supply of provisions, than those who live in large villages.   The people of these three lodges have gathered a quantity of sun-flower seed, and also of the lambs-quarter [*Chenopodium*], which they pound and mix with service-berries, and make of the composition a kind of bread, which appears capable of sustaining life for some time.   On this bread and the fish they take out of the river, these people, who appear to be the most wretched of the human species, chiefly subsist.— GASS (pp. 177, 178; cf. 183).

mountain for 3 miles and Encamped on the lower p⸍ of an Island we attempted to gig fish without Suckcess caught but one Small one.   The last Creek or Small river is on the right Side and "a road passes up it & over to the Missouri" (*to Wisdom*) (*From Several of these Streams roads go across to Wisdom River*) in this day passed Several womin and Children gathering and drying buries of which they were very kind and gave us a part.   the river rapid and Sholey maney Stones Scattered through it in different directions.   I saw to day [a] Bird of the woodpecker kind which fed on Pine burs its Bill and tale white the wings black every other part of a light brown, and about the Size of a robin.   Some fiew Pine scattered in the bottoms & Sides of the Mountains (the Top of the Mt⸍ to the left Covered & inaxcessable)   I saw one which would make a Small Canoe.

[Lewis:] [1]   *Friday August 23ʳᵈ 1805.*

This morning I arrose very early and despatched two hunters on horseback with orders to extend their hunt to a greater distance up the S. E. fork than they had done heretofore, in order if possible to obtain some meet for ourselves as well as the Indians who appeared to depend on us for food and our store of provision is growing too low to indulge them with much more corn or flour.   I wished to have set out this morning but the cheif requested that I would wait untill another party of his nation arrived which he expected today, to this I consented from necessity, and therefore sent out the hunters as I have mentioned.   I also laid up the canoes this morning in a pond near the forks; sunk them in the water and weighted them down with stone, after taking out the plugs of the gage holes in their bottoms; hoping by this means to guard against both the effects of high water, and that of the fire which is frequently kindled in these plains by the natives.   the Indians have promised to do them no intentional injury and [I] beleive

[1] Lewis's entries for August 23–26 are made on a few loose sheets, designated by Coues as Codex Fb. — ED.

they are too laizy at any rate to give themselves the trouble to raise them from their present situation in order to cut or birn them.   I reminded the chief of the low state of our stores of provision and advised him to send his young men to hunt, which he immediately recommended to them and most of them turned out.   I wished to have purchased some more horses of them but they objected against disposing of any more of them untill we reach their camp beyond the mountains.   the Indians pursued a mule buck[1] near our camp   I saw this chase for about 4 miles it was really entertaining,   there were about twelve of them in pursuit of it on horseback, they finally rode it down and killed it.   the[y] all came in about 1. P. M. having killed 2 mule deer and three goats.   this mule buck was the largest deer of any kind I had ever seen.   it was nearly as large as a doe Elk.   I observed that there was but little division or distribution of the meat they had taken among themselves.   some familes had a large stock and others none. this is not custumary among the nations of Indians with whom I have hitherto been acquainted.   I asked Cameahwait the reason why the hunters did not divide the meat among themselves; he said that meat was so scarce with them that the men who killed it reserved it for themselves and their own families. my hunters arrived about 2 in the evening with two mule deer and three common deer.   I distributed three of the deer among those families who appeared to have nothing to eat.   at three P. M. the expected party of Indians arrived, about 50 men women and children.   I now learnt that most of them were thus far on their way down the valley towards the buffaloe country, and observed that there was a good deel of anxiety on the part of some of those who had promised to assist me over the mountains to accompany this party; I felt some uneasiness on this subject but as they still said they would return with me as they had promised I said nothing to them but resolved to set out in the morning as early as possible.   I dispatched two hunters this evening into the cove to hunt and leave the meat they might kill on the rout we shall pass tomorrow.

---

[1] Meaning a buck of the mule, or black-tailed, deer (*Cariacus macrotis*). — ED.

INDIANS HUNTING THE BISON

The metal which we found in possession of these people consi[s]ted of a few indifferent knives, a few brass kettles some arm bands of iron and brass, a few buttons, woarn as ornaments in their hair, a spear or two of a foot in length and some iron and brass arrow points which they informed me they obtained in exchange for horses from the Crow or Rocky Mountain Indians on the yellowstone River. the bridlebits and stirreps they obtained from the Spaniards, tho these were but few. many of them made use of flint for knives, and with this instrument, skined the animals they killed, dressed their fish and made their arrows; in short they used it for every purpose to which the knife is applyed. this flint is of no regular form, and if they can only obtain a part of it, an inch or two in length that will cut they are satisfyed. they renew the edge by flecking off the flint by means of the point of an Elk's or deer's horn. with the point of a deer or Elk's horn they also form their arrow points of the flint, with a quickness and neatness that is really astonishing. we found no axes nor hatchets among them; what wood they cut was done either with stone or Elk's horn. the latter they use always to rive or split their wood. their culinary eutensils exclusive of the brass kettle before mentioned consist of pots in the form of a jar made either of earth, or of a white soft stone which becomes black and very hard by birning, and is found in the hills near the three forks of the Missouri betwen Madison's and Gallitin's rivers.[1] they have also spoons made of the Buffaloe's horn and those of the Bighorn. Their bows are made of ceader or pine and have nothing remarkable about them. the back of the bow is covered with sinues and glue and is about 2½ feet long. much the shape of those used by the Siouxs Mandans Minnetares &c. their arrows are more slender generally than those used by the nations just mentioned but much the same in construction. Their sheild is formed of buffaloe hide, perfectly arrow proof, and is a circle of 2 feet 4 I. or 2 F. 6 I. in diameter. this is frequently painted with varios figures and ornamented around the edges with feather[s] and a fringe of

---

[1] These people make willow baskets so close, and to such perfection, as to hold water, for which purpose they make use of them. —GASS (p. 183).

dressed leather. they sometimes make bows of the Elk's horn and those also of the bighorn. those of the Elk's horn are made of a single peice and covered on the back with glue and sinues like those made of wood, and are frequently ornamented with a stran[d] wrought [of] porcupine quills and sinues raped around them for some distance at both extremities. the bows of the bighorn are formed of small peices laid flat and cemented with gleue, and rolled with siniws, after which, they are also covered on the back with sinews and glew, and highly ornamented as they are much prized. forming the sheild is a cerimony of great importance among them, this implement would in their minds be devested of much of its protecting power were it not inspired with those virtues by their old men and jugglers. their method of preparing it is thus, an entire skin of a bull buffaloe two years old is first provided; a feast is next prepared and all the warriors old men and jugglers invited to partake. a hole is sunk in the ground about the same in diameter with the intended sheild and about 18 inches deep. a parcel of stones are now made red hot and thrown into the hole water is next thrown in and the hot stones cause it to emit a very strong hot steem, over this they spread the green skin which must not have been suffered to dry after taken off the beast. the flesh side is laid next to the groround and as many of the workmen as can reach it take hold on it's edges and extend it in every direction. as the skin becomes heated, the hair seperates and is taken of[f] with the fingers, and the skin continues to contract untill the who[l]e is drawn within the compas designed for the shield, it is then taken off and laid on a parchment hide where they pound it with their heels when barefoot. this operation of pounding continues for several days or as long as the feast lasts when it is delivered to the propryeter and declared by the jugglers and old men to be a sufficient defence against the arrows of their enimies or even bullets if [the] feast has been a satisfactory one. many of them beleive implisitly that a ball cannot penitrate their sheilds, in consequence of certain superna[t]ural powers with which they have been inspired by their jugglers. The Poggâmoggon is an instrument with a handle of wood

covered with dressed leather about the size of a whip handle
and 22 inches long; a round stone of 2 pounds weight is also
covered with leather and strongly united to the leather of the
handle by a throng of 2 inches long; a loop of leather united
to the handle passes arond the wrist. a very severe blow may
be given with this instrument. They have also a kind of
armor which they form with many foalds of dressed [an]telope's
skin, unite with glue and sand. with this they cover their
own bodies and those of their horses. these are sufficient
against the effects of the arrow. the quiver which contains
their arrows and implements for making fire is formed of
various skins. that of the Otter seems to be prefered. they
are but narrow, of a length suffucent to protect the arrow from
the weather, and are woarn on the back by means of a strap
which passes over the left sholder and under the wright arm.
their impliments for making fire is nothing more than a blunt
arrow and a peice of well seasoned soft spongey wood such as
the willow or cottonwood. the point of this arrow they apply
to this dry stick so near one edge of it that the particles of
wood which are seperated from it by the friction of the arrow
falls down by it's side in a little pile. the arrow is held between
the palms of the hand with the fingers extended, and being
pressed as much as possible against the peice is briskly rolled
between the palms of the hands backwards and forwards by
pressing the arrow downwards   the hands of course in rolling
[the] arrow also decend; they bring them back with a quick
motion and repeat the operation till the dust by the friction
takes fire; the peice and arrow are then removed and some
dry grass or dooted [rotted] wood is added. it astonished me
to see in what little time these people would kindle fire in this
way. in less than a minute they will produce fire.[1]

Capt. Clark set out this morning very early and poroceeded
but slowly in consequence of the difficulty of his road which
lay along the steep side of a mountain over large irregular

---

[1] Cf. the account by Gass (pp. 182, 183). For aboriginal methods and implements used in fire-making, see *Jes. Relations*, vi, p. 217; xii, 117, 272; xxii, 267,
319; and Hough's "Fire-making apparatus," in *U. S. Nat. Mus. Rep.*, 1887–88,
pp. 531–587. —ED.

and broken masses of rocks which had tumbled from the upper part of the mountain. it was with much wrisk and pain that the horses could get on. at the distance of four miles he arrived at the river and the rocks were here so steep and juted into the river [in] such manner that there was no other alternative but passing through the river, this he attempted with success tho' water was so deep for a short distance as to swim the horses and was very rapid; he continued his rout one mile along the edge of the river under this steep Clift to a little bottom, below which the whole current of the river beat against the Star.^d shore on which he was, and which was formed of a solid rock perfectly inaccessible to horses. here also the little track which he had been pursuing, terminated. he therefore determined to leave the horses and the majority of the party here and with his guide and three men to continue his rout down the river still further, in order more fully to satisfy himself as to it's practicability. accordingly he directed the men to hunt and fish at this place untill his return. they had not killed anything today but one goose, and the ballance of the little provision they had brought with them, as well as the five salmon they had procured yesterday were consumed last evening; there was of cour[s]e no inducement for his halting any time, at this place; after a few minutes he continued his rout clambering over immence rocks and along the sides of lofty precepices on the border of the river to the distance of 12 miles, at which place a large creek discharged itself on the No[r]th side 12 yd.^s wide and deep. a short distance above the entrance of this creek there is a narrow bottom which is the first that he had found on the river from that in which he left the horses and party. a plain indian road led up this creek which the guide informed him led to a large river that ran to the North, and was frequented by another nation who occasionally visited this river for the purpose of taking fish. at this place he saw some late appearance of Indians having been encamped and the tracks of a number of horses. Capt. C. halted here about 2 hours, caught some small fish, on which, with the addition of some berries, they dined. the river from the place at which he left the party to his present station was one continued rapid, in which there were five shoals neither of which could be passed with loaded canoes nor even run with empty ones. at those several places therefore it would be necessary to unload and transport the baggage for a considerable distance over steep and almost inaccessable rocks where there was no possibility of employing horses for the releif of the men; the canoes would next have to be let down by cords and even with this precaution Capt. C. conceived there would be much wrisk of both canoes and men. at one of those shoals the lofty perpendicular rocks which from [form] the bases of the mountains approach the river so nearly on each side, as to prevent the possibility of a portage, or passage for the canoes without expending much labour in removing rocks and cuting away the earth in some places. to surmount These difficulties, precautions must be observed which in their execution must necessarily consume much time and provision, neither of which we can command. the season is now [too] far advanced to remain in these mountains as the Indians inform us we shall shortly have snow; the salmon have so far declined that they are themselves haistening from the country and not an animal of any discription is to be seen in this difficult part of the river larger than a pheasant or a squirrel and they not abundant; add to this that our stock of provision is now so low that it would not support us more than ten days. the bends of the river are short and the currant beats from side to side against the rocks with great violence. the river is about 100 yd^s wide and so deep that it cannot be foarded but in a few places; and the rocks approach the river so near in most places that there is no possibility of passing between them and the water; a passage therefore with horses along the river is also impracticable. The sides of these mountains present generally one barren surface of confused and broken masses of stone. above these are white or brown and towards the base of a grey colour and so hard that when struck with a steel, yeald fire like flint. those he had just past were scarcely releived by the appearance of a tree; but those below the entrance of the creek were better covered with timber, and there were also some tall pine near the river. The sides of the mountains are very steep, and the torrents of water which roll down their sides at certain seasons appear to carry with them vast quantities of the loose stone into the river. after dinner Cap! C. continued his rout down the river and at ½ a mile pased another creek not so large as that just mentioned, or about 5 yards wide. here his guide informed him that by ascending this creek some distance they would have a better road and would cut off a considerable bend which the river made to the south; accordingly he pursued a well beaten Indian track which led up this creek about six miles, then leaving the creek on the wright he passed over a ridge, and at the distance of a mile arrived at the river where it passes through a well timbered bottom of about eighty acres of land; they passed this bottom and asscended a steep and elivated point of a mountain, from whence the guide shewed him the brake of the river through the mountains for about 20 miles further. this view was terminated by one of the most lofty mountains, Cap! C. informed me, he had ever seen which was perfectly covered with snow. the river directed it's course immediately to this stupendous mountain at the bace of which the gu[i]de informed him those difficulties of which -himself and nation had spoken, commenced. that after the river reached this mountain it continued it's rout to the North for many miles between high and perpendicular rocks, roling foaming and beating against innumerable rocks which crouded it's channel; that then it penetrated the mountain through a narrow gap leaving a perpendicular rock on either side as high as the top of the mountain which he beheld. that the river here making a bend they could not see through the mountain, and as it was impossible to decend the river or clamber over that vast mountain covered with eternal snow neither himself nor any of his nation had ever been lower in this direction, than in view of the place at which the river entered this mountain; that if Cap! C. wished him to do so, he would conduct him to that place, where he thought they could probably arrive by the next evening. Cap! C. being now perfictly satisfyed as to the impracticability of this rout either by land or water, informed the old man, that he was convinced of the varacity of his assertions and would now return to the village from whence they had set out where he expected to meet myself and party. they now returned to the upper part of the last creek he had passed, and encamped. it was an hour after dark before he reached this place. a small river falls into this fork of the Columbia just above the high mountain through which it passes on the south side.

[Clark:]   *August 23ʳᵈ Friday 1805*

We Set out early   proceed on with great dificuelty as the rocks were So sharp large and unsettled and the hill sides Steep that the horses could with the greatest risque and dificulty get on,   no provisions as the 5 Sammon given us yesterday by the Indians were eaten last night,   one goose killed this morning; at 4 miles we came to a place the horses Could not pass without going into the river,   we passed one mile to a verry bad riffle the water confined in a narrow Channel & beeting against the left Shore,   as we have no parth further and the Mount⁹ jut So close as to prevent the possibility of horses proceeding down, I Deturmined to delay the party here and with my guide and three men proceed on down to examine if the river continued bad or was practi[c]able,   I set out with three men directing those left to hunt and fish untill my return. I proceeded on.   Sometimes in a Small wolf parth & at other times Climing over the rocks for 12 miles to a large Creek on the right Side   above the mouth of this Creek for a Short distance is a narrow bottom & the first, below the place I left my party.   a road passes down this Creek which I understood passed to the water of a River which run to the North & was the ground of another nation,   Some fresh Sign about this Creek of horse[s] and Camps.   I delay⁹ 2 hours to fish, Cought Some Small fish on which we dined. The River from the place I left my party to this Creek is almost one continued rapid, five verry considerable rapids   the passage of either with Canoes is entirely impossible, as the water is Confined between huge Rocks & the Current beeting from one against another for Some distance below &c. &c.   at one of those rapids the mountains close so Clost as to prevent a possibility of a portage with [out] great labour in cutting down the Side of the hill removeing large rocks &c. &c.   all the others may be passed by takeing every thing over slipery rocks, and the Smaller ones Passed by letting down the Canoes empty with Cords, as running them would certainly be productive of the loss of Some Canoes,   those dificulties and necessary precautions would delay us an emence time in which provisions would be necessary.   (we have but little and nothing to be procured in this quarter except *Choke Cheres & red haws*   not an animal of any kind to be Seen and only the track of a Bear)   below this Creek the lofty Pine is thick in the bottom hill Sides on the mountains & up the runs.   The river has much the resemblance of that above   bends Shorter and no passing after a few miles between the river & the mountains & the Current so Strong that [it] is dangerous crossing the river, and to proceed down it would ren.ᵈ it necessary to Cross almost at every bend   this river is about 100 yards wide and can be forded but in a few places.   below my guide and maney other Indians tell me that the Mountains Close and is a perpendicular Clift on each Side, and Continues for a great distance and that the water runs with great violence from one rock to the other on each Side foaming & roreing thro rocks in every direction, So as to render the passage of any thing impossible.   those rapids which I had Seen he said was Small & trifleing in comparrison to the rocks & rapids below, at no great distance & The Hills or mountains were not like those I had Seen but like the Side of a tree Streight up.   Those Mountains which I had passed were Steep Contain a white, a brown, & low down a Grey hard stone which would make fire,   those Stone were of different Sizes all Sharp and are continuly Slipping down, and in maney places one bed of those Stones inclined from the river bottom to the top of the mountains.   The Torrents of water which come down after a rain carries with it emence numbers of those Stone[s] into the river[1]   about ½ a mile below the last mentioned

---

[1] The rest of this paragraph was evidently written at a later time — probably when Clark and Biddle were preparing the MSS. for publication. — Ed.

Creek another Creek falls in, my guide informed me that our
rout was up this Creek by which rout we would Save a considerable bend of the river to the South. we proceeded on a
well beeten Indian parth up this creak (Berry Creek) about
6 miles and passed over a ridge 1 mile to the river in a Small
vally through which we passed and assended a Spur of the
Mountain from which place my guide Shew[ed] me the river
for about 20 miles lower & pointed out the dificulties[1] we
returned to the last creek & camped about one hour after
dark.

(*There my guide Shewed me a road from the N Which came
into the one I was in which he Said went to a large river which
run to the north on which was a nation he called Tushapaws,[2] —
he made a map of it.*)

[Lewis:]   *Saturday August 24th 1805.*

As the Indians who were on their way down the Missouri
had a number of spare ho[r]ses with them I thought it probable that I could obtain some of them and therefore desired
the Cheif to speak to them and inform me whether they would
trade. they gave no positive answer but requested to see the
goods which I was willing to give in exchange. I now produced some battle axes which I had made at Fort Mandan
with which they were much pleased. knives also seemed in
great demand among them. I soon purchased three horses

---

[1] This point was on the Salmon River, 52 miles below its confluence with the
Lemhi. Finding it impossible to go further by this route, the expedition was compelled to march northward through the mountains over nearly two degrees of latitude,
to a point almost west of the Missouri " gates of the Rockies," before it could again
strike for the waters of the Columbia. — ED.

[2] Who having no salmon in their river, came by these roads to the fish weirs on
Lewis's river. He had himself been among these Tushepaws, and having once accompanied them on a fishing party to another river he had there seen Indians who had
come across the rocky mountains. — BIDDLE (i, p. 402).

This tribe (named Tussapa by Gass, and Tut-see'-wâs in Lewis's " Statistical
View ") belonged to the Salishan family, which includes numerous tribes, commonly
known as Flatheads ; their habitat extended from western Montana to the Pacific
coast, and north to the 53rd parallel. At present, about one-third of them live on
reservations in Washington, the rest in British Columbia. See Powell's account of
them in *U. S. Bur. Ethnol. Rep.*, 1885–86, pp. 102–105. — ED.

and a mule. for each horse I gave an ax a knife handkercheif and a little paint; & for the mule the addition of a knife
a shirt handkercheif and a pair of legings; at this price which
was quite double that given for the horses, the fellow who
sold him made a merit of having bestoed [on] me one of his
mules. I consider this mule a great acquisition. these Indians
soon told me that they had no more horses for sale and I
directed the party to prepare to set out. I had now nine
horses and a mule, and two which I had hired made twelve
these I had loaded and the Indian women took the ballance
of the baggage. I had given the Interpreter some articles
with which to purchase a horse for the woman which he had
obtained. at twelve Oclock we set out and passed the river
below the forks, directing our rout towards the cove along the
track formerly mentioned. most of the horses were heavily
laden, and it appears to me that it will require at least 25
horses to convey our baggage along such roads as I expect we
shall be obliged to pass in the mountains. I had now the
inexpressible satisfaction to find myself once more under way
with all my baggage and party. an Indian had the politeness
to offer me one of his horses to ride which I accepted with
cheerfullness as it enabled me to attend better to the march of
the party. I had reached the lower part of the cove when an
Indian rode up and informed me that one of my men was very
sick and unable to come on. I directed the party to halt at a
small run which falls into the creek on Lar⁴ at the lower part
of the Cove and rode back about 2 Miles where I found
Wiser very ill with a fit of the cholic. I sent Serg⁴ Ordway
who had remained with him for some water and gave him a
doze of the essence of Peppermint and laudinum which in the
course of half an hour so far recovered him that he was enabled
to ride my horse and I proceeded on foot and rejoined the
party. the sun was yet an hour high but the Indians who had
for some time impatiently waited my return at length unloaded
and turned out their horses and my party had followed there
example. as it was so late and the Indians had prepared their
camp for the night I thought it best to acquiess and determined also to remain. we had traveled only about six miles.

after we encamped we had a slight shower of rain.   Goodrich who is our principal fisherman caught several fine trout. Drewyer came to us late in the evening and had not killed anything.   I gave the Indians who were absolutely engaged in transporting the baggage, a little corn as they had nothing to eat.   I told Cameahwait that my stock of provision was too small to indulge all his people with provision and recommended it to him to advise such as were not assisting us with our baggage to go on to their camp to morrow and wait our arrival ; which he did accordingly.   *Cameahwait* literally translated is *one who never walks.*   he told me that his nation had also given him another name by which he was signalized as a warrior which was Too-et'-te-can'-e or *black gun.*   these people have many names in the course of their lives, particularly if they become distinguished characters.   for it seems that every important event by which they happen to distinguish themselves intitles them to claim another name which is generally scelected by themselves and confirmed by the nation.   those distinguishing acts are the killing and scalping an enemy, the killing a white bear, leading a party to war who happen to be successfull either in destroying their enemies or robing them of their horses, or individually stealing the horses of an enemy. these are considered acts of equal heroism among them, and that of killing an enemy without scalping him is considered of no importance ; in fact the whole honour seems to be founded in the act of scalping, for if a man happens to slay a dozen of his enemies in action and others get the scalps or first lay their hand on the dead person the honor is lost to him who killed them and devolves on those who scalp or first touch them. Among the Shoshones, as well as all the Indians of America, bravery is esteemed the primary virtue ; nor can any one become eminent among them who has not at some period of his life given proofs of his possessing this virtue.   with them there can be no preferment without some warlike achievement, and so completely interwoven is this principle with the earliest Elements of thought that it will in my opinion prove a serious obstruction to the restoration of a general. peace among the nations of the Missouri.   while at Fort Mandan I was one day addressing some cheifs of the Minetares w[h]o visited us and pointing out to them the advantages of a state of peace with their neighbours over that of war in which they were engaged.   the Chiefs who had already geathered their ha[r]vest of larals [laurels], and having forceably felt in many instances some of those inconveniences attending a state of war which I pointed out, readily agreed with me in opin[i]on.   a young fellow under the full impression of the Idea I have just suggested asked me if they were in a state of peace with all their neighbours what the nation would do for Cheifs : ? and added that the cheifs were now oald and must shortly die and that the nation could not exist without cheifs.   taking as granted that there could be no other mode devised for making Cheifs but that which custom had established through the medium of warlike ac[h]ievements.

The few guns which the Shoshones have[1] are reserved for war almost exclusively and the bow and arrows are used in hunting.   I have seen a few skins among these people which have almost every appearance of the common sheep.   they inform me that they finde this animal on the high mountains to the West and S. W. of them.   it is about the size of the common sheep, the wool is reather shorter and more intermixed with long hairs particularly on the upper part of the neck.   these skins have been so much woarn that I could not form a just Idea of the animal or it's colour.   the Indians however inform me that it is white and that it's horns are lunated comprest twisted and bent backward as those of the common sheep.   the texture of the skin appears to be that of the sheep.   I am now perfectly convinced that the sheep as well as the Bighorn exist in these mountains.   (*Cap*: *C saw one at a distance to day*)

The usual caparison of the Shoshone horse is a halter and saddle.   the 1ˢᵗ consists either of a round plated or twisted cord of six or seven strands of buffaloe's hair, or a throng of raw hide made pliant by pounding and rubing.   these cords of bufaloe's hair are about the size of a man's finger and remarkably strong.   this is the kind of halter which is prefered

---

1 They have but four guns in the nation. — GASS (p. 179

by them. the halter of whatever it may be composed is
always of great length and is never taken from the neck of
the horse which they commonly use at any time. it is first
attatched at one end about the neck of the horse with a knot
that will not slip, it is then brought down to his under jaw
and being passed through the mouth imb[r]aces the under jaw
and tonge in a simple noose formed by crossing the rope inder-
neath the jaw of the horse. this when mounted he draws up on
the near side of the horse's neck and holds in the left hand,
suffering it to trail at a great distance behind him — sometimes the halter is attatched so far from the end that while the
shorter end serves him to govern his horse, the other trails on
the grond as before mentioned. they put their horses to their
full speed with those cords trailing on the ground. when they
turn out the horse to graze the noose is mearly loosed from
his mouth. the saddle is made of wood and covered with
raw hide which holds the parts very firmly together. it is
made like the pack saddles in uce among the French and
Spaniords. it consists of two flat thin boards which fit the
sides of the horses back, and are held firm by two peices
which are united to them behind and before on the outer side
and which rise to a considerable hight terminating sometimes
in flat horizontal points extending outwards, and alwas in an
accute angle or short bend underneath the upper part of these
peices. a peice of buffaloe's skin with the hair on, is usually
put underneath the saddle ; and very seldom any covering on
the saddle (*but when they ride they throw on a piece of skin*).
stirrups when used are made of wood and covered with leather.
these are generally used by the elderly men and women ; the
young men scarcely ever use anything more than a small pad
of dressed leather stuffed with hair, which is confined with a
leather thong passing around the body of the horse in the
manner of a girth. they frequently paint their favorite horses,
and cut their ears in various shapes. they also decorate their
mains and tails, which they never draw or trim, with the
feathers of birds, and sometimes suspend at the breast of the
horse the finest ornaments they possess. the Spanish bridle
is prefered by them when they can obtain them, but they

[31]

never dispence with the cord about the neck of the horse, which serves them to take him with more ease when he is runing at large. They are excellent horsemen and extreemly expert in casting the cord about the neck of a horse. (*make a noose & catch him running &c.*) the horses that have been habituated to be taken with the cord in this way, however wild they may appear at first, surrender the moment they feel the cord about their necks. There are no horses in this quarter which can with propriety be termed wild. there are some few which have been left by the indians at large for so great a length of time that they have become shye, but they all shew marks of having been in possession of man. such is that one which Cap! Clark saw just below the three forks of the Missouri, and one other which I saw on the Missouri below the entrance of the Mussle shell river. Cap! Clark set out very early this morning on his return, he traveled down the creek to it's entrance by the same Indian track he had ascended it; at the river he marked his name on a pine tree, then ascended to the bottom above the second creek, and brekfasted on burries, which occupyed them about one hour. he now retraced his former track and joined the party where he had left them at 4 P. M. on his way Cap! C. fell from a rock and injured one of his legs very much. the party during his absence had killed a few pheasants and caught a few small fish on which together with haws and Serviceburies they had subsisted. they had also killed one cock of the mountain. Cap! Clark now wrote me a discription of the river and country, and stated our prospects by this rout as they have been heretofore mentioned (*related the information of his gu[i]de & recom[d] to me to purchase horses &c he had learned from his guid[e] that he had been on the river to the N. where he saw people from the other side [of] the mountains and there was a road, the route he shewed in the sand, which gave me hope of finding a route across the m.[ountains] in that direction*) and dispatched Colter on horseback with orders to loose no time reaching me. he set out late with the party continued his rout about two miles and encamped. Capt Clark had seen some trees which would make small canoes but all of them

some distance below the Indian Ca[m]ps which he passed at
the entrance of fish Creek.

[Clark:]   *August 24ᵗʰ Satturday* 1805

Set out verry early this morning on my return passed
down the [Berry] Creek   at the Mouth Marked my name
on a pine Tree,   proceed[ed] on to the bottom above the
Creek & Brackfast on buries & delayed 1 hour,   then proceeded on up the river by the Same rout we decended to the
place I left my party where we arrived at 4 oClock, (I sliped
& bruised my leg verry much on a rock)   the party had killed
several phesents and cought a fiew Small fish on which they
had Subsisted in my absence.   also a heath hen, near the size
of a Small turkey.

I wrote a letter to Capᵗ Lewis informing him of the prospects before us and information rec[ei]ved of my guide which
I thought favourable &c. & Stating two plans one of which
for us to pursue &c. and despatched one man & horse and
directed the party to get ready to march back,   every man
appeared disheartened from the prospects of the river, and
nothing to eate,   I Set out late and Camped 2 miles above,
nothing to eate but Choke Cherries & red haws, which act in
different ways So as to make us Sick,   dew verry heavy, my
beding wet   in passing around a rock the horses were obliged
to go deep into the water.

The plan I stated to Capᵗ Lewis if he agrees with me we
shall adopt is.   to procure as many horses (one for each man)
if possible and to hire my present guide who I sent on to him
to interigate thro' the Intptʳ and proceed on by land to Some
navagable part of the *Columbia* River, or to the *Ocean*, depending on what provisions we can procure by the gun aded to the
Small Stock we have on hand depending on our horses as
the last resort.

a second plan to divide the party one part to attempt this
deficuelte river with what provisions we had, and the remainde[r]
to pass by Land on ho[r]se back Depending on our gun &c.
for Provisions &c. and come together occasionally on the

river.[1]   the 1ˢᵗ of which I would be most pleased with &c.
I saw Several trees which would make Small Canoes and by
putting 2 together would make a Siseable one, all below the
last Indian Camp Several miles

[Lewis:]   *Sunday August 25ᵗʰ 1805.*

This morning loaded our horses and set out a little after
sunrise; a few only of the Indians unengaged in assisting us
went on as I had yesterday proposed to the cheif.   the others
flanked us on each side and started some Antelope which they
pursued for several hours but killed none of them.   we proceeded within 2 Mˢ of the narrow pass or seven miles from
our camp of last evening and halted for dinner.   Our hunters
joined us at noon with three deer the greater part of which I
gave the indians.   sometime after we had halted, Charbono
mentioned to me with apparent unconcern that he expected to
meet all the Indians from the camp on the Columbia tomorrow
on their way to the Missouri.   allarmed at this information I
asked why he expected to meet them.   he then informed me
that the 1ˢᵗ Cheif had dispatched some of his young men this
morning to this camp requesting the Indians to meet them
tomorrow and that himself and those with him would go on
with them down the Missouri, and consequently leave me and
my baggage on the mountain or thereabouts.   I was out of
patience with the folly of Charbono who had not sufficient
sagacity to see the consequencies which would inevitably flow
from such a movement of the indians, and altho' he had been
in possession of this information since early in the morning
when it had been communicated to him by his Indian woman
yet he never mentioned it untill the after noon.   I could not
forbear speaking to him with some degree of asperity on this
occasion.   I saw that there was no time to be lost in having
those orders countermanded, or that we should not in all probability obtain any more horses or even get my baggage to the

---

[1] In the MS. is written, then crossed out, the following : " A third to devide.
one party to attempt to pass the mountains by turns, and the other to return to the
Missouri collect provisions & go up Medeson river &c." — ED.

waters of the Columbia. I therefore Called the three Cheifs together and having smoked a pipe with them, I asked them if they were men of their words, and whether I could depent on the promises they had made me; they readily answered in the affirmative; I then asked them if they had not promised to assist me with my baggage to their camp on the other side of the mountains, or to the place at which Cap! Clark might build the canoes, should I wish it. they acknowledged that they had. I then asked them why they had requested their people on the other side of the mountain to meet them tomorrow on the mountain where there would be no possibility of our remaining together for the purpose of trading for their horses as they had also promised. that if they had not promised to have given me their assistance in transporting my baggage to the waters on the other side of the mountain that I should not have attempted to pass the mountains but would have returned down the river and that in that case they would never have seen anymore white men in their country. that if they wished the white men to be their friends and to assist them against their enemies by furnishing them with arms and keeping their enemies from attacking them that they must never promis us anything which they did not mean to perform. that when I had first seen them they had doubted what I told them about the arrival of the party of whitemen in canoes, that they had been convinced that what I told them on that occasion was true, why then would they doubt what I said on any other point. I told them that they had witnessed my liberality in dividing the meat which my hunters killed with them; and that I should continue to give such of them as assisted me a part of whatever we had ourselves to eat. and finally concluded by telling them if they intended to keep the promises they had made me to dispatch one of their young men immediately with orders to their people to remain where they were untill our arrival. the two inferior cheifs said that they wished to assist me and be as good as their word, and that they had not sent for their people, that it was the first Chief who had done so, and they did not approve of the measure. Cameahwait remained silent for some time, at length he told me that he knew he had done wrong but that he had been induced to that measure from seeing all his people hungry, but as he had promised to give me his assistance he would not in future be worse than his word.   I then desired him to send immediately and countermand his orders; accordingly a young man was sent for this purpose and I gave him a handkerchief to engage him in my interest.   this matter being arranged to my satisfaction I called all the women and men together who had been assisting me in the transportation of the baggage and gave them a billet for each horse which they had imployed in that service and informed them when we arrived at the plaice where we should finally halt on the river I would take the billet back and give them merchandize for it. every one appeared now satisfyed and when I ordered the horses loaded for our departure the Indians were more than usually allert.   we continued our march untill late in the evening and encamped at the upper part of the cove where the creek enters the mountains; here our hunters joined us with another deer which they had killed,   this I gave to the women and Children, and for my own part remained supperless.   I observed considerable quantities of wild onions in the bottom lands of this cove.   I also saw several large hares and many of the cock of the plains.

Cap: Clark set out early this morning and continued his rout to the indian camp at the entrance of fish Creek; here he halted about an hour; the indians gave himself and party some boiled salmon and berries (*tho' not half Sufficient &c*). these people appeared extreemly hospitable tho' poor and dirty in the extreem.   he still pursued the track up the river by which he had decended and in the evening arrived at the bluff on the river where he had encamped on the 21:st Ins:t   it was late in the evening before he reached this place.   they formed their camp, and Cap: C. sent them in different directions to hunt and fish.   some little time after they halted a party of Indians passed by on their way down the river, consisting of a man a woman and several boys; from these people the guide obtained 2 salmon which together with some small fish they caught and a beaver which Shannon killed furnished them with a plentifull supper. the pine grows pretty abundantly high up on the sides of the mountains on the opposite side of the river. one of the hunters saw a large herd of Elk on the opposite side of the river in the edge of the timbered land. Winsor was taken very sick today and detained Cap! C. very much on his march. three hunters whom he had sent on before him this morning joined him in the evening having killed nothing ; they saw only one deer.

The courses and distances, of Cap! Clark's rout down this branch of the Columbia below this bluff, commencing opposite to an Island, are as follow.

N. 30° W. 2 To the top of a mountain   the river 1 m. on the left.

N. 45° W. 10. With the general cou[r]se of the river; passing over the spurs of four mountains, almost inaccessible, and two small runs from the wright, to some Indian lodges at the entrance of fish creek which discharges itself on the N. Side. a large Indian road passes up this creek. on this course Cap! C. also passed several Islands, and some small bottoms between the river and the mountains.

West 3. along the river to the ascent of a mountain, passing one spur of the same. also 2 Islands and a bottom in which there was an abundance of berries.

S. 45° W. 5. to a very bad rapid, opposite which, a small run discharges itself on N. side. passing perpendicular clifts where the [y] were compelled to pass through the water; passed over loose fragments of rocks on the side of a steep mountain   also passed one Island and a number of small rapids.

N. 45° W. 3. high clifts on either side of the river, no road.

West 2. no road. passed several bad rapids which it would be scarcely possible either to ascend or decend with empty canoes.

N. 45° W. 6. to a large Creek on the N. side; passing several bad rappids and a number of riffles. the mountains high steep and very rocky. no bottom except a little above the entrance of this Creek.

South 1. to the entrance of a small run on N. side opposite to a small island and a bad rapid.

N. 45. W.	6.	up the run along an indian road through a piney country; steep and lofty hills on each side.
S. 45° W.	1.	to the river at a small bottom, passing a gap in the mountain from the top of which can be seen the break of the river through the mountains for 20 miles to a very high mountain on the South, at which place the guide informed Cap.t C. that the
Miles	39	impassable part of the river commenced, and was in[fi]nitely worse than any part he had yet seen.

This morning while passing through the Shoshone cove Frazier fired his musquet at some ducks in a little pond at the distance of about 60 yards from me; the ball rebounded from the water and pased within a very few feet of me.   near the upper part of this cove the Shoshonees suffered a very severe defeat by the Minnetares about six years since.   this part of the cove on the N. E. side of the Creek has lately been birned by the Indians as a signal on some occasion.

[Clark:]   *August 25.th Sunday 1805*

Set out verry early and halted one hour at the Indian Camp, they were kind gave us all a little boiled Sammon & dried buries to eate, ab.t half as much as I could eate,   those people are kind with what they have but excessive pore & Durtey. we proceeded on over the mountains we had before passed to the Bluff we Encamped at on the 21.st instant where we arrived late and turned out to hunt & fish,   Cought Several Small fish,   a party of Squars & one man with Several boys going down to guathe[r] berries below,   my guide got two Sammon from this party which made about half a Supper for the party, after Dark Shannon came in with a beaver which the Party suped on Sumptiously.   one man verry Sick to day which detained us verry much   I had three hunters out all day, they saw one Deer, killed nothing.   one of the Party Saw 9 Elk on a Mountain to our right assending, amongst the Pine timber which is thick on that side

Course & Distance Down Columbia [Lemhi and Salmon] river by
    Land, as I Decended &c.

N. W.	18	miles from the Indian Camp to the forks [of Salmon R]

[Aug 20]
    crossed the [Lemhi] river twice, passed Several old
    camps on the East Side and a Camp of Several lodges
[Aug 21]
    at a were [weir] on the west Side, passed a roade on
    the left leading up the main West fork [i.e. Salmon
    above the Lemhi] below the last Camp, Several Small
    branches falls in on each Side [of the Lemhi], a high
    mountain on each Side, [of Salmon and Lemhi together]

N. 15° W. 14 miles to a Island passed [a] high red Clift on the right
    Side passed a large [*Tower*] Creek [*on the right*] at
[Aug 21]
[Aug 22]
    9 miles up which a roade passes   large bottom below.
    Several Spring runs falling from the mountains on the
    left.   passed a Creek on the right.

N. 30° W. 2 to the top of a mountain the river one mile to the left

NW 10 miles with the general Course of the river,   passed
    over the Spurs of four mountains almost inexcessable
[Aug. 22]
    and two Small runs on the right to Some Indian
    Camps at the mouth of a Small river [*Fish cr.*] on the
    right up which a road passes   passed Several Islands,
    and Small bottoms between the mountains.

West 3 miles on the right Side to the assent of a mountain,
    passed over one Spur of the Same Mountain   passed
    2 Islands, & a bottom in which berris were plenty.

S.W. 5 miles to a verry bad rapid & *Camped*, a Small run on
    the left.   passed perpendicular Clift where we were
[Aug. 22]
    obliged to go into the water   passed Several places on
    Stones & sides of Mountains, one Island & several
    rapids,   all the way rapids at intervales

N.W. 3 miles high Clifts on each Side   no road [*left men here*]

West 2 Miles d° d°.   passed bad rapids Scercely possible to
[Aug. 23]
    pass down or up

N.W. 6 miles to a large Creek on the Right Side,   passed verry
    bad rapids & a number of riffles,   Mountains high
    and Steep verry Stoney   no bottoms except the Creek
    & a little above

South 1 Mile to the Mouth of a Small run   on the right a Small
    Island and rapid

N.W. 6 Miles up the Run [*Berry Creek Aug. 23*] thro a piney
    countrey   large & lofty hills high

S.W.   1 m. to the river at a Small bottom   passed over a gap
              in the Mount.[ns] from the top of which I could See the
              hollers of the river for 20 miles to a verry high
[*End of recon-* Mountain on the left, at which place my guide made
noissance][1]   Signs that the bad part of the river Com.[sd] and much
              worst than any I saw &c. &c.

miles   70
              returned.   6 bad rapids.   many others

[Lewis :]   *Monday August 26.th 1805.*

This morning was excessively cold; there was ice on the vessels of water which stood exposed to the air nearly a quarter of
an inch thick.   we collected our horses and set out at sunrise.
we soon arrived at the extreem source of the Missouri; here I
halted a few minutes, the men drank of the water and consoled
themselves with the idea of having at length arrived at this
long wished for point.   from hence we proceeded to a fine
spring on the side of the mountain where I had lain the evening before I first arrived at the Shoshone Camp.   here I halted
to dine and graize our horses, there being fine green grass on
that part of the hillside which was moistened by the water of
the spring while the grass on the other parts was perfectly dry
and parched with the sun.   I directed a pint of corn to be
given each Indian who was engaged in transporting our baggage and about the same quantity to each of the men which
they parched pounded and made into supe.   one of the women
who had been assisting in the transportation of the baggage
halted at a little run about a mile behind us, and sent on the
two pack horses which she had been conducting by one of her
female friends.   I enquired of Cameahwait the cause of her
detention, and was informed by him in an unconcerned manner
that she had halted to bring fourth a child and would soon
overtake us; in about an hour the woman arrived with her
newborn babe and passed us on her way to the camp apparently

1 The bracketed emendations in this "Course and Distance" are in pencil, and
apparently in Coues's handwriting. — ED.

as well as she ever was.   It appears to me that the facility and ease with which the women of the aborigines of North America bring fourth their children is reather a gift of nature than depending as some have supposed on the habitude of carrying heavy burthens on their backs while in a state of pregnacy. if a pure and dry air, an elivated and cold country is unfavourable to childbirth, we might expect every difficult incident to that operation of nature in this part of the continent; again as the snake Indians possess an abundance of horses, their women are seldom compelled like those in other parts of the continent to carry burthens on their backs, yet they have their children with equal convenience, and it is a rare occurrence for any of them to experience difficulty in childbirth. I have been several times informed by those who were conversant with the fact, that the indian women who are pregnant by whitemen experience more difficulty in childbirth than when pregnant by an Indian. if this be true it would go far in suport of the opinion I have advanced. the tops of the high and irregular mountains which present themselves to our view on the opposite side of this branch of the Columbia are yet perfectly covered with snow; the air which proceeds from those mountains has an agreeable coolness and renders these parched and South hillsides much more supportable at this time of the day it being now about noon.   I observe the indian women collecting the root of a speceis of fennel [1] which grows in the moist grounds and feeding their poor starved children; it is really distressing to witness the situation of those poor wretches the radix of this plant is of the knob kind, of a long ovate form terminating in a single radicle, the whole being about 3 or four inches in length and the thickest part about the size of a man's little finger. it is white firm and crisp in it's present state, when dryed and pounded it makes a fine white meal; the flavor of this root is not unlike that of annis seed but not so pungent; the stem rises to the hight of 3 or four feet is jointed smooth and cilindric; from 1 to 4 of those knobed roots are attatched to the base of this stem. the leaf is sheathing, sessile, and

---

[1] The dill (*Carum*), called "yamp" or "yampah" by the Indians (see p. 13, *note* 1, *ante*). — ED.

pultipartite,[1] the divisions long and narrow; the whole is of a deep green. it is now in blume; the flowers are numerous, small, petals white, and are of the umbellaferous kind. several small peduncles put forth from the main stock one at each joint above the sheathing leaf. it has no root leaves. the root of the present year declines when the seeds have been matured and the succeeding spring other roots of a similar kind put fourth from the little knot which unites the roots and stem and grow and decline with the stem as before mentioned. The sunflower is very abundant near the watercourses the seeds of this plant are now rip[e] and the natives collect them in considerable quantities and reduce them to meal by pounding and rubing them between smooth stones. this meal is a favorite food their manner of using it has been beforementioned. after dinner we continued our rout towards the village. on our near approach we were met by a number of young men on horseback. Cameahwait requested that we would discharge our guns when we arrived in sight of the Village, accordingly when I arrived on an eminence above the village in the plain I drew up the party at open order in a single rank and gave them a runing fire discharging two rounds. they appeared much gratifyed with this exhibition. we then proceeded to the village or encampment of brush lodges 32 in number. we were conducted to a large lodge which had been prepared for me in the center of their encampment which was situated in a beautifull level smooth and extensive bottom near the river about 3 miles above the place I had first found them encamped. here we arrived at 6 in the evening arranged our baggage near my tent and placed those of the men on either side of the baggage facing outwards. I found Colter here who had just arrived with a letter from Cap! Clark in which Cap! C. had given me an account of his perigrination and the description of the river and country as before detailed [*advised the purchase of horses and the pursute of a rout he had learned from his guide who had promised to pilot ous to a road. to the North &c.*[2]] from this view of the subject I found it a folly to think of attemp[t]ing to

<hr>

1 Probably intended for " multipartite " — Biddle gives it as "polipartite."—ED.

2 These bracketed emendations are in Clark's handwriting. — ED.

decend this river in canoes and therefore determined to commence the purchase of horses in the morning from the indians
in order to carry into execution the design we had formed of
[*Cap! C had recomended in*] passing the rocky Mountains.
I now informed Cameahwait of my intended expedition overland to the great river which lay in the plains beyond the
mountains and told him that I wished to purchase 20 horses
of himself and his people to convey our baggage. he observed
that the Minnetares had stolen a great number of their horses
this spring but hoped his people would spear me the number
I wished.   I also asked a (*another*) guide, he observed that he
had no doubt but the old man who was with Cap! C. would
accompany us if we wished him and that he was better informed
of the country than any of them.   matters being thus far arranged I directed the fiddle to be played and the party danced
very merily much to the amusement and gratification of the
natives, though I must confess that the state of my own mind
at this moment did not well accord with the prevailing mirth
as I somewhat feared that the caprice of the indians might sud-
denly induce them to withhold their horses from us without
which my hopes of prosicuting my voyage to advantage was
lost; however I determined to keep the indians in a good
humour if possible, and to loose no time in obtaining the
necessary number of horses.   I directed the hunters to turn
out early in the morning and indeavor to obtain some meat.
I had nothing but a little parched corn to eat this evening.

This morning Cap!`C. and party [1]

[Clark:]   *August 26th Monday 1805 —*

a fine morning   Despatched three men a head to hunt,   our
horses missing Sent out my guide and four men to hunt them,
which detained me untill 9 oClock a.m. at which time I set out

---

[1] Here follow two memoranda, both apparently in Clark's writing, but in different
inks: "This Comes into N° 7 betwen the 23rd and 26 August 1805," and "This
has been Copied from W. C. Journal and Coms in as above in N° 7." By "No. 7"
is meant Codex G (Clark's), which Biddle called No. 7.   At this point ends Codex
Fb, and with it Lewis's record of the journey (except for three short fragments) until
Jan. 1, 1806. — ED.

and proceeded on by way of the forks to the Indian Camps at the first were [weir]   not one mouthfull to eate untill night as our hunters could kill nothing and I could See & catch no fish except a few Small ones.   The Indians gave us 2 Sammon boiled which I gave to the men,   one of my men Shot a Sammon in the river about Sunset those fish gave us a Supper.   all the Camp flocked about me untill I went to Sleep.   and I beleve if they had a Sufficency to eate themselves and any to Spare they would be liberal of it

I derected the men to mend their Mockessons to night and turn out in the morning early to hunt Deer fish birds &c. &c. Saw great numbers of the large Black grasshopper.   Some har[e]s which were verry wild, but few Birds, a number of ground Lizards, Some fiew Pigions

CHAPTER XVII

DOWN THE LOLO TRAIL

Clark's Journal, August 27—October 10, 1805
Entries by Lewis, September 9, 10, 18–22

[Clark:]   *August 27ᵗʰ Tuesday* 1805

SOME frost this morning   every Man except one, out hunting,[1]   a young man Came from the upper Village & informed me that Cap' Lewis would join me ab. 12 oClock to day.   one man killed a Small Sammon, and the Indians gave me another which afforded us a Sleight brackfast. Those Pore people are here depending on what fish they can catch, without anything else to depend on; and appere contented,   my party hourly Complaining of their retched Situation and [word illegible in MS. — Ed.] doubts of Starveing in a Countrey where no game of any kind except a fiew fish can be found,   an Indian brough[t] in to the Camp 5 Sammon, two of which I purchased which afforded us a Supper

August 28ᵗʰ Wednesday 1805

a frost this morning.   The Ind. Cought out of their traps Several Sammon and gave us two.   I purchased two others which we made last us to day.   Several — a Camp of about 40 Indians came from the West fork and passed up to day, nothing killed by my party with every exertion in all places where game probably might be found.   I dispatched one man[2]

---

[1] I observed some flax growing in the bottoms on this river, but saw no clover or timothy, as I had seen on the Missouri and Jefferson river.   There is a kind of wild sage or hyssop, as high as a man's head, full of branches and leaves, which grows in these bottoms. — GASS (pp. 181, 182).

[2] I went on to the upper village, where I found Captain Lewis and his party buying horses.   They had got 23, which, with two we had, made in the whole 25.   I then returned to our camp, a distance of 15 miles, and arrived there late. — GASS (p. 182).

[45]

to the upper Camps to enquire if Cap. Lewis was comeing &c.
he returned after night with a letter from Cap? Lewis informing
me of his Situation at the upper Village, and had precured 22
horses for our rout through by land on the plan which I had
preposed in which he agreed with me in; and requ[e]sted me
to ride up, and get the horses the Indians informed him they
had reserved for me &c.   I purchased Some fish roe[1] of those
pore but kind people with whome I am Encamped for which I
gave three Small fish hooks, the use of which they readily pro-
seved; one Indian out all day & killed only one Sammon with
his gig; My hunters killed nothing; I had three pack
Saddles made to day for our horses which I expected Cap'
Lewis would purchase &c. Those Sammon which I live on
at present are pleasent eateing, notwithstanding they weaken
me verry fast and my flesh I find is declineing

Course Distance & [c.] over the portage from the Waters of the
Missouri to the Waters of the Columbia River.

N. 60? W.   5 Miles to a Point of a hill on the right   Passed Several
points of high land   bottom wide   only 3 Small trees

S. 80? W   10 Miles to a place the high lands approach within 200
yards, Creek 10 yds. wide

S. W.   5 miles to a narrow part of the bottom   passed a Creek
on each Side,   a place the Indians were masserced
[massacred],   a road coms in on the right

S. 70? W.   2 miles to a Creek on the right

S. 80? W   3 Miles to a rockey point ops? a Pine thicket on the left,
passed a run from the right

West   3 Miles to the head Spring of the Missouri near the top
of a deviding mountain at a gap

S. 80? W   6 miles to a run from the right,   passed Several Small
Streams & Spring runs running to my left, and down
a Drean,

N. 80? W.   4 miles to the East fork of the Lewis's River 40 y?? Wide

Miles   38   an Indian Snake Camp of 25 Lodges   passed over
hilley land all the way from the deviding ridge.

---

[1] Which, when dried and pounded, make the best of soup. — GASS (p. 183).

August 29ᵗʰ Thursday 1805 —

a Cold morning Some frost.   the Wind from the South,   I left our baggage in possession of 2 men and proceeded on up to join Capᵗ Lewis at the upper Village of Snake Indians where I arrived at 1 oClock   found him much engaged in Councelling[1] and attempting to purchase a fiew more horses. I Spoke to the Indians on various Subjects endeavoring to impress on theire minds the advantage it would be to them for to sell us horses and expedite the [*our*] journey the nearest and best way possibly that we might return as soon as possible and winter with them at Some place where there was plenty of buffalow,   our wish is to get a horse for each man to carry our baggage and for Some of the men to ride occasionally, The horses are handsom and much acustomed to be changed as to their Parsture,   we cannot calculate on their carrying large loads & feed on the Grass which we may calculate on finding in the Mountain thro' which we may expect to pass on our rout   Made Some Selestial observations, the Latᵈ of this part the Columbia River is [blank space in MS.] North. Longtᵈ [blank space in MS.] W.

I purchased a horse for which I gave my Pistol 100 Balls Powder & a Knife.   our hunters Killed 2 Deer near their Camp to day 2 yesterday & 3 the day before,   this meet was a great treat to me as I had eate none for 8 days past

August 30ᵗʰ Friday 1805

a fine Morning,   finding that we Could purchase no more horse[s] than we had for our goods &c. (and those not a Sufficint number for each of our Party to have one which is our wish) I Gave my Fuzee to one of the men & Sold his musket for a horse which Completed us to 29 total horses,   we Purchased pack cords Made Saddles & Set out on our rout down the [*Lemhi*] river by land guided by my old guide [and] one

---

[1] The Biddle text states (i, p. 435) that the guide's assertion of a practicable route up Berry Creek was " contradicted by all the Shoshonees ; " but the explorers ascribed this to the Indians' desire to retain their white guésts through the winter, and consume their merchandise. — ED.

other who joined him,   the old gu[i]de's 3 Sons followed him, before we Set out our hunters killed three Deer   proceeded on 12 Miles and encamped on the river South Side.[1]   at the time we Set out from the Indian Camps the greater Part of the Band Set out over to the waters of the Missouri. we had great attention paid to the horses, as they were nearly all Sore Backs, and Several pore, & young   Those horses are indifferent, maney Sore backs and others not acustomed to pack, and as we cannot put large loads on them are Compelled to purchase as maney as we can to take our Small propotion of baggage of the Parties, (& Eate if necessary)   Proceeded on *12* Miles to day

August 31*st* 1805 *Satturday.*

A fine morning   Set out before Sun rise,   as we passed the lodges at which place I had encamped for thre[e] nights and left 2 men,[2] those 2 men joined us and we proceeded on in the Same rout I decended the 21*st* Instant,   halted 3 hours on Sammon Creek[3] to Let our horses graze   the wind hard from the S.W.   I met an Indian on horse back who fled with great Speed to Some lodges below & informed them that the Enemies were Coming down, arm*d* with guns &c.   the inhabitents of the Lodges indisceved him,   we proceeded on the road on which I had decended as far as the 1*st* *run* [*Tower Cr.*][4] below & left the road & Proceeded up the Run in a tolerable road 4 miles & Encamped in Some old lodges at the place the road

----

[1] This camping-place was on the Lemhi River, about eight miles above the forks of Salmon River. — ED.

[2] 29th. — Capt. Clarke and all the men, except myself and another, who remained to keep camp and prepare packsaddles, went up to Capt. Lewis's camp.

30th. — We remained here all day, and in the evening the whole of the corps came down within a mile of our camp, and remained there all night, being a good place for grass. — GASS (pp. 182, 183).

[3] See Clark's map in our Atlas volume, where he calls this "Salmon Run." This is the first affluent of the Lewis (Salmon) River below the forks, and probably the one now called Carmen Creek. — ED.

[4] The emendations in bracketed Italics which appear in this part of the journal are written in pencil, apparently by Coues. — ED.

leaves the Creek and assends the high Countrey   Six Indians
followed us four of them the Sons of our guide,   our hunters
killed one Deer a goose & Prarie fowl.   This day warm and
Sultrey, Praries or open Valies on fire in Several places.   The
Countrey is Set on fire for the purpose of Collecting the different bands, and a Band of the *Flat heads* to go to the Missouri where they intend passing the winter near the Buffalow
Proceeded on 22 miles to Day, 4 miles of which up a run [1]

Course and Distance by land from the Columbia River 14 miles
below the forks.   August 31ˢᵗ 1805.

N. 35° E 2 miles up Tower Creek to a hill
N. 10° E 2   dᵒ   dᵒ   dᵒ   passed remarkable rock resem-
___
4   bling Pirimids on the Left Side

September 1ˢᵗ Sunday 1805

a fine morning Set out early and proceeded on over high
ruged hills passing the heads of the Small runs which fall into
the river on our left to a large Creek which falls into the river
6 miles to our left and encamped, in the bottom,[2]   Some rain
to day at 12 and in the evening which obliges us to Continue
all night   despatched 2 men to the mouth of the Creek to
purchase fish of the Indians at that place, they returned with
Some dried,   we giged 4 Sammon & killed one Deer to Day.
the Countrey which we passed to day is well watered & broken
Pore Stoney hilly country except the bottoms of the Creek
which is narrow,   all the Indians leave us except our Guide,
one man Shot two bear this evining unfortunately we Could
git neither of them

---

[1] The encampment for this night was at some distance from the river at the head
of Tower (Boyle's) Creek upon what Clark designates on his map as a "nakid
mour." — ED.

[2] In the low ground there are most beautiful tall straight pine trees of different
kinds, except of white pine. . . . The country is very mountainous and thickly
timbered, mostly with spruce pine. — GASS (p. 187).

Septr 1st Sunday

N. 80.° W   1½   Miles to the top of a high hill

N 65.° W   1½   to the of a hill passing the heads of dreans passing to our left

N. 55.° W. 3½   miles to the top of a high hill   pass^d two forks of a Crek, the first large & bold the 2^d Small

S. 80.° W. 1½   mile down a raveen to a run

N. 70.° W. 3½   to the top of a high hill passing a branch at ¼ & over a hill at 1 mile

N. 35.° W. 2½   to the top of a high hill

N. 25.° W. 1½   to ditto   passed a branch at ½ mile which passes to the left

N. 80.° W. 2½   decending a Steep winding hill to a large Creek which we Call Fish Creek & runs into the river at Some lodge 6 miles below South [1]

N. 12.° W. 2   Miles up the Creek to a bluff Point. [2]

   20

September 2nd Monday 1805

a Cloudy Morning, raind Some last night we Set out early and proceeded on up the [*Fish*] Creek, Crossed a large fork from the right and one from the left; and at 8 [7½] miles left the roade on which we were pursuing and which leads over to the Missouri, [3] and proceeded up a West fork [*of Fish Creek*] without a roade proceded on thro' thickets in which we were obliged to Cut a road, over rockey hill Sides where our horses were in [per]peteal danger of Slipping to their certain distruction & up & Down Steep hills, where Several horses fell, Some turned over, and others Sliped down Steep hill Sides, one horse Crippeled & 2 gave out. with the greatest dificuelty risque &c. we made five miles 7½ & Encamped on the left Side of the Creek in a Small Stoney bottom. after night Some time before the rear Came up, one Load left about 2 miles back, the horse on which it was carried crippled. Some rain at night

1 Fish Creek is now known as the North fork of the Salmon. — ED.

2 From the encampment for this night (see Clark's map) the trail crossed Fish Creek, but recrossed to the east bank a short distance above. — ED.

3 By way of Datang Creek and Big Hole Pass. — ED.

Sept. 2nd Monday

North	1½	to a large fork which falls in on the left in a pine bottom
N. 45° E	2½	Miles to a large fork which falls in on the right Hills Cov.d with Pine
North	3½	miles to the forks of the Creek passed a leavel pine bottom & pine hills maney beaver Dams across the Creek
N. 60° W	2½	miles up the west fork leaving the road on our right which passes to the Missouri by the East fork
N. 35° W	3	miles up the west fork Crossed it Several times & passing thro' thickets brush & over rocks.
N. 50° W	2	miles over hills rocks & Steep points & hill Sides on the left of the Creek Crossing a run at 1 mile
	15	

September 3rd Tuesday 1805 —

A Cloudy morning,   horses verry Stiff   Sent 2 men back with the horse on which Cap.t Lewis rode for the load left back last night which detained us untill 8 oClock at which time we Set out.   The Country is timbered with Pine Generally, the bottoms have a variety of Srubs & the fur trees in Great abundance,   hills high & rockey on each Side,   in the after part of the day the high mountains closed the Creek on each Side and obliged us to take on the Steep Sides of those Mountains, So Steep that the horses Could Scur[ce]ly keep from Slipping down,   Several sliped & Injured themselves verry much,   with great dificuelty we made [blank space in MS.] miles (*about 8 m. see Courses & Dist*) & Encamped on a branch of the Creek we assended after crossing Several Steep points & one mountain,   but little to eate I killed 5 Pheasents & the hunters 4 with a little Corn afforded us a kind of Supper,   at dusk it began to Snow, at 3 oClock Some rain.   The mountains (*we had passed*) to the East Covered with Snow.   we met with a great misfortune, in haveing our last Th[er]mometer broken, by accident   This day we passed over emence hils and Some of the worst roads that ever horses passed,   our horses frequently fell   Snow about 2 inches deep when it began to rain which termonated in a Sleet [storm]   our gen.l Courses nearly North from the R

[51]

Sept! 3rd Tuesday 1805

N. 25° W. 2½ Miles to a Small fork on the left Hilley and thick
assending

N. 15° W. 2   miles to a fork on the right assending

N. 22° W. 2½ miles to a fork on the left passing one on the left
Several Spring runs on the right   Stoney hills &
much falling timber

N. 18° E. 2   miles passing over Steep points & winding ridges to a
high Point   passed a run on the right

N. 32° W. 2   miles to the top of a high hill   passed 2 runs from the
left, passing on the Side of a Steep ridge.   no road

N. 40° W 3   miles leaveing the waters of the Creek to the right &
    ——   passing over a high pine Mount? to the head of
    14   a Drean running to the left

September 4th Wednesday 1805 —

a verry cold morning every thing wet and frosed,   we [were]
detained untill 8 oClock to thaw the covering for the baggage
&c. &c.   Groun[d] covered with Snow,   we assended a
mountain & took a Divideing ridge[1] which we kept for Several Miles & fell on the head of a Creek which appeared to
run the Course we wished to go,   I was in front, & saw
Several of the Argalia or Ibex   decended the mountain by
verry Steep decent takeing the advantage of the points and
best places to the Creek, where our hunters killed a Deer
which we made use of, and prosued our Course down the
Creek[2] to the forks about 5 miles where we met a part[y] of
the Tushepau nation, of 33 Lodges   about 80 men 400 Total
and at least 500 horses,   those people rec[e]ved us friendly,
threw white robes over our Sholders & Smoked in the pipes
of peace,   we Encamped with them & found them friendly
but nothing but berries to eate a part of which they gave us,

---

1 One of the Bitter Root range, which divides the waters of the Salmon and Bitter
Root rivers.   At this point the explorers again enter Montana, but are still on the
Pacific slope. — ED.

2 Proceeded down a small valley about a mile wide with a rich black soil; in
which there are a great quantity of sweet roots and herbs, such as sweet myrrh,
angelica, and several others, that the natives make use of. — GASS (p. 188).

those Indians are well dressed with Skin shirts & robes,   they
[are] Stout & light complected more So than Common for
Indians, The Chief harangued untill late at night, Smoked
in our pipe and appeared Satisfied.   I was the first white man
who ever wer on the waters of this river.[1]

September 4th Wednesday 1805

N. 10° W. 6 miles on a Direct Course over a high Snow mountain &
          down a Drean of Flat head River to a fork on the
          right. (our rout on a Dividing ridge to the right 9 m[s]
          about.   bad road

N. 18° W. 3 down the run to a run on the left

N. 35° W 3 miles down the run to the river which Coms from the
          East, a wide Vallie.   33 tents of Flat heads.[2]

ml[s]   12
        ─────
        53 ½ [65]

September 5[th] Thursday 1805

a cloudy morning   we assembled the Chiefs & warriers and
Spoke to them (with much dificuel[t]y as what we Said had to
pass through Several languages before it got into theirs, which
is a gugling kind of language Spoken much thro the throught
[throat][3]) we informed them who we were, where we came

---

[1] Traditions current among the present generation of Flathead Indians regarding
this visit of Lewis and Clark are presented by O. D. Wheeler in *Wonderland*, 1900,
pp. 43–45. — ED.

[2] In ascending Fish Creek the party kept to the East side of that stream ; and
their direction of travel was, with one immaterial exception, always to the west of
north, often considerably so.   This, I think, brought them out on the head of a
branch of Camp Creek, instead of on the main stream, and to the northwest of the
latter's head.   The camp of the Indians and of the explorers from Sept. 4 to Sept. 6
was unquestionably on Camp Creek, and not on Ross's Fork.   I think that the last
course-reading of Clark on Sept. 4, which he gives as " N. 35° W. 3m. down this
run," should probably read " N. 35. E. ; " this would reconcile the apparent dis-
crepancies, and justify the above conclusion. — O. D. WHEELER.

[3] Their words have all a remarkably guttural sound, and there is nothing which
seems to represent the tone of their speaking more exactly than the clucking of a
fowl, or the noise of a parrot.   This peculiarity renders their voices scarcely audible,
except at a short distance, and when many of them are talking, forms a strange confusion of sounds. — BIDDLE (i, p. 441).

from, where bound and for what purpose &c. &c. and requested to purchase & exchange a fiew horses with them, in the Course of the day I purchased 11 horses & exchanged 7 for which we gave a fiew articles of merchendize, those people possess ellegant horses.[1] we made 4 Chiefs [to] whome we gave meadels & a few Small articles with Tobacco, the women brought us a few berries & roots to eate and the Principal Chief a Dressed Brarow, Otter & two Goat & antilope Skins

Those people wore their hair as follows the men Cewed [queued] with otter Skin on each Side falling over the Sholders forward, the women loose promisquisly over ther Sholders & face long shirts which come to their anckles & tied with a belt about their waste with a roabe over, the[y] have but fiew ornaments and what they do were [wear] are Similar to the Snake Indians, They Call themselves Eoote-lash-Schute (*Oat la shoot*)[2] and consist of 450 Lodges in all and divided into Several bands on the heads of Columbia river & Missouri, Some low down the Columbia River

September 6ͭͪ Friday 1805 —

Some little rain, purchased two fine horses & took a Vocabelary of the language litened our loads & packed up, rained cont.ᵈ untill 12 oClock, we Set out at 2 oClock at the Same time all the Indians Set out on their way to meet the Snake Indians at the 3 forks of the Missouri. Crossed a Small river from the right we call (*this was the main river or Clarks*) Soon after Setting out, also a Small Creek from the North all three forks Comeing together below our Camp at which place the Mountains Close on each Side of the river, We proceeded on N 30 W. Crossed a Mountain and Struck the river Several miles down, at which place the Indians had

---

[1] And so numerous that this party had with them at least five hundred. — BIDDLE (*ut supra*).

[2] And represent themselves as one band of a nation called Tushepaws, a numerous people of four hundred and fifty tents, etc. — BIDDLE (i, pp. 440, 441).

Encamped two days before, we Proceeded on down the River
which is 30 y^{ds} wide Shallow & Stoney Crossing it Several
times & Encamped in a Small bottom on the right side.
rained this evening nothing to eate but berries, our flour out,
and but little Corn, the hunters killed 2 pheasents only. all
our horses purchased of the flat heads (*oote-lash-shutes*) we
Secured well for fear of their leaveing of us, and Watched them
all night for fear of their leaving us or the Indians prosuing &
Steeling them.

Course Distance &c. Down Clark's river Septr 6th 1805

N. 30° W. 5   miles crossing the river & a creek at 1½ m. & thro a
                vallie to the top of a mountain covered with pine
N. 80° W. 1 ½ miles down a reveen & Steep hill Sides to the river at
                an old Encampment. a creek left
West   1 ½ miles down the Creek, bottoms narrow.
N. 35° W. 2   miles down the River which is 25 yards wide passed
                a run on each side.

          10

September 7th Satturday 1805 —

A Cloudy & rainie Day the greater Part of the day dark &
Drisley we proceeded on down the river thro a Vallie passed
Several Small Runs on the left (*right*) & *3* creeks on the left
The Vallie from 1 to 2 miles wide the Snow top mountains
to our left, open hilley Countrey on the right,[1] Saw 2 horses
left by the Indians those horses were as wild a[s] Elk. One
of our hunters came up this morning without his horse, in the
course of the night the horse broke loose & cleared out. we
did not make camp untill dark, for the want of a good place,
one of our hunters did not join us this evening. he haveing
killed an elk packed his horse & could not overtake us

---

[1] The explorers are now in the valley of the Bitter Root River (sometimes known
as St. Mary's Fork). At Missoula this unites with Hellgate River to form Missoula
River, which becomes Clark's Fork of the Columbia. — ED.

Sept! 7th Satturday 1805

N. 40.° W. 3 miles down the River aforesaid

N. 80.° W. 3 miles down the River to a large Creek on the left. bottoms narrow.

N. 45.° W. 4 down the river to a Creek on the left. bottoms wider, hills on the right is bald, mountains on our left is high and the tops Covered with Snow

North   4 miles to a Creek which runs from the Snow toped mountains, passed one on the left at 1 mile & Several Small runs on the right, and left, one Drean

N. 25.° E. 8 miles down the River, passed a large Creek on the left at 2 miles. the Vallie thro which we passed about 2 miles wide, lands pore & Stoney   The foot of the Snow toped mountains approach near the river on the left   the river 50 yards wide Shallow & Stoney.   no fish to be Seen.   2 Deer 2 crains & 2 Phesents killed to day.[1]

_____

22

September 8th Sunday 1805 —

a Cloudy morning   Set out early and proceeded on through an open Vallie for 23 miles passed 4 Creeks on the right Some runs on the left,   the bottoms as also the hills Stoney bad land,   Some pine on the Creeks and mountains, an[d] partial on the hills to the right hand Side   two of our hunters came up with us at 12 oClock with an Elk, & Buck,   the wind from the N.W. & Cold.   The foot of the Snow mountains approach the River on the left Side.   Some Snow on the mountain to the right also,   proceeded on down the Vallie which is pore Stoney land and encamped on the right Side of the river   a hard rain all the evening   we are all Cold and wet.   on this part of the river (*on the head of Clarks River*) I observe great quantities of a peculiar Sort of Prickly peare grow in Clusters ovel & about the Size of a Pigions egge with strong thorns which is So birded [bearded] as to draw the

_____

[1] This is one of the most fertile valleys in Montana, now covered with orchards. The camp for this night was a few miles south of Grantsdale, apparently just above Weeping Child Creek. — O. D. WHEELER.

UPPER BITTERROOT VALLEY, MONTANA

Pear from the Cluster after penetrating our feet. Drewyer killed a Deer, I killed a prarie fowl we found 2 mears and a Colt, the mears were lame, we ventered to let our late purchase of horses loose to night

September 8th Sunday

North   11 miles to a small run on the right Side, passed a large Creek at 1 mile one at 4 miles & a Small one at 8 miles, thro' a open Vally of 4 or 5 miles wide Call'd Horse Vally

N. 12° W 12 through the Said Vallie to a large Creek from the right divided into 4 different Channels, i. e. scattered Creek[1]

———
23

[Lewis :][2]   *Monday September 9th 1805.*

Set out at 7 A.M. this morning and proceeded down the Flathead river leaving it on our left, the country in the valley of this river is generally a prarie and from five to 6 miles wide the growth is almost altogether pine principally of the long-leafed kind, with some spruce and a kind of furr resembleing the scotch furr. near the wartercourses we find a small proportion of the narrow leafed cottonwood; some redwood honeysuckle and rosebushes form the scant proportion of underbrush to be seen. at 12 we halted on a small branch which falls into the river on the E. side, where we breakfasted on a scant proportion of meat which we had reserved from the hunt of yesterday added to three geese which one of our hunters killed this morning. two of our hunters have arrived, one of them brought with him a redheaded woodpecker of the large kind common to the U States. this is the first of the kind I have seen since I left the Illinois. just as we were seting out Drewyer arrived with two deer. we continued our rout down the valley about 4 miles and crossed the river; it is hear a handsome stream about 100 yards wide and affords

———
[1] Coues identifies " scattered Creek " with the present Burnt Fork, near whose mouth is the town of Stevensville. The encampment for this night must have been near Fort Owen, named for the earliest ranchers in the valley. — ED.

[2] These entries by Lewis for Sept. 9 and 10 are contained in Codex Fc. — ED.

a considerable quantity of very clear water, the banks are low and it's bed entirely gravel. the stream appears navigable, but from the circumstance of their being no sammon in it I believe that there must be a considerable fall in it below. our guide could not inform us where this river discharged itself into the columbia river, he informed us that it continues it's course along the mountains to the N. as far as he knew it and that not very distant from where we then were it formed a junction with a stream nearly as large as itself which took it's rise in the mountains near the Missouri to the East of us and passed through an extensive valley generally open prarie which forms an excellent pass to the Missouri.[1] the point of the Missouri where this Indian pass intersects it, is about 30 miles above the *gates of the rocky Mountain,* or the place where the valley of the Missouri first widens into an extensive plain after entering the rockey Mountains. the guide informed us that a man might pass to the missouri from hence by that rout in four days. we continued our rout down the W. side of the river about 5 miles further and encamped on a large creek which falls in on the West. as our guide inform[ed] me that we should leave the river at this place and the weather appearing settled and fair I determined to halt the next day rest our horses and take some scelestial Observations. we called this Creek *Travellers rest.*[2] it is about 20 yards wide a fine bould clear runing stream the land through which we passed is but indifferent a could white gravley soil. we estimate our journey of this day at 19. M.

at the creek where we dined I took the Meridian Alt.ᵈ of ☉'s U. L. with Sextant fore obsᵗⁿ 98°. 1′. 30″.
Latitude deduced from this Observation 46°. 41′. 38.9

Point of observation N.° *46.*

At our encampment of this evening observed time and distance of the Moon's western limb from *a* Aquila ✳. West. with Sextant.

---

1 The Hellgate River. — Ed.
2 Now called the Lo Lo (or Lou Lou) fork of the Bitter Root River ; at its mouth is a town of the same name. — Ed.

Time		Distance		Time		Distance	
h	m	s			h	m	s	
P.M. 9.	52.	47.	63°. 33′. —″	P.M. 10.	6.	1.	63°. 38. 30
".	56.	58.	". 35. 15	"	7.	46.	". 39. 45
".	59.	41.	". 36. 30	"	9.	24.	". 40. 30
10.	3.	48.	". 37. 45	"	11.	2.	". 41. —
".	6.	1.	". 38. 30	"	13.	27.	". 41. 45

this set of observations cannot be much depended on as through mistake I brought the Moons Western limb in contact with the star, instead of her Eastern limb she having passed into her third quarter and of course her Western limb somewhat imperfect.

[Clark:]   *September 9th Monday 1805 —*

a fair morning Set out early and proceeded on thro' a plain as yesterday down the valley Crossed a large Creek (*called*) Scattering (on which Cotton trees grew) at 1½ miles, a Small one at 10 miles, both from the right, the main river at 15 miles & Encamped on a large Creek from the left which we call Travelers rest Creek. killed 4 deer & 4 Ducks & 3 prarie fowls. day fair Wind NW. (See Suplement)

September 9th Monday

N. 15° W. 15 miles Thro a open vallie to the River, leaveing the road to our right Crossed a Small Creek from the left at 9 miles, and the river which is 100 yards wide, & passed through a pine bottom after Crossing the (*Clarks*) River

N. 40° W. 2 miles passing thro' a pine bottom after crossing the river to a large road on the left of the river in an open Vallie

N. 10° W. 4 miles Through an open Valle to a large Creek from the left. (caled *Travelers rest* and Encamped the 9th & 10th

21

9th Sept. Cont.

North 12 Miles to the mouth of a lark [large] fork which Joins from the right and heads up near the Missouri Some distance below the 3 forks, this River has extinsive Vallies and is a good rout to the Missouri which the Indians say may be traveled in 4 days and is a good rout. The Vallie near the mouth of this fork, is about 7 or 8 miles wide leavel & open, but little timber on this fork in Sight.

[Lewis:]   *Tuesday September 10th 1805*

The morning being fair I sent out all the hunters, and directed two of them to procede down the river as far as it's junction with the Eastern fork which heads near the missouri, and return this evening. this fork of the river we determined to name the Valley plain river. (we called the Eastern fork of Clarkes river.) I think it most probable that this river continues it's course along the rocky M.ts Northwardly as far or perhaps beyond the scources of Medecine river and then turning to the West falls into the Tacootchetessee.[1] The Minetares informed us that there wass a large river west of, and at no great distance from the sources of Medicine river, which passed along the Rocky Mountains from S. to N. this evening one of our hunters returned accompanyed by three men of the Flathead nation whom he had met in his excurtion up *travellers rest* Creek. on first meeting him the Indians were alarmed and prepared for battle with their bows and arrows, but he soon relieved their fears by laying down his gun and advancing towards them. the Indians were mounted on very fine horses of which the Flatheads have a great abundance; that is, each man in the nation possesses from 20 to a hundred head. our guide could not speake the language of these people but soon engaged them in conversation by signs or jesticulation, the common language of all the Aborigines of North America, it is one understood by all of them and appears to be sufficiently copious to convey with a degree of certainty the outlines of what they wish to communicate. in this manner we learnt from these people that two men which they supposed to be of the Snake nation had stolen 23 horses from them and that they were in pursuit of the theaves. they told us they were in great hast, we gave them some boiled veni-

---

1 This "eastern fork" was Hellgate River. The name Tacootchetessee evidently refers to the Columbia River, although it was really applied to the river afterward called Fraser's; see Alexander Mackenzie's *Voyages through N. America* (London, 1801), at the end of which is a map showing the "Tacoutche Tesse or Columbia River," its lower course hypothetically traced by a dotted line — indicating that he supposed Fraser's (which he had seen only in its upper reaches) to end in the Columbia. — ED.

son, of which the[y] eat sparingly. the sun was now set, two of them departed after receiving a few small articles which we gave them, and the third remained, having agreed to continue with us as a guide, and to introduce us to his relations whom he informed us were numerous and resided in the plain below the mountains on the columbia river, from whence he said the water was good and capable of being navigated to the sea ; that some of his relation[s] were at the sea last fall and saw an old whiteman who resided there by himself and who had given them some handkerchiefs such as he saw in our posses- sion. he said it would require five sleeps[1]

[Clark:]   *September* 10*ᵗʰ* *Tuesday* 1805 —

A fair morning Concluded to Delay to day and make Some observations, as at this place the rout which we are to prosue will pass up the *Travelers rest Creek*, The day proved fair and we took equal altitudes & some luner observations. The Lat*ᵈ* *46° – 48′ – 28″* as the guide report[s] that no game is to be found on our rout for a long ways, ads an addi- tion to the cause of our delay to precure Some meat, des- patched all our hunters in different directions, to hunt the Deer which is the only large game to be found they killed 4 deer a Beaver & 3 Grouse which was divided, one of the hunters Colter, met with 3 flatheads [*Tushapaw*] Indians who were in pursuit of 2 Snake Indians that hade taken from ther Camps on the Columbia [*head of Kooskooske*] River 21 horses, Those Indians came with Colter to our Camp & informed by Signs of their misfortune & the rout to their villages &c. &c. one of them Concluded to return with us. I (*we*) gave them a ring fish hook & tied a pece of ribin in the hare of each, which appeared to please them verry much, Cap Lewis gave them a Steel & a little Powder to make fire, after eating 2 of them proceeded on in pursute of their horses. men all much engaged preparing mockersons &c. &c. The Countrey about this place is already described in that above.

---

[1] Five sleeps, or days' journey.— BIDDLE (i. p. 446).

[Clark:]   *September 11ᵗʰ Wednesday 1805 —*

A fair morning wind from the NW   we set out at 3 oClock
and proceeded on up the *Travelers rest Creek* accompanied by
the Flat head (*or Tushapaws*) Indian   about 7 miles below
this Creek a large fork comes in from the right and heads up
against the waters of the Missouri below the three forks,   this
river has extensive Vallies of open leavel land, " and passes in
its Whole Course thro' a Valie" they call it Valie Plain
River (*Chicarlusket we call it the east fork of Clark's river*)
our guide tels us a fine large roade passes up this river to the
Missouri.   The loss of 2 of our horses detained us un! 3
oClock. P.M.   our *Flat head* Indian being restless thought
proper to leave us and proceed on alone,   Sent out the hunters to hunt in advance as usial.   (we have Selected 4 of the
best hunters to go in advance to hunt for the party.   This
arrangement has been made long since)   we proceeded on up
the Creek [*Travelers rest*] on the right [*hand*] Side [*left bank*]
thro a narrow valie and good road for 7 miles and Encamped
at Some old Indian Lodges,   nothing killed this evening
hills on the right high & ruged,   the mountains on the left
high & Covered with Snow.   The day Verry worm

[Courses & distances] September 11ᵗʰ Tuesday, 1805 [1]

S. 45° E. 1½ miles up Travelers rest Creek to a road which passes up
           on the lower side & is the road to the Missouri
West   5½ miles up the Creek on the right side   hills on the right
           high & rugid   Snow toped mountains on the left &
           we passed in the vallie which is about ½ᵐ Wide [2]

[Clark: *September 12ᵗʰ Thursday 1805.*

a white frost   Set out at 7 oClock & proceeded on up the
Creek, passed a Fork on the right on which I saw near an old
Indian encampment a Swet (*Sweat*) house Covered with earth,
at 2 miles assended a high hill & proceeded through a hilley

---

¹ The courses and distances as given by Clark Sept. 11–20, 1805, with the accompanying maps are found in Clark-Voorhis field-book.   For a description of this
interesting MS. see Preface. — ED.

² The first eight or ten miles up this stream (Lolo) is through a fine bottom now
occupied by ranches. — O. D. WHEELER.

Map from Clark Field-book, showing Course and Camping places,
September 11, 12, 1805.

and thickly timbered Countrey for 9 miles & on the Right [*hand side*] of the Creek, passing Several branches from the right of fine Clear water and Struck at a fork at which place the road forks, one passing up each fork. The Timber is Short & long leaf Pine Spruce Pine & fur. The road through this hilley Countrey is verry bad passing over hills & thro' Steep hollows, over falling timber &c. &c. continued on & passed Some most intolerable road on the Sides of the Steep Stoney mountains, which might be avoided by keeping up the Creek which is thickly covered with under groth & falling timber,[1] Crossed a Mountain 8 miles with out water & encamped on a hill Side on the Creek after Decending a long Steep mountain,   Some of our Party did not get up untill 10 oClock P M.   I mad[e] camp at 8   on this roade & particularly on this Creek the Indians have pealed a number of Pine for the under bark which they eate at certain Seasons of the year,   I am told in the Spring they make use of this bark our hunters Killed only one Pheasent this afternoon.   Party and horses much fatigued.

[Courses and distances] Sept.ʳ 12ᵗʰ

N. W   11 miles to the forks of the Creek   road passing through a hilley countrey thickly timbered with the long leaf short leaf Spruce Pine   crossed 6 branches which runs from the left the 1ˢᵗ the largest   Killed 3 [words illegible] this morning Dined at the forks,   passed a Hot hous cov.ᵈ with Earth on the 1ˢᵗ fork.

S. 75° W 12 miles to the Creek striking the creek at 4 mile and passing over a high mountain for 8 miles   no water   the hills steep & rockey & thickly timbered   [one line illegible]

September 13ᵗʰ *Wednesday* (*Friday*) 1805 —

a cloudy morning   Cap.ᵗ Lewis and one of our guides lost their horses, Cap.ᵗ Lewis & 4 men detained to hunt the horses,   I proceeded on with the partey up the Creek   at 2 miles passed Several Springs which I observed the Deer

---

[1] This corresponds to the description of recent travellers, who say that the cañon is narrow, bushy, and rough, but the hills are rugged and difficult. — ED.

Elk &c. had made roads to, and below one of the Indians had made a whole to bathe, I tasted this water and found it hot & not bad tasted   The last [blank space in MS.]   in further examonation I found this water nearly boiling hot at the places it Spouted from the rocks (which [are] a hard Corse Grit, and of great size   the rocks on the Side of the Mountain of the Same texture)   I put my finger in the water, at first could not bare it in a Second.[1]   as Several roads led from these Springs in different derections, my guide took a wrong road and took us out of our rout 3 miles through intolerable rout,   after falling into the right road   I proceeded on thro [a] tolerable rout for ab: 4 or 5 miles and halted to let our horses graze as well as wate for Cap: Lewis who has not yet come up,   The pine Countrey falling timber &c. &c. Continue. This Creek is verry much damed up with the beaver, but we can see none,   dispatched two men back to hunt Cap: Lewis horse, after he came up, and we proceeded over a mountain to the head of the Creek which we left to our left and at 6 miles from the place I nooned it, we fell on a Small Creek from the left which Passed through open glades Some of which [were] ½ a mile wide;   we proceeded down this Creek about 2 miles to where the mountains Closed on either Side crossing the Creek Several times & Encamped.[2]

---

[1] There are two sets of hot springs here. Less than two miles above the explorers' camp of the 12th, Traveler's Rest Creek forks, the northern branch bearing the name of Granite Creek — on which, just above the forks, among a maze of huge granite boulders, the Granite Hot Springs pour forth. On the other fork, Traveler's Rest or Lolo Creek proper, — half a mile, perhaps, by the trails across the hill, and somewhat farther by the creek, — are what are known as Boyle's Springs, and these are they to which the narrative refers — its description agreeing well with the present appearance of the latter springs. There is now (1903) a good road up Lolo Creek to both springs, and a daily stage-coach to and from Missoula. — O. D. WHEELER.

[2] The expedition at this point crossed the divide between the waters of Clark's Fork (Lolo Creek) and those of the Lewis (Snake) River. Glade Creek is one of the sources of the Clearwater (or Kooskooskee) River, whose waters Lewis and Clark follow in the main to its junction with Lewis River at Lewiston, Idaho. The pass is that known as the Lolo or Northern Nez Percé trail, and follows a ridge north of the Clearwater valley through the northern portion of the Bitter Root Forest Reserve. This trail was explored in 1854 by Lieut. John Mullan, and his account is given in Stevens's report, vol. xii of *Explorations and Surveys for R. R. to Pacific Ocean*

Map from Clark Field-book, showing Course and Camping places.
September 13–16, 1805.

One Deer & Some Pheasants killed this morning,　I shot 4 Pheasents of the Common Kind except the tale was black. The road over the last mountain was thick Steep & Stoney as usial,　after passing the head of Travelers rest Creek, the road was verry fine leavel open & firm　Some mountains in view to the SE & SW Covered with Snow.

Course & Distance &c Sept. 13th 1805

S. W.	2 miles up the Said Creek through an emencely bad road, rocks, steep hill sides & fallen timber inumerable　The snow toped mountains at a long distance from S W to S E　none else to be seen in any other Directions to hot springs on the right.　Those springs come out in maney places in the rocks and nearly boiling hot
S. 30° W.	3 miles to the creek　passed　a round about of 3 miles to our left of intolerable road timber &c as usial　halted to noon it & wate for Capt Lewis who lost his horse
S. 30° W.	7 miles over a mountain & a Dividing ridge of flat gradey [gladey] land to a Creek from the left passing thro a glade of ½ a mile in width, keeping down the Creek 2 mile & Encamped.　The country as usial except the Glades which is open & boggey, water clare and sandey.　Snow toped mountains to the S E. at the head of this Creek which we call [blank in MS.] Creek. The after part of the day cloudy.　I killed 4 Pheasents & Shields killed a Black tail Deer.　a horse found in the glades left lame by some Indians &c
m　12	

September 14th Thursday (Saturday) 1805

a cloudy day　in the Valies it rained and hailed, on the top of the mountains Some Snow fell　we Set out early and Crossed a high mountain on the right of the Creek for 6 miles to the forks of the Glade Creek (*one of the heads of the Koos koos kee*)

(Washington, 1860).　General O. O. Howard made a military trail through this region in 1876–77, during the Nez Percé War.　This followed the Indian trail, save where cut-offs made the route more practicable.　The details of Lewis and Clark's route have been much discussed.　The best modern map and description is that of John B. Leiberg, "The Bitterroot Forest Reserve," in the United States Geological Survey, *Report*, 1898–99, vol. v, pp. 317–410.　The recently discovered map made by Clark (see our Atlas volume) will serve to decide many topographical puzzles. — ED.

the right hand fork which falls in is about the size of the other, we crossed to the left Side at the forks, and cross^d a verry high Steep mountain for 9 miles to a large fork from the left which appears to head in the Snow toped mountains Southerley and S.E.   we Cross^d Glade Creek above its mouth, at a place the *Tushepaws or* Flat head Indians have made 2 *Wears* across to Catch Sammon and have but latterly left the place   I could see no fish, and the grass entirely eaten out by the horses,   we proceeded on 2 miles & Encamped opposit a Small Island at the mouth of a branch on the right side of the river which is at this place 80 yards wide, Swift and Stoney,   here we were compelled to kill a Colt for our men & Selves to eat for the want of meat & we named the South fork Colt killed Creek,[1] and this river we Call *Flat head* River   the flat head name is Koos koos ke   The Mountains which we passed to day much worst than yesterday the last excessively bad & thickly Strowed with falling timber & Pine Spruce fur Hackmatak & Tamerack,[2] Steep & Stoney   our men and horses much fatigued,   The rain [blank space in MS.]

Course Distance &^{c} Sept. 14$^{th}_{''}$ 1805

S. 20° W. 6 miles over a high mountain countrey thickley covered with pine to the forks of the Creek one of equal size from the right side, passed much falling timber   this Mountain is covered with Spruce & Pitch pine fir, & what is called to the Northard Hackmatack & Tamerack,   The Creeks are verry stoney and has much fall

S. 60° W. 9 miles over a high mountain steep & almost inaxcessible much falling timber which fatigues our men & horses

---

[1] After reaching the forks of Glade Creek, the party in some way left the regular Lolo Trail which ascends the ridge to the left and for a long distance runs nearly due west. L. & C. took a side trail to the southwest which led them over a mountain into the Lochsa cañon at the mouth of Whitesand, i. e. Colt-killed Creek.   This trail is used still by Indians and by trappers on the upper Lochsa.   The trail down the Lochsa is good and probably always has been as the timber is open.   We were easily able to locate the camp " opposit a Small Island at the mouth of a branch on the right side of the river."   Just before reaching this branch is a small prairie of about five acres on which we may suppose the horses grazed, if indeed the camp itself were not there. — C. V. PIPER.

[2] These are both varieties of *Larix occidentalis.* — C. V. PIPER.

S. 60° W — exceedingly, in stepping over so great a number of logs added to the steep assents and decents of the mountains to the forks of the Creek, the one on our left which we had passed down falling into one still larger from the left which heads in the Snowey Mountains to the S. E. & South, those two Creeks form a river of 80 yards wide, containing much water, verry stoney and rapid. The Creek we came Down I call Glade Creek. the left hand fork the Killed Colt Creek from our killing a *Colt* to eate, above the mouth of Glade fork, the *Flatheads* has a were [weir] across to catch sammon [one line in MS. gone]

S. 70° W — 2 miles down the [blank space in MS.] River to the mouth of a run on the right side opposit an Island & camped

m 17 — turned our horses on the Island rained snowed & hailed the greater part of the day all wet and cold

Wednesday (Sunday) Sept. 15th 1805

We set out early, the morning Cloudy and proceeded on Down the right Side of (*koos koos kee*) River over Steep points rockey & buschey as usial for 4 miles to an old Indian fishing place,[1] here the road leaves the river to the left and assends a *mountain* winding in every direction to get up the Steep assents & to pass the emence quantity of falling timber which had [been] falling from dift causes i e fire & wind and has deprived the greater part of the Southerley Sides of this mountain of its green timber, 4[2] miles up the mountain I found a Spring and halted for the rear to come up and to let our horses rest & feed, [in] about 2 hours the rear of the party came up much fatigued & horses more So, Several horses Sliped and roled down Steep hills which hurt them verry much the one which Carried my desk & Small trunk Turned over & roled down a mountain for 40 yards & lodged against a tree, broke the Desk

[1] This fishing place is still used by the Indians; it is a beautiful little prairie of two or three acres at the moutn of a fine creek. — C. V. PIPER.

[2] Just below the fishing place is a cañon two or three miles long, impassable to horses. The vertical distance from the fishing place to the Lolo trail is about 4000 feet. Lewis and Clark easily lost more than a day's time by losing the main trail at the forks of Glade Creek. All of the trails up the cañon wall of the Lochsa are *very steep*. — C. V. PIPER.

the horse escaped and appeared but little hurt   Some others verry much hurt,   from this point I observed a range of high mountains Covered with Snow from S E. to S W with their tops bald or void of timber,   after two hours delay we proceeded on up the mountain Steep & ruged as usial, more timber near the top,   when we arrived at the top As we Conceved, we could find no water and Concluded to Camp and make use of the Snow we found on the top to cook the remn.t of our Colt & make our Supe,   evening verry cold and cloudy. Two of our horses gave out, pore and too much hurt to proceed on and left in the rear.   nothing killed to day except 2 Phest.t

From this mountain I could observe high ruged mountains in every direction as far as I could see.   with the greatest exertion we could only make 12 miles up this mountain (*and encamped on the top of the mountain near a Bank of old Snow about 3 feet deep lying on the Northern Side of the mountain and in Small banks on the top & leavel parts of the mountain,   we melted the Snow to drink, and cook our horse flesh to eat*).

September 15th Friday 1805

West   4 mile down the creek bottoms Passing over 4 steep high hills to a run at an old Indian Camp at a fishing place, where we wer some time e'er we found the proper road which assends a high mountain   road excessively bad. I take the wrong road

N. W.   4 miles assending a high steep ruged mountain winding in every direction,   the timber has been burnt & lies in every direction, several horses roled down much hurt   my portable desk broken,   from the top of those mountains a snow mountain from S E to S W.   we leave the river to our left hand,   found a spring on the top of the mountain where we halted to Dine & wate for the party.   rained

N. W.   4 miles assend a steep ruged mountain passing over high stoney
 —— 12   knobs   maney parts bare of timber, the[y] haveing burnt it down & as it lies on the ground in every direction   we could find no water deturmined to camp as it was late and make use of snow for to boil our coalt meat & make supe.   we camped on a high Pinical of the mountain Two of our horses gave out to day and left.   the road as bad as it can possibly be to pass.

Saturday (Monday) Sept.ʳ 16.ᵗʰ 1805

began to Snow about 3 hours before Day and continued all
day   the Snow in the morning 4 inches deep on the old Snow,
and by night we found it from 6 to 8 inches deep,   I walked
in front to keep the road and found great dificuelty in keeping
it as in maney places the Snow had entirely filled up the track,
and obliged me to hunt Several minits for the track,   at 12
oClock we halted on the top of the mountain to worm & dry
our Selves a little as well as to let our horses rest and graze a
little on Some long grass which I observed,   (*on*) The (*South*)
Knobs Steep hill Sides & falling timber Continue to day, and
a thickly timbered Countrey of 8 different kinds of pine, which
are so covered with Snow, that in passing thro' them we are
continually covered with Snow,[1]   I have been wet and as cold
in every part as I ever was in my life, indeed I was at one time
fearfull my feet would freeze in the thin Mockirsons which I
wore,   after a Short Delay in the middle of the Day,[2] I took
one man and proceeded on as fast as I could about 6 miles to
a Small branch passing to the right, halted and built fires for
the party agains[t] their arrival which was at Dusk, verry cold
and much fatigued,   we Encamped at this Branch in a thickly
timbered bottom which was scurcely large enough for us to lie
leavil,   men all wet cold and hungary.   Killed a Second Colt
which we all Suped hartily on and thought it fine meat.

I saw 4 (*Black tail*) Deer to day (*before we set out which came
up the mountain*) and what is singular Snaped 7 times at a large
buck.   it is singular as my gun has a Steel fuzee and never
Snaped 7 times before,   in examining her found the flint loose.
to describe the road of this day would be a repitition of yesterday except the Snow which made it much worse (*to prosue as we*

---

[1] The following kinds of pine occur along the Lolo trail : *Pinus albicaulis* Engalm. ;
Pinus contorta var. murrayana ; *Tsuga pattoniana* ; *Picea engalmanni* ; *Abies subal-
pina (A. lasiocarpa)* ; *Abies grandis* ; *Pseudo tsuga taxifolia* ; *Thuya gigantea* Nutt.
(*T. plicata* Dou.) ; *Taxus brevisfolia* Nutt. (rare). — C. V. Piper.

[2] Their noon camp this day was at or near a point known as " Indian Post-offices,"
two piles or mounds of stone.   These mounds were there when Lewis and Clark
passed, but they probably did not see them, owing to the peculiarity of the trail.   On
the return journey they mention one such mound farther to the west. — O. D.
Wheeler.

had in maney places to derect our way by the appearence of the rub-bings of the Packs[1] *against the trees which have limbs quiet low and bending downwards)*

Sept. 16th Satturday 1805
Course &c.

S. 75° W 13 miles over the mountain passing emince Dificuelt knobs stoney   much falling timber and emencely steep   with great dificulty we proceeded on.   The *snow* began to fall about 3 hours before Day and cont.d all day.   I found great dificulty in finding the road in the evining as the snow had fallen from 6 to 8 Inches deep, verry cold and the pine which in maney places verry thick so covered with snow, as in passing I became wet,   discover 8 distinct kinds of pine on those

13   mountains   We encamped on a small branch running to the right.   Killed a Coalt & eate it

Sunday (Tuesday) 17th Sept. 1805 —

Cloudy morning   our horses much Scattered which detained us untill one oClock P. M. at which time we Set out *(the falling Snow &)* Snow falling from the trees which kept us wet all the after noon   passed over Several high ruged Knobs and Several dreans & Springs passing to the right, & passing on the ridge devideing the waters of two Small rivers.   road exceesively bad   Snow on the Knobs,   no Snow in the Vallies Killed a fiew Pheasents which was not sufficient for our Supper which compelled us to kill Something, a Coalt being the most useless part of our Stock he fell a Prey to our appetites.   The after part of the day fare,   we made only 10 miles to day   two horses fell & hurt themselves very much   we Encamped on the top of a high Knob of the mountain at a run passing to the left.[2] *(we proceed on as yesterday, & with dificulty found the road)*

---

[1] The burdens of the Indian horses. — BIDDLE (i, p. 450).

[2] I think this must be Bald Mountain, an absolutely necessary camp, as there is no grass for long distances each way.   This location accords well with the distances in advance. — C. V. PIPER.

Map from Clark Field-book, showing Course and Camping places,
September 16–18, 1805.

Course Dist. &ᶜ 17ᵗʰ Septʳ 1805 Sunday

S. 50° W. 12 miles over high knobs of the mountains passed three
    Dreans to right and encamped on one to the left.
    Springs at all those dreans &ᶜ road emencely bad as
    usial, no snow in the hollers all the high knobs of
    the mountains covered passed on a Dividing ridge
    on which we had to cross over emencely high knobs.
    road bad   Killed a few Phesants only.   Killed a colt
    to eate.

[Lewis :] [1]   *Wednesday September 18ᵗʰ 1805*

Cap Clark set out this morning to go a head with six hunters.
there being no game in these mountains we concluded it would
be better for one of us to take the hunters and hurry on to the
leavel country a head and there hunt and provide some provisions while the other remained with and brought on the party.
the latter of these was my part ; accordingly I directed the
horses to be gotten up early being determined to force my
march as much as the abilities of our horses would permit.
the negligence of one of the party (Willard) who had a spare
horse, in not attending to him and bringing him up last evening was the cause of our detention this morning untill ½ after
8 A. M. when we set out.   I sent willard back to serch for his
horse, and proceeded on with the party   at four in the evening
he overtook us without the horse,   we marched 18 miles this
day and encamped on the side of a steep mountain ;   we suffered for water this day passing one rivulet only ; we wer[e]
fortunate in finding water in a steep raviene about ½ maile
from our camp.   this morning we finished the remainder of
our last coult.   we dined & suped on a skant proportion of
portable soupe, a few canesters of which, a little bears oil and
about 20 lbˢ of candles [2] form our stock of provision, the only

---

[1] The entries by Lewis for Sept. 18–22 are found in Codex Fd. — ED.
[2] Bear's oil, instead of candles, according to Biddle. — ED.

recources being our guns & packhorses.   the first is but a poor dependance in our present situation where there is nothing upon earth ex[c]ept ourselves and a few small pheasants, small grey Squirrels, and a blue bird of the vulter kind about the size of a turtle dove or jay bird.   our rout lay along the ridge of a high mountain *course* S. 20. W.   18 m.   used the snow for cooking.

[Clark:]   *Monday (Wednesday) 18*^th^. *Sept*^r^. 1805 —

a fair morning cold   I proceeded on in advance with Six hunters (*and let it be understood that my object was*) to try and find deer or Something to kill (*& send back to the party*) (*The want of provisions together with the dificul[t]y of passing those emence mountains dampened the sperits of the party which induced us to resort to Some plan of reviving ther sperits.   I deturmined to take a party of the hunters and proceed on in advance to Some leavel Country, where there was game kill Some meat & send it back &c.*)

we passed over a countrey Similar to the one of yesterday more fallen timber   passed Several runs & Springs passing to the right,   from the top of a high part of the mountain at 20 miles I had a view of an emence Plain and *leavel* Countrey to the S W. & West.[1]   at a great distance a high mountain in advance beyond the Plain,   Saw but little (*no*) Sign of deer and nothing else,   much falling timber,   made 32 miles and Encamped on a bold running Creek passing to the left which I call *Hungery* Creek[2] as at that place we had nothing to eate. I halted only one hour to day to let our horses feed on Grass (*Grassy hill side*) and rest

---

1 This high part of the mountain must be Rocky Ridge, the first point on the trail from which the prairie country of the Clearwater can be descried. — C. V. PIPER.

2 Hungry Creek is an unnamed creek that flows south, southeast, and south again into the Lochsa fork.   It rises directly south of Weitus Meadow — a low divide south of Rocky Ridge. — O. D. WHEELER.

Map from Clark Field-book, showing Course and Camping places,
September 18–20, 1805.

Course Distance 18ᵗʰ Sepᵗ 1805 Monday

S. 85 W. 32 miles nearly   I proceeded on with the hunters to a creek
running from the right which I call hungary Creek as
we have nothing to eate   passed a run & several
springs which pass to the right,   keep on a Dividing
ridge & crossed several high and Steep knobs   a great
quantity of falling timber   at 20 miles I beheld a wide
and extencive vallie in a West & S W Direction about
[blank space in MS.] miles.   a high mountain beyond.
Drewyer shot at a Deer we did not get it.   Killed
nothing in those emence mountains of stones falling
timber & brush.

[Lewis:]   *Thursday September 19ᵗʰ 1805.*

Set out this morning a little after sun rise and continued our
rout about the same course of yesterday or S. 20. W. for 6
miles when the ridge terminated and we to our inexpressable
joy discovered a large tract of Prairie country lying to the S.
W. and widening as it appeared to extend to the W.   through
that plain the Indian informed us that the Columbia river, (in
which we were in surch) run.   this plain appeared to be about
60 Miles distant, but our guide assured us that we should
reach it's borders tomorrow   the appearance of this country,
our only hope for subsistance greately revived the sperits of the
party already reduced and much weakened for the want of food.[1]
the country is thickly covered with a very heavy growth of pine
of which I have ennumerated 8 distinct species.   after leaving
the ridge we asscended and decended several steep mountains in
the distance of 6 miles further when we struck a Creek about
15 yards wide, our course being S. 35. W.   we continued our
rout 6 miles along the side of this creek upwards passing 2 of
it's branches which flowed in from the N.   1ˢᵗ at the place we
struck the creek and the other 3 miles further.   the road was
excessively dangerous along this creek being a narrow rockey
path generally on the side of [a] steep precipice, from which
in many places if e[i]ther man or horse were precipitated they

[1] The plain to the southwest was not the Weippe Country, but the now well-
known Kamas prairie plateau beyond the Kooskooskee or Clearwater. — O. D.
WHEELER.

[73]

would inevitably be dashed in pieces.   Fraziers horse fell from this road in the evening, and roled with his load near a hundred yards into the Creek.   we all expected that the horse was killed but to our astonishment when the load was taken off him he arose to his feet & appeared to be but little injured, in 20 minutes he proceeded with his load.   this was the most wonderfull escape I ever witnessed, the hill down which he roled was almost perpendicular and broken by large irregular and broken rocks.   the course of this Creek upwards due W. we encamped on the Star. side of it in a little raviene, having traveled 18 miles over a very bad road.   we took a small quantity of portable soup, and retired to rest much fatiegued. several of the men are unwell of the disentary.   brakings out, or irruptions of the Skin, have also been common with us for some time.

[Clark:]   *Tuesday (Thursday) 19ᵗʰ Sept.ʳ 1805*

Set out early proceeded on up the [*Hungry*] Creek passing through a Small glade at 6 miles at which place we found a horse.   I derected him killed and hung up for the party after takeing a brackfast off for our Selves which we thought fine after Brackfast proceed on up the Creek two miles & left it to our right   passed over a mountain, and the heads of a branch of hungary Creek, two high mountains, ridges and through much falling timber (which caused our road of to day to be double the derect distance on the Course   Struck a large Creek passing to our left which I Kept down for 4 miles and left it to our left & passed over a (*down the*) mountain bad falling timber to a Small Creek passing to our left and Encamped.[1]   I killed 2 Pheasents, but fiew birds (*are to be seen*); Blue jay, Small white headed hawk, Some Crows & ravins & large hawks   road bad. (*as we decend the mountain the heat becomes more proseptable every mile*)

---

1 Clark went up Hungry Creek eight miles, wound about its headwaters and came down on the north side of the eastern branch of Collins Creek, followed its course four miles, crossed the mountain, once more on the main trail, and camped on the north branch of Collins Creek, now Lolo Creek, some miles above the forks. — O. D. WHEELER.

Cours Distance &c 19th Sept.r Tuesday

S 60. W nearly 22 miles on a Direct Course & at double the distance
wind around falling timber to a branch running to the Left
& camped. at 6 miles found a horse on the head of the
Creek in some glades, he was not fat the me[n] beg
leave to kill him which I granted, after they filled themselves, I had the ballance hung up for Cap.t Lewis and
proceeded on in the time the one half of the party was
skining cooking &c. the others were hunting, without seeing
a track of any animal. The road up this creek is much wors
than any other part as the hills sides are steep and at maney
places obliged for several y.ds to pass on the sides of rocks
where one false step of a horse would be certain destruc-
tion. Crossed over a mountain and the heads of a branch
of hungary Creek over ridges and much falling timber, and
a 2.d high mountain of like description to a large creek running west for 4 miles then turned South. I keped down
4 miles & turned up to the right over a mountain which
was bad as usial to a branch which runs to the left and
camped. The road to day wors than usial owing to the
falling timber &c. we killed 2 phs.ts but few birds. the
Blue jay and small white headed Hawk some crows &
ravens

[Lewis:]   *Friday September 20.th 1805.*

This morning my attention was called to a species of bird
which I had never seen before. (*Copy for Dr. Barton*) It was
reather larger than a robbin, tho' much it's form and action.
the colours were a blueish brown on the back the wings and
tale black, as wass a stripe above the croop ¾ of an inch wide
in front of the neck, and two others of the same colour passed
from it's eyes back along the sides of the head. the top of the
head, neck brest and belley and butts of the wing were of a
fine yellowish brick reed [red]. it was feeding on the buries
of a species of shoemake or ash which grows common in [this]
country & which I first observed on 2.d of this month. I have
also observed two birds of a blue colour both of which I believe
to be of the haulk or vulter kind. the one of a blue shining
colour with a very high tuft of feathers on the head a long tale,

[75]

it feeds on flesh the beak and feet black.   it's note is chă-ăh, chă-ăh.   it is about the size of a pigeon, and in shape and action resembles the jay bird.   another bird of very similar genus, the note resembling the mewing of the cat, with a white head and a light blue colour is also common, as are a black species of woodpecker about the size of the lark woodpecker. Three species of Phesants, a large black species, with some white feathers irregularly scattered on the brest neck and belley — a smaller kind of a dark uniform colour with a red stripe above the eye, and a brown and yellow species that a gooddeel resembles the phesant common to the Atlantic States.   we were detained this morning untill ten oclock in consequence of not being enabled to collect our horses. we had proceeded about 2 Miles when we found the greater part of a horse which Cap! Clark had met with and killed for us.   he informed me by note that he should proceed as fast as possible to the leavel country which lay to the S. W. of us, which we discovered from the hights of the mountains on the 19th   there he intended to hunt untill our arrival.   at one oclock we halted on a small branch runing to the left and made a hearty meal on our horse beef much to the comfort of our hungry stomachs.   here I larnt that one of the Packhorses with his load was missing and immediately dispatched Baptiest Lapage who had charge of him, to surch for him.   he returned at 3 OC. without the horse.   The load of the horse was of considerable value consisting of merchandize and all my stock of winter cloathing.   I therefore dispatched two of my best woodsmen in surch of him, and proceeded with the party.   Our rout lay through a thick forrest of large pine the general course being S. 25. W. and distance about 15. miles.   our road was much obstructed by fallen timber particularly in the evening. we encamped on a ridge where ther was but little grass for our horses, and at a distance from water.   however we obtained as much as served our culinary purposes and suped on our beef. the soil as you leave the hights of the mountains becomes gradually more fertile.   the land through which we passed this evening is of an excellent quality tho' very broken,   it is a dark grey soil. a grey free stone appearing in large masses

above the earth in many places. (*Copy for Dr. Barton*) saw
the hucklebury, honeysuckle, and alder common to the Atlantic states, also a kind of honeysuckle which bears a white bury
and rises about 4 feet high not common but to the western
side of the rockey mountains. a growth which resembles the
choke cherry bears a black bury with a single stone of a sweetish
taste, it rises to the hight of 8 or 10 feet and grows in thick
clumps. the Arborvita is also common and grows to an immence size, being from 2 to 6 feet in diameter.[1]

[Clark:]   *Wednesday (Friday) 20ᵗʰ September 1805*

    I set out early and proceeded on through a Countrey as
ruged as usial   passed over a low mountain into the forks of
a large Creek which I kept down 2 miles and assended a high
Steep mountain leaveing the Creek to our left hand · passed
the head of several dreans on a divideing ridge, and at 12
miles decended the mountain to a leavel pine Countrey   proceeded on through a butifull Countrey for three miles to a
Small Plain[2] in which I found maney Indian lodges, at the
distance of 1 mile from the lodges, I met *3* (*Indian*) boys,
when they saw me [they] ran and hid themselves, (*in the grass*)
(*I desmounted gave my gun and horse to one of the men,*) searched
(*in the grass and*) found (*2 of the boys*) gave them Small pieces
of ribin & Sent them forward to the village (*Soon after*) a man
Came out to meet me, [*with great caution*] & Conducted me
[*us*] to a large Spacious Lodge which he told me (by Signs)
was the Lodge of his great Chief who had Set out 3 days pre-

---

    [1] The huckleberry here mentioned (*Vaccinium membraceum*) was met again in
this region June 16, 1806.   The honeysuckle (*Louicera ciliosa* Poir.) is often mentioned as the " vining honeysuckle ; " the white-berried honeysuckle is *Symphoricarpus
raceinosus* L.   The choke-cherry is *Prunus demissa* Nutt. ; and the arbor vitae,
Thuya plicata Don. (*T. gigantea* Nutt.).   The alder is not the same as the black
alder referred to Nov. 6, 1805, and other times, but *Alnus sinuata* Rydt. — C. V.
PIPER.

    [2] Captain Clark's route this day was, apparently, down Lolo, or the north branch
of Collins Creek, to the junction with the eastern branch, then down the creek and
across to the headwaters of Musselshell and Brown creeks, but not as the trail of
to-day runs.   From here he followed through the more open country, and came out
into the wide and beautiful prairie country. — O. D. WHEELER.

vious with all the Warriers of the nation to war on a South
West derection & would return in 15 or 18 days. the fiew
men that were left in the Village and great numbers of women
geathered around me with much apparent signs of fear, and
ap! pleased   they those people gave us a Small piece of
Buffalow meat, Some dried Salmon beries & roots in different
States, Some round and much like an onion which they call
Pas she co [*quamash.*[1] *the Bread or Cake is called Pas-shi-co*]
Sweet, of this they make bread & Supe   they also gave us,
the bread made of this root all of which we eate hartily,   I
gave them a fiew Small articles as preasents, and proceeded on
with a Chief to his Village 2 miles in the Same Plain,   where
we were treated kindly in their way and continued with them
all night Those two Villages consist of about 30 double
lodges, but fiew men a number of women & children,   They
call themselves *Cho pun-nish* or *Pierced noses*[2] Their diolect
appears verry different from the flat heads, [*Tushapaws*], altho
origineally the Same people,   They are darker than the Flat
heads I have seen [*Tushapaws Their*] dress Similar, with more
beads white & blue principally, brass & Copper in different
forms, Shells and ware their haire in the Same way. they
are large Portley men Small women & handsom featured

---

[1] The quamash, or camas (with many other variants of the name), is an important
article of food among the Northwestern Indian tribes. It is the bulbous root of a
liliaceous plant (*Camassia* — of two species, *esculenta* and *leuchlini*; also named
Quamasia quamash, Coville) which grows in moist places from California to Montana and British Columbia; it is dug in June and July, and may be eaten raw or
cooked. It is agreeable to the taste, nutritious, and when cooked and dried can be
kept for a year or more. Granville Stuart says — *Montana as it Is* (N. Y., 1865),
pp. 28, 58 — that its Shoshoni name " pah'-see'-go," means " water seego," as distinguished from the " seego " that grows on high lands; and that the same name is
applied to dried apples or peaches. See also *Report*, 1870, of U. S. Commissioner
of Agriculture, p. 408, and plate xix. — ED.

[2] The Chopunnish, or Nez Percés, were located on the Salmon and Snake rivers;
they were the principal tribe of the Shahaptian family, which formerly extended along
a considerable part of the lower Columbia and its tributaries, as far east as the Bitter
Root Mountains. The Nez Percés were always friendly to the whites until 1877,
when the so-called " Chief Joseph's war " occurred — a revolt of the " non-treaty "
members of the tribe; they were subdued by United States troops, and the remnant
of the band placed on a reservation. See O. O. Howard's account of this war, in
his *Nez Percé Joseph* (Boston, 1881); he says of this tribe, " There are few Indians
in America superior to the Nez Percés." — ED.

Map from Clark Field-book, showing Course and Camping places,
September 20–October   , 1805.

Emence quantity of the [*quawmash or*] *Pas-shi-co* root[1] gathered & in piles about the plain, those roots grow much like an onion in marshey places the seed are in triangular Shells, on the Stalk. they sweat them in the following manner i.e. dig a large hole 3 feet deep, cover the bottom with Split wood on the top of which they lay Small Stones of about 3 or 4 Inches thick, a Second layer of Splited wood & Set the whole on fire which heats the Stones, after the fire is extinguished they lay grass & mud mixed on the Stones, on that dry grass which Supports the Pâsh-shi-co root a thin Coat of the Same grass is laid on the top, a Small fire is kept when necessary in the Center of the kill &c.

I find myself verry unwell all the evening from eateing the fish & roots too freely Sent out hunters they killed nothing Saw Some Signs of deer.

Course Dist? Friday 20th Sept? 1805

Nearly S W	12 miles over a mountain to a low ridgey countrey covered with large pine, passed into the forks of a large creek which we kept down about 2 miles & left it to the left hand and crossed the heads of some Dreans of the creek & on a ruged Deviding ridge, road as bad as usial no game of sign to day
West	3 miles to an Indian camp in a leavel rich open Plain I met 3 boys who I gave a pice of ribin to each & sent them to the Villages, I soon after met a man whome I gave a handkerchief and he escorted me to the grand Chiefs Lodge, who was with the most of the nation gone to war those people treated us well gave us to eate roots dried roots made in bread, roots boiled, one sammon, Berries of red haws some dried, my arrival raised great confusion, all running to see us, after a Delay of an hour I deturmined to go lower & turn out & hunt, a principal man informed me his camp was on my way and there was fish I concluded to go to his village and set out accomp? by about 100 men womin & boys 2 mile across the Plains, & halted turned out 4 men to

---

[1] Gass says (p. 202) of the bread made with this root: "It is good and nourishing, and tastes like that sometimes made of pumpkins." — ED.

hunt,   he gave us a sammon to eate,   I found that
his situation was not on the river as I expected &
that his sammon was dried, & but fiew.   this course
is N. 70°. W 2 miles across a rich leavel Plain in
which great quantites of roots have been geathered
and in heaps.   those roots are like onions, sweet
when Dried, and tolerably good in bread,   I eate
much & am sick in the evening.   those people have
an emence quantities of Roots which is their Principal
food.   The hunters discovered some signs but killed
nothing.

17

[Lewis:]   *Saturday September 21st 1805.*

We were detained this morning untill 11 OC^k. in consequence of not being able to collect our horses.   we then set
out and proceeded along the ridge on which we had encamped,
leaving which at 1-½ we passed a large creek [Collins — ED.]
runing to the left just above it's junction with another which
run parrallel with and on the left of our road before we struck
the creek ; through the level wide and heavy timbered bottom
of this creek we proceeded about 2-½ miles when bearing to
the right we passed a broken country heavily timbered great
quantities of which had fallen and so obstructed our road
that it was almost impracticable to proceed in many places.
th[r]ough these hills we proceeded about 5.M^s when we passed
a small creek on which Capt Clark encamped on the 19th
passing this creek we continued our rout 5. M^s thro' a similar
country when we struck a large creek at the forks, passed the
Northern branch and continued down it on the West side
1 mile and encamped in a small open bottom where there was
tolerable food for our horses.   I directed the horses to be
hubbled to prevent delay in the morning being determined to
make a forced march tomorrow in order to reach if possible
the open country.   we killed a few Pheasants, and I killed a
prarie woolf which together with the ballance of our horse
beef and some crawfish which we obtained in the creek enabled
us to make one more hearty meal, not knowing where the
next was to be found. (*Copy for Dr. Barton*) the Arborvita

increases in quantity and size.　I saw several sticks today large enough to form eligant perogues of at least 45 feet in length.　I find myself growing weak for the want of food and most of the men complain of a similar deficiency, and have fallen off very much.　the general course of this day S. 30 W. 15. M.

[Clark, first draft :]　　　　　　　　　　*Sept.ʳ 21.ˢᵗ Saturday 1805* [1]

a fine morning　sent out all the hunters early in different directions to kill something and delayed with the Indians to prevent suspicion & to acquire as much information as possible　one of them Drew me a chart of the river & nations below　informed of one falls below which the white men lived from whome they got white beeds cloth &.ᶜ &.ᶜ　The day proved warm, 2 Chiefs of Bands visited me to day.　the hunters all returned without any thing,　I collected a horse load of roots &ˏ3 Sammon & sent R Fields with one Indian to meet Cap.ᵗ Lewis　at 4 oClock set out with the other men to the river, passed thro a fine Pine countrey decended a steep ruged hill verry long to a small river which comes from our left and I suppose it to be [blank space in MS.] River passed down the river 2 miles on a steep hill side　at 11 oClock P. M. arrived at a camp of 5 squars a boy & 2 children　those people were glad to see us & gave us dried sammon　one had formerly been taken by the Minitarries of the north & seen white men,　our guide called the chief who was fishing on the other side of the river, whome I found a cherfull man of about 65.　I gave him a Medal.

Thursday (Saturday) 21.ˢᵗ₁₁ Sept.ʳ 1805

A fine Morning　Sent out all the hunters in different directions to hunt deer,　I my self delayed with the Chief to prevent Suspission and to Collect by Signs as much information as possible about the river and Countrey in advance.　The Chief drew me a kind of chart of the river, and informed me

---

[1] The first draft entries made by Clark, Sept. 21–Dec. 31, 1805, are found in the Clark-Voorhis field-book. — ED.

that a greater Chief than himself was fishing at the river half a days march from his Village called the twisted hare [hair], and that the river forked a little below his Camp and at a long distance below & below 2 large forks one from the left & the other from the right the river passed thro' the mountains at which place was a great fall of the Water passing through the rocks, at those falls white people lived from whome they precured the white Beeds & Brass &c. which the womin wore ; a Chief of another band visit[ed] me to day and Smoked a pipe, I gave my handkerchief & a Silver Cord with a little Tobacco to those Chiefs, The hunters all return without any thing, I purchased as much Provisions as I could with what fiew things I chan[c]ed to have in my Pockets, Such a[s] Salmon Bread roots & berries, & Sent one man R Fields with an Indian to meet Cap⁺ Lewis, and at 4 oClock P.M. Set out to the river, met a man at dark on his way from the river to the Village, whome I hired and gave the neck handkerchief of one of the men, to polit [pilot] me to the Camp of the twisted hare, we did not arrive at the Camp of the Twisted hare but opposit, untill half past 11 oClock P.M. found at this Camp five Squars & 3 Children. my guide called to the Chief who was Encamped with 2 others on a Small Island in the river, he Soon joinᵈ me, I found him a Chearfull man with apparant siencerity, I gave him a Medal &c. and Smoked untill 1 oClock a. m. and went to Sleep. The Countrey from the mountains to the river hills is a leavel rich butifull Pine Countrey badly watered, thinly timbered & covered with grass. The weather verry worm after decending into the low Countrey, the river hills are Verry high & Steep, Small bottoms to this little river which is Flat head [Clearwater] & is 160 yards wide and Sholey This river is the one we killed the first Coalt on near a fishing *were*

I am verry sick to day and puke which relive me

[Lewis :]   *Sunday September 22ⁿᵈ 1805.*

Notwithstanding my positive directions to hubble the horses last evening one of the men neglected to comply. he plead[ed] ignorance of the order.   this neglect however detained us untill ½ after eleven OC^k. at which time we renewed our march, our course being about west.   we had proceeded about two and a half miles when we met Reubin Fields one of our hunters, whom Capt. Clark had dispatched to meet us with some dryed fish and roots that he had procured from a band of Indians, whose lodges were about eight miles in advance.   I ordered the party to halt for the purpose of taking some refreshment. I divided the fish roots and buries, and was happy to find a sufficiency to satisfy compleatly all our appetites.   Fields also killed a crow   after refreshing ourselves we proceeded to the village — due West 7-½ Miles where we arrived at 5 OCk in the afternoon   our rout was through lands heavily timbered, the larger wood entirely pine.   the country except the last 3 miles was broken and decending.   the pleasure I now felt in having tryumphed over the rockey Mountains and decending once more to a level and fertile country where there was every rational hope of finding a comfortable subsistence for myself and party can be more readily conceived than expressed, nor was the flattering prospect of the final success of the expedition less pleasing.   on our approach to the village which consisted of eighteen lodges most of the women fled to the neighbouring woods on horseback with their children, a circumstance I did not expect as Capt. Clark had previously been with them and informed them of our pacific intentions towards them and also the time at which we should most probably arrive.[1]   the men seemed but little concerned, and several of them came to meet us at a short distance from their lodges unarmed.[2]

---

[1] There is a tradition among the Nez Percé Indians that when Lewis and Clark first visited the Chopunnish, the latter were inclined to kill the white men, — a catastrophe which was averted by the influence of a woman in that tribe.   She had been captured by hostile Indians, and carried into Manitoba, where some white people enabled her to escape ; and finally she returned to her own tribe, although nearly dead from fatigue and privations.   Hearing her people talk of killing the explorers, she urged them to do no harm to the white men, but to treat them with kindness and hospitality — counsel which they followed. — O. D. WHEELER.

[2] The following memoranda appear at the end of this fragment (Codex Fd) :

" (This a part of Book N°. 7. to be referred to and examined after the 9th Sep^t. 1805.   W. C."
" Look forward 4 leaves "

[Clark, first draft:]   *September 22ⁿᵈ Sunday 1805*

our first course of yesterday was nearly

N. 80° W.   winding thro a grassy Pine Country of fine land for 12
miles

N. 70 W.   3 miles down a steep hill & on a hill side a creek to the
right to the river from the left at a rapid

West   2 miles down the N side of the River and encamped, in
the morning proceeded down to the Chief ['s] Lodge
miles   7   on an Island, found 3 men fishing hot day

a fine morning I proceed on down the little river to
about 1½ a mile & found the chi[e]f in a canoe comeing to
meet me I got into his canoe & crossed over to his camp on
a small Island at a rapid Sent out the hunters leaving one
to take care of the baggage, & after eating a part of a sammon
I set out on my return to meet Capt Lewis with the Chief &
his son at 2 miles met Shields with 3 Deer, I took a small
pice & changed for his horse which was fresh & proced on this
horse threw me 3 times which hurt me some. at Dark met
Capt Lewis Encamped at the first Village men much fatigued
& reduced, the Supply which I sent by R Fields was timely,
they all eate hartily of roots & fish, 2 horses lost 1 Days
journey back[1]

Friday (Sunday) 22ⁿᵈ Sept. 1805

a verry worm day the hunters Shi[e]lds killed 3 Deer this
morning, I left them on the Island and Set out with the
Chief & his Son on a young horse for the Village at which
place I expected to meet Capt Lewis this young horse in
fright threw himself & me 3 times on the Side of a Steep hill
& hurt my hip much, Cought a Coalt which we found on
the roade & I rode it for Several miles untill we saw the Chiefs
horses, he Cought one & we arrived at his Village at Sunset,
& himself and mys[el]f walked upto the 2ᵈ Village where I
found Capt Lewis & the party Encamped, much fatigued, &

1 The Biddle text here states (i, p. 457) that after proceeding a few miles the
party was joined by the two men who had been sent back after a horse two days
earlier. They had lost the horse, and were exhausted with fatigue. — ED.

hungery, much rejoiced to find something to eate of which
they appeared to partake plentifully   I cautioned them of the
Consequences of eateing too much &c.

The planes appeared covered with Spectators viewing the
white men and the articles which we had,   our party weakened
and much reduced in flesh as well as Strength,   The horse I
left hung up they receved at a time they were in great want,
and the Supply I Sent by R. Fields proved timely and gave
great encouragement to the party with Captⁿ Lewis. he lost
3 horses one of which belonged to our guide.   Those Indians
Stole out of R.F. Shot pouch his knife wipers Compas &
Steel, which we could not precure from them,   we attempted
to have Some talk with those people but could not for the
want of an Interpreter thro' which we could Speake,   we
were Compelled to converse alltogether by Signs.   I got the
Twisted hare to draw the river from his Camp down which he
did with great Cherfullness on a white Elk skin,   from the
1ˢᵗ fork which is few miles below, to the large fork on which
the *So So ne* or Snake Indians fish, is South 2 Sleeps ;   to a
large river which falls in on the N W. Side and into which
The *Clarks river* empties itself is 5 Sleeps   from the mouth
of that river to the *falls* is 5 Sleeps   at the falls he places
Establishments of white people &c. and informs that great
numbers of Indians reside on all those fo[r]ks as well as the
main river ;   one other Indian gave me a like account of the
Countrey.   Some few drops of rain this evening.   I precured
maps of the Country & river with the Situation of Indians,
Towns from Several men of note Seperately which varied
verry little.

[Clark, first draft :]   *Septʳ 23ʳᵈ Sunday*

Traded with the Indians,   made 3 chiefs and gave them
meadels & Tobacco & Handkerchif & knives, one a flag & left
a Flag & handkerchief for the great chief when he returns from
War,   in the evening proceeded to the 2ᵈ Vilg 2 miles,   a
hard wind and rain at dark,   traded for some root Bread &
skins to make shirts.   hot day

Saturday (Monday) 23.ᵈ *Sept*ʳ 1805

We assembled the principal Men as well as the Chiefs and by Signs informed them where we came from where bound our wish to inculcate peace and good understanding between all the red people &c.   which appeared to Satisfy them much,   we then gave 2 other Medals to other Chefs of bands, a flag to the *twisted hare*,   left a flag & Handkerchief to the grand Chief   gave a Shirt to the *Twisted hare* & a knife & Handkerchief with a Small pece of Tobacco to each.   Finding that those people gave no provisions to day we deturmined to purchase with our Small articles of Merchindize, accord[ingly] we purchased all we could, Such as roots dried, in bread, & in their raw State, Berries of red Haws[1] & *Fish* and in the evening Set out and proceeded on to the 2ᵈ Village 2 miles dist. where we also purchased a few articles all amounting to as much as our weak horses could carry to the river,   Cap. Lewis & 2 men Verry Sick this evening,   my hip Verry Painfull,   the men trade a few old tin Canisters for dressed Elk Skin to make themselves Shirts.   at dark a hard wind from the S W accompanied with rain which lasted half an hour.   The *twisted hare* envited Cap. Lewis & myself to his lodge which was nothin[g] more than Pine bushes & bark, and gave us Some broiled dried *Salmon* to eate,   great numbers about us all night.   at this village the women were busily employed in gathering and drying the *Pas-she-co* root of which they had great quantities dug in piles

[Clark, first draft :]   *Sept*ʳ. 24ᵗʰ *Monday* 1805

Set out early for the river and proceeded on the same road I had previously gone to the Island at which place I had found the Chief & formed a Camp   several 8 or 9 men sick,   Cap. Lewis sick   all Complain of a *Lax* & heaviness at the stomack, I gave rushes Pills to several   hot day.   maney Indians & thier gangues of horses follow us   hot day   Hunters had 5 Deer

---

[1] The red-berried hawthorn common along the Clearwater is *Cratægus Piperi Britt.* — C. V. PIPER.

Sunday (Tuesday) 24*th* *Sept*. 1805

a fine morning   collected our horses   despatched J. Colter
back to hunt the horses lost in the mountains & bring up Some
Shot left behind, and at 10 oClock we all Set out for the river
and proceeded on by the Same rout I had previously traveled,
and at Sunset we arrived at the Island on which I found the
Twisted hare, and formed a Camp on a large Island a little below,[1]   Cap. Lewis scercely able to ride on a jentle horse which
was furnished by the Chief,   Several men So unwell that they
were Compelled to lie on the Side of the road for Some time
others obliged to be put on horses.   I gave rushes Pills to the
Sick this evening.   Several Indians follow us.

[Clark, first draft:]   *Sept*. 25*th*

I with the Chief & a young man went down to hunt timber
for canoes   proceeded on down to the forks 4 miles N 70. W 2
miles S. 75° W 2 miles,   halted   young man cought 6 Sammon,   the forks nearly the same size,   crossed the South fork
& found Timber large Pine in a bottom   Proceeded up the
South side   *3* parts of Party sick   Cap. Lewis verry sick   hot
day

Monday (Wednes?) 25*th* *of September* 1805 —

a verry hot day,   most of the Party Complaining and 2 of
our hunters left here on the 22.nd Verry sick,   they had killed
only two Bucks in my absence.   I Set out early with the Chief
and 2 young men to hunt Some trees Calculated to build
Canoes, as we had previously deturmined to proceed on by
water,   I was furnished with a horse and we proceeded on
down the river   Crossed a Creek at 1 mile from the right
verry rockey which I call rock dam Creek & Passed down on
the N side of the river to a fork from the North which is
about the Same size and affords about the Same quantity of

---

[1] This route led down the Jim Ford Creek of the present day to the Clearwater or
Kooskooskee. — O. D. WHEELER.

water with the other fork,[1] we halted about an hour, one of the young men took his guig and killed 6 fine Salmon two of them were roasted and we eate, two Canoes Came up loaded with the furniter & provisions of 2 families, those Canoes are long Stedy and without much rake, I crossed the South fork and proceeded up on the South side, the most of the way thro' a narrow Pine bottom in which I Saw fine timber for Canoes one of the Indian Canoes with 2 men with Poles Set out from the forks at the Same time I did and arrived at our Camp on the Island within 15 minits of the Same time I did, not withstanding 3 rapids which they had to draw the Canoe thro' in the distance, when I arrived at Camp found Cap![t] Lewis verry Sick, Several men also verry Sick, I gave Some Salts & Tarter *emetic*, we deturmined to go to where the best timber was and there form a Camp

[Clark, first draft :] *Sept!* 26th

Set out early and proceeded down the river to the bottom on the S Side opposit the forks & formed a camp had ax handled ground &[c]. our axes all too small. Indians caught sammon & sold us, 2 Chiefs & their families came & camped near us several men bad, Cap[t] Lewis sick I gave Pukes Salts &[c]. to several, I am a little unwell. hot day

Tuesday (Thursday) 26th. *Sept!* 1085

Set out early and proceeded on down the river to a bottom opposit the forks of the river on the South Side and formed a Camp. Soon after our arrival a raft Came down the N. fork on which was two men, they came too, I had the axes distributed and handled and men apotn[ed] [apportioned] ready to commence building canoes on tomorrow, our axes are Small & badly calculated to build Canoes of the large Pine, Cap[t] Lewis Still very unwell, Several men taken Sick on the way

---

This is the junction of the Middle and North forks of the Kooskooskee (Clearwater). The explorers called the North Fork the Chopunnish. See Clark's map in our Atlas volume. — ED.

down, I administered *Salts* Pils Galip, [jalap] Tarter emetic
&c.   I feel unwell this evening,   two Chiefs & their families
follow us and encamp near us,   they have great numbers
of horses.[1]   This day proved verry hot,   we purchase fresh
Salmon of the Indians

[Clark, first draft:]   *Sept.ʳ 27ᵗʰ Thursday 1805*

Set all the men able to work ab.ᵗ building canoes,   Colter
returned and found one horse & the canister of shot left in
the mountains   he also killed a Deer ½ of which he brought
hot day   men sick

                                                  27ᵗʰ Sept.ʳ (Friday) 1805

All the men able to work comen[c]ed building 5 Canoes,
Several taken Sick at work, our hunters returned Sick without
meet.   J. Colter returned he found only one of the lost horses,
on his way killed a Deer, half of which he gave the Indians
the other proved nourishing to the Sick   The day verry hot,
we purchase fresh Salmon of them   Several Indians come up
the river from a Camp Some distance below   (*Cap.ᵗ Lewis
very sick   nearly all the men sick.   our Shoshonee Indian Guide
employed himself makeing flint points for his arrows*)

[Clark, first draft:]   *Sept.ʳ 28ᵗʰ Friday*

Several men sick,   all at work which is able,   nothing killed
to day   Drewyer sick   maney Indians visit us   worm day

                                      Thursday (Saturday) 28ᵗʰ Sept.ʳ 1805

Our men nearly all Complaining of their bowels, a heaviness
at the Stomach & Lax,   Some of those taken first getting

---

[1] According to Gass (pp. 205, 206), most of the warriors of this band had gone
to attack some tribe to the northwest of this village ; they returned on the 27th, but
the white men, not having an interpreter, could learn but little of what they had
accomplished. — ED.

better,   a number of Indians about us gazeing &c. &c   This day proved verry worm and Sultery,   nothing killed   men complaining of their diat of fish & roots   all that is able working at the Canoes,   Several Indians leave us to day,   the raft continued on down the river,   one old man informed us that he had been to the white peoples fort at the falls & got white beeds &c.   (*his Story was not beleved as he could explain nothing*).

[Clark, first draft:]   *Septr 29th Satterday*

Drewyer killed 2 deer Collins 1 deer   men cont^e sickly   at work all able to work.

(Friday) Sunday 29th Septr 1805

a cool morning   wind from the S W   men Sick as usial,[1] all the men (*that are*) able to (*at*) work, at the Canoes   Drewyer killed 2 Deer Colter killed 1 Deer,   the after part of this day worm   (*Capt Lewis very Sick, and most of the men Compla[in]ing very much of their bowels & Stomach*)

[Clark, first draft:]   *Sunday 30th Septr 1805   Forks*

a fine morning   our me[n] recruteing a little,   cool,   all at work doing some thing except 2 which are verry sick,   Great numbers of small duck passing up and down the river this morning

Took equal altitudes with Sextent at Camp opposit the Junction of [blank space in MS.]   River and [blank space in MS]   River

Sunday 30th Septr 1805

	H	M	S		H	M	S
A.M	8	49	32 5	P M	4	5	23.5
"	"	51	17 5		4	7	9
"	"	53	8 5		4	8	58 5

Altitude produced from this observation is 42°–50'–45"

---

1 In weather diary for this date (Codex I, p 27), Clark says "¾ of the party sick " — ED

Observed time and distance of Sun and Moon nearest Limbs ☉ West.
with Sextent

	Time		distance		
	H	m	s			
P M	4	21	44	91°	57′	00″
"		22	53	91	57	30
"		23	52	91	58	0
"		24	37	91	58	15
"		25	35	91	58	15
"		26	42	91	58	30
"		27	39	91	58	45
"		28	17	91	59	15
"		29	43	91	59	45
"		31	10	92	50	0
"		32	15	92	0	15
"		33	8	92	0	45
"		34	23	92	1	15
"		35	30	92	1	30
"		36	20	92	1	45

Error of Enstrement 8′ 45″ sub Cronometer too fast

Septͬ. 30ᵗʰ Satturday (Monday) 1805

a fine fa[i]r morning   the men recruiting a little,   all at
work which are able[1]   Great number of Small Ducks pass
down the river this morning.   maney Indians passing up and
down the river.[2]

[Clark, first draft:]   *October 1ˢͭ 1805 Tuesday*

a cool morning wind from the N.E   I examine & Dry all
our article clothes & nothing to eat except Dried fish verry bad
diet Capᵗ Lewis getting much better than for several days past
Several Indians visit us from the different villages below and on
the main fork, S.   nothing killed

---

[1] But the greater number are very weak   To save them from hard labour, we
have adopted the Indian method of burning out the canoes — GASS (p 207)

[2] Here follow the astronomical observations, which being the same as those in the
first draft are omitted   In Codex G, pp 130–134, are found the "Courses and
distances" Sept 11–25, which are also omitted as being transcripts of those from
the Clark-Voorhis field-book — ED

October 1st Monday (Tuesday) 1805 —

A cool Morning wind from the East had Examined and dried all our Clothes and other articles, and laid out a Small assortment of such articles as those Indians were fond of to trade with them for Some provisions (they are remarkably fond of Beeds) nothin to eate except a little dried fish which they men complain of as working of them as (*as much as*) a dost of Salts. Capt Lewis getting much better. Several Indians visit us from the different tribes below. Some from the main South fork. our hunters killed nothing to day worm evening

[Clark, first draft :] *Octr 2nd 1805 Wednesday*

dispatch 2 men & an Indian up to the villages we first came too to purchase roots fish &.^c nothing to eat but roots. gave a small pice of Tobacco to the Indians, 3 broachs & 2 rings with my Handkerchif divided between 5 of them. I walked on the hills to hunt to day, saw only one deer, could kill nothing day excesively hot in the river bottoms wind North, Burning out the holler of our canoes, men something better nothing except a small Prarie wolf killed to day, our Provisions all out except what fiew fish we purchase of the Indians with us; we kill a horse for the men at work to eate &.^c &.^c

October 2nd Tuesday (Wednesday) 1805 —

despatched 2 men Frasure & S. Guterich back to the village with 1 Indian & 6 horses to purchase dried fish, roots &c. We have nothing to eate but roots, which give the men violent pains in their bowels after eating much of them. To the Indians who visited us yesterday I gave [presents] divided my Handkerchief between 5 of them, with a Small piece of tobacco & a pece of riebin & to the 2 principal men each a ring & brooch. I walked out with my gun on the hills which is verry steep & high could kill nothing, day hot wind N. Hunters killed nothing excep a Small Prarie wolf. Provisions all out, which compells us to kill one of our horses to eate (*and make Suep for the Sick men.*)

[Clark, first draft:]   *October 3ʳᵈ Thursday 1805 Canoe Run*

a fair cool morning wind from the East   all our men gitting well and at work at the canoes &ᶜ.

Took equal altitudes with Sextent

	H.	M.	S.			H.	M.	
A M.	9	8	14		P M.	3	57	8
	9	10	8			3	58	58.5
	9	11	59			4	0	5

Altitude produced 44° 53′ 45″

P M Observed time and distance of the *Moons* western Limb from *a Arietis* ✳ East of the ☾

		Time			distance	
	Hᵒ.	Mᵒ.	Sdᵒ.			
P M	8	11	49	78°	4′	00″
	"	21	6	"	2	30
	"	23	21	"	2	15
	"	25	7	"	1	45
	"	27	40	"	1	30
	"	30	10	77	59	00
	"	33	34	"	58	45
	"	35	1	"	58	15
	"	37	1	"	58	00
	"	38	28	"	57	30

October 3ʳᵈ⸗ (Thursday) 1805 —

a fine morning   cool wind East   all our men getting better in helth, and at work at the Canoes &c.   The Indians who visited us from below Set out on their return early.   Several others Come from different directions [1]

[Clark, first draft:]   *October 4ᵗʰ⸗ 1805 Friday*

This morning is a little cool wind from the East.   I displeased an Indian by refuseing to let him have a pice of Tobacco.   three Indians from the S. fork visit us   Fraser and Gutrich return from the village with fish, roots &ᶜ which they purchased

---

[1] The astronomical observations, being a transcript of those in the first draft, are here omitted. — Eᴅ.

October 4ᵗʰ (Friday) 1805 —

a cool wind from off the Eastern mountains, I displeased an Indian by refuseing him a pice of Tobacco which he tooke the liberty to take out of our Sack. Three Indians visit us from the Great River South of us. The two men Frasure and Guterich return late from the Village with Fish roots &c. which they purchased as our horse is eaten we have nothing to eate except dried fish & roots which disagree with us verry much. The after part of this day verry worm. (*Capᵗ Lewis Still Sick but able to walk about a little.*)

[Clark, first draft :]   *October 5ᵗʰ Saturday 1805*

a cool morning wind from the East, collected all our horses, & Branded[1] them 38 in Nᵒ. and delivered them to the men who were to take charge of them, each of which I gave a Knife & one a wampom-shell gorget, The Lattᵈ. of this place the mean of 2 observations is 46° − 34′ − 56″. 3 North. nothing to eat but dried roots & Dried fish, Capᵗ Lewis & my self eate a supper of roots boiled, which filled us so full of wind, that we were scercely able to Breathe all night feel the effects of it. Lanc[h]ed 2 canoes to day one proved a little leakey the other a verry good one

October 5ᵗʰ Friday Satᵞ 1805

Wind Easterley and Cool, had all our horses 38 in number Collected and branded Cut off their fore top and delivered them to the 2 brothers and one son of one of the Chiefs who intends to accompany us down the river to each of those men I gave a Knife & Some Small articles &c. they promised to be attentive to our horses untill we Should return.

---

[1] In 1892 was found, on an island 3½ miles above the Dalles of the Columbia, a branding-iron used by Lewis and Clark ; it contained the words " U. S. Capt. M. Lewis." It is now in possession of George H. Himes, of the Oregon Historical Society, Portland, Ore. See *Wonderland*, 1900, p. 50. — ED.

Lattitude of this place from the mean of two observations is *46°– 34'– 56".3* North.

Nothing to eate except dried fish & roots. Capt Lewis & myself eate a Supper of roots boiled, which Swelled us in Such a manner that we were Scercely able to breath for Several hours. finished and lanced (*launched*) 2 of our canoes this evening which proved to be verry good our hunters with every diligence Could kill nothing. The hills high and ruged and woods too dry to hunt the deer which is the only game in our neighbourhood. Several Squars Came with fish and roots which we purchased of them for Beeds, which they were fond of. *Capt Lewis not So well to day as yesterday*

[Clark, first draft:]   *October 6th Sunday* 1805

A cool morning wind East for a short time, which is always a cool wind,   had a *cach* made for our saddles and buried them on the side of a Pond.

Magnetic azmuth of Sun A. M.

Time			azm^{th}	altitude		
H.	M.	S.				
9	6	27	S 75° E	42°	58'	00''
9	18	21	S. 73 E	45	46	45

finish all the Canoes late. I am verry sick all night,   Pane in Stomach & the bowels oweing to my diet

Equal altitudes 6th Sept^r [Oct.] with Sextent

	H.	m.	s		H.	m	s
A. M.	9	16	21.5	P M.	3	45	34.5
	ˮ	18	20.5		ˮ	47	34.5
	ˮ	20	17.5		ˮ	49	26.5

Altitude produced 45° 46' 45''

Took time and distance of moons Western Limb and *a* Arquilé, [Aquilæ] Star West.

[95]

P. M.	Time			distance		
	H.	M.	S.	°	′	″
8	25	55	58	54	15
"	28	34	"	55	30
"	32	47	"	56	45
"	34	40	"	57	0
"	36	53	"	57	45
"	38	41	"	58	30
"	40	35	"	59	15
"	42	14	"	59	45
"	43	37	59	1	00
"	45	21	"	1	45

Took time and Distance of Moons Western Limb from Alberian [Aldebaran] Star East

Time			distance		
h.	m	s	°	′	″
9	9	52	65	29	15
"	12	6	"	28	00
"	13	47	"	27	15
"	16	8	"	27	15
"	18	2	"	28	00
"	19	49	"	24	30
"	21	12	"	24	00
"	22	44	"	23	30

October 6th Saturday [*Sunday*] 1805

A Co[o]l Easterley wind which Springs up in the latter part of the night and continues untill about 7 or 8 oClock A.M. had all our Saddles Collected a whole dug and in the night buried them, also a Canister of powder and a bag of Balls at the place the Canoe which Shields made was cut from the body of the tree. The Saddles were buried on the Side of a bend about ½ a mile below. all the Canoes finished this evening ready to be put into the water. I am taken verry unwell with a pain in the bowels & Stomach, which is certainly the effects of my diet which last all night.

The winds blow cold from a little before day untill the Suns gets to Some hight from the Mountains East as they did from the Mountains at the time we lay at the falls of Missouri from the West

The river below this forks is Called *Kos-kos-kee*   it is Clear rapid with Shoals or Swift places

The open Countrey Commences a fiew miles below this on each side of the river, on the Lard Side below the 1ˢᵗ Creek. with a few trees Scattered near the river.[1]

[Clark, first draft:]   7ᵗʰ Octʳ 1805 *Monday*

I feel myself verry unwell,   all the canoes in the water,   we Load and set out, after fixing all our Poles &ᶜ. &ᶜ. The after noon Cloudy   proced on   passing maney bad rapids,   one canoe that in which I went in front sprung a Leak in passing the 3ʳᵈ. rapid.

Set out at	3	oClock P M & proceeded on
N. 80° W.	1	mile, passed a bad rappid
S. W.	1½	mile to the L. Side bend
West	½	mile to R. Sᵈ passᵈ a rapid
S W.	1	mile to a Left hand bend
N. 70 W.	1½	miles passed a rapid R.
S. 60 W.	1½	miles dᵒ. bad to L. S.
West	3	miles passᵈ a rapid ½ a Creek on the left at 2 miles to a right hand bend
S. 10° E	1½	mile to a Left B. passed a rapid
N. 60 E	1½	m. to a R. bend passed a rapid
South	1	To a bend on the Left Side passed a bad rapid
West	1	in the left hand bend
N W.	½	a mile to a bad rapid
S. 70° W	1½	miles to a bend on the right
S W.	2	miles to a bend on the left at the mo. of a run opposit to which we camped, [blank space in MS.] from water Encamped on a pool [to the] right, narrows
	20	above for 6 miles all [w]ay

[1] The astronomical observations are omitted, as they are transcripts of those found in the first draft. — ED.

*October 7*ᵗʰ *Monday* 1805 —

I continue verry unwell but obliged to attend every thing all the Canoes put into the water and loaded, fixed our Canoes as well as possible and Set out   as we were about to Set out we miss⁴ both of the Chiefs who promised to accompany us, I also missed my Pipe Tomahawk which could not be found.

The after part of the day cloudy   proceded on passed 10 rapids which wer dangerous   the Canoe in which I was Struck a rock and Sprung a leak in the 3ʳᵈ rapid,   we proceeded on 20 [*19*] miles and Encamped on a Star⁴ point opposit a run. passed a Creek small on the Lar⁴ Side at 9 miles,   a Short distance from the river at 2 feet 4 Inches N. of a dead toped pine Tree had buried 2 Lead Canisters of Powder

Had the Canoes unloaded examined and mended a Small leake which we discovered in a thin place in her Side   passed Several Camps of Indians to day

our Course and distance Shall be given after I get to the forks. &c. which the Indians Say is the last of the bad water untill we get to the great falls 10 day below, where the white people live &c.   [*The Lodges are of Sticks set in form of roof of a house & covered with mats and straw*]

[Clark, first draft :]   8ᵗʰ *Oct*ʳ. 1805 *Tuesday*

a cloudy morning   changed canoes and buried 2 Lead canisters of Powder 2 foot 4 In. North of a dead toped pine opposit our camp & opposit the mouth of a run   after repareing leaks in the canoes sprung comeing over the rapids yesterday set out at 9 oClock

N. W.	1	mile to a riffle in the S. bend
South	¼	thro a verry bad rappid all way
S. 70° W.	½	to a L. bend good water
N.W.	¼	thro a rapid in a Star⁴ bend
West	2 ½	miles to a Star⁴ bend passed a bad rapid at 1 mile p⁴ a rap⁴ at 2 miles
South	1 ½	to a L. bend ops⁴ a bottom of stone
S. 70° W.	2 ½	mile to a Star⁴ bend passed an Island on the Lar⁴ Side, a rapid at head & foot of Island end of the course

S.W.	2	miles to a Lar^d bend passed a rapid & Ind camp (3 Lodges) & fishing place, Low^r p^t of Is^d at which place we dined & bought fish Passed Lower p^t Is^d on Star^d Side
West	2 ½	miles passed an Island on which 3 Lodges of Indians were encamped ops^d on the La^d Side a small creek at the Lower p^t on St^d Side 6 Lodges of Inds. we halted and took in our 2 chiefs and bought fish & roots Ps^d 2 rapids
S W	1 ½	m. to a bend on St^d passed a rapid
S. 40^b E.	1	to a bend on Lar^d. ps^d a rapid
S. 60° W.	2 ½	miles to a bend St^d Side passing an Is^d on the Lar^d. & bad rapid
S W	1 ½	miles to a Star^d bend passed an Is^d on Ld Side a rapid at upper point and lower p^t canoe [c]racked, a creek falls in on the Star^d Side[1]
West	1 ½	to the upper p^t of a Island St^d Side
	21	

October 8th Tuesday 1805 —

A Cloudy morning loaded our Canoes which was unloaded last night and Set out at 9 oClock passed 15 rapids four Islands and a Creek on the Star^d Side at 16 miles just below which one canoe in which Serg^t. Gass was Stearing and was nearle turning over, she Sprung a leak or Split open on one side and Bottom filled with water & Sunk on the rapid, the men, Several of which Could not Swim hung on to the Canoe, I had one of the other Canoes unloaded & with the assistance of our Small Canoe and one Indian Canoe took out every thing & toed the empty Canoe on Shore, one man Tompson a little hurt, every thing wet particularly the greater part of our Small Stock of Merchandize, had every thing opened, and two Sentinels put over them to keep off the Indians, who are enclined to theave haveing Stole Several Small articles those people appeared disposed to give us every assistance in their power during our distress. We passed Several Encamp-

---

1 The explorers (in revision, Codex G) named this Colter Creek ; it is now Pot-latch Creek, the principal tributary of the lower Clearwater. — ED.

ments of Indians on the Islands and those near the rapids in which places they took the Salmon,   at one of those Camps we found our two Chiefs who had promised to accompany us, we took them on board after the Serimony of Smokeing

[Clark, first draft :]   *Octo. 9ᵗʰ*

  all day drying our roots good[s] & articles which got wet in the canoe last night.   our 2 Snake Indian guides left us without our knowledge,   The Indians troublesom stole my spoon which they returned   men merrey at night & singular acts of a Indⁿ

October 9ᵗʰ Wednesday 1805 —

  The morning Cool as usial   the greater part of the day proved to be Cloudy, which was unfavourable for drying our things &c. which got we[t] yesterday.   In examoning our Canoe found that by putting Knees & Strong peces pined (*pieces primed*) to her Sides and bottom &c.   She could be made fit for Service in by the time the goods dried,   Set 4 men to work at her, Serjⁿ Pryor & Gass, Jo Fields & Gibson, others' to collect rosin,   at 1 oClock she was finished stronger than ever   The wet articles not sufficiently dried to pack up obliged us to delay another night   dureing the time one man was tradeing for fish for our voyage,   at Dark we were informed that our old guide & his son had left us and had been Seen running up the river Several miles above,   we could not account for the cause of his leaveing us at this time, without receiving his pay for the services he had rendered us, or letting us know anything of his intention.[1]

  we requested the Chief to Send a horseman after our old guide to come back and receive his pay &c. which he advised us not to do as his nation would take his things from him before he passed their camps.   The Indians and our party were verry mery this after noon   a woman fainᵈ madness &c. &c.

---

[1] I suspect he was afraid of being cast away passing the rapids.   At dark one of the squaws, who keep about us, took a crazy fit, and cut her arms from the wrists to the shoulders, with a flint ; and the natives had great trouble and difficulty in getting her pacified. — GASS (p. 209).

Singular acts of this woman in giveing in small po[r]tions all
she had & if they were not received (*or she had no more to give
pitied by Indians she sang*)   She would Scarrify her self in a
horid manner &c.   Capt Lewis recovering fast.

[Clark, first draft :]   *Octr 10th 1805 Thursday*

Set out at 7 oClock

South	1	mile passed a bad rapid at the head of an Is^d on Ld Side
S. 20° W.	1 ½	miles to a L^d bend, passed a Is^d on Ld Side. rapid at the head bad. passed Lower p^t of the other [island] at the mouth of a run on Star^d
West	½	to a St^d bend passed a small Is^d Ld Side and a rapid
S. 30° W.	3	miles to a L^d bend passed a creek coming [in] on the Ld Side at ½ a mile on which is cotton wood bottoms Ind^s camp below the Creek
West	2	miles to the head of an Is^d at a bad rapid on both side current on the right side
S. 30° W.	4	mile p^d a rapid at Lower point of Is^d & rapid at 1 mile, a rapid at 1 ½ miles rockey bottoms on each side a rapid at 2 ½ miles a run & (Indn camp) on Star^d Side at 3 miles a rapid at 3 ½ miles to a Lar^d bend, low plain 100 ft
West	2	mile to a Star^d bend, (passed an Indian bathing in hot bath) rapid an Island on the L. S. shole waters at the head ops^d to which a verry bad rapid we call ragid rapid one canoe struck & lodged sprung a Leak onload Passed several Ind^s camps on the Island. Took meridian altitude on the Island with Sextent made it 74° 26' Lat^d 46° 29' 21'' 7/10 North
S. W.	1	mile to a bend on the St Side ps^d a rapid
South	1	mile to the L. bend passed 2 rapids a large bottom on each side
S. 80° W.	3	miles to the mouth of a Large fork caled by the Ind^s Ki-moo-e-nen [1] passed 2 rapids Is^d in mouth

---

[1] As understood by the Nez Percé of to-day, the name Kimooenim — or Kah-móo-enim, as it is given to me — is applied, strictly speaking, to the South Fork of the Lewis or Snake River, although it is sometimes used for the entire stream.   The junction of the Kooskooskee and Lewis rivers is called (according to Stuart) Asotin — a name also applied to a lateral stream of the Lewis River, and to a town and county in Washington. — O. D. WHEELER.

West   1   mile to a St^d bend ps^d a shole in the mouth. Wind
high which obliged us to stop. Kimooenem has
two forks on the South Side, & camps of Ind^s all the
way up 2^d fork called *Pâr-nash-te* about 50 miles
camped on St^d Side to make observations.

$\overline{58^1}$

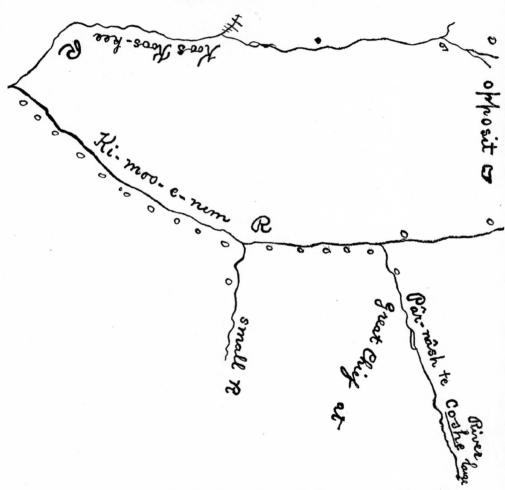

a verry worm day,   Indians continue all day on the banks to
view us as low as the forks.   Two Indians come up in a canoe
who means to accompany us to the Great rapids,   Could get
no observations,   worm night. The water of the South fork
is of a bluish green colour

---

[1] In the revision in Codex G, Clark makes this distance 60 miles. — ED.

October 10ᵗʰ Wednesday (Thursday)

a fine Morning   loaded and Set out at 7 oClock   at 2½ miles passed a run on the Star.ᵈ Side haveing passed 2 Islands and two bad rapids   at 3 miles lower passed a Creek[1] on the Lar.ᵈ with wide cotton willow bottoms haveing passed an Island and a rapid   an Indian Camp of three Lodges below the Creek   at 8½ miles lower we arrived at the heade of a verry bad riffle at which place we landed near 8 Lodges of Indians (*Choponnesh*) on the Lar.ᵈ Side to view the *riffle*, haveing passed two Islands & Six rapids Several of them verry bad   after viewᵍ this riffle two Canoes were taken over verry well ; the third stuck on a rock which took us an hour to get her off which was effected without her receving a greater injurey than a Small Split in her Side which was repaired in a Short time,   we purchased fish & dogs[2] of those people, dined and proceeded on. here we met with an Indian from the falls at which place he Sais he saw white people, and express.ᵈ an inclination to accompany us,[3]   we pass.ᵈ a few miles above this riffle 2 Lodges and an Indian batheing in a hot bath made by hot stones thrown into a pon[d] of water.   at this riffle which we Call ragid rapid took Meridian altitude of the Suns upper Limb with Sex.ᵗ 74.° 26' 0″ Lat.ᵈ produced [blank space in MS.] North   at five miles lower and Sixty miles below the forks arived at a large southerly fork which is the one we were on with the *Snake* or *So-So-nee* nation (haveing passed 5 rapids) This South fork or *Lewis's River*[4] which has two forks which

---

[1] This is Lapwai Creek.   Up this stream is the site of Fort Lapwai, Idaho.   The military post was discontinued about 1886, and its buildings used for the schools, etc., of the Indian agency there.   The first settlement at this place was made (about 1836) by a missionary, Dr. Spalding ; he had a printing-office, and printed the New Testament in the Nez Percé language'; his press is preserved in the State Library at Salem, Ore.   This mission was abandoned in 1847.   The town of Spalding, Idaho, now stands at the mouth of Lapwai Creek. — ED.

[2] We have some Frenchmen, who prefer dog-flesh to fish ; and they here got two or three dogs from the Indians. — GASS (*ut supra*).

[3] An offer which, however, we declined. — BIDDLE (i, p. 466).

[4] At this point the expedition reaches the junction of the Clearwater (or Kooskooskee) River with the Snake River.   The stream which Clark first reached on the Pacific slope was the Lemhi, a tributary of the Salmon, and this latter of the Snake. It was the Salmon to which he gave the name Lewis's River, but intended it to apply

fall into it on the South the 1ˢᵗ Small the upper large and about 2 days march up imediately parrelal to the first villages we Came to and is called by those Indians *Pâr-nash-te*[1] on this fork a little above its mouth resides a Chief who as the Indian say has more horses than he can count and further sayeth that Louises River is navagable about 60 miles up with maney rapids at which places the Indians have fishing Camps and Lodges built of an oblong form with flat ruffs. below the 1ˢᵗ river on the South Side there is ten established fishing places on the 1ˢᵗ fork which fall[s] in on the South Side is one fishing place, between that and the *Par-nashte River*, five fishing places, above two; and one on that river all of the *Cho-pun-nish* or Pierced nose *Nation* many other Indians re-side high up those rivers The Countrey about the forks is an open Plain on either Side. I can observe at a distance on the lower Larᵈ Side a high ridge of Thinly timbered Countrey the water of the South fork is a greenish blue, the north as clear as cristial

Imediately in the point is an Indian Cabin & in the South fork a Small Island, we came to on the Starᵈ Side below with a view to make some luner observations, the night proved cloudy and we were disapointed. The Indians Came down all the Cou[r]ses of this river on each side on horses to view us as we were decending. The man whome we saw at the *ruged rapid* and expressed an inclination to accompany us to the great rapids, came up with his son in a Small Canoe and procisted in his intentions. worthey of remark that not one stick of timber on the river near the forks and but a fiew trees for a great distance up the River we decended I think Lewis's

---

to the entire stream as far as its junction with the Columbia. The camping place of the explorers for this night was near the site of the present city of Lewiston, Idaho. O. D. Wheeler cites a letter of George E. Cole of Spokane, Wash., at one time governor of Washington Territory, as follows : "Col. Lyle, Capt. Ainsworth, Law-rence Co., Vic Trevett, and myself selected the location and named the place Lewis-ton, in the latter part of May or the first part of June, in 1861, in honor of Capt. Lewis of the Lewis and Clark expedition." In recent years, Clark has been similarly honored in the name of Clarkston a young city of Washington, on the Lewis River opposite Lewiston. — ED.

1 The first of these, the southern, is the Grande Ronde River ; the second (Pâr-nash-te), the Salmon River. — ED.

[Snake] River is about 250 yards wide, the *Koos koos ke*[1] River about 150 yards wide and the river below the forks about 300 yards wide a miss understanding took place between Shabono one of our interpreters and Jo & R Fields which appears to have originated in just [jest]. our diet extremely bad haveing nothing but roots and dried fish to eate, all the Party have greatly the advantage of me, in as much as they all relish the flesh of the dogs, Several of which we purchased of the nativs for to add to our store of fish and roots &c. &c. — [2]

The *Cho-pun-nish* or Pierced nose Indians are Stout likely men, handsom women,[3] and verry dressey in their way, the dress of the men are a White Buffalow robe or Elk Skin dressed with Beeds which are generally white, Sea Shells & the Mother of Pirl hung to the[i]r hair & on a piece of otter skin about their necks hair Ceewed in two parsels hanging forward over their Sholders, feathers, and different Coloured Paints which they find in their Countrey Generally white, Green & light Blue. Some fiew were a Shirt of Dressed Skins and long legins & Mockersons Painted, which appears to be their winters dress, with a plat of twisted grass about their Necks.

The women dress in a Shirt of Ibex or Goat [*Argalia*] Skins which reach quite down to their anckles with[4] a girdle, their heads are not ornemented, their Shirts are ornemented with quilled Brass, Small peces of Brass Cut into different forms, Beeds, Shells & curious bones &c. The men expose those parts which are generally kept from few [view] by other nations but the women are more perticular than any other nation which I have passed [*in s[e]creting the parts*]

Their amusements appear but fiew as their Situation requires the utmost exertion to pr[o]cure food they are generally employed in that pursute, all the Summer & fall fishing for the

---

[1] The natives call this eastern branch Koos-koos-ke, and the western Ki-mo-ee-nem. — GASS (p. 210).

[2] "Courses and distances" for Oct. 7–10 (pp. 146–148 of Codex G) are omitted, being transcripts of those in the first draft. — ED.

[3] The complexion of both sexes is darker than that of the Tushepaws. — BIDDLE (i, p. 468).

[4] "Without," in Biddle text. In Clark's MS. this word was first written, and then "out" was crossed out with ink. — ED.

Salmon, the winter hunting the deer on Snow Shoes in the plains and takeing care of ther emence numbers of horses, & in the Spring cross the mountains to the Missouri to get Buffalow robes and meet &c.   at which time they frequent[ly] meet with their enemies & lose their horses & maney of their people.[1]

Their disorders are but fiew and those fiew of a s[c]rofelous nature.   they make great use of Swetting.   The hot and cold bathes,   They are verry Selfish and Stingey of what they have to eate or ware, and they expect in return Something for everything give[n] as presents or the survices which they doe let it be however Small, and fail to make those returns on their part.[2]

---

[1] Though originally the same people, their dialect varies very perceptibly from that of the Tushepaws. — BIDDLE (i, p. 469).

[2] Here ends Codex G.   The narrative is continued by Clark in Codex H, which covers the period from Oct. 11 to Nov. 19, 1805.— ED.

Chapter XVIII

THE RAPIDS OF THE SNAKE AND COLUMBIA

Clark's Journal, October 11–20, 1805

[Clark, first draft:]   *Octr. 11th 1805 Friday*[1]

a cloudy morning   wind   set out early   course

S. 40° W. 1½ miles to p^t of rocks on the Lb^d below a bottom &
                ops^d one ps^d an old Lodge in the L^d bottom

West   2   miles to a Star^d bend passed a rapid at ½ a mile   2
                large Indⁿ houses in a bottom on the Star^d Side
                above & below the rapid, rockey hill sides

S. 40° W. 3   miles to the mouth of a branch on the Lar^d bend,
                several Lodges at the branch and a house opposit
                vacant,   we Purchased 7 dogs & fish roots &^c to eat

S. 75° W. 1½ mile in the Lar^d bend passed a rapid Point swift water

N. 40° E 1   mile to a bend St^d at a rapid ps^d a large Indⁿ house
                St^d Side

N. 60° W. 2   miles to a Lar^d bend at a rapid bad   no timber except
                a fiew low Hackburries & a fiew willows. we
                Purch^d Dried cherries Pashequar root and *Pashequar
                marsh* [mash] or bread.   Prise the shells *verry much*,
                also Iron wire

N. 10° W. 2   miles to a Star^d bend at a rapid,   2 Ind. Huts on the
                St^d Side

N. 40° W. 4   mile to a St^d bend ps^d a St^d point to an Indian camp
                of 3 Lodges on the Star^d Side,   Dined & purchased
                3 Dogs and a fiew dried fish for our voyage down,
                one Indian accompanyed us

S. 60° W. 2   mile to a Star^d bend passed a Star^d point and 2 Indian
                Houses all the houses are deserted   the owners out
                in the plains killing the antelope,   saw gees &
                Ducks

---

[1] The first draft entries of this chapter are from the Clark-Voorhis field-book. — ED.

S 30°. W	1	to a Lard bend ops.ᵈ old Indian Camp
N. 60. W	2	miles to clift in a Starᵈ bend psᵈ a rapid at ½ mile, an Indian cabin on the Stᵈ Side
West	½	a mile to a Larᵈ bend
N. 10° W	1½	miles to a St.ᵈ bend pass.ᵈ a cabin S.
West	2½	miles to a Lar.ᵈ bend passed a rapid ops.ᵈ a stoney Island from Starᵈ opsᵈ which S is an Indian Cabin, a rapid at the Lower point of Isᵈ
N. W.	3½ / 30	miles to the mouth of a run in the Star.ᵈ Bend at 2 Indian Lodges, here we camped, met an Indian from below Purchased 3 dogs and a fiew dried fish, this is a great fishing place a house below evacuated wind a head

October 11ᵗʰ Friday 1805 [1]

a cloudy morning wind from the East.   We set out early
and proceeded on   passed a rapid at *two* miles,   at 6 miles
we came too at Some Indian lodges and took brackfast,   we
purchased all the fish we could and Seven dogs of those people
for Stores of Provisions down the river   at this place I saw a
curious Swet house underground, with a Small whole at top
to pass in or throw in the hot Stones, which those in [side]
threw on as much water as to create the temperature of heat
they wished   at 9 mile passed a rapid   at 15 miles halted at
an Indian Lodge, to purchase provisions of which we pre-
c[u]red some of the *Pash-he-quar* roots five dogs [2] and a few
fish dried,   after takeing Some dinner of dog &c. we proceeded
on.   Came to and encamped at 2 Indian Lodges at a great
place of fishing [3]   here we met an Indian of a nation near the
mouth of this river.   (*Qu*) we purchased three dogs and a
fiew fish of those Indians,   we Passed today nine rapids all
of them great fishing places,   at different places on the river
saw Indian houses and Slabs & Spilt [Split] timber raised from
the ground being the different parts of the houses of the natives

---

1 This is the beginning of Codex H (Clark's); also of vol. ii of the Biddle edition. — ED.

2 Most of our people having been accustomed to meat, do not relish the fish, but prefer dog-meat, which, when well cooked, tastes very well. — GASS (p. 210).

8 Almota Creek, in Whitman County, Washington. — ED.

when they reside on this river for the purpose of fishing   at
this time they are out in the Plain on each side of the river
hunting the antilope as we are informed by our Chiefs,   near
each of those houses we observe grave yards picketed, or pieces
of wood stuck in permiscuesly over the grave or body which is
covered with earth, [*wrap up dead, put them in earth & throw
over earth & picket the ground about*]   The Country on either
Side is an open plain leavel & fertile after ascending a Steep
assent of about 200 feet,   not a tree of any kind to be Seen
on the river   The after part of the day the wind from the
S. W. and hard.   The day worm.

[Clark, first draft :]   *October 12th 1805 Saturday*

   a fair cool morning wind from E   after purchaseing all the
dried fish those people Would spear, from their hole in which
they were buried we Set out at 7 oClock and proceeded on

S W.	3	miles passed 4 Islands at 1½ miles 3 nearly opposit a bad rapid on the Lar.ᵈ Side of those Islands, and swift water around them to a Lar.ᵈ point passed a Starᵈ point
West	3	miles to a Larᵈ Bend passed a small rapid & Island on the Lar.ᵈ also an Indian cabin.
N. W.	2	miles to a Star.ᵈ Bend the bottoms are narrow from the points, the bends & high lands have clifts of ruged rock to the river, & bottoms
S. 70.° W.	2	miles to a bend at a rapid on the Star.ᵈ Isᵈ ops.ᵈ passed a rapid on the St.ᵈ Side of a stoney Island, ops.ᵈ to which on the Std. Side below the rapid a small creek falls in. saw an Indian on the high land at a distance no timber in view
South	2	miles to a p.ᵗ in Lar.ᵈ bend here the Plains become low on both sides river about 400 yards wide
S. 30.° W.	2½	miles to the mouth of a creek enter[ing] in a Lar.ᵈ bend ops.ᵈ a small Island on the Larᵈ Side
S. 85° W	2½	to the Starᵈ bend at a swift place about half the distance of this course Cᵖ L took meridian altitude on L.ᵈ Side 72° 30' 0"
S. 10.° W.	1½	to a Larᵈ Bend, (low open country)

S. 88. W. 3½ to a Star.ᵈ Bend   wind S W. and hard.   plain country
                rise gradually on each side   passed Islands and rapid
                an Indian house on the Star.ᵈ some Indians at it &.ᶜ

S. 60.° W. 6   miles to a Star.ᵈ bend passed an Island at 4 miles & one
                at 5 miles, swift water, and sholey

S. 30.° W. 1   mile to a Lard bend passed a rapid the upper p.ᵗ of
                a small stoney Is.ᵈ

West   1   mile to a Star.ᵈ bend ops.ᵈ a small Island close under the
       ‾‾‾‾
         30   Lard shore passed a run on the St.ᵈ side.   here we
                came too to view a falls or very bad rapid imediately
                below.   (Camped) which the Ind.ˢ informed us was
                very bad,   we found it bad.   Sent our small canoe
                over.

October 12ᵗʰ Saturday 1805

A fair Cool morning wind from the East   after purchaseing
every Sp[e]cies of the provisions those Indians could spare we
set out and proceeded on   at three miles passed 4 Islands,
Swift water and a bad rapid opposit to those Islands on the
Larᵈ side   at 14-½ miles passed the mouth of a large Creek
on the Larᵈ side opposit a Small Island   here the Countrey
assends with a gentle assent to the high plains, and the River
is 400 yards wide   about 1 mile below the Creek on the Same
Side took Meridian altitude which gave 72° 30′ 00″ Latitude
produced   °   ′   ″ [blank spaces in MS.] North   in the
afternoon the wind shifted to the S. W. and blew hard   we
passed today [blank space in MS.] rapids several of them very
bad and came to at the head of one (at 30 miles) on the Starᵈ
Side   to view it before we attemptᵈ to d[e]send through it[1]
The Indians had told us [it] was very bad   we found [it] long
and dangerous about 2 miles in length, and maney turns necessary to Stear Clare of the rocks, which appeared to be in every
direction   The Indians went through & our small canoe followed them,   as it was late we deturmined to camp above
untill the morning   we passed several stoney Islands today
Country as yesterday open plains, no timber of any kind,

---

[1] The Texas rapids; at their head is the town of Riparia, on the southern
shore. — ED.

a fiew Hackberry bushes & willows[1] excepted, and but few drift trees to be found, So that fire wood is verry Scerce The hills or assents from the water is faced with a dark ruged Stone. The wind blew hard this evening.

[Clark, first draft:]   *October 13ᵗʰ Sunday 1805*

Rained a little before day, and all the morning a hard wind from the S West untill 9 oClock, the rained seased & wind luled, and Capᵗ Lewis with two canoes set out & passed down the rapid The others soon followed and we passed over this bad rapid safe. We should make more portages if the season was not so far advanced and time precious with us.

Course & Distance 13ᵗʰ

S. 20° W	2	miles to a Larᵈ Bend passed in the Greater part of the distance thro a bad rapids, rocks in every derection. Channel on the Lard Side about the center of the long rapid
S. 70° W	3	miles to a large Creek in the Lᵈ bend. passed a bad rockey rapid at 2 miles many rocks
N. 50° W.	5	miles to a large creek Stᵈ bend at 2 Indian cabins passed a bad rapid for 4 miles water compressed in a narrow channel not more than 25 yards for about 1½ miles saw several Indians, this place may be called the narrows or narrow rapids great fishery
N. 75° W.	2	miles to the Starᵈ bend
S W.	2½	miles to a Larᵈ bend
N. 80° W.	3	miles to a Starᵈ bend
S. 60° W.	2	miles on the Stᵈ side passed a rapid
S. 40° W.	3½	miles to a Larᵈ bend high clifts the parts of an Indian house scaffoled up on the Larᵈ Sᵈ opposit a Picketed grave yard. we came to on the Starᵈ Side & camped. Two Indians whom we left at the forks over took us on horsback & wishes to accompany us. no game.
	23	

The wife of Shabono our interpreter we find reconsiles all the Indians, as to our friendly intentions a woman with a party of men is a token of peace

---

[1] The hackberry is *Celtis occidentalis*. The common species of willow on the banks of the Snake are *Salix amygdaloides* And., and *Salix exigua* Nutt. *S. lasiandra var. caudata* Sudw. is less common, but becomes plentiful along the Columbia. — C. V. Piper.

October 13ᵗʰ Sunday 1805

A windey dark raney morning   the rain commenced before day and continued moderately untill near 12 oClock   we took all our Canoes through this rapid without any injurey   a little below passed through another bad rapid   at [blank space in MS.] miles passed the Mo: of a large Creek [*at 5 m in the Larᵈ bend we call Ki-moó-e-nimm*[1] *Creek*]   At *10 Mᵉ* [a] little river in a Starᵈ bend, imediately below a long bad rapid [*Drewyers River*][2] in which the water is confined in a Chanel of about 20 yards between rugid rocks for the distance of a mile and a half, and a rapid rockey chanel for 2 miles above. This must be a verry bad place in high water,   here is great fishing place,   the timber of Several houses piled up, and a number of wholes of fish, and the bottom appears to have been made use of as a place of deposit for their fish for ages past,   here two Indians from the upper forks over took us and continued on down on horse back, two others were at this mouth of the Creek.   we passed a rapid about 9 mile lower. at dusk came to on the Stᵈ Side & Encamped.   Th[e] two Indˢ on horse back Stayed with us.   The Countery thro' which we passed to day is Similar to that of yesterday open plain no timber   passed several houses evacuated at established fishing places, wind hard from the S. W. in the evening and not very cold[3]

[Clark, first draft :]   *October 14ᵗʰ Monday 1805*

a verry cool morning   wind from West   set out at 8 oClock proceeded on

---

[1] This creek is now called Tukenon ; at its mouth are old Fort Taylor and the town of Grange City. — ED.

[2] Now the Palouse River ; the largest tributary of the Snake below the Clearwater. — ED.

[3] Some of the Flat-head nation of Indians live all along the river thus far down. There are not more than four lodges in a place or village, and these small camps or villages are eight or ten miles apart : at each camp there are five or six small canoes.   Their summer lodges are made of willows and flags, and their winter lodges of split pine, almost like rails, which they bring down on rafts to this part of the river where there is no timber. — GASS (p. 212).

West	2 ½	miles to a Star^d bend swift water ops.^d a rock on L.^d p.^t like a ship
S. 10° W.	2 ½	miles to a Lar.^d bend passed a rapid
S.W.	3	miles to a Star.^d bend passed a rapid and small Island on the Star^d Side
S. 10° E.	2 ½	miles to a Lar.^d bend ps.^d small Is.^d S.
S. 70° W.	1 ½	miles to a Starboard bend, wind cold & from the S W
South 18° W	3	miles to a Lar.^d bend passed a long bad rapid on which 3 canoes struck, with 2 rockey Islands in it killed 8 ducks good dinner off the Lar.^d Point at 3 miles, a cave in which the Indians have lived below on the Star.^d Side near which is
m.^s 15		a grave yard above an Island and bad rapid on both sides at this rapid the canoe a stern steared by drewyer struck a rock turned the men got out on a rock the stern of the canoe took in water and she sunk the men on the rock hel[d] her,

a number of articles floated   all that could be cought were taken by 2 of the other canoes,   Great maney articles lost among other things 2 of the mens beding shot pouches Tomahaw[k]s &.^c &.^c and every article wet.   of which we have great cause to lament as all our loose Powder two Canisters, all our roots prepared in the Indian way, and one half of our goods, fortunately the lead canisters which was in the canoe was tied down, otherwise they must have been lost as the canoe turned over   we got off the men from the rock towd our canoe on Shore after takeing out all the stores &.^c we could & put them out to dry on the Island on which we found some wood which was covered with stones,   this is the Parts of an Indian house, which we used for fire wood, by the wish of our two chiefs. Those chee[f]s, one of them was in the canoe, swam in & saved some property.   The Ind.^s have buried fish on this Isl.^d which we are cautious not to touch,   our small canoe & three Indians in another was out of sight at the time our misfortune hapined, and did not join us.   Wind hard S W.

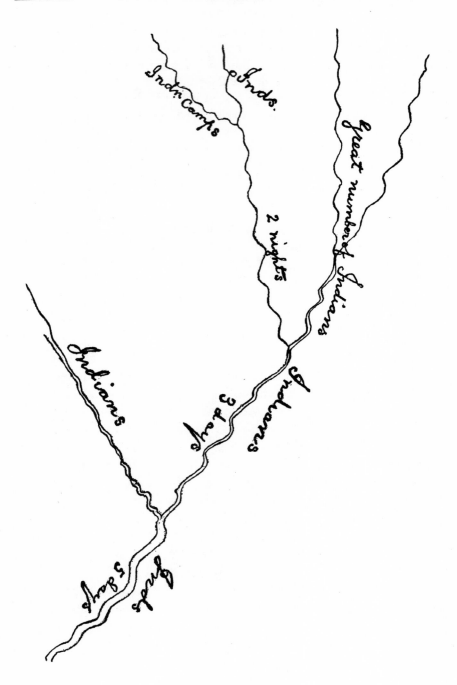

October 14.ᵗʰ Monday 1805

a verry Cold morning wind from the West and Cool untill about 12 oClock when it Shifted to the S. W. at 2-½ miles passed a remarkable rock verry large and resembling the hill [hull] of a Ship Situated on a Lar.ᵈ point at some distance from the assending Countrey   passed rapids at 6 and 9 miles. at 12 miles we came too at the head of a rapid which the Indians told me was verry bad, we viewed the rapid found it bad in decending three Stern Canoes stuck fast for some time on the head of the rapid and one struck a rock in the worst part, fortunately all landed Safe below the rapid which was nearly 3 miles in length.   here we dined, and for the first time for three weeks past I had a good dinner of Blue wing Teel,   after dinner we Set out and had not proceded on two miles before our Stern Canoe in passing thro a Short rapid opposit the head of an Island,[1] run on a Smothe rock and turned broad Side,   the men got out on the [rock] all except one of our Indian Chiefs who swam on Shore, The canoe filed and sunk a number of articles floated out, Such as the mens bedding clothes & skins.   the Lodge &c &c. the greater part of which were cought by 2 of the Canoes, whilst a 3.ʳᵈ was unloading & Steming the Swift current to the relief of the men on the rock, who could with much dificuelty hold the Canoe   however in about an hour we got the men an[d] canoe to shore with the Loss of Some bedding Tomahaw[k]s shot pouches skins Clothes &c &c. all wet   we had every article exposed to the Sun to dry on the Island,   our loss in provisions is verry considerable all our roots was in the canoe that Sunk, and Cannot be dried Sufficient to save, our loose powder was also in the Canoe and is all wete.   This I think may be saved, [*we shall save*]   In this Island we found some Spilt [Split] timber the parts of a house which the Indians had verry securely covered with Stone, we also observed a place where the Indians had buried their fish,   we have made it a point at all times not to take any thing belonging to the Indians even their wood.   but at this time we are Compelled to violate that

---

[1] These were the Pine-tree Rapids, some 30 miles below Palouse River. — ED.

rule and take a part of the split timber we find here bur[i]ed for fire wood, as no other is to be found in any direction. our Small Canoe which was a head returned at night with 2 ores which they found floating below. The wind this after noon from the S. W. as usial and hard.

[Clark, first draft :]   *October 15th Tuesday 1805*

a fair morning after a cold night. Some frost this morning and Ice. Several hunters out saw nothing Cap't Lewis assended the hills & saw Mountain a head bearing S. E. & N W. a high point to the West. Plains wavering. Set out at 3 oClock

Course

South	4 ½	miles to the lower point of a Island, close under the St'd Side passed one on the Lard. & one other in the middle of the river, 4 small rapids at the lower p't of 1st Is'd ops'd 2nd & 3rd Islands
S. E.	1 ½	miles to the lower point of an Is'd. close under the Lar'd bend ops'd. the upper p't of an Is'd. on St'd. point a small rapid opposit
S. 35° W.	9	miles to a Point of rocks on Lar'd. S'd passed a place of swift water at the lower point of the 1st Island a small rapid a little below a Lar'd. point at 2 miles a Star'd point at 4 miles, a Lar'd. point at 5 miles a Star'd point 3 small Is'd. ops'd on Lar'd. & 2 on Star'd. Side at 6½ a small rapid, several scafles of split timber on the Star'd. Side in the bottom below the
	15	Islands a Island in the river at 8½ miles on St'd Side a fishing timber scaffeled a willow bottom on the Lard Side above the point country lower each side 90 to 100 feet is the hite of the plains some swift water at the last Is'd.
South	5	miles to an Island in the head of a rapid Passed for 3 miles through good water inclosed in clifts of rocks 100 feet high. below which the river widens into a Bay nearly round. we Encamped at three
	20	scaffles of split timber on the Star'd Side. here we found our Pilot & one man wateing for us to show us the best way thro those rapids. the evening cool, we saw no timber to day, except small willow & srub of Hackberry Killed 2 Teel this evening.

Map from Clark Field-book, locating
Indian tribes.

*October 15*th *Tuesday 1805*

a fair morning sent out hunters to hunt in the plains, about 10 oClock they returned and informed that they could not See any Signs of game of any kind. Cap!. Lewis walked on the plains and informs that he could plainly See a rainge of mountains which bore S. E. & N. W. the nearest point south about 60 miles, and becoms high toward the N. W.[1] The plaines on each side is wavering. Labiesh killed 2 gees & 2 Ducks of the large kind. at two oClock we loaded & Set out, our Powder & Provisions of roots not sufficently dry. but we shall put them out at the forks or mouth of this river which is at no great distance, and at which place we Shall delay to make some selestial observations &c. passed Eleven Island[s] and Seven rapids today Several of the rapids verry bad and dificuelt to pass, The Islands of different sizes and all of round Stone and Sand, no timber of any kind in Sight of the river, a fiew small willows excepted; in the evening the countrey becomes lower not exceding 90 or 100 feet above the water and back is a wavering Plain on each Side, passed thro: narrows for 3 miles where the clifts of rocks juted to the river on each side compressing the water of the river through a narrow chanel; below which it widens into a kind of bason nearly round without any proceptiable current. at the lower part of this bason is a bad dificuelt and dangerous rapid to pass, at the upper part of this rapid we over took the three Indians who had Polited [piloted] us thro the rapids from the forks. those people with our 2 Chiefs had proceeded on to this place where they thought proper to delay for us to warn us of the difficulties of this rapid. we landed at a parcel of split timber, the timber of a house of Indians out hunting the *Antilope* in the plains; and raised on scaffolds to save them from the spring floods. here we were obliged for the first time to take the property of the Indians without the consent or approbation of the owner. the night was cold & we made use of a part of those boards and split logs for fire wood. Killed two teel this

---

[1] Apparently a spur of the Blue Mountains, which run through Columbia and Asotin counties, in southeast Washington. — ED.

evening.   Examined the rapids which we found more dificuelt to pass than we expected from the Indians information — a suckcession of sholes, appears to reach from bank to bank for 3 miles which was also intersepted with large rocks Sticking up in every direction, and the chanel through which we must pass crooked and narrow.   We only made 20 miles today,[1] owing to the detention in passing rapids &c.

[Clark, first draft:]   *Oct*. 16*th* 1805 *Wednesday*

a cool morning   set out early   passed the rapid with all the canoes except Serj: Pryors which run on a rock near the lower part of the rapid and stuck fast,   by the assistance of the 3 other canoes she was unloaded and got off the rock without any further injorey than the wetting the greater part of her loading.   loaded and proceeded on   I walked around this rapid

Course

S. 12.° E 3	miles to the Lar.d bend passed a bad rapid all the way. here one canoe stuck bad rapid
S. 60.° W. 3	miles to a Star.d bend to a scaffel of split timber on an Island ops.d 2 other Is.ds on Lar.d
S. 10.° W. 3	miles to a Point of rocks at a rapid ops.d the upper part of small Island on the Lar.d Side, passed a rapid at the lower point of the 3 first Is.ds one at the Lar.d p.t 1½ m.s below swift water
S. 50.° W. 6	miles to Lar.d p.t ops.d a rapid & a p.t of an Island the countrey low on both sides, Passed a rapid at 3 miles, passed a verry Bad rapid or falls, obliged to unload at 5 miles at the lower point of a small Island Star.d dined Loaded 5 Ind.s came to us
S. 28 W. 6 ½	miles to the Junction of Columbia in the Stard Point & Passed the rapid opposit the upper Point of the said Island and Passed a small Is.d on Lar.d Side opposit, passed the lower point of the Island on Star.d Side at 2½ miles a gravelley bare [bar] in the river at 3 miles, river wide Countrey on each side low, a rainge of hills on the west imedeately in front on the opposit side of Columbia

[1] Their camp was on Rattlesnake Flats just above Fish-hook Rapids. — ED.

Columbia River and its waters, showing fishing establishments,
sketch-map by Clark.

We halted a short time above the point and smoked with the Indians, & examined the point and best place for our camp, we camped on the Columbia River a little above the point   I saw about 200 men comeing down from their villages & were turned back by the Chief,   after we built our fires of what wood we could collect, & get from the Indians, the Chief brought down all his men singing and danceing as they came, formed a ring and dancd for some time around us   we gave them a smoke, and they returned [to] the village a little above, the chief & several delay untill I went to bead.   bought 7 dogs & they gave us several fresh salmon & some horse dried

October 16th. Wednesday 1805

A cool morning,   deturmined to run the rapids,   put our Indian guide in front our Small Canoe next and the other four following each other,   the canoes all passed over Safe except the rear Canoe which run fast on a rock at the lower part of the Rapids,   with the early assistance of the other Canoes & the Indians, who was extreamly ellert every. thing was taken out and the Canoe got off without any enjorie further than the articles [with] which it was loaded [getting] all wet.   at 14 miles passed a bad rapid at which place we unloaded and made a portage of ¾ of a mile[1] haveing pass^d 4 Smaller rapids, three Islands and the parts of a house above,   I Saw Indians & Horses on the South Side below   five Indians came up the river in great haste, we Smoked with them and gave them a piece of tobacco to Smoke with their people and sent them back, they Set out in a run & continued to go as fast as they could run as far as we could see them.   after getting Safely over the rapid and haveing taken Diner Set out and proceeded on Seven miles to the junction of this river and the Columbia which joins from the N. W.   pass^d a rapid two Islands and a graveley base, and imediately in the mouth a rapid above an Island.   In every direction from the junction of those rivers the countrey is one continued plain low and rises from the water gradually, except a range of high Countrey which runs

---

1 Now called the Five Mile Rapids from their distance above the forks. — ED.

from S.W. & N. E. and is on the opposit Side about 2 miles distant from the Collumbia and keeping its derection S. W. untill it joins a S. W. range of mountains.

We halted above the point on the river Kimooenim[1] to smoke with the Indians who had collected there in great numbers to view us, here we met our 2 Chiefs who left us two days ago and proceeded on to this place to inform those bands of our approach and friendly intentions towards all nations &c. we also met the 2 men who had passed us Several days ago on horsback, one of them we observed was a man of great influence with those Indians, harranged them; after Smokeing with the Indians who had collected to view us we formed a camp at the point near which place I saw a fiew pieces of Drift wood   after we had our camp fixed and fires made, a Chief came from this camp which was about ¼ of a mile up the Columbia river at the head of about 200 men singing and beeting on their drums Stick and keeping time to the musik, they formed a half circle around us and Sung for Some time, we gave them all Smoke, and Spoke to their Chief as well as we could by signs informing them of our friendly disposition to all nations, and our joy in Seeing those of our Children around us,   Gave the principal chief a large Medal, Shirt and Handkf.   a 2nd. Chief a Meadel of Small size, and to the Cheif who came down from the upper villages a Small *Medal* & Handkerchief.

The Chiefs then returned with the men to their camp; Soon after we purchased for our Provisions *Seven* Dogs,   Some fiew of those people made us presents of fish and Several returned and delayed with us untill bedtime.   The 2 old chiefs who accompanied us from the head of the river precured us Some fuil Such as the Stalks of weed[s] or plant[s] and willow bushes. one man made me a present of a about 20ᴸᵇ of verry fat Dried horse meat.

great quantities of a kind of prickley pares,[2] much worst than

---

[1] The Columbia here is 860 yards wide, and the Ki-moo-ee-nem (called Lewis's River from its junction with the Koos-koos-ke) 475. — GASS (p. 217).

[2] There is but one species of prickly pear that grows in this neighborhood, *Opuntia polyacantha* Haworth. — C. V. PIPER.

Map from Clark Field-book, showing Course and Camping places,
October 16–18, 1805.

any I have before seen of a tapering form and attach themselves
by bunches.[1]

[Clark, first draft:]   *October 17th Thursday 1805 Forks of Columbia*

Took altitude with Sextant as follows

A M.

	h	m	s	
	7	40	13	
"		42	58	} altitude produced 22° − 25' − 15''
	43	44		

Observed time and distance of Son and Moons nearest Limbs the Sun
East (at the Point)

		Time			distance	
	H.	M.	S.			
A.M.	7	51	43	60°	47'	15''
	"	53	33	"	46	30
	"	54	35	"	45	45
	"	55	55	"	45	
	"	57	37	"	45	00
	"	58	29	"	44	00
	8	00	26	"	43	45
	"	1	22	"	43	15
	"	3	8	"	43	00
	"	4	43	"	42	30
	"	6	5	"	43	
	"	7	52	"	41	30

Magnetick azmoth.   Time and distance of the Sun &c.

Azmth			Time			distance		
			H.	M	s			
S	75°	E	8	15	45	33°	4'	30''
S.	74°	E	8	19	43	34	13	"

Took Equal altitudes

	H.	m	s			h	m	s
A M.	8	23	00		PM.	3	21	53
	"	24	55			"	23	50
	"	26	49			"	25	42

Altitude produced is 35° − 9' − 30''

----

[1] "Courses and distances," and "Celestial observations" which here follow are
omitted, being transcripts from those in the first draft. — ED.

This morning after the Luner observations, the old chief came down, and several men with dogs to sell & womin with fish &.ͨ the Dogs we purchased the fish not good.

I took 2 men and set out in a small canoe with a view to go as high up the Columbia river as the 1.ˢᵗ fork which the Indians made signs was but a short distance, I set out at 2 oClock first course was N. 83° W 6 miles to the lower point of a Island on the Lar.ᵈ Side, passed an Island in the middle of the river at 5 miles, at the head of which is a rapid not bad at this rapid 3 Lodges of mats on the Larᵈ emence quantites of dried fish. Then West 4 miles to the Lower point of an Island on the Star.ᵈ Side 2 lodges of Indians large and built of mats, passed 3 verry large mat lodges at 2 mile on the Starᵈ Side large scaffols of fish drying at every lodge, and piles of salmon lying, the squars engaged prepareing them for the scaffol. a squar gave me a dried salmon. from those lodges on the Island an Indian showed me the mouth of the river which falls in below a high hill on the Lar.ᵈ N. 80.° W. 8 miles from the Island. The river bending Lar.ᵈ This river is remarkably clear and crouded with salmon in maney places, I observe in assending great numbers of salmon *dead* on the shores, floating on the water and in the Bottom which can be seen at the debth of 20 feet, the cause of the emence numbers of dead salmon I can't account for so it is I must have seen 3 or 400 dead and maney living the Indians, I believe made us[e] of the fish which is not long dead as, I struck one nearly dead and left him floating, some Indians in a canoe behind took the fish on board his canoe

The bottoms on the South side as high as the Tarcouche tesse[1] is from 1 to 2 miles wide, back of the bottoms rises to hilly countrey, the Plain is low on the North & Easte for a great distance no wood to be seen in every direction.

The Tarcouche tesse bears South of West, the Columbia N W above [a] range of hills on the West Parralel a range of mountains to the East which appears to run nearly North & South distance not more than 50 miles. I returned to the point at Dusk followed by three canoes of Indians 20 in num-

1 The Columbia, see note p. 60, *ante.* — ED.

ber.   I killed a Fowl of the Pheasent kind as large as a small
turkey.   The length from his Beeck to the end of its tail
2 feet 6 ¾ Inches, from the extremity of its wings across 3 feet
6 Inches.   the tail feathers 13 Inches long,   feeds on grasshoppers, and the seed of wild Isoop   Those Indians are
orderly, badly dressed in the same fashions of those above
except the women who wore short shirts and a flap over their
22ᵈ   Fishing houses of Mats robes of Deer, Goat & Beaver.

October 17ᵗʰ Thursday 1805

A fair morning   made the above observations during which
time the principal Chief came down with Several of his principal men and smoked with us ;   Several men and woman offered
Dogs and fish to Sell, we purchased all the dogs we could, the
fish being out of season and dieing in great numbers in the
river, we did not think proper to use them,   send out Hunters
to shute the Prarie Cock a large fowl which I have only Seen
on this river, several of which I have killed,   they are the size
of a Small turkey, of the pheasant kind,   one I killed on the
water[s] edge to day measured from the Beak to the end of the
toe 2 feet 6 &·¾ Inches ; from the extremities of its wings
3 feet 6 inches ; the tale feathers is 13 inches long :   they feed
on grasshoppers and the Seed of the wild plant which is also
peculiar to this river and the upper parts of the Missoury
somewhat resembling the whins.   Capᵗ Lewis took a Vocabelary of the Language of those people who call themselves
Sokulk, and also one of the language of a nation resideing on
a Westerly fork of the Columbia which mouthes a fiew miles
above this place who Call themselves *Chim-nâ-pum*   Some fiew
of this nation reside with the *Sokulks* nation.   Their language
differ but little from either the Sokulks or the *Chô-pun-nish* (or
pierced nose) nation which inhabit the Koskoskea river and
Lewis's R below.[1]

I took *two* men in a Small canoe and assended the Columbia
river 10 miles to an Island near the Starᵈ Shore on which two

---

[1] This would indicate that the tribes here named were of the Shahaptian family.
The river on which the Chim-nâ-pum lived is the Yakima, also mentioned below as
the Tâpetêtt (in Biddle text, Tapteal and Tapteet). — Eᴅ.

large Mat Lodges of Indians were drying Salmon, (as they
informed me by Signs for the purpose of food and fuel, & I do
not think [it] at all improbable that those people make use of
Dried fish as fuel,   The number of dead Salmon on the Shores
& floating in the river is incrediable to say — and at this Season
they have only to collect the fish Split them open and dry them
on their Scaffolds on which they have great numbers,   how far
they have to raft their timber they make their scaffolds of
I could not lern ; but there is no timber of any sort except
Small willow bushes in sight in any direction.   from this Island
the natives showed me the enterance of a large Westerly fork
which they Call *Tâpetêtt* at about 8 miles distant,   the evening
being late I deturmined to return to the forks, at which place
I reached at Dark.[1]   from the point up the Columbia River is
N. 83° W. 6 miles to the lower point of an Island. near the
Lar⁴ Side, passed a Island in the middle of the river at 5 miles
at the head of which is a rapid, not dangerous   on the Lar⁴ Side
opposit to this rapid is a fishing place 3 Mat Lodges, and great
quanᵗˢ of Salmon on scaffolds drying.   Saw great numbers of
Dead Salmon on the Shores and floating in the water, great
numbers of Indians on the banks viewing me. and 18 canoes
accompanied me from the point.   The waters of this river is
clear, and a Salmon may be seen at the deabth of 15 or 20 feet.
West 4 miles to the lower point of a large Island near the
Star⁴ Side at 2 Lódges, passed three large lodges on the Star⁴
Side near which great number of Salmon was drying on scaffolds   one of those Mat lodges I entered   found it crouded
with men women and children and near the enterance of those
houses I saw maney squars engaged [in] splitting and drying
Salmon.   I was furnished with a mat to set on, and one man
set about prepareing me something to eate,   first he brought
in a piece of a Drift log of pine and with a wedge of the elks
horn, and a malet of Stone curioesly carved he Split the log
into Small pieces and lay'd it open on the fire on which he put
round Stones,   a woman handed him a basket of water and

---

1 At the confluence of the Columbia and Snake is the town of Ainsworth.   Clark
visited the Indians where now the river is spanned by the Northern Pacific Railway
bridge between the towns of Pasco and Kennewick. — ED.

a large Salmon about half Dried, when the Stones were hot he put them into the basket of water with the fish which was soon sufficently boiled for use it was then taken out put on a platter of rushes neetly made, and set before me they boiled a Salmon for each of the men with me, dureing those preparations, I smoked, with those about me who chose to smoke which was but fiew, this being a custom those people are but little accustomed to and only Smok thro: form. after eateing the boiled fish which was delicious, I set out & halted or come too on the Island at the two Lodges, Several fish was given to me, in return for Which I gave Small pieces of ribbond from those Lodges the natives Showed me the mouth of *Tap teel* River about 8 miles above on the West Side this western fork appears to beare nearly West, the main Columbia river N. W. a range of high land to the S. W. and parralal to the river and at the distance of 2 miles on the Lard. Side, the countrey Low on the Stard. Side, and all coverd. with a weed or plant about 2 & three feet high and resembles the whins. I can proceive a range of mountains to the East which appears to bare N. & South distant about 50 or 60 miles. no wood to be Seen in any derection, on my return I was followd. by 3 canoes in which there was 20 Indians I shot a large Prairie Cock Several grouse, Ducks and fish. on my return found Great numbs. of the nativs with Capt. Lewis, men all employ[e]d in dressing ther skins mending their clothes and putting their arms in the best order the latter being always a matter of attention with us. The Dress of those natives differ but little from those on the Koskoskia and Lewis's rivers, except the women who dress verry different, in as much as those above ware long leather Shirts which [are] highly ornimented with beeds shells &c. &c. and those on the main Columbia river only ware a truss or pece of leather tied around them at their hips and drawn tite between ther legs and fastened before So as bar[e]ly to hide those parts which are so sacredly hid & s[e]cured by our women. Those women are more inclined to Co[r]pulency than any we have yet Seen, with low Stature broad faces, heads flatened and the foward [forehead] compressed so as to form a Streight line from the nose to the Crown of the head, their eyes are of a Duskey black, their hair of a corse black without orniments of any kind braded as above

The orniments of each Sects are Similar, Such as large blue & white beeds, either pendant from their ears or incircling their necks, wrists & arms. they also ware bracelets of Brass, Copper & horn, and trinkets of Shells, fish bones and curious feathers. Their garments consists of a short shirt of leather and a roabe of the Skins of Deer or the antilope, but fiew of them ware Shirts all have Short robes. Those people appears to live in a State of comparitive happiness : they take a great[er] share [in the] labor of the woman, than is common among Savage tribes, and as I am informed [are] content with one wife (as also those on the Ki moo e nim river) Those people respect the aged with Veneration. I observed an old woman in one of the Lodges which I entered, She was entirely blind as I was informed by signs, had lived more than 100 winters, She occupied the best position in the house, and when She Spoke great attention was paid to what she Said. Those people as also those of the *flat heads* which we had passed on the Koskoske and Lewis's rivers are subject to sore eyes, and many are blind of one and Some of both eyes. this misfortune must be owing to the reflections of the sun &c. on the waters in which they are continually fishing during the Spring Summer & fall, & the snows dureing the, winter Seasons, in this open countrey where the eye has no rest. I have observed amongst those, as well in all other tribes which I have passed on these waters who live on fish maney of different sectes who have lost their teeth about middle age, Some have their teeth worn to the gums, perticelar[ly] those of the upper jaw, and the tribes generally have bad teeth the cause of it I cannot account [for], sand attach.^d to the roots & the method they have of useing the dried Salmon, which is mearly worming it and eating the rine & scales with the flesh of the fish, no doubt contributes to it.

The Houses or Lodges of the tribes of the main Columbia river is of large Mats made of rushes, those houses are from 15 to 60 feet in length generally of an Oblong squar form, Supported by poles on forks in the in[n]er Side, Six feet high, the top is covered also with mats leaveing a Seperation in the whole length of about 12 or 15 inches wide, left for the purpose of admitting light and for the Smok of the fire to pass which is made in the middle of the house. The roughfs are nearly flat, which proves to me that rains are not common in this open Countrey.

Those people appear of a mild disposition and friendly disposed. They have in their huts independant of their nets gigs & fishing tackling each bows & large quivers of arrows on which they use flint Spikes. Their ammusements are similar to those of the Missouri. they are not beggerley, and receive what is given them with much joy.

I saw but fiew horses they appeared [to] make but little use of those animals principally useing Canoes for their uses of procuring food &c.

[Clark, first draft :]   *October 18th Friday 1805*

a cold morning faire & wind from S E   several Heath hens or large Pheasents lit near us & the men killed six of them.

Took one altitude of the Suns upper Limb *28° . 22′ . 15″* at *8. 1. 24.* A. M.   Several Indian canoes come down & joind those with us.   made a second Chief by giveing a Meadel & Wampom   I also gave a string of wampom to the old Chief who came down with us and informed the Indians of our views and intentions in a council

Observed time and distance of Sun & Moons nearest Limbs Sun East

	Time			distance	
H.	m	s			
9	37	46	47°	15′	30″
"	40	32	"	14	15
"	41	47	"	14	00
"	42	55	"	13	30
"	43	44	"	12	45
"	46	2	"	12	30
"	47	18	"	12	00
"	48	35	"	11	45
"	49	44	"	11	15
"	50	53	"	11	00
"	52	00	"	.9	30
"	53	46	"	9	30

Took a second altitude of the Suns upper Limb *58° – 34 – 45″* at *10 – 3 – 59*^{h m s} Measured the width of the Columbia River from the Point across to a Point of View is S 22° W. from the Point up the Columbia to a Point of view is N. 84.° W. 148 poles, thence across to the 1ˢᵗ point of view is S 28 ½ E.

Measured the width of *Ke-moo-e-nim* River, from the Point across to an object on the opposit side is N. 41 ½ E from the Point up the river is N. 8. E. 82 poles thence across to the Point of view is N. 79.° East

Distance across the *Columbia* 960 ¾ yards water

Distance across the *Ki-moo-e-nim* 575 yds water

Names of this nation above the mouth of the *Ki-moo-e-nim* is *So-kulk* Perced noses   The Names of the nation on the Ki-mooenim River is *Cho-pun-nish* Piercd noses at the Prarie   the name of a nation at the Second forks of the *Tape tett* River, or *Nocktosh* fork *Chim-nâ-pum*, some of which reside with the *Sokulks* above this and at a few miles distance   4 men in a canoe come up from below stayed a fiew minits and returned.

Took a meridian altitude *68° – 57′ – 30″* the suns upper Limb.   the Lattitude produced is *46° – 15′ – 13″* ⁹/₁₀ North, Capᵗ Lewis took a vocabillary of the Sokulk or Pierced noses Language and *Chim-nâ-pum* Language whic[h] is in some words different but orriginally the same people,   The Great Chief *Cuts-sâh nem* gave me a sketch of the rivers & Tribes above on the great river & its waters on which he put great numbers of villages of his nation & friends, as noted on the sketch.

The fish being very bad those which was offerd to us we had every reason to believe was taken up on the shore dead we thought proper not to purchase any,   we purchased forty dogs for which we gave articles of little value, such as beeds, bells & thimbles, of which they appeared verry fond,   at 4 oClock we set out down the Great Columbia accompanied by our two old Chiefs,   one young man wished to accompany us, but we had no room for more, & he could be of no service to us.

The great chief continued with us untill our departure.

Course

S. 55° E. 12   miles a Lard. bend lower part of a bad rapid and several
little stony Islands   passed. an Island imediately in
the mouth of the *Kimoo-e nim* one in the mid river at
8 miles   this Island of corse gravel and 3 miles
long,   the Columbia more than a mile wide, banks
low not subject to overflow   an Island on the Star.ᵈ
Side from op.ᵈ the center the last 3½ miles long.
no timber in view   ops.ᵈ the center of this Island
and below the larst a Island in the middle with 9
Lodges and a great quantity of fish on its upper
point,   a small Island imediately below ops.ᵈ the
upper P.ᵗ of which the rapid commences   several
small [islands] on the Lar.ᵈ Side

S. 20° E.   2½   miles to 2 Lodges of Indians on a small Island Star.ᵈ
point

S. E   1½   miles to mo. of a river 40 yds wide under a high clift
in the Lar.ᵈ bend   here the river enters the high
countrey rising ab.ᵗ 200 feet above the water   large
black rocks makeing out from Lar.ᵈ half across the
river and some distance from Star.ᵈ Side.

S. 12° W.   4   miles to a point of rocks in a Lar.ᵈ bend,   passed a
small Is.ᵈ   passed a 2.ᵈ at 2 miles, on its upper Point
2 Lodges of Indians fishing at a rapid   ops.ᵈ the
lower point ps.ᵈ 9 Lodges of Indians fishing on an
Island on the Star.ᵈ Side   below about 1 mile 5
Lodges on the Star.ᵈ Side,   passed a Island in middle

21   of river at 3 m.

we Encamped a little below & ops.ᵈ the lower point of the
Island on the Lar.ᵈ Side[1]   no wood to be found   we were.
obliged to make use [of] small dried willows to cook.   our
old chief informed us that the great chief of all the nations
about lived at the 9 Lodges above and wished us to land &.ᶜ
he said he would go up and call him over   they went up and
did not return untill late at night,   about 20 came down &
built a fire above and stayed all night.   The chief brough[t] a
basket of mashed berries.

---

[1] The camp for this day was on or barely over the border of Washington. — ED.

October 18ᵗʰ Friday 1805

This morning Cool and fare wind from the S. E.   six of the large *Prarie cock* killed this morning.   Several canoes of Indians came down and joined those with us, we had a council with those in which we informed of our friendly intentions towards them and all other of our red children, of our wish to make a piece between all of our red Children in this quarter &c. &c.   this was conveyed by signs thro: our 2 Chiefs who accompanied us, and was understood, we made a 2ᵈ Chief and gave Strings of wompom to them all in remembrance of what we Said.   four men in a Canoe came up from a large encampment on an Island in the River about 8 miles below, they delayed but a fiew minits and returned, without Speaking a word to us.

The Great Chief and one of the *Chim-nâ-pum* nation drew me a sketch of the Columbia above and the tribes of his nation, living on the bank[s], and its waters, and the *Tâpe-tett* river which falls in 18 miles above on the westerly side See sketch below for the number of villages and nations &c. &c.¹

we thought it necessary to lay in a Store of Provisions for our voyage, and the fish being out of Season, we purchased forty dogs for which we gave articles of little value, such as bells, thimbles, knitting pins, brass wire and a few beeds [with] all of which they appeared well Satisfied and pleased.

every thing being arranged we took in our Two Chiefs, and set out on the great Columbia river, haveing left our guide and the two young men two of them enclined not to proceed on any further, and the 3ᵈ could be of no service to us as he did not know the river below

Took our leave of the Chiefs and all those about us and proceeded on down the great Columbia river   passed a large

---

¹ They drew it with a piece of coal on a robe, and as we afterwards transferred to paper, it exhibited a valuable specimen of Indian delineation. — BIDDLE (ii, p. 17).

[In the fire of 1895] was burned a map of Oregon presented by the Indians to Lewis and Clark. It was on dressed skin, and showed, by the number of snow-shoes, the relative population of the villages, etc., in that section.— P. B. BON-INGER (University of Virginia).

Junction of Columbia and Lewis's Rivers,
sketch-map by Clark.

Island at 8 miles about 3 miles in length, a Island on the Star.^d
Side the upper point of which is opposit the center of the last
mentioned Island and reaches 3-½ miles below the 1.st Island
and opposit to this near the middle of the river nine Lodges
are Situated on the upper point at a rapid which is between the
lower point of the 1.st Island and upper point of this; great
numbers of Indians appeared to be on this Island, and emence
quantites of fish scaffold[s]   we landed a few minits to view a
rapid which commenced at the lower point,   pass.^d this rapid
which was verry bad, between 2 Small Islands, two Still Smaller
near the Lar.^d Side, at this rapid on the Star.^d Side is 2 Lodges
of Indians Drying fish, at 2-½ miles lower and 14-½ below
the point passed an Island Close under the Star.^d Side on which
was 2 Lodges of Indians drying fish on Scaffolds as above   at
16 miles from the point the river passes into the range of high
Countrey, at which place the rocks project into the river from
the high clifts which is on the Lar.^d Side about ⅓ of the way
across and those of the Star.^d Side about the same distance,
the countrey rises here about 200 feet above the water and is
bordered with black rugid rocks,   at the Commencement of
this high countrey on Lar.^d Side a Small riverlet falls in which
appears to [have] passed under the high count.^y in its whole
co[ur]se.   saw a mountain bearing S. W. conocal form Covered
with Snow.[1]   passed 4 Islands, at the upper point of the 3.rd is
a rapid,   on this Island is *two* Lodges of Indians, drying fish,
on the fourth Island close under the Star.^d Side is *nine* large
Lodges of Indians Drying fish on scaffolds as above   at this
place we were called to to land,   as it was near night, and no
appearance of wood, we proceeded on about 2 miles lower to
Some Willows, at which place we observed a drift log   formed
a camp on the Lar.^d Side under a high hill nearly opposit to
five Lodges of Indians; Soon after we landed, our old Chiefs
informed us that the large camp above " was the Camp of the
1.st Chief of all the *tribes* in this quarter, and that he had called
to us to land and Stay all night with him, that he had plenty of
wood for us &c."   This would have been agreeable to us if it

---

[1] The "small riverlet" is the Walla Walla River ; the snow-covered conical mountain, Mount Hood, of which this was the explorer's first glimpse. — ED.

had have been understood perticelarly as we were compelled to use drid willows for fuel for the purpose of cooking, we requested the old Chiefs to walk up on the Side we had landed and call to the chief to come down and Stay with us all night which they did, late at night the Chief came down accompanied by 20 men, and formed a camp a short distance above, the chief brought with him a large basket of mashed berries which he left at our Lodge as a present. I saw on the main land opposit those Lodges a number of horses feeding, we made 21 miles to day.

[Clark, first draft:]   *October 19ᵗʰ Saturday*

The Great Chief 2ᵈ Chief and a Chief of a band below came and smoked with us we gave a meadel a string of Wampom & handkerchef to the Great Chief by name *Yel-lep-pit*¹   The 2ᵈ Chief we gave a string of wampom, his name is [blank space in MS.]   The 3ᵈ who lives below a string of wampom his name I did not learn.   the Chief requested us to stay untill 12 we excused our selves and set out at 9 oClock

Course

S W.   14 miles to a rock in a Larᵈ resembling a hat just below a rapid at the lower Point of an Island in the middle of the river 7 Lodges and opposit the head of one on the Star Side 5 Lodges   passed an Island at 8 miles 6 miles long close to Larᵈ Side   no water on Larᵈ   a small one opsᵈ and at the lower point no water   Larᵈ passed an Islᵈ in middle at 8 miles on which 5 Indian Lodges, deserted   at the end of this course a bad rockey place plenty of water rocks in the river. passed a Starᵈ point at 4 miles country a little lower

¹ The following list of chiefs was found on a separate leaf at the back of the Clark-Voorhis field-book. — ED.

> *To-mar-lar-pom*   Grand Chief
> *Wal lar war lar*   N[ation]
> *Yel lep pet*   Chief
> made a Chief and gave a small medal by name of
>   *Ar-lo-quat*   of the Chopunnish Nation
> made a Chief by name Tow-wall.

S. 80° W.   7 miles to a Point of rocks on the Star^d bend   Passed the
Island on St^d side   at 1 mile passed a verry bad rapid
above the end of this course.   2 miles in length with
several small Islands in it & Banks of Mussle shells
in the rapids.   here the lower countrey commences.
Saw a high mountain covered with snow *West*   this
we suppose to be Mt St Helens

S. 70° W.   12 miles to & passed 20 Lodges of Indians scattered allong
the Star^d Side drying fish & Prickley pares (to Burn
in winter)   I went on shore in a small canoe a head,
landed at the first 5 Lodges,   found the Indians much
fritened,   all got into their lodges and when I went
in found some hanging down their heads, some crying
and others in great agitation,   I took all by the hand
and distributed a few small articles which I chanced
to have in my pockets and smoked with them which
expelled their fears, soon after the canoes landed &
we all smoked and were friendly.   I gave a string of
Wampom to the Principal man,   we dined on dryed
salmon & set out.   I am confident that I could have
tomahawked every Indian here.   The Language is
the same as those above, those Lodges can turn out
350 men.   I shot a Crain & 2 Ducks and opposit
to a Lodge on the Star^d Side, one mile below a rapid.
a high Mountain S. W. from the Muscle Shell rapid.

S. W.   3 miles to a few willow Trees on the Lar^d Side below the
lower p^t of an Is^d L^d opposit 24 Lodges of Indians
fishing.   here we came too and camped, 19 of them
on the Star^d Side and 5 on an Island in the middle of
the river,   about 100 Ind^s come over some brought
wood and we gave smoke to all which they were
pleased at

_____
36

P. Crusat played on the violin which pleased and astonished
those [w]reches who are badly clad, ¾ with robes not half
large enough to cover them,   they are homeley high cheeks,
and but fiew orniments.   I suped on the crane which I killed
to day.

October 19th Saturday 1805

The great chief *Yel-lep-pit* two other chiefs, and a chief of [a] Band below presented themselves to us verry early this morning. we Smoked with them, enformed them as we had all others above as well as we could by signs of our friendly intentions towards our red children perticelar those who opened their ears to our Councils. we gave a Medal, a Handkercheif & a String of Wompom to *Yelleppit* and a String of wompom to each of the others. *Yelleppit* is a bold handsom Indian, with a dignified countenance about 35 years of age, about 5 feet 8 inches high and well perpotiond. he requested us to delay untill the Middle of the day, that his people might come down and see us, we excused our Selves and promised to stay with him one or 2 days on our return which appeared to Satisfy him; great numbers of Indians came down in Canoes to view us before we Set out which was not untill 9 oClock A. M. we proceeded on passed a Island, close under the Lar.d Side about six miles in length opposit to the lower point of which two Isd.s are situated on one of which five Lodges vacent & S[c]affolds [of] dryed fish at the upper point of this Island Swift water. a Short distance below passed two Islands, one near the middle of the river on which is Seven lodges of Indians drying fish, at our approach they hid themselves in their Lodges and not one was to be seen untill we passed, they then came out, in greater numbers than is common in Lodges of their Size, it is probable that the inhabitants of the 5 Lodges above had in a fright left their lodges and decended to this place to defend themselves if attackted there being a bad rapid opposit the Island thro which we had to pass prevented our landing on this Island and passifying those people, about four miles below this fritened Island we arrived at the head of a verry bad rapid,[1] we came too on the Lard.d Side to view the rapid before we would venter to run it, as the Chanel appeared to be close under the opp.d Shore, and it would be necessary to liten our canoe, I deturmined to walk down on the Lar.d Side, with the 2 chiefs the interpreter & his

---

[1] The Umatilla Rapid, near the mouth of the river of that name. — ED.

Map from Clark Field-book, showing Course and Camping place,
October 19, 1805.

woman, and derected the Small canoe to pr[o]cede down on
the Lar.ᵈ Side to the foot of the rapid which was about 2 miles
in length - I sent on the Indian chief &c. down. and I
assended a high clift about 200 feet above the water from the
top of which is a leavel plain extending up the river and off
for a great extent, at this place the countrey becoms low on
each Side of the river, and affords a pros[pect] of the river and
countrey below for great extent both to the right and left;
from this place I descovered a high mountain of emence hight
covered with Snow, this must be one of the mountains laid
down by Vancouver, as seen from the mouth of the Columbia
River, from the course which it bears which is *West* I take it
to be Mᵗ Sᵗ Helens, destant about 120 miles a range of
mountains in the Derection crossing a conical mountain S. W.
toped with snow,[1]   This rapid I observed as I passed opposit
to it to be verry bad intersep[t]ed with high rock and Small
rockey Islands, here I observed banks of Muscle Shells
banked up in the river in Several places, I delayed at the
foot of the rapid about 2 hours for the canoes which I could
see met with much dificuelty in passing down the rapid on the
oposit Side maney places the men were obliged to get into
the water and haul the canoes over sholes while Setting on
a rock wateing for Capᵗ Lewis I shot a crain which was flying
over of the common kind. I observed a great number of
Lodges on the opposit Side at some distance below, and
Several Indians on the opposit bank passing up to where
Capᵗ Lewis was with the Canoes, others I saw on a knob
nearly opposit to me at which place they delayed but a Short
time, before they returned to their Lodges as fast as they could
run, I was fearfull that those people might not be informed of
us, I deturmined to take the little canoe which was with me
and proceed with the three men in it to the Lodges, on my
aproach not one person was to be seen except three men off

---

[1] The mountain was not Mt. St. Helens, but Mt. Adams.   The latter is east
of the main Cascade range ; the former (which is 2,500 feet lower than Mt. Adams)
is west of the range, and would not be visible from the locality where Clark was,
unless from some very lofty and exceptional spot.   Other explorers have, like Clark,
confused the identity of these two peaks. — O. D. WHEELER.

in the plains, and they sheared off as I saw approached near the Shore,   I landed in front of five Lodges which was at no great distance from each other, Saw no person   the enterance or Dores of the Lodges wer Shut with the Same materials of which they were built a Mat,   I approached one with a pipe in my hand entered a lodge which was the nearest to me   found 32 persons men, women and a few children Setting permiscuisly in the Lodge, in the greatest agutation, Some crying and ringing there hands, others hanging their heads.   I gave my hand to them all and made Signs of my friendly dispo[si]tion and offered the men my pipe to Smok and distributed a fiew Small articles which I had in my pockets,   this measure passified those distressed people verry much,   I then sent one man into each lodge and entered a Second myself the inhabitants of which I found more fritened than those of the first lodge   I destributed Sundrey Small articles amongst them, and Smoked with the men, I then entered the third 4.ᵗʰ & fifth Lodge which I found Somewhat passified, the three men, Drewer Jo. & R. Fields, haveing useed everey means in their power to convince them of our friendly disposition to them,   I then Set my self on a rock and made signs to the men to come and Smoke with me   not one come out untill the canoes arrived with the 2 chiefs, one of whom spoke aloud, and as was their custom to all we had passed.   the Indians came out & Set by me and smoked   They said we came from the clouds[1] &c. &c. and were not men &c. &c.   this time Capt. Lewis came down with the canoes in which the Indian[s were],   as Soon as they Saw the Squar wife of the interperter they pointed to her and informed those who continued yet in the Same position I first found them,   they imediately all came out and appeared to assume new life,   the sight of This Indian woman, wife to one of our interprs. confirmed those people of our friendly intentions, as no woman ever accompanies a war party of Indians in this

---

[1] The Biddle text explains this notion : these Indians had seen the birds which Clark had shot fall from the sky ; and, connecting this with the fact that some clouds were floating above, they imagined that he had dropped from the clouds ; the sound of his gun (a weapon which they had never seen), and his use of a burning-glass to make fire, confirmed their superstitious dread. — ED.

quarter. [*See Descriptions*] Capt Lewis joined us and we smoked with those people in the greatest friendship, dureing which time one of our Old Chiefs informed them who we were from whence we came and where we were going giveing them a friendly account of us,   those people do not speak prosisely the same language of those above but understand them,   I saw Several Horses and persons on horsback in the plains maney of the men womin and children came up from the Lodges below, all of them appeared pleased to see us,   we traded some fiew articles for fish and berries,   Dined, and proceeded on   passed a Small rapid and 15 Lodges below the five, and Encamped[1] below an Island close under the Lar.^d Side, nearly opposit to 24 Lodges on an Island near the middle of the river, and the Main Star.^d Shore   Soon after we landed which was at a fiew willow trees about 100 Indians came from the different Lodges, and a number of them brought wood which they gave us,   we Smoked with all of them, and two of our Party Peter Crusat & Gibson played on the *violin* which delighted them greatly,   we gave to the principal man a String of wompon   treated them kindly for which they appeared greatfull, This Tribe [*a branch of the nation called Pisch quit pás*][2] can raise about 350 men   their Dress are Similar to those at the fork except their robes are smaller and. do not reach lower than the waste ¾ of them have scercely any robes at all,   the women have only a Small pece of a robe which covers their Sholders neck and reaching down behind to their wastes, with a tite piece of leather about the waste,   the brests are large and hang down verry low illy Shaped, high Cheeks flattened heads, & have but fiew orniments,   they are all employed in fishing and drying fish of which they have great quantities on their scaffolds,   their habits customs &c. I could not lern.   I killed a Duck that with the Crain afforded us a good Supper.   the Indians continued all night at our fires.   This day we made *36* miles.

---

[1] Six or seven miles below the mouth of Umatilla River. — ED.

[2] Probably the Salishan tribe now known as Pishquow. — ED.

[Clark, first draft :]   *October 20ᵗʰ 1805 Sunday*

A very cold morning wind S W. about 100 Indians come over this morning to see us, after a smoke, a brackfast on Dogs flesh we set out, [There are] about 350 men [of these Indians.]

West	6 miles to a Stᵈ bend head of a rapid passed the Island at 1 mile 3 Indⁿ Lodges on Larᵈ
S. 20° W.	10 miles passed rockey bad rapid on the Starᵈ a chain of rocks from the Stᵈ several small Isᵈ on the Larᵈ good water. passed an Indian fishing camp of 4 Lodges deserted, fish hanging on scaffels (saw great numbers of Pelicans & comerants, black) To a Larᵈ Bend opsᵈ a large Isᵈ on the Starᵈ Side
S. 60° W.	8 miles to the commencement of a high countrey on the Starᵈ Side, passed 3 Islands nearly opposit, 2 furst on the Starᵈ Side Indians encamped on each Island. we came to at some camps on the lower point of the 1ˢᵗ & dined. purchased a fiew indifferent fish & some berries examined a vault &ᶜ &ᶜ passed 4 Lodges on a Island near the Starᵈ side opsᵈ a bad rapid at the lower point of the Island
S. W.	18 miles to a Point of high land in the Stᵈ bend Passed a large Island in the middle of the R at 8 miles one on the Larᵈ & one on the Starᵈ below both small, one other imedeately below in the middle, passed a Larᵈ point at 10 miles high uneavin lands on the Starᵈ low and leavil on the Larᵈ Side
42	Passed 5 Islands small on the Starᵈ Side and 5 on the Larᵈ Side a small one in the middle of the river at 16 miles. The land is higher on the Lard. side
42	passed a small riffle at the head of the 12 Islands in this day

Killed 2 large speckle guls 4 Duck in malade [mallard] small ducks the flavour of which much resembles the canvis back. no timber of any kind on the river, we saw in the last Lodges acorns of the white oake which the Indˢ inform they precure above the falls. The men are badly dressed, some have scarlet & blue cloth robes. one has a salors jacket, The women have a short indiferent shirt, a short robe of Deer

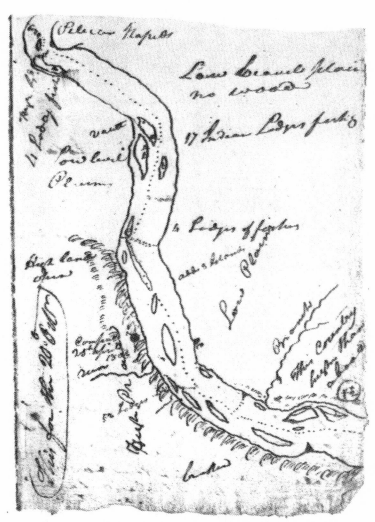

Map from Clark Field-book, showing Course and Camping place,
October 20, 1805.

or Goat skin, & a small skin which they fasten tite around their bodies & fasten between the legs to hide the [blank space in MS.]

October 20th Sunday 1805

A cool morning wind S. W. we concluded to delay untill after brackfast which we were obliged to make on the flesh of dog. after brackfast we gave all the Indian men Smoke and we Set out leaveing about 200 of the nativs at our Encampment, pass.d three Indian Lodges on the Lar.d Side a little below our camp which lodges I did not discover last evening, passed a rapid at seven miles one at a Short distance below we passed a verry bad rapid, a chane of rocks makeing from the Star.d Side and nearly chokeing the river up entirely with hugh black rocks, an Island below close under the Stard. Side on which was *four* Lodges of Indians drying fish, here I saw a great number of Pelicons on the wing, and black Comerants. at one oClock we landed on the lower point of an Island at Some Indian Lodges, a large Island on the Star.d Side nearly opposit and a Small one a little below on the Lar.d Side, on those three Island[s] I counted *seventeen* Indian lodges, those people are in every respect like those above, prepareing fish for theire winter consumption, here we purchased a fiew indifferent Dried fish & a fiew berries on which we dined (on the upper part of this Island we discovered an Indian Vault,[1] our curiosity induced us to examine the method those nativs practiced in depos[it]eing the dead, the vau[l]t was made by broad poads [*boards*] and pieces of Canoes leaning on a ridge pole which was Suported by 2 forks Set in the ground six feet in hight in an easterly and westerly direction and about 60 feet in length, and 12 feet wide, in it I observed great numbers of humane bones of every description perticularly in a pile near the center of the vault, on the East End 21 Scul bomes forming a circle on Mats; in the westerley part of the *Vault* appeared to be appropriated for those of more resent death, as many of the bodies of the

---

[1] These islands are known as Memaloose Islands, i. e., the "place of the departed." — O. D. WHEELER.

deceased *raped* up in leather robes, lay [*in rows*] on board[s] covered with mats, &c [*when bones & robes rot, they are gathered in a heap & sculls placed in a circle*] we observed, independant of the canoes which served as a covering, fishing nets of various kinds, Baskets of different Sizes, wooden boles, robes Skins, trenchers, and various kind of trinkets, in and suspended on the ends of the pieces forming the vault; we also Saw the Skeletons of Several Horses at the vault a great number of bones about it, which convinced me that those animals were Sacrefised as well as the above articles to the Deceased.) after diner we proceeded on to a bad rapid at the lower point of a Small Island on which four Lodges of Indians were Situated drying fish; here the high countrey commences again on the Star.ᵈ Side leaveing a vallie of 40 miles in width, from the mustle shel rapid. examined and passed this rapid close to the Island at 8 miles lower passed a large Island near the middle of the river, a brook on the Star.ᵈ Side and 11 Isld.ˢ all in view of each other below, a riverlit [*rivulet*] falls in on the Lar.ᵈ Side behind a Small Island a Small rapid below, The Star Side is high rugid hills, the Lar.ᵈ Side a low plain and not a tree to be Seen in any Direction except a fiew Small willow bushes which are scattered partially on the Sides of the bank

The river to day is about ¼ of a mile in width, this evening the countrey on the Lar.ᵈ Side rises to the hight of that on the Starboard Side, and is wavering we made 42 miles to day; the current much more uniform than yesterday or the day before. Killed 2 Speckle guls sever.ˡ ducks of a delicious flavour.

Map from Clark Field-book, showing position of Indian lodges, and places of Encampment for October 20, and the return journey, April 24, 1806.

ORIGINAL JOURNALS

OF THE

LEWIS AND CLARK EXPEDITION

1804-1806

WITH FACSIMILES, MAPS, PLANS, VIEWS, PORTRAITS, AND A BIBLIOGRAPHY

VOLUME THREE

PART II

Journals and Orderly Book of Lewis and Clark, from the Encampment on the Columbia River near the Mouth of the Umatilla River to Fort Clatsop October 21, 1805 — January 20, 1806

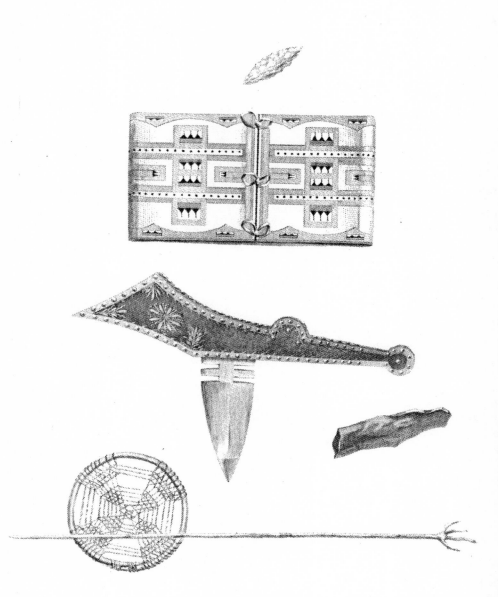

INDIAN UTENSILS AND ARMS

ORIGINAL JOURNALS

OF THE

LEWIS AND CLARK EXPEDITION

1804-1806

PRINTED FROM THE ORIGINAL MANUSCRIPTS
in the Library of the American Philosophical Society and
by direction of its Committee on Historical Documents

TOGETHER WITH

MANUSCRIPT MATERIAL OF LEWIS AND CLARK
from other sources, including Note-Books, Letters, Maps, etc.,
and the Journals of Charles Floyd and Joseph Whitehouse

NOW FOR THE FIRST TIME PUBLISHED IN FULL
AND EXACTLY AS WRITTEN

Edited, with Introduction, Notes, and Index, by

REUBEN GOLD THWAITES, LL.D.

Editor of " The Jesuit Relations and Allied Documents," etc.

VOLUME THREE
PART II

NEW YORK

DODD, MEAD & COMPANY

1905

THE UNIVERSITY PRESS
CAMBRIDGE, U. S. A.

CONTENTS TO VOL. III

PART II

PAGE

CHAPTER XIX. — DESCENDING THE COLUMBIA TO THE
RAPIDS 141
Clark's Journal, October 21—November 1, 1805.

CHAPTER XX. — FROM THE RAPIDS TO THE SEA 188
Clark's Journal, November 2–21, 1805.

CHAPTER XXI. — AT FORT CLATSOP 243
Clark's Journal, November 22, 1805—January 6, 1806.
Lewis's Journal, November 29—December 1, 1805, and January 1–6, 1806.
Orderly Book, January 1, 1806.

CHAPTER XXII. — AT FORT CLATSOP 318
Lewis's Journal, January 7–20, 1806.
Clark's Journal, January 7–20.

LIST OF ILLUSTRATIONS

Vol. III — Part II

Indian Utensils and Arms . . . . *Frontispiece*

PAGE

Map from Clark Field-book, showing Course and Camping place,
October 21, 1805 142

Great Falls of the Columbia River, sketch-map by Clark . . . 148

Shape of Hut Door (Clark, text cut) 154

Long and Short Narrows of the Columbia River, sketch-map by
Clark 158

Clark's Map of Indian Tribes on the Columbia River 168

Great Rapids of the Columbia River, sketch-map by Clark . . 172

Shape of Hut Door (Clark, text cut) 183

Map by Clark, showing location of Indian Tribes, interwoven with
entry for November 1, 1805 (text cut) 184

Cape Horn, Columbia River 188

Sketch of a Flounder (Clark, text cut) 231

Mouth of the Columbia River, sketch-map by Clark 234

Point Adams, sketch by Clark in Lewis's Journal (text cut) . . 261

Map by Clark, showing position and plan of Fort Clatsop, interwoven with entry for December 7, 1805 (text cut) . . . 268

The Site of Fort Clatsop 272

Map by Clark, showing site of Fort Clatsop, and the trail to
Clatsop Village (text cut) 282

MS. page by Clark, dated December 25, 1805 290

Sketch of a Native Hat (first draft, by Clark, text cut) . . . 294

LIST OF ILLUSTRATIONS

PAGE

Sketch of a Native Hat (second draft, by Clark, text cut) . . . 296

Plan by Clark of Fort Clatsop, from the elk-skin cover of his
Field-book (text cut) 298

Two Swords, a Bludgeon, and a Paddle, apparently drawn by
Lewis 326

Sketch of Barb (Lewis, text cut). 347

Sketch of Barb (Clark, text cut) 349

Sketch of Fish-Hook and line (Lewis, text cut) 350

Sketch of Fish-Hook and line (Clark, text cut) 352

CHAPTER XIX

DESCENDING THE COLUMBIA TO THE RAPIDS

Clark's Journal, October 21—November 1, 1805

[Clark, first draft:]   *October 21ˢᵗ 1805 Monday* [1]

A VERRY cold morning   we set out early   wind from the SW.   we could not cook brackfast before we embarked as usial for the want of wood or something to burn.

South   3 miles to a Lar^d Bend
S 55° W.   17 miles to a Lar^d Bend below a bad rapid high ruged rocks
          Passed a small Island at 2½ miles one at 4 miles, in
          the middle of the river, at 2 more swift water   an
          Ind^n camp of 8 Lodges on the St^d Side ops^d the Lower
          point where we Brackfast, and bought some fine fish
          & Pounded ro[o]tes.   people well disposed   passed
          a rapid at 10 miles.   Rocks out in the water   passed
          a Star^d point & a Lar^d point at 15   passed 5 Lodges
          of Indians, & 2 Lodges some distance above on St^d
N. 45° W.   4 miles to a star^d bend pass^d the lower p^t of the Is^d at 1
          mile and 2 Lodges of fishers below on the Star^d Side,
          the rocks on the Lar^d appear as if sliped from the
          clifts under which they are   passed emence rocks in
          different parts of the river which were large and too
          noumerous to notice.   Fowl of all kinds more plenti-
          ful than above.   passed a verry bad rapid at 2 miles,
          this rapid is crouded with Islands of bad rocks dificult
          & crooked passage   2 Lodges of Indians below on
          St^d Side.   I saw some fiew small Pine on the tops of
          the high hills and bushes in the hollers

---

[1] The first draft entries in this chapter are from the Clark-Voorhis field-book.— ED.

[141]

S. 60° W.   5 miles to the Star.ᵈ Bend,   passed maney ruged black rocks in different parts of the river, and a bad rapid at 2 miles & river narrow.   Several canoes loaded with Indians (*Pierce Noses*) came to see us.   at the expiration of this course a river falls in on the Lar.ᵈ 40 yds. wide Islands of rocks in every direction in the river & rapids

S. 52° W.   13 miles to upʳ point of a rocky Island 80 feet high   a rapid above   passed the little river rapid thro narrow channels between the rocks   4 Lodges of Indians on the Star.ᵈ side opposit á round toped mountain imediately in front and is the one we have been going towards & which bore S.W. from the 2.ᵈ course below the Forks   passed the lower point of an Island on the Starᵈ at 2 miles   landed at 5 Lodges of Pierced noses Indians at 4 miles where we encamped and

————
42

purchased a little wood to boil our Dogs & fish, Those Indians are the relations of [those at] the falls below,   fortunately for us the night was worm   fine water for 7 miles   passed a rapid of rocks nearly across above which at 6 miles passed 6 Lodges.   at 9 miles passed a bad rapid, & Lodges of Indians on St.ᵈ Side   20 piles of fish on an Island drying, several Indians in canoes fishing in canoes & gigs &.ᶜ

Collins made some excellent beer of the *Pasheco quarmash* bread of roots which was verry good.   obliged to purchase wood at a high rate.

October 21.ˢᵗ Monday 1805

A verry cool morning wind from the S. W.   we set out verry early and proceeded on,   last night we could not collect more dry willows the only fuel, than was barely Suffi[ci]ent to cook Supper, and not a sufficency to cook brackfast this morning,   pass.ᵈ a Small Island at 5½ miles a large one 8 miles in the middle of the river, some rapid water at the head and Eight Lodges of nativs opposit its Lower point on the Star.ᵈ Side, we came too at those lodges, bought some wood and brackfast, Those people recived us with great kindness, and examined us

Map from Clark Field-book, showing Course and Camping place,
October 21, 1805.

with much attention, their employments customs, Dress and appearance Similar to those above, Speak the Same language, here we Saw two scarlet and a blue cloth blankets, also a Salors Jacket the Dress of the men of this tribe only a Short robe of Deer or Goat Skins, and that of the women is a short piece of Dressed Skin which fall from the neck so as to cover the front of the body as low as the waste, a Short robe, which is of one Deer or antilope Skin, and a flap around their waste and Drawn tite between their legs as before described, their orniments are but fiew, and worn as those above.

we got from those people a fiew pounded roos [*roots*] fish and *Acorns*[1] of white oake, those Acorns they make use of as food raw & roasted and inform us they precure them of the natives who live near the falls below which place they all discribe by the term *Timm*[2] at 2 miles lower passed a rapid large rocks stringing into the river of large Size, opposit to this rapid on the Star. Shore is Situated *two* Lodges of the Nativs drying fish here we halted a fiew minits to examine the rapid before we entered it which was our Constant Custom, and at all that was verry dangerous put out all who Could not Swim to walk around, after passing this rapid we proceeded on passed anoother rapid at 5 miles lower down, above this rapid on the Star. Side *five* Lodges of Indians fishing &c above this rapid maney large rocks on each Side at Some distance from Shore, [at] one mile passed an Island close to the Star. Side, below which is *two* Lodges of nativs, a little below is a bad rapid which is bad crouded with hugh [huge] rocks scattered in every Direction which renders the pasage verry Difficult a little above this rapid on the Lar. Side emence piles of rocks appears as if Sliped from the clifts under which they lay, passed great number of rocks in every direction scattered in the river. 5 Lodges a little below on the Star. Side, and one lodge on an Island near the Star. Shore opposit to which is

---

[1] We saw among them some small robes made of the skins of grey squirrel, some racoon skins, and acorns, which are signs of a timbered country not far distant. — GASS (p. 220).

[2] Which they pronounce so as to make it perfectly represent the sound of a distant cataract. — BIDDLE (ii, p. 28).

a verry bad rapid, thro which we found much dificuelty in passing, the river is crouded with rocks in every direction, after Passing this dificult rapid to the mouth of a Small river on the Larboard Side 40 yards wide descharges but little water at this time, and appears to take its Sourse in the open plains to the S. E.[1] from this place I proceved some fiew Small pines on the tops of the high hills and bushes in the hollars. imediately above & below this little river comences a rapid which is crouded with large rocks in every direction, the pasage both crooked and dificuelt, we halted at a Lodge to examine those noumerous Islands of rock which ap.d to extend maney miles below, great numb.r of Indians came in canoes to View us at this place, after passing this rapid which we accomplished without loss; winding through between the hugh rocks for about 2 miles. (from this rapid the Conical mountain is *S.W.* which the Indians inform me is not far to the left of the great falls; this I call the *Timm* or falls mountain it is high and the top is covered with snow) imediately below the last rapids there is four Lodges of Indians on the Star.d Side, proceeded on about two miles lower and landed and encamped near *five* Lodges of nativs, drying fish those are the relations of those at the *great falls*, they are pore and have but little wood which they bring up the river from the falls as they Say, we purchased a little wood to cook our Dog meat and fish; those people did not receive us at first with the same cordiality of those above, they appear to be the Same nation Speak the Same language with a little curruption of maney words Dress and fish in the same way, all of whome have *pierced noses* and the men when Dressed ware a long taper'd piece of Shell or beed put through the nose.[2]

---

[1] We gave it the name of Lepage's river from Lepage one of our company. — BIDDLE (ii, p. 29).

This is now the John Day's River, named for a Virginia backwoodsman who was a member of the overland expedition to Astoria in 1811–12. See Bradbury's *Travels* (Thwaites' ed., Cleveland, 1904), *note* 104. — ED.

[2] Inserting two small, tapering white shells, about two inches long, through the lower part of the cartilaginous division of the nose. These shells are of the genus *dentalium*, they inhabit the Pacific shore, and are an article of traffic among the natives. — SAMUEL PARKER (*Journal*, p. 143).

this part of the river is furnished with fine Springs which either rise high up the Sides of the hills or on the bottom near the river and run into the river. the hills are high and rugid a fiew scattering trees to be Seen on them either Small pine or Scrubey white oke.

The probable reason of the Indians residing on the Star.ᵈ Side of this as well as the waters of Lewis's River is their fear of the *Snake Indians* who reside, as they nativs say on a great river to the South, and are at war with those tribes, one of the Old Chiefs who accompanies us pointed out a place on the Lar.ᵈ Side where they had a great battle, not maney years ago, in which maney were killed on both Sides, One of our party J. Collins presented us with Some verry good *beer* made of the *Pa-shi-co-quar-mash* bread, which bread is the remains of what was laid in as a part of our Stores of Provisions, at the first flat heads or Cho-pun-nish Nation at the head of the *Kosskoske* river which by being frequently wet molded & sowered &c. we made 33 miles to day.

[Clark, first draft :]   *October 22ⁿᵈ Tuesday* 1805

a fine morning calm we set out at 9 oClock and on the Course S. 52.° W. 10 miles passed lodges & Indians and rapids as mentioned in the course of yesterday, from the expiration of

S. 30.° W.   3 miles to the mouth of a large river in the Lar.ᵈ bend 200 yᵈˢ. wide   great rapids in it a ¼ up it long and impracticable of assent   Passed a point of rock Island at 2 miles on the Star.ᵈ 3 Islands in the mouth of this river no bottoms a little up

West   4 miles to a bend on Star.ᵈ side passed the Island of rocks at 2 miles   at Lower point 8 large Lodges, on the Star.ᵈ Side 10 Lodges,   below at the end of the course 6 more Lodges passed a Island on the Stᵈ Side

S. W.   2 miles to a rocky Lar.ᵈ bend from the mouth of the river at the fall or commencement of the Pitch where we made a portage of 457 yards & down a steep

19

Took our Baggage & formed a camp below the rapids in a cove on the Star.ᵈ Side   the distance 1200 yards haveing passed at the upper end of the portage 17 Lodges of Indians below the rapids & above camp 5 large Lodges of Indians,   great numbers of baskets of Pounded fish on the rocks Islands & near their Lodges   those are neetly pounded & put in verry new baskets of about 90 or 100 pounds w[e]ight.   hire Indians to take our heavy articles across the portage · purchased a Dog for supper   Great numbers of Indians view us,   we with much dificuelty purchased as much wood as cooked our dog this evening,   our men all in helth.   The Indians have their grave yard on an Island in the rapids.   The Great Chief of those Indians is out hunting.   no Indians reside on the Larᵈ Side for fear of the Snake Indians with whome they are at war and who reside on the large fork on the lar.ᵈ a little above

October 22ᵈ Tuesday 1805

A fine morning calm and fare   we set out at 9 oClock passed a verry bad rapid at the head of an Island close under the Star.ᵈ side   above this rapid on the Starᵈ side is six Lodges of nativs Drying fish,   at 9 ml.ˢ passed a bad rapid at the head of a large Island of high & uneaven [rocks], jutting over the water,   a Small Island in a Star.ᵈ Bend opposit the upper point, on which I counted 20 parcels of dryed and pounded fish ; on the main Star.ᵈ Shore opposit to this Island *five* Lodges of Indians are Situated, Several Indians in canoes killing fish with gigs &c.   opposit the center of this Island of rocks which is about 4 miles long we discovered the enterence of a large river on the Lar.ᵈ Side which appeared to come from the *S. E.*   we landed at some distance above the mouth of this river and Cap.ᵗ Lewis and my Self set out to view this river above its mouth,   as our rout was intersepted by a deep narrow Chanel which runs out of this river into the Columbia a little below the place we landed, leaveing a high dry rich Island of about 400 yards wide and 800 yards long   here we Seperated, I proceeded on to the river and Struck it at the foot of a verry Considerable rapid,   here I beheld an emence body of water compress.ᵈ in

[146]

a narrow chanel of about 200 yds in width, fomeing over rocks maney of which presented their tops above the water, when at this place Cap! Lewis joined me haveing delayed on the way to examine a root of which the nativs had been digging great quantities in the bottoms of this River. at about two miles above this river appears to be confined between two high hils below which it [is] divided by numbers of large rocks, and Small Islands covered with a low groth of timber, and has a rapid as far as the narrows, three Small Islands in the mouth of this River, this River haveing no Indian name that we could find out, except " the River on which the Snake Indians live ",[1] we think it best to leave the nameing of it untill our return.

we proceeded on pass[ed] the mouth of this river at which place it appears to discharge 1/4 as much water as runs down the Columbia. at *two* miles below this River passed Eight Lodges on the Lower point of the Rock Island aforesaid at those Lodges we saw large logs of wood which must have been rafted down the *To wor-ne hi ooks* River, below this Island on the main Stard. Shore is 16 Lodges of nativs, here we landed a fiew minits to Smoke, the lower point of one Island opposit which heads in the mouth of *Towornehiooks* River which I did not observe untill after passing these lodges about 1/2 a mile lower passed 6 more Lodges on the Same Side and 6 miles below the upper mouth of *Towornehiooks* River the comencement of the pitch of the great falls,[2] opposit on the Star! Side is 17 Lodges of the nativs we landed and walked down accompanied by an old man to view the falls, and the best rout for to make a portage which we Soon discovered was much nearest on the Star! Side, and the distance 1200 yards one third of the way on a rock, about 200 yards over a loose Sand collected in a hollar blown by the winds from the bottoms below which was disagreeable to pass, as it was steep and loose. at the lower part of those rapids we arrived at 5 Large Lod[g]es of nativs drying and prepareing fish for market, they gave

---

[1] The Indians called this Towahnahiooks River. It is now known as the Des Chutes. — ED.

[2] Now known as Celilo Falls ; at their head is the town of Celilo, Ore. — ED.

us Philburts,[1] and berries to eate.   we returned droped down to the head of the rapids and took every article except the Canoes across the portag[e] where I had formed a camp on [an] ellegable Situation for the protection of our Stores from thieft, which we were more fearfull of, than their arrows.   we despatched two men to examine the river on the opposit Side, and [they] reported that the canoes could be taken down a narrow Chanel on the opposit Side after a Short portage at the head of the falls, at which place the Indians take over their Canoes.   Indians assisted us over the portage with our heavy articles on their horses,[2] the waters is divided into Several narrow chanels which pass through a hard black rock forming Islands of rocks at this Stage of the water,   on those Islands of rocks as well as at and about their Lodges I observe great numbers of Stacks of pounded Salmon neetly preserved in the following manner, i. e. after [being] suffi[c]ently Dried it is pounded between two Stones fine, and put into a speces of basket neetly made of grass and rushes better than two feet long and one foot Diamiter, which basket is lined with the Skin of Salmon Stretched and dried for the purpose,   in this it is pressed down as hard as is possible, when full they Secure the open part with the fish Skins across which they fasten th[r]o. the loops of the basket that part very securely, and then on a Dry Situation they Set those baskets the corded part up,   their common custom is to Set 7 as close as they can Stand and 5 on the top of them, and secure them with mats which is raped around them and made fast with cords and covered also with mats,   those 12 baskets of from 90 to 100^{lbs} each form a Stack. thus preserved those fish may be kept Sound and sweet Several years, as those people inform me,   Great quantities as they inform us are sold to the whites people who visit the mouth of this river as well as to the nativs below.[3]

---

[1] The only species of filberts of the Columbia region is *Corylus californica* Dc. — C. V. Piper.

[2] "But for this service they repaid themselves so adroitly" (Biddle) that the explorers had to take the precaution mentioned in the second preceding sentence. — Ed.

[3] Almost, if not quite, along the very ground over which Lewis and Clark dragged their canoes around the falls, the railway trains of the Oregon Railroad and Navigation Company run. . . . I have stood on the river bank and have seen stacks of fish standing waiting until the Indians were ready to use them. — O. D. Wheeler.

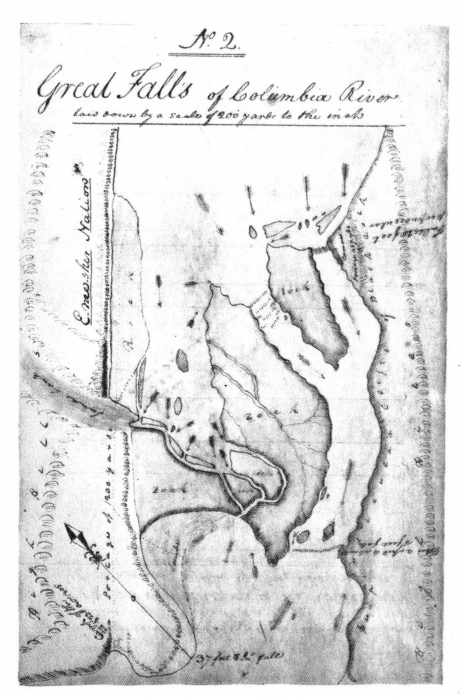

Great Falls of the Columbia River,
sketch-map by Clark.

on one of those Island[s] I saw Several tooms but did not visit them   The principal Chiefs of the bands resideing about this Place is out hunting in the mountains to the S. W.   no Indians reside on the S. W. side of this river for fear (as we were informed) of the Snake Indians, who are at war with the tribes on this river.   they represent the Snake Indians as being verry noumerous, and resideing in a great number of villages on Towornehiooks River which falls in 6 miles above on the Lar.ᵈ Side and it reaches a great ways and is large a little abov its mouth at which part it is not intersepted with rapids,   they inform that one considerable rapid & maney Small ones in that river, and that the Snake live on Salmon, and they go to war to their first villages in 12 days,   the Course they pointed is S. E. or to the S of S. E.   we are visited by great numbers of Indians to Day to view us,   we purchased a Dog for Supper, some fish and with dificuelty precured as much wood as cooked Supper, which we also pur̤-chased   we made 19 miles to day.

[Clark, first draft:]   *October 23ʳᵈ Wednesday 1805*

Took the canoes over the Portage on the Lar.ᵈ Side with much dificulty,   description on another Paper   one canoe got loose & cought by the Indians which we were obliged to pay our old Chiefs over herd the Indians from below say they would try to *kill* us & informed us of it,   we have all the arms examined and put in order, all the Indians leave us early. Great numbers of flees on the Larᵈ Side.   Shot a Sea Orter [otter] which I did not get,   Great Numbers about those rapids   we purchased 8 dogs, Small & fat for our party to eate,   the Indians not verry fond of selling their good fish, compells us to make use of dogs for food.   Exchanged our small canoe for a large & verry new one built for riding the waves   obsᵈ Merᵈⁿ Altᵈ 66° 27' 30".   Latᵈ prodsᵈ *45° 42' 57"3/₁₀* North.

October 23ᵈ Wednesday 1805

a fine morning,   I with the greater part of the men crossed in the canoes to opposit side above the falls and hauled them across the portage of 457 yards which is on the Larᵈ Side and certainly the best side to pass the canoes,   I then decended through a narrow chanel of about 150 yards wide forming a kind of half circle in it[s] course of a mile to a pitch of 8 feet in which the chanel is divided by 2 large rocks,   at this place we were obliged to let the Canoes down by strong ropes of Elk Skin which we had for the purpose,   one Canoe in passing this place got loose by the cords breaking, and was cought by the Indians below.   I accomplished this necessary business and landed Safe with all the canoes at our Camp below the falls by 3 oClock P. M.   nearly covered with flees which were so thick amongst the Straw and fish Skins at the upper part of the portage at which place the nativs had been Camped not long since ; that every man of the party was obliged to Strip naked dureing the time of takeing over the canoes, that they might have an oppertunity of brushing the flees of[f] their legs and bodies.   Great numbers of *Sea Otters* in the river below the falls, I shot one in the narrow chanel to day which I could not get.   Great numbers of Indians visit us both from above and below.   one of the old Chiefs who had accompanied us from the head of the river, informed us that he herd the Indians Say that the nation below intended to kill us.   we examined all the arms &c. complete the amunition to 100 rounds.   The nativs leave us earlyer this evening than usial, which gives a Shadow of confermation to the information of our old Chief,   as we are at all times & places on our guard, are under no greater apprehention than is common.

we purchased 8 Small fat dogs for the party to eate ; the nativs not being fond of Selling their good fish, compells us to make use of Dog meat for food, the flesh of which the most of the party have become fond of from the habits of useing it for Some time past.   The altitude of this day 66°. 27′. 30″ gave for Latᵈ 45°. 42′. 57 . ³/₁₀ N.

I observed on the beach near the Indian Lodges two butifull canoes of different Shape & Size to what we had Seen

above wide in the midd[l]e and tapering to each end, on the
bow curious figures were cut in the wood &c.   Cap! Lewis
went up to the Lodges to See those Canoes and exchanged
our Smallest canoe for one of them by giveing a Hatchet &
few trinkets to the owner who informed that he purchased it
of a white man below for a horse,   these canoes are neeter
made than any I have ever Seen and calculated to ride the
waves, and carry emence burthens,   they are dug thin and
are suported by cross pieces of about 1 inch diamieter tied
with Strong bark thro' holes in the Sides.   our two old chiefs
appeared verry uneasy this evening.

[Clark, first draft :]   *October 24th Thursday 1805*

a fine morning   the Indians approached us with caution,
our 2 old Chiefs deturmine to return home, saying they were
at war with Indians below and they would kill them   we pur-
swaded them to stay 2 nights longer with us, with a view to
make a peace with those Indians below as well as to have them
with us dureing our Delay with this tribe.   Cap' Lewis went
to view the falls   I set out with the party at 9 oClock a m   at
2½ miles passed a rock which makes from the Star^d Side
(4 Lodges above 1 below) and confined the river in a narrow channel of about 45 yards   this continued for about ¼ of
a mile & widened to about 200 yards,   in those narrows the
water was agitated in a most shocking manner boils swells &
whorlpools,   we passed with great risque It being impossible
to make a portage of the canoes,   about 2 miles lower passed
a verry Bad place between 2 rocks one large & in the middle
of the river   here our canoes took in some water   I put all
the men who could not swim on shore, & sent a fiew articles
such as guns & papers, and landed at a Village of 21 houses
on the Star^d Side in a Deep bason where the river appeared to
be blocked up with emence rocks.   I walked down and examined the passage found it narrow, and one verry bad place
a little below the houses   I pursued this channel which is
from 50 to 100 yards wide and swels and boils with a most
tremendeous manner, prosued this channel 5 ms. & returned

found Capt Lewis & a Chief from below with maney of his men on a visit to us,   one of our Party Pete Crusat played on the *violin* which pleased the savage,   the men danced,   Great numbers of Sea Orter Pole Cats about those fishings   the houses of those Indians are 20 feet square and sunk 8 feet under ground & covered with bark with a small door round at top rose about 18 Inches above ground, to keep out the snow I saw 107 parcels of fish stacked, and great quantites in the houses.

October 24th. Thursday 1805

The morning fare after a beautifull night,   the nativs approached us this morning with great caution.   our two old chiefs expressed a desire to return to their band from this place, Saying " that they could be of no further Service to us, as their nation extended no further down the river than those falls, (*they could no longer understand the language of those below the falls, till then not much difference in the vocab.*) and as the nation below had expressed hostile intentions against us, would certainly kill them; perticularly as they had been at war with each other ;"   we requested them to Stay with us *two* nights longer, and we would See the nation below and make a peace between them, they replied they " were anxious to return and See our horses "   we insisted on their staying with us two nights longer to which they agreed ;   our views were to detain those Chiefs with us, untill we should pass the next falls, which we were told were very bad, and at no great distance below, that they might inform us of any designs of the nativs, and if possible to bring about a peace between them and the tribes below.

The first pitch of this falls is 20 feet perpendecular, then passing thro' a narrow chanel for 1 mile to a rapid of about 8 feet fall below which the water has no perceptable fall but verry rapid   *See Sketch* N° 1.   It may be proper here to remark that from Some obstruction below, the cause of which we have not yet learned, the water in high fluds (which are in the Spring) rise below these falls nearly to a leavel with the water above the falls; the marks of which can be plainly trac^d around the

falls[1]:   at that Stage of the water the Salmon must pass up
which abounds in such great numbers above.   below those falls
we[re] Salmon trout, and great numbers of the heads of a
Species of trout Smaller than the Salmon,   those fish they
catch out of the Salmon Season, and are at this time in the act
of burrying those which they had drid for winter food.   the
mode of bur[y]ing those fish is in holes of various Sizes, lined
with Straw on which they lay fish Skins in which they inclose
the fish which is laid verry close, and then covered with earth
of about 12 or 15 inches thick.   Cap[t] Lewis and three men
crossed the river and on the opposit Side to view the falls which
he had not yet taken a full view of.   At 9 oClock a. m. I Set
out with the party and proceeded on down a rapid Stream of
about 400 yards wide   at 2-½ miles the river widened into
a large bason to the Star[d] Side on which there is five Lodges of
Indians.   here a tremendious black rock Presented itself high
and Steep appearing to choke up the river; nor could I See
where the water passed further than the current was drawn with
great velocity to the Lar[d] Side of this rock at which place
I heard a great roreing.   I landed at the Lodges and the
natives went with me to the top of this rock which makes from
the Star[d] Side, from the top of which I could See the dificuelties
we had to pass for Several miles below ; at this place the water
of this great river is compressed into a chanel between two rocks
not exceeding *forty five* yards wide and continues for a ¼ of
a mile when it again widens to 200 yards and continues this
width for about 2 miles when it is again intersepted by rocks.
This obstruction in the river accounts for the water in high
floods riseing to Such a hite at the last falls.   The whole of the
Current of this great river must at all Stages pass thro' this
narrow chanel of 45 yards wide.[2]   as the portage of our canoes
over this high rock would be impossible with our Strength, and
the only danger in passing thro those narrows was the whorls

---

[1] The reason of the rise in the water below the falls is, that for three miles down,
the river is so confined by rocks (being not more than 70 yards wide), that it cannot
discharge the water, as fast as it comes over the falls, until what is deficient in breadth
is made up in depth. — GASS (p. 222).

[2] The so-called Short Narrows of the Columbia. — ED.

and swills [swells] arriseing from the Compression of the water, and which I thought (as also our principal watermen Peter Crusat) by good Stearing we could pass down Safe, accordingly I deturmined to pass through this place notwithstanding the horrid appearance of this agitated gut swelling, boiling & whorling in every direction, (which from the top of the rock did not appear as bad as when I was in it; however we passed Safe to the astonishment of all the Ind.ᵃ of the last Lodges who viewed us from the top of the rock. passed one Lodge below this rock, and halted on the Star.ᵈ Side to view a very bad place, the current divided by 2 Islands of rocks the lower of them large and in the midal of the river, this place being verry bad I sent by land all the men who could not Swim and such articles as was most valuable to us such as papers Guns & amunition, and proceeded down with the canoes two at a time to a village of 20 wood houses in a Deep bend to the Star.ᵈ Side below which [was] a rugid black rock about 20 feet hiter ['higher] than the Common high fluds of the river with Several dry chanels which appeared to Choke the river up quite across; this I took to be the 2.ᵈ falls or the place the nativs above call *timm*, The nativs of this village re[ce]ived me verry kindly, one of whome envited me into his house, which I found to be large and comodious, and the first wooden houses in which Indians have lived Since we left those in the vicinty of the Illinois, they are scattered permiscuisly on a elivated Situation near a mound of about 30 feet above the Common leavel, which mound has Some remains of houses and has every appearance of being artificial. those houses are about the Same Shape Sise and form 20 feet Square, [*wide and 30 feet long*] with one Dore raised 18 Inches above ground, they [the doors — Ed.] are 29-½ inches high & 14 wide, forming in a half circle above, ⌂ those houses were Sunk into the earth six feet, the roofs of them was Supported by [*a ridge pole resting on*] three Strong pieces of Split timber on which, [*thro' one of which the dore was cut*] that and the walls, the top of which was just above ground Supported a certain number of Spars which are Covered with the Bark of the white Ceadar, or *Arber Vitea;* and the whole attached and Secured by the fibers

of the Cedar. the eaves at or near the earth, the gable ends
and Side Walls are Secured with split boards which is Seported
on iner Side with Strong pieces of timber under the eves &c.
to keep those pieces errect & the earth from without pressing
in the boards, Suported by Strong posts at the corners to
which those poles were attached to give aditional Strength,
small openings were left in the roof above the ground, for the
purpose, as I conjectured, of deschargeing their arrows at a be-
siegeing enimey ; Light is admited thro' an opening at top which
also Serves for the Smoke to pass through,[1]   one half of those
houses is apropriated for the storeing away Dried & pounded
fish which is the principal food, the other part next the dore is
the part occupied by the nativs who have beds raised on either
side, with a fire place in the center of this Space   each house
appeared to be occupied by about three families; that part
which is apropriated for fish was crouded with that article, and
a fiew baskets of burries.   I dispatched a Sufficent number of
the good Swimers back for the 2 canoes above the last rapid,
and with 2 men walked down three miles to examine the river
Over a bed of rocks, which the water at verry high fluds passes
over,   on those rocks I Saw Several large scaffols on which the
Indians dry fish,   as this is out of Season the poles on which
they dry those fish are tied up verry Securely in large bundles
and put upon the scaffolds,   I counted 107 stacks of dried
pounded fish in different places on those rocks which must
have contained 10.000 lb of neet fish,   The evening being late
I could not examine the river to my Satisfaction,   the chanel
is narrow and compressed for about 2 miles, when it widens
into a deep bason to the Star.d Side, & again contracts into a narrow chanel divided by a rock.   I returned through a rockey
open countrey infested with pole-cats to the village where I met
with Cap.t Lewis the two old Chiefs who accompanied us & the
party & canoes who had all arrived Safe ; the Canoes haveing
taken in some water at the last rapids.   here we formed a camp

---

[1] This village has better lodges than any on the river above ; one story of which
is sunk under ground and lined with flag mats.   The upper part, about 4 feet above
ground, is covered over with cedar bark, and they are tolerably comfortable houses. —
GASS (p. 223).

near the village,   The principal chief from the nation below
with Several of his men visited us, and afforded a favourable
oppertunity of bringing about a Piece and good understanding
between this chief and his people and the two chiefs who accompanied us which we have the Satisfaction to say we have accomplished, as we have every reason to believe, and that those two
bands or nations are and will be on the most friendly terms
with each other,   gave this great chief a Medal and some other
articles, of which he was much pleased.   Peter Crusat played
on the *violin* and the men danced which delighted the nativs,
who Shew every civility towards us.   we Smoked with those
people untill late at night, when every one retired to rest.

[Clark, first draft:]   *October 25ᵗʰ Friday 1805*

A cold morning   we deturmined to attempt the chanel after
brackfast   I took down all the party below the bad places with
a load & one canoe passed well,   a 2ᵈ passed well   I had men
on the shore with ropes to throw in in case any accidence happened at the whirl &ᶜ   The Indˢ on the rocks viewing us
the 3ʳᵈ canoe nearly filled with water   we got her safe to shore.
the last canoe came over well which to me was truly gratifying
set out and had not passed 2 miles before 3 canoes run against
a rock in the river with great force no damage   met with a
2ᵈ Chief of the nation from hunting,   we smoked with him
and his party and gave a medal of the small size & set out
passed great numbers of rocks,   good water and came to at
a high point of rocks below the mouth of a creek which falls
in on the Larᵈ Side and head up towards the high snow mountain to the S W.   this creek is 20 yards wide and has some
beaver signs at its mouth   river about ½ a mile wide and
crouded with sea otters, & Drum [fish] was seen this evening,
we took possession of a high Point of rocks to defend our
selves in case the threts of those Indians below should be put
in execution against us.   Sent out some hunters to look if any
signs of game,   one man killed a small deer & several others
seen   I killed a goose, and suped hartily on venison & goose
Camped on the rock.   guard under the hill

Courses from the upper rapids

West 2 miles passing a Lar.ᵈ point of Sand and a Star.ᵈ point & 3 Lodges a deep bason to the Star.ᵈ to a pt of rocks, above a chanel

S. 75.° W. 2 miles to a rock Island in the middle of the river at a bad rapid & who[r]ls, passed thro a narrow bad chanel 45 yds wide for ¼ of a mile. a Lodge below on Star.ᵈ Side. halted to lookout

S. 50.° W. 2 miles to a rock at the head of a narrow chanel, a deep bason to the Star.ᵈ on which a village of 21 Lodges passed a large rock Island in the middle of the river. The channel nearest the Lar.ᵈ Side

Oct. 25

S. 34.° W. 3 miles thro a narrow swift bad chanel from 50 to 100 yards wide, of swels whorls & bad places a verry bad place at 1 mile, a rock in the middle at 2 miles to a rock, above a Deep bason to the Star.ᵈ Side above the rock

S. 20.° W. 2 miles to a high rock passed thro a narrow channel on the St.ᵈ Side of a rock in the middle of the chanel

N. 60.° W 1 mile to a bend, passed a bason to the Lar.ᵈ Side, and large ruged rocks on both sides

S. 60.° W. 4 miles to large Creek [in] a Lar.ᵈ bend under a timbered bottom & the first timber we have seen near the river for a long distance, Pine & white Oake

October 25ᵗʰ. Friday 1805

A cool morning Cap.ᵗ Lewis and my Self walked down to See the place the Indians pointed out as the worst place in passing through the gut, which we found difficuelt of passing without great danger, but as the portage was impracti[c]able with our large canoes, we concluded to Make a portage of our most valuable articles and run the canoes thro.[1] accordingly on our return divided the party Some to take over the Canoes, and others to take our Stores across a portage of a mile to a place on the chanel below this bad whorl & Suck, with Some

1 The Long Narrows. — ED.

others I had fixed on the Chanel with roapes to throw out to
any who Should unfortunately meet with difficuelty in passing
through ; great number of Indians viewing us from the high
rocks under which we had to pass,   the 3 fir[s]t canoes passed
thro very well, the 4.th nearly filled with water, the last passed
through by takeing in a little water,   thus Safely below what
I conceved to be the worst part of this chanel felt my self
extreamly gratified and pleased.   We loaded the Canoes & set
out, and had not proceeded more than 2 mile[s] before the
unfortunate Canoe which filled crossing the bad place above,
run against a rock and was in great danger of being lost ;   this
Chanel is through a hard rough black rock, from 50 to 100
yards wide, swelling and boiling in a most tremendious maner
Several places on which the Indians inform me they take the
Salmon as fast as they wish ; we passed through a deep bason
to the Star.^d Side of 1 mile below which the River narrows and
[is] divided by a rock   the curent we found quit[e] gentle,
here we met with our two old chiefs who had been to a village
below to smoke a friendly pipe and at this place they met the
Chief & party from the village above on his return from hunting all of whome were then crossing over their horses,   we
landed to Smoke a pipe with this Chief whome we found to be
a bold pleasing looking man of about 50 years of age dress.^d in
a war jacket a cap Legins & mockesons. he gave us some
meat of which he had but little and informed us he in his rout
met with a war party of Snake Indians from the great river of
the S. E. which falls in a few miles above and had a fight. we
gave this Chief a Medal, &c. [had] a parting Smoke with our
two faithful friends the chiefs who accompanied us from the
head of the river, (who had purchased a horse each with 2
rob[e]s and intended to return on horseback) we proceeded
on down   the water fine, rocks in every derection for a fiew
miles when the river widens and becoms a butifull jentle Stream
of about half a mile wide,   Great numbers of the Sea orter
[or Seals] about those narrows and both below and above. we
came too, under a high point of rocks on the Lar.^d Side below
a creek of 20 yards wide and much water,   as it was necessary
to make Some Selestial observations we formed our camp on

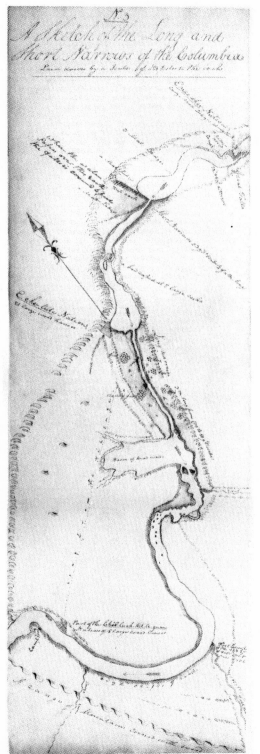

Long and Short Narrows of the Columbia River,
sketch-map by Clark.

the top of a high point of rocks, which forms a kind of fortification in the Point between the river & creek, with a boat
guard,[1] this Situation we conceived well Calculated for Defence, and conveniant to hunt under the foots of the mountain
to the West & S. W. where timber of different kinds grows,
and appears to be handsom coverts for the Deer, in oke woods,
Sent out hunters to examine for game. G. D. Killed a Small
Deer & other[s] Saw much sign, I killed a goose in the creek
which was verry fat. one of the guard saw a Drum fish to day
he conceved, our Situation will calculated to defend our selves
from any designs of the natives, Should they be enclined to
attack us.

This little creek heads in the range of mountains which runs
S. S. W. & N. W. for a long distance on which is scattering
pine white oake &c. The Pinical of the round toped mountain which we Saw a Short distance below the forks of this
river is S. 43° W. of us and ab' 37 miles, it is at this time
toped with Snow we called this the *falls mountain* or *Timm
mountain.* [*this the Mount Hood or Vancouver*] The face of
the Countrey on both Side of the river above and about the
falls, is Steep ruged and rockey open and contain[s] but a Small
preportion of [h]erbage, no timber a fiew bushes excepted.
The nativs at the upper falls raft their timber down *Towarne-
hooks* River & those at the narrows take theirs up the river to
the lower part of the narrows from this Creek, and carry it over
land 3 miles to their houses[2] &c. at the mouth of this creek
Saw Some beaver Sign, and a Small wolf in a Snare set in the
willows The Snars of which I saw Several made for to catch
wolves, are made as follows vz. a long pole which will Spring
is made fast with bark to a willow, on the top of this pole a
string (*Described elsewhere*)

---

[1] The point at which the expedition camped is just below the steamboat landing
at Dalles City, and across Mill Creek or Quenett (Quinett), as the explorers understood the Indians to say. — O. D. WHEELER.

On their return journey the explorers named this Rock Fort Camp. — ED.

[2] This region, now called the Dalles of the Columbia, was a great resort of the
natives, who rallied here not only to fish but to levy tribute upon all who passed the
river. Only the size of the Lewis and Clark party protected them on their outward
journey ; upon the return they were nearly involved in battle with the Indians. — ED.

[Clark, first draft :]   *October 26th 1805 Saturday*

a fine morning   sent out six men to hunt deer & collect
rozin to Pitch our canoes,   had all our articles put out to dry.
Canoes drawed out and repaired, the injories receved in drawing them over the rocks,   every article wet in the canoe which
nearly sunk yesterday

Took the Azmuth of the Sun & time this morning

Azmuth		Time			distance		
		h	m	s			
S.	64° E	8	41	6	41°	1'	0"
S.	63° E	8	45	32	42	6	30
S.	62° E	8	51	8	43	28	15

Took equal altitudes with Sextant

	H.	M.	S.		h	m	s
A M	8	54	22	P M	2	9	44
	8	56	41	"	12	5	
	8	59	1				

Altitude produced from this observation 44° − 14' − 15"
a number of Indians came to the opposit side and shew great anxiety
to come over.   they delayed untill late
Took time and distance of Sun and moon   Sun West P. M.

h	m	s			
2	21	12	49°	51'	15"
"	25	45	49	51	00
"	29	4	49	52	00
"	31	43	49	52	30
"	33	9	49	52	45
"	36	2	49	53	30
"	37	49	49	54	30
"	39	5	49	55	00
"	40	23	49	55	30
"	41	36	49	56	00

Took time and distance of Moons Western limb & Fulenhalt
[Fomalhaut.]   Star East

		Time			distance		
		h	m	s			
P M	6	34	0		67°	36'	15"
	"	36	4		67	35	15
	"	39	2		67	34	30

In the evening 2 chief[s] and 15 men came over in a single canoe, those chiefs proved to be the 2 great chiefs of the tribes above, one gave me a Dressed Elk Skin, and gave us some deer meet, and 2 cakes of white bread made of white roots, we gave to each chief a meadel of the small size a red silk handkerchief a knife to the 1st a arm ban[d] & a pice of Paint & a comb to his son a Pice of riben tied to a tin gorget and 2 hams of Venison They deturmined to stay with us all night, we had a fire made for them & one man played on the violin which pleased them much my servent danced. our hunters killed five Deer, 4 verry large gray squirrels, a goose & Pheasent, one man giged a *Salmon trout* which we had fried in a little Bears oil which a Chief gave us yesterday and I think the finest fish I ever tasted, saw great numbers of white crains flying in Different directions verry high. The river has rose nearly 8 Inches to day and has every appearance of a tide, from what cause I can't say. our hunters saw Elk & bear signs to day in the white oake woods the countrey to the Lard is broken Countrey thinly timbered with pine and white oake, a mountain which I must call *Timm* or *falls* mountain rises verry high and bears to S.W. the course it has bore since we first saw it, our men danced to night. dried all our wet articles and repaired our canoes.

The flees my self and the men got on them in passing thro the plains the Indians had lately lived in Lodges on the Lard Side at the falls, are very troublesom and with every exertion the men can't get rid of them, perticularly as they have no clothes to change those which they wore. Those Indians are at war with the Snake Indians on the river which falls in a few miles above this and have lately had a battle with them, their loss I cannot lern

October 26th Saturday 1805.

A fine morning Sent Six men out to hunt Deer, and collect rozin to pitch the canoes which has become verry leakey by frequently hauling them over rocks &c. as well [as] Striking rocks frequently in passing down. all our articles we have exposed to the Sun to Dry; and the Canoes drawn out and turned up. maney of our Stores entirely spoiled by being repeetedly wet,[1]

A number of Indians came to the oposit side of the river in the fore part of the day and Shew[ed] that they were anxious to cross to us, we did not think proper to cross them in our Canoes and did not Send for them. in the evening *two* chiefs and 15 men came over in a Small Canoe, those two chiefs proved to be the two Principal Chiefs of the tribes above at the falls, and above, who was out hunting at the time we passed their bands; one of those Chiefs made Cap! Lewis and my self each a Small present of Deer meat, and small cakes of white bread made of roots. we gave to each chief a Meadel of the Small Size a red Silk handkerchief, arm band, Knife & a piece of Paint, and acknowledged them as chiefs; as we thought it necessary at this time to treat those people verry friendly & ingratiate our Selves with them, to insure us a kind & friendly reception on our return, we gave Small presents to Several, and half a Deer to them to eate. we had also a fire made for those people to sit around in the middle of our camp, and Peter Crusat Played on the violin, which pleased those nativs exceedingly. (*Yorke danced for the Ind*!) the two Chiefs and several men deturmined to delay all night with us all the others returned, leaving the horses for those who staied on the opposit Side. our hunters returned in the evening Killed five Deer, four verry large grey Squirels and a grouse. one of the guard at the river guiged a Salmon Trout, which we had fried in a little Bears oil which the Chief we passed below the narrows gave us: this I thought one of the most delicious fish I have ever tasted

Great numbers of white crain flying in different Directions verry high. The river rose 8 inches to day from what cause I cannot Say certainly, as the tides cannot effect the river here as there is a falls below, I conjecture that the rise is owing to the winds which has Set up the river for 24 hours past

our hunters inform that the country back is broken, stoney and thinly timbered with pine and white Oake. They saw

---

[1] The astronomical data, being a transcript of those in the first draft, are here omitted. — Ed.

Elk & Bear sign in the mountains.   Dried all our wet articles and repaired our canoes to day, and the Party amused themselves at night danceing.   The *Flees* which the party got on them at the upper & great falls, are very troublesom and dificuelt to get rid of, perticularly as the me[n] have not a Change of Clothes to put on,   they strip off their Clothes and kill the flees, dureing which time they remain nakid.

The nations in the vicinity of this place is at War with the Snake Indians who they Say are noumerous and live on the river we passed above the falls on the Same Side on which we have encamped, and, the nearest town is about four days march they pointed nearly S. E. and informed that they had a battle with those Ind! laterly, their loss I could not assertain.

[Clark, first draft:]   *October 27ᵗʰ Sunday 1805*

a verry windy night and morning wind from the West and hard

Took time and distance of Suns and moons nearest Limbs. Sun West

		Time		distance		
	h	m	s			
P M	3	20	37	61°	0′	0 ″
"		22	33	61	0	45
"		23	23	61	1	15
"		24	24	61	1	45
"		25	25	61	2	15
"		26	22	61	2	30
"		27	25	61	2	30
"		28	23	61	3	15
"		29	9	61	3	30
"		29	50	61	3	30

Send out hunters and they killed 4 deer 1 pheasent and a squirel the 2 Chiefs and party continue with us, we treat them well give them to eate & smoke, they were joined by seven others, from below. who stayed about 3 hours and returned down the river in a pet, soon after the Chiefs deturmined to go home we had them put across the river the wind verry high, we took a vocabelary of the Languages of

the 2 nations, the one liveing at the Falls call themselves
E-nee-shur   The other resideing at the levels or narrows in a
a village on the St.ᵈ side call themselves *E-chee-lute*   not withstanding those people live only 6 miles apart, [they understand]
but fiew words of each others language the language of those
above having great similarity with those tribes of flat heads we
have passed.   all have the clucking tone anexed which is pro-
dominate above, all flatten the heads of their female children
near the falls, and maney above follow the same custom   The
language of the *Che-luc-it-te-quar* a fiew miles below is different
from both in a small degree.   The wind increased in the
evening and blew verry hard from the same point W   day
fair and cold.   The creek at which we are Encamped is called
by the natives *Que-nett*   Some words with Shabono about
his duty   The pinical of Falls mountain bears S 43.° W. about
35·miles

October 27ᵗʰ. Sunday 1805

Wind hard from the west all the last night and this morning.[1]
Some words with Shabono our interpreter about his duty.
Sent out Several hunters who brought in *four Deer*, one
Grouse and a *Squirel*.   The two Chiefs & party was joined by
seven others from below in two canoes,   we gave them to eate
& Smoke   Several of those from below returned down the river
in a bad humer, haveing got into this pet by being prevented
doeing as they wished with our articles which was then exposed
to dry.   we took a Vocabelary of the Languages of those two
chiefs which are verry different notwithstanding they are Situated
within six miles of each other,   Those at the *great falls* call
themselves *E-nee-shur* and are understood on the river above:
Those at the Great Narrows call themselves *E-che-lute* and is
understood below,[2]   maney words of those people are the Same,

---

[1] The astronomical data are here omitted, as being transcripts of those in the first
draft. — ED.

[2] The Eneeshurs were a tribe of the Shahaptian family, now extinct, or else un-
known by that name.   The Echeloot is one of the leading tribes of the Chinookan
family, which formerly occupied the lower Columbia, from this encampment of the
expedition to the river's mouth, and for some distance along the Pacific coast. — ED.

and common to all the *flat head* Bands which we have passed
on the river, all have the *clucking* tone anexed which is pro-
domonate above all the Bands flatten the heads of the female
children, and maney of the male children also.[1] Those two
Chief[s] leave us this evening and returned to their bands,
the wind verry high & from the west, day proved fair and
cool.

The natives call this creek near which we are encamped
Que-nett.

[Clark, first draft :]   *October* 28$\frac{th}{11}$ *Monday* 1805

a windey morning loaded our canoes and set out at 9 oClock.
A M. *3* canoes came down from the village above & 2 from
that below. in one of those canoes a Indian wore his hair cued
[queued], and had on a round hat.   Wind from West

Course Distance

N. 50° W. 2 miles [to a] cove in a Lar.ᵈ bend Clift of rocks on each
        side of 90 feet high, fiew pine
N. 10° W. 2 miles to an Indian village of the *Chee-luck-it-tee-quar*
        nation of 8 houses in the form of those above, passed
    4   the mouth of a small creek

Those Indians have a musket & sword, and several Brass
Tea kittles which they appear to be verry fond of We purchased of those people five small dogs, and some Dried beries
& white bread of roots, the wind rose and we were obliged to
lie by about 1 mile below on the Lar.ᵈ Side

North 1 mile to a rock Island on the Star.ᵈ Side. we had
not landed long be[fo]r an Indian canoe came from below with
3 Indians in it. those Indians make verry nice canoes of Pine.
Thin with aperns & carve on the head imitation of animals &
other heads; The Indians above sacrifice the property of the
Deceased towit horses, canoes, bolds [bowls] Basquets of which
they make great use to hold water boil their meet &.ᶜ &.ᶜ great

---

[1] We now begin to observe that the heads of the males, as well as of the other sex,
are subjected to this operation, whereas among the mountains the custom has confined
it almost to the females. — BIDDLE (ii, p. 45).

many Indians came down from the upper Village & sat with us [and] smoked, rained all the evening & blew hard from the West, encamped on the Lard Side ops.d an Rock in the river   Bad place

A cool windey morning   we loaded our canoes and Set out at 9 oClock, a. m.   as we were about to set out 3 canoes from above and 2 from below came to view us   in one of those canoes I observed an Indian with round hat Jacket & wore his hair cued [*he said he got them from Indians below the great rapid who bought them from the whites*] we proceeded on   river inclosed on each Side in high clifts of about 90 feet of loose dark Coloured rocks   at four miles we landed at a Village of 8 houses on the Star.d Side under some rugid rocks,   Those people call themselves *Chil-luckit-te-quaw*,[1] live in houses similar to those described, Speake somewhat different language with maney words the Same & understand those in their neighbourhood   Cap.t Lewis took a vocabilary of this Language   I entered one of the houses in which I saw a British musket, a cutlash and Several brass Tea kittles of which they appeared verry fond   Saw them boiling fish in baskets with Stones,   I also Saw [*badly executed*] figures of animals & men cut & painted on boards in one Side of the house which they appeared to prize, but for what purpose I will not venter to say, here we purchased five Small Dogs, Some dried buries, & white bread made of roots,   the wind rose and we were obliged to lie by all day at 1 mile below on the Lar.d Side.   we had not been long on Shore before a Canoe came up with a man woman & 2 children, who had a fiew roots to Sell,   Soon after maney others joined them from above,   The wind which is the cause of our delay, does not retard the motions of those people at all, as their canoes are calculated to ride the highest waves,   they are built of white cedar or Pine verry light wide in the middle and tapers at each end, with aperns, and heads of animals

---

[1] Coues says (*L. and C.*, ii, p. 673), "No Indians are now known by this name" — apparently a *lapsus calami*, since Powell includes among the Chinookan tribes the Chilluckquittequaw (*U. S. Bur. Ethnol. Rep.*, 1885–86, p. 66). — ED.

carved on the bow, which is generally raised. Those people make great use of Canoes, both for transpo[r]tation and fishing, they also [make] use of bowls & baskets made of grass & [*bark*] Splits to hold water and boil their fish & meat. maney of the nativs of the last Village come down [to] Sit and Smoke with us, wind blew hard accompanied with rain all the evening, our Situation not a verry good one for an encampment, but such as it is we are obliged to put up with, the harbor is a Safe one, we encamped on the Sand, wet and disagreeable one Deer killed this evening, and another wounded near our Camp.

[**Clark, first draft :**]   *October 29*[th] *Tuesday 1805*

A Cloudy morning wind still from the West not hard, we set out at day light proceeded on about 5 miles and came too at a Lodge of a chief which we made at the upper Village at the *falls* about his house there is six others This chief gave us to eate *Sackacomme* burries Hasel nuts fish Pounded, and a kind of Bread made of roots. we gave to the women pices of ribon, which they appeared pleased with. those houses are large 25 feet sq[r] and contain about 8 men, say 30 inhabitants

Course

N. 55° W. 4 miles to a Lar[d] point, pas[d] a run on Lar[d] Side
West   8 miles to Rock Island near the middle of River, passed
          7 Houses of Indians about 50 men at 1 mile on the
____   Star[d] Side. Brackfast Those people fish at the last
 12   narrows, & have but little pounded fish, some dried and
          berries

Those people are friendly gave us to eate fish Beries, nuts bread of roots & Dr[i]ed beries and we call this the friendly Village We purchased 12 dogs of them & 4 Sacks of Pounded fish, and some fiew Dried Berries, and proceeded on at 4 miles further we landed to smoke a pipe with the people of a village of 11 houses we found those people also friendly Their village is Situated imediately below the mouth of a River of 60 yards water which falls in on the Star[d] Side and heads in the mountains to the N. & N. E. the Indians inform us that

this river is long and full of falls no salmon pass up it. They
also inform that 10 nations live on this river by hunting and
on buries &.ᶜ The Countrey begins to be thinly timbered with
Pine & low white Oake verry rocky and hilley. We purchased at this village 4 dogs. at the end of this Course is
3 rocks, in the river and a rock point from the Lard. the
middle rock is large and has a number of graves on it we call
it the Sepulchar Island. The last River we call Caterack River
from the number of falls which the Indians inform is on it
The Indians are afraid to hunt or be on the Larᵈ Side of this
Columbia river for fear of the Snake Indˢ who reside on a fork
of this river which falls in above the falls. a good situation for
winter quarters if game can be had is just below Sepulchar rock
on the Larᵈ Side, high & pine and oake timber the rocks ruged
above, good hunting Countrey back, as it appears from the
river Indian village opsᵈ of 2 Lodges river ½ mile wide at
least

12 miles brought forward

S. 60.° W. 5 miles to a point of rocks Island in a Lard bend, passed
2 rocks in the river. passed 2 Houses at 1 mile on the
Starᵈ Side and 2 at 4 miles on the Starᵈ Side Countrey
on the Lard. Side has more timber than common and
looks well for hunting high and ruged.

S. 80.° W. 6 miles to 4 Houses in a point of a timbered bottom on the
Larᵈ Side at a large creek or River 40 yᵈˢ passed a
bottom on the Starᵈ Side the distance in which there is
14 Indian houses. The falls mountain covered with
snow is South

S. 70.° W. 6 miles to a high clift of rocks Stᵈ bend passed a large
creek at 1 mile on the Starᵈ Side in which the Indians
catch fish a large sand bar from the Larᵈ Side for 4
miles, at which place a small stream of water falls over
a rock of 100 feet on the Larᵈ Side passed 4 Indian
Houses at 5 miles in a bottom on the Larᵈ Side

The robes of those Indians are of wolf deer elk, wild cats,
some fox, & Deer I saw one of the mountain sheep, the wool
thick and long corse hair on the back, resembling bristles.
those animals live among the rocks in those mountains below,

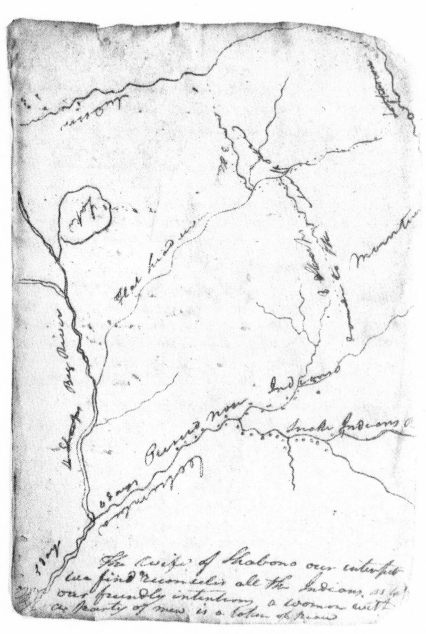

Map from Clark Field-book, showing location of Indian tribes
on the Columbia River.

orter is much valued by those people   they cew their hair on
each side with it and ware it about the necks with the tail
in front

S. 56° W. 6 miles to a point of timbered bottom on the Lar.ᵈ Side,
         pass.ᵈ a Star.ᵈ point at 2 miles   Here the mountains are
         high on each side, the high points of those to the
         Lar.ᵈ has snow

Came too at 3 miles on this course at 3 Houses of flatheads
and Encamped on the Starᵈ Side, a Pond lies back of those
people in which we saw great numbers of the small swan.   we
Purchased of those people 3 Dogs   they gave us High bush
cramburies, bread of roots [blank space in MS.] and roots, they
were pleased with musick of the violin.

October 29ᵗʰ Tuesday 1805

A cloudy morning wind from the west but not hard,   we Set
out at day light, and proceeded on about *five* miles   came too
on the Star.ᵈ Side at a village of 7 houses built in the Same form
and materials of those above,   here we found the Chief we had
Seen at the long narrows named [blank space in MS.]   we entered his lodge and he gave us to eate Pounded fish, bread
made of roots, Filbert nuts, & the berries of Sackecomme.
[*Sác de Commis*]   we gave to each woman of the lodge a brace
of Ribon of which they were much pleased.   each of those
houses may be calculated to contain 8 men and 30 Soles,   they
are hospitable and good humered Speak the Same language of
the inhabitants of the last village,   we call this the friendly village.   I observed in the lodge of the chief sundery articles
which must have been precured from the white people, Such
[as] a Scarlet & blue cloth Sword Jacket & hat.   I also observed two wide Split boards w[i]th images on them cut and
painted in emitation of a man ; I pointed to this image and
asked a man to what use he put them to, he Said Something
the only word I understood was " good," and then Steped to
the image and took out his Bow & quiver to Show me, and
Some other of his war emplemints, from behind it.   The Chief

then directed his wife to hand him his medison bag which he opened and Showed us 14 fingers [*different fingers not little or middle fingers*] which he said was the fingers of his enemies which he had taken in war, and pointed to S. E. from which direction I concluded they were Snake Indians, this is the first Instance I ever knew of the Indians takeing any other trofea of their exploits off the dead bodies of their Enimies except the Scalp.   The chief painted those fingers with Several other articles which was in his bag red and securely put them back,[1] haveing first mad[e] a short harrang which I suppose was bragging of what he had done in war.   we purchased 12 Dogs and 4 Sacks of fish, & some fiew ascid berries,   after brackfast we proceeded on,   the mountains are high on each side, containing scattering pine white Oake & under groth, hill Sides Steep and rockey ;   at 4 miles lower we observed a small river falling in with great rapidity on the Star.ᵈ Side below which is a village of 11 houses,   here we landed to Smoke a pipe with the nativs and examine the mouth of the river, which I found to be 60 yards wide rapid and deep,   The inhabitants of the village are friendly and chearfull ; those people inform us as also those at the last village that this little river is long and full of falls, no Salmon pass up it, it runs from N. N. E.,   that *ten* nations live on this river and its waters, on buries, and what game they can kill with their Bow & arrows

we purchased 4 dogs and set out. (this village is the of the Same nation of the one we last passed) and proceeded on.   The countrey on each side begin[s] to be thicker timbered with Pine and low white oake ; verry rockey and broken.   passed three large rocks in the river   the middle rock is large long and has Several Squar vaults on it, we call this rockey Island the Sepulchar.[2]   The last river we passed we shall call the *Cataract* River[3] from the number of falls which the Indians say is on it,   passed 2 Lodges of Indians a short distance below the

---

[1] After an harangue . . . the fingers were carefully replaced among the valuable contents of the red medicine-bag. — BIDDLE (ii, p. 47).

[2] One of the best known Indian burial-places, still showing many remains in the shape of skulls and bones.   O. D. Wheeler describes a grave and monument of a well-known Oregon pioneer, Trevitt, upon this island. — ED.

[3] Now Klickitat River, in the county of the same name, in Washington. — ED.

sepulchor Island on the Star.^d Side.   river wide, at 4 mile passed 2 houses on the Star.^d Side,   six miles lower passed 4 houses above the mouth of a Small river 40 yards wide on the Lar.^d Side a thick timbered bottom above & back of those houses,   those are the first houses which we have seen on the South Side of the Columbia River, (and the axess to those dificuelt) for fear of the approach of their common enemies the Snake Indians,   passed 14 houses on the St.^d Side scattered on the bank,   from the mouth of this little river which we shall Call Labeasche River,[1] the *falls mountain* [*Mount Hood*] is South and the top is covered with Snow.   one mile below pass the mouth of a large rapid Stream on the Star.^d Side, opposit to a large Sand bar,   in this creek the Indians above take their fish,   here we saw Several canoes, which induc[e]d us to call this Canoe Creek   it is 28 yards wide,   about 4 miles lower and below the Sand bar is a butifull cascade falling over a rock of about 100 feet [high],   a Short distance lower passed 4 Indian houses on the Lar.^d Side in a timbered bottom,   a fiew miles further we came too at 3 houses on Star.^d Side, back of which is a pond in which I Saw great numbers of Small Swan, Capt Lewis and [I] went into the houses of those people who appeared Somewhat surprised at first   Their houses are built on the Same Construction of those above, Speak the Same language and Dress in the Same way, robes of the Skins of wolves, Deer, Elk, wild cat, or Loucirvia & fox,   I also Saw a mountain Sheap [2] skin the wool of which is long, thick, & corse with long corse hare on the top of the neck and back something resembling bristles of a goat, the skin was of white hare, those animals these people inform me by signs live in the mountains among the rocks, their horns are Small and streight, Orter Skins are highly prised among those people as well as those on the river above,   They cue their hare which is divided on each sholder, and also ware small strips about their necks with the tale hanging down in front.   Those people gave us,

---

[1] Now named for the mountain, Hood's River.   "Canoe Creek" is now White Salmon River. — Ed.

[2] Not a sheep, but the mountain goat (*Haplocerus montanus*).   "Loucirvia" is only a corruption of the Fr. *loup cervier*; the lynx. — Ed.

High bush cramberries, [*described hereafter not H. B. Cr.*] bread made of roots, and roots; we purchased three dogs for the party to eate; we Smoked with the men, all much pleased with the violin.   Here the mountains are high on each side, those to the Lar.^d Side has Some Snow on them at this time, more timber than above and of greater variety.

[Clark, first draft:]   *October* 30th *Wednesday* 1805

A cloudy morning.   Some little rain all night,   after eating a slight brackfast of venison we set out.   The rocks project into the river in maney places and have the appearance of haveing fallen from the high hills   those projected rocks is common & small Bays below & nitches in the rocks.   passed 4 cascades or small streams falling from the mountains on Lar.^d

S. 70.° W.   3 miles to a point of rocks on the Star.^d Side, passed a number of stumps at some distance in the water
This part of the river resembles a pond partly dreaned leaving many stumps bare both in & out of the water, current about 1 mile p.^r Hour
S. 74.° W   2 miles to a point of a timbered bottom on Star.^d Side halted to Dine, killed a Deer & 3 ducks & a squirel of the mountains   we can plainly here the roreing of the grand Shute below,   saw the large Buzard white head and part of the wings white
West   4 miles to the mouth of a river on the Star.^d Side of about 60 yards wide   passed St.^d point & many large rocks promiscuously in the river both above and below this river a large sand bar on the Lard Side

The bottom above the river is about ¾ of a mile wide and rich,   some deer & bear sign.   rained moderately all day, we are wet and cold.   Saw several species of wood which I never saw before, some resembling Beech & other Poplar.   Day dark and disagreeable

S. 45.° W.   2 miles to a large rock in the river, passed several rocks and a large sand bar on the Lar.^d Side   verry large rock near the Star.^d Side   High Mountains on each side, ruged and covered with a variety of timber such as Pine Spruce Seder Cotton wood oake

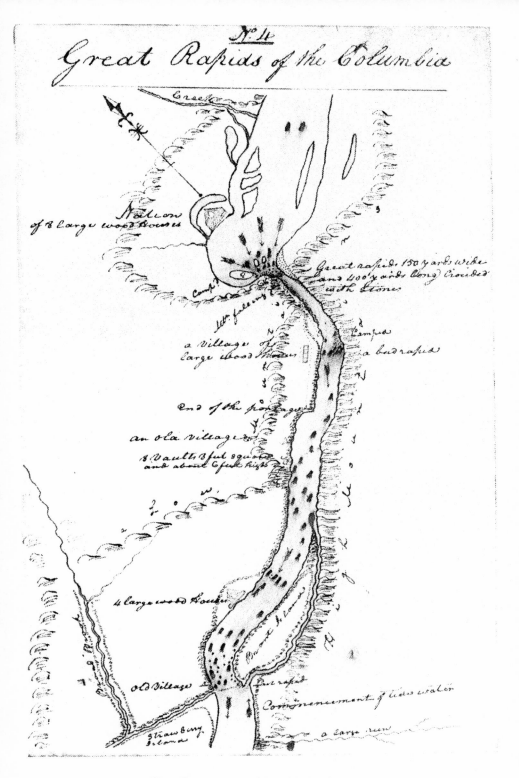

Great Rapids of the Columbia River,
sketch-map by Clark.

S. 30 W 4 miles to a Island, at the commencement of the grand
shute and the Star.^d Side where we camped, passed
maney large rocks in the river,[1] a large creek on the
St^d Side at 2 miles, with an Island in the mouth.

15

passed 3 Islands on the Star.^d one on the Lard above 2
small Islands ops.^d to us on which there grows large
Pine, 4 rock Islands which almost chokes up the river.
a deep bay to the Star^d on which the Indians live in 8
large worm Houses 2 ponds back of them on the
Stard 1 above the Islands, one on the Lar^d side. several
small rocks in dif.^t p.^{ts}

I with 2 men proceeded down the river 2 miles on an old
Indian parth to view the rapids, which I found inpassible for
our canoes without a portage, the roade bad at 1 mile I
saw a Town of Houses entirely abandoned, on an elevated situa-
tion, ops.^d a 2.^d shute, returned at dark. Capt Lewis and 5
men went to the Town found them kind they gave Beries &
nuts, but he c.^d get nothin[g] from them in the way of Information, the greater part of those people out collecting roots
below, rained all the evining Those people have one gun &
maney articles which they have purchased of the white people
their food is principally fish

*October 30*th*. Wednesday 1805*

A cool morning, a moderate rain all the last night, after
eating a partial brackfast of venison we Set out passed several
places where the rocks projected into the river & have the
appearance of haveing Seperated from the mountains and fallen
promiscuisly into the river, Small nitches are formed in the
banks below those projecting rocks which is comon in this
part of the river, Saw 4 Cascades caused by Small Streams
falling from the mountains on the Lar.^d Side, a remarkable
circumstance in this part of the river is, the Stumps of pine
trees are in maney places, are at Some distance in the river,
and gives every appearance of the river being damed up below
from some cause which I am not at this time acquainted with,

---

1 Word illegible. — ED.

the current of the river is also verry jentle not exceeding 1-½ mile p. hour and about ¾ of a mile in width,   Some rain,   we landed above the mouth of a Small river on the Star.d Side and Dined,   J. Shields Killed a Buck & Labeash 3 Ducks,   here the river widens to about one mile large Sand bar in the middle, a great [rock] both in and out of the water, large Stones or rocks are also permiscuisly scattered about in the river,   this day we Saw Some fiew of the large Buzzard   Cap.t Lewis Shot at one,   those Buzzards are much larger than any other of ther Spece or the largest Eagle white under part of their wings &c.   The bottoms above the mouth of this little river [1] is m[u]ch covered with grass & firn & is about ¾ of a mile wide rich and rises gradually,   below the river (which is 60 yards wide above its mouth,) the Countery rises with steep assent. we call this little river from a Speces of Ash [*new Timbered*] that wood [Ash] which grows on its banks [is] of a verry large [size] and different [kind] from any we had before Seen, and a timber resembling the beech in bark but different in its leaf which is Smaller, and the tree Smaller.[2]   passed maney large rocks in the river and a large creek on the Star.d Side in the mouth of which is an Island [3]   passed on the right of 3 Islands near the Stard. Side, and landed on an Island close under the Star.d Side at the head of the great Shute, and a little below a village of 8 large houses on a Deep bend on the Star.d Side, and opposit 2 Small Islands imediately in the head of the Shute, which Islands are covered with Pine,   maney large rocks also, in the head of the Shute.   Ponds back of the houses, and countrey low for a short distance.   The day proved cloudy dark and disagreeable with some rain all day which kept us wet.   The countary a high mountain on each side thickly covered with timber, such as Spruce, Pine, Cedar, oake Cotton &c. &c.   I took two men and walked down three miles to

---

1 This is the present Wind River, Washington.   As an afterthought, the explorers gave it the name of " Cruzatte," which did not persist. — ED.

2 The first tree is the broad-leaved maple (*Acer macrophyllum*).   The only tree closely resembling the beech is the Oregon alder, but Lewis and Clark call this the "black alder," Mar. 28, and June 10, 1806.   The "growth resembling the beech" may be the "Indian plum," *Nuttallia cerasiformis* T. & G. — C. V. PIPER.

3 Now Rock Creek, just above the Cascades. — ED.

examine the Shute and river below   proceeded along an old
Indian path, pass.^d an old village at 1 mile on an ellevated
Situation of,   this village contained verry large houses built in
a different form from any I had seen, and laterly abandoned,
and the most of the boa[r]ds put into a pond of water near the
village, as I conceived to drown the flees, which was emensely
noumerous about the houses,   I found by examonation that
we must make a portage of the greater perpotion of our stores
2-½ miles, and the canoes we could haul over the rocks,   I
returned at Dark   Capt Lewis and 5 men had just returned
from the village,   Capt L. informed me that he found the
nativs kind, they gave him berries, nuts & fish to eate ; but he
could get nothing from them in the way of information.   The
greater part of the inhabitants of this Village being absent
down the river Some distance colecting roots   Capt L. Saw
one gun and Several articles which must have been precured
from the white people.   a wet disagreeable evening, the only
wood we could get to burn on this little Island on which we
have encamped is the newly discovered *Ash*, which makes a
tolerable fire.   we made fifteen miles to daye.

[Clark, first draft :]   *October 31*st *Thursday* 1805

   a cloudey raney morning   I proceed down the river to view
it more at leasure,   I took Jos. Fields & Peter Crusat and proceeded on down,   Send Crusat back at 2 m.^s to examine the rapid
near the shore & I proceeded on down about 10 miles to a very
high rock in a bottom on the Star.^d ops.^d 2 Islands covered with
timber on which I saw Ind.^s at a distance ;   found the river rocky
for 6 miles, after which the current became uniform.   at 1 mile
I passed an old deserted village on a Pond on a high situation
of 8 Houses.   at 3½ miles one house the only rem.^t of an antient village   ½ a mile lower I saw 8 vaults for the Dead which
was nearly square 8 feet closely covered with broad boa[r]ds
curiously ingraved,   the bones in some of those vaults were 4
feet thick,   in others the Dead was yet layed side of each other
nearly East & west, [w]raped up & bound securely in robes,

[175]

great numbers of trinkets Brass kittles, sea shells, Iron Pan Hare &c. &c. were hung about the vaults and great maney wooden gods, or Imeges of men cut in wood, set up around the vaults, some of those so old and worn by time that they were nearly worn out of shape, and some of those vaults so old that they were roted entirely to the ground. not withstanding they [the] wood is of Pine & [word illegible. — ED.] or Seder as also the wooden gods. I can not learn certainly if those people worship those wooden emiges, they have them in conspicuous parts of their houses at 5 miles I passed 4 large houses on the Stard Side a little above the last rapid and opposit a large Island which is Situated near the Lard Side. The enhabitents of those houses had left them closely shut up, They appeared to contain a great deel of property and Provisions such as those people use. I did not disturb any thing about those houses, but proceed[ed] on down below the rapid which I found to be the last, a large village has at some period been on the Stard Side below this rapid The bottom is high stoney and about 2 miles wide covered with grass, here is the head of a large Island in high water, at this time no water passes on the Stard Side I walked thro this Island which I found to be verry rich, open & covered with Strawberry vines, and has greatly the appearance of having at some period been cultivated, The natives has dug roots in some parts of this Isl. which is about 3 miles long & 1 wide, a small Island covered with timber opposit the lower point no water runs on the Stard Side of it below and in the middle of the river is a large Island covered with tall trees opposit the Strawberry Island on its Stard Side a creek falls in which has no running water at present, it has the appearance of throwing out emence torents. I saw 5 Indians in a canoe below. Jo [Fields] killed a Sand hill Crane & we returned by the same rout to camp at the grand Shute where I found several Indians, I smoked Two canoes loaded with fish for the Trade below come down & unloaded The after noon fare

S. 30° E   1 mile to a Lar^d Bend passing the Grand Shute which is ¼
of a mile and the water confined within about 150
yards, passing with Tremendeous force,   great number
of rocks in the upper p^t of this shute,   a low pine
mountain on the Sta^d Side, high one on the Lar^d Side.

S. 30° W. 1 mile to a Lar^d bend passed several rocks in the river & a
rapid at ¾ of a mile the water being confined between
large rocks, maney of which is under water.   an old
village of 8 houses on the Star^d Side on the hill opposit.

S. 45° W   2 miles to a high rock above the upper point of a large
Isl^d on the Lar^d Side, passed maney rocks in different
derections, a house on the Star^d at 1 mile   just below is
8 Indian *Vaults* in which is great number of dead, raped
up   their trinkets, & wooden Gods are placed around
the vaults, they lie East & west

S. 60° W   2 miles to a large black rock in a Star^d bend at the commencement of a rapid ops^d lower point of an Island
Lar^d passed a rapid at ½ m^l not bad.   several large
rocks in the river permiscusly,   4 large Ind. houses
without inhabitents on the Star^d Side at 1½ mile   a
Island on the Lar^d Side   extensive high stoney bottoms
on the Star^d Side

South   2 miles to a creek under a Bluff in a Lar^d bend passed the
rapid ¼ of a mile long.   the upper point of a large
Island on the Star^d Side no running water on the Star^d
Side of it at present   this Island high rich and open
covered with Strawbery vines   a narrow open bottom
on the Lar^d Side

Those Indians cut off the hands of those they kill & pre-
serve the fingers.

October 31st *Thursday* 1805

A cloudy rainey disagreeable morning   I proceeded down
the river to view with more attention [*the rapids*] we had to
pass on the river below,   the two men with me.   Jo. Fields &
Peter Crusat proceeded down to examine the rapids   the Great
Shute[1] which commenced at the Island on which we encamped

---

[1] Fr. *chute*, "fall."   This is known as the Cascades of the Columbia.   The Cas-
cades cover a stretch of water several miles long where the river breaks through the
Cascade Mountains.   The Upper Cascades are those Lewis and Clark called the
"Great Shute."   The entire fall for three miles is sixty feet. — ED.

continued with great rapidity and force thro a narrow chanel much compress.ᵈ and interspersed with large rocks for ½ a mile, at a mile lower is a verry considerable rapid at which place the waves are remarkably high,   and proceeded on in a old Indian parth 2-½ miles by land thro a thick wood & hill Side, to the river where the Indians make a portage,   from this place I Dispatched Peter Crusat (our principal waterman) back to follow the river and examine the practibility of the canoes passing, as the rapids appeared to continue down below as far as I could See,   I with Jo Fields proceeded on,   at ½ a mile below the end of the portage passed a house where there had been an old town for ages past   as this house was old Decayed and a place of flees I did not enter it,   about ½ a mile below this house in a verry thick part of the woods is 8 Vaults, which appeared closely covered and highly deckerated with orniments.   Those vaults are all nearly the Same size and form 8 feet square, 6 feet high, sloped a little so as to convey off the rain, made of Pine or cedar boards Closely Connected & s[e]curely Covered with wide boards, with a Dore left in the East side which is partially stoped with wide boards curiously engraved.   In Several of those vaults the dead bodies w[e]re raped up verry securely in Skins tied around with cords of grass and bark, laid on a mat, all east & west and some of those vaults had as maney as 4 Bodies laying on the Side of each other.   the other Vaults containing bones only, Some contained bones for the debth of 4 feet.   on the tops and on poles attached to those vaults hung Brass kittles & frying pans pearced through their bottoms, baskets, bowls of wood, sea Shels, skins, bits of Cloth, hair, bags of Trinkets & Small pieces of bone &c. and independant of the [*Hieroglyphics, figures of men & animals*] curious engraveing and Paintings on the boards which formed the Vaults I observed Several wooden Images, cut in the figure[s] of men and Set up on the Sides of the vaults all round,   Some of those so old and worn by time, that they were nearly out of Shape,[1]   I also observed the remains of

---

[1] Wooden and stone images like those here mentioned were found in great numbers by the early settlers, and many have been preserved.   They suggest the figures of idols which are brought from foreign lands. — EVA E. DYE.

Vaults rotted entirely into the ground and covered with moss. This must bee the burrying place for maney ages for the inhabitants of those rapids, the vaults are of the most lasting timber Pine & Cedar. I cannot say certainly that those nativs worship those wooden idols as I have every reason to believe they do not; as they are Set up in the most conspicious parts of their houses, and treated more like orniments than objects of adoration. at 2 miles lower and 5 below our Camp I passed a village of 4 large houses, abandon^d by the nativs, with their dores bared up, I looked into those houses and obsirved as much property as is usial in the houses of those people which induced me to conclude that they w[e]re at no great distance, either hunting or Colecting roots, to add to their winter subsistance. from a Short distance below the vaults the mountain which is but low on the Star^d Side, leave[s] the river, and a leavel stoney open bottom suckceeds on the Said St^d Side for a great Distance down, the mountains high and rugid on the Lar^d Side this open bottom is about 2 miles a Short distance below this village is a bad Stoney rapid and appears to be the last in view I observed at this lower rapid the remains of a large and antient Village which I could plainly trace by the Sinks in which they had formed their houses, as also those in which they had buried their fish. from this rapid to the lower end of the portage the river is crouded with rocks of various sises between which the water passes with great velociety createing in maney places large waves, an Island which is Situated near the Lar^d Side occupies about half the distance the lower point of which is at this rapid. immediately below this rapid the high water passes through a narrow chanel through the Star^d Bottom forming an Island of 3 miles Long & one wide; I walked through this Island which I found to be verry rich land, and had every appearance of haveing been at some distant period cultivated at this time it is covered with grass intersperced with strawberry vines, I observed Several places on this Island where the nativs had dug for roots and from its lower point I observed 5 Indians in a Canoe below the upper point of an Island near the middle of the river covered with tall timber, which induced me to believe that a village was at no great distance below,   I could not see any rapids below in the extent of my view which was for a long distance down the river, which from the last rapids widened and had everry appearance of being effected by the tide [*this was in fact the first tide water*] I deturmind to return to camp 10 miles distant,   a remarkable high detached rock Stands in a bottom on the Star.ᵈ Side near the lower point of this Island on the Star.ᵈ Side about 800 feet high and 400 paces around, we call the *Beaten* [*Beacon*] *rock*.¹   a Brook falls into the narrow chanel which forms the [*what we call*] Strawberry Island, which at this time has no running water, but has every appearance of dischargeing emence torrents &c. &c.   Jo. Fields shot a Sand hill Crane.   I returned by the Same rout on our Indian parth passing up on the N. W. Side of the river to our Camp at the Great Shute   found Several Indians from the village, I Smoked with them ;   Soon after my return two canoes loaded with fish & Bear grass for the trade below, came down from the village at the mouth of the Catterack River,   they unloaded and turned their canoes up Side down on the beech, & camped under a Shelving rock below our Camp.

One of the men shot a goose above this Great Shute, which was floating into the Shute, when an Indian observed it, plunged ! into the water & swam to the Goose and brought in on shore, at the head of the Suck, [*great danger, rapids bad, a descent close by him (150 feet off,) of all Columbia River, current dashed among rocks, if he had got in the Suck — lost*]   as this Indian richly earned the goose I suffered him to keep it which he about half picked and Spited it up with the guts in it to roste.

This Great Shute or falls is about ½ a mile, with the water of this great river compressed within the space of 150 paces in which there is great numbers of both large and Small rocks, water passing with great velocity forming [foaming] & boiling in a most horriable manner, with a fall of about 20 feet,   below it widens to about 200 paces and current gentle for a Short distance.   a Short distance above is three Small rockey Islands

---

¹ This rock is a well-known landmark on the lower river, and stands to-day as it did in the time of Lewis and Clark.   It has been called Pillar Rock, but is now usually known as Castle Rock. — ED.

and at the head of those falls, three Small rockey Islands are Situated crosswise the river, Several rocks above in the river & 4 large rocks in the head of the Shute; those obstructions together with the high Stones which are continually braking loose from the mountain on the Star.⁴ Side and roleing down into the Shute aded to those which brake loose from these Islands above and lodge in the Shute, must be the cause of the rivers daming up to such a distance above, where it shows such evidant marks of the common current of the river being much lower than at the present day.

[Clark, first draft:]   *November 1ˢᵗ Friday 1805*

a verry cold morning   wind from N.E. and hard

Took equal altitudes of Sun

	h	m	s		h	m	s
A. M.	9	22	51	P. M.	3	12	21
"	"	25	6	"		14	38
"	"	27	24	"		16	47

Altitude produced 36° – 22' – 15"

Set all hands packing the loading over the portage which is below the grand shute and is 940 yards of bad way over rocks & on the slipery hill sides   The Indians who came down in 2 canoes last night packed their fish over a portage of 2½ miles, to avoid a 2ᵈ *Shute*   four of them took their canoes over the 1ˢᵗ portage and run the 2ᵈ *Shute*,   great numbers of sea otters,   they are so cautious that I with deficuelty got a shute at one today, which I must have killed but could not get him as he sunk

Lattitude : 45° – 44' – 3". North
Cronomiter is 3ᵐ 27ˢ too slow M. Time
1ˢᵗ Nov.ʳ P M

Observed time and distance of the Moons Western Limb from *Antares* ✱ West

[181]

Time			Distance		
h	**m**	**s**			
P.M. 7	5	33	91°	50′	45″
"	8	25	"	50	15
"	10	53	"	52	00
"	17	1	"	52	30
"	18	59	"	52	30

The mountains is so high that no further observations can be made with this ✳
observed time and distance of Moon's Western Limb from a *Arietis*
✳ East

Time			distance		
H	**m**	**s**			
PM. 7	29	34	58°	4′	30″
"	33	12	"	4	00
"	35	21	"	3	15
"	37	16	"	2	00
"	39	2	"	1	00
"	40	35	"	0	15

We got all our canoes and baggage below the Great Shute, 3 of the canoes being Leakey from injures receved in hauling them over the rocks, obliged us to delay to have them repaired a bad rapid just below us,   three Indian canoes loaded with pounded fish for the trade down the river arrived at the upper end of the portage this evening.   I can't lern whether those Indians trade with white people or Ind⁵ below for the Beeds & copper which they are so fond of.   They are nearly necked prefuring beeds to any thing.   Those Beeds they trafick with Indians still higher up this river for skins robes &ᶜ &ᶜ   The Indians on those waters do not appear to be sickly, sore eyes are common and maney have lost their eyes, some one and maney both, they have bad teeth, and the greater perpotion of them have worn their teeth down, maney into the gums. They are rather small high cheeks, women small and homely, maney of them have sweled legs, large about the knees owing to the position in which they set on their hams, They are nearly necked only a piece of leather tied about their breech and a small robe which generally comes to a little below their wastes and scercely sufficently large to cover arround them when confined they are all fond of clothes but more so of Beeds perticularly blue & white beeds. They are durty in the extreme both in their cooking and in their houses.

Those at the last Village raise the beads about five feet from the earth, under which they store their Provisions. Their houses is about 33 feet to 50 feet square, the dore of which is about 30 Inches high and 16 Inches wide in this form Ω cut in a wide part of Pine board, they have maney imeges cut in wood, generally in the figure of a man. Those people are high with what they have to sell, and say the white people below give them great Prices for what they sell to them. Their noses are all Pierced, and the[y] wear a white shell maney of which are 2 Inches long pushed thro' the nose. all the women have flat heads pressed to almost a point at top. The[y] press the female childrens heads between 2 bords when young untill they form the skul as they wish it which is generally verry *flat*. This amongst those people is considered as a great mark of buty, and is practised in all the tribes we have passed on this river more or less. Men take more of the drugery off the women than is common with Indians.

Names of Tribes

E-neê-Shur at the falls
E-chee-lute at the lower whorl
Che-luck-it-te-quar below
Chim-ná-pum Nation above
Qua-ba-ha — near.

November 1st Friday 1805

A verry cool morning wind hard from the N. E. The Indians who arrived last evening took their Canoes on ther Sholders and carried them below the Great Shute, we Set about takeing our Small canoe and all the baggage by land 940 yards of bad slippery and rockey way. The Indians we discoverd took ther loading the whole length of the portage 2-½ miles, to avoid a second Shute which appears verry bad to pass, and thro' which they passed with their empty canoes. Great numbers of Sea Otters, they are so cautious that I with dificuelty got a Shot at one today, which I must have killed, but could not get him as he Sunk.

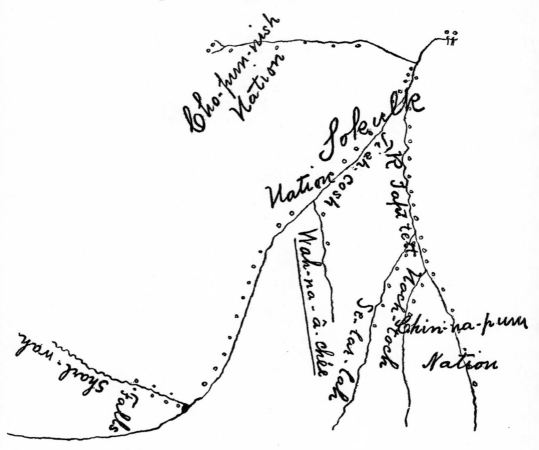

We got all our baggage over the Portage of 940 yards, after which we got the 4 large canoes over by slipping them over the rocks on poles placed across from one rock to another, and at some places along partial Streams of the river. in passing those canoes over the rocks &c. three of them rec[ei]ved injuries which obliged us to delay to have them repared.

Several Indian Canoes arrived at the head of the portage, Some of the men acompanied by those from the village come down to Smoke with us,   they appear to Speak the same language with a little different axcent[1]

I visited the Indian Village found that the construction of the houses [was] Similar to those abov[e] described, with this difference only, that they are larger say from 35 to 50 feet by 30 feet, raised about 5 feet above the earth, and nearly as much below   the Dores in the Same form and size cut in the wide post which supports one end of the ridge pole and which is carved and painted with different figures & Hieroglyphics. Those people gave me to eate nuts berries & a little dried fish, and Sold me a hat of their own taste without a brim, and baskets in which they hold their water.   Their beads [beds] are raised about 4-½ feet, under which they Store away their dried fish,   between the part on which they lie and the back wall, they Store away their roots burries nuts and valuable articles on mats, which are Spread also around the fireplace which is Sunk about one foot lower than the bottom flore of the house,   this fireplace is about 8 feet long and Six feet wide secured with a fraim,   those houses are calculated for 4, 5 & 6 families, each familey haveing a nice painted ladder to assend up to their beads.   I Saw in those houses Several wooden *Images* all cut in imitation of men, but differently fasioned and placed in the most conspicious parts of the houses, probably as an orniment

I cannot lern certainly as to the traffick those Ind: carry on below, if white people or the indians who trade with the whites who are either settled or visit the mouth of this river.   I believe mostly with the latter as their knowledge of the white people appears to be verry imperfect, and the articles which they appear to trade mostly i. e. Pounded fish, Beargrass, and roots; cannot be an object of comerce with furin merchants. however they git in return for those articles Blue and white *beeds* copper [Tea] Kettles, brass arm bands, some scarlet and blue robes and a fiew articles of old clothes,   they prefer beeds to any thing, and will part with the last mouthfull or articles

---

1 Astronomical data here omitted, being a transcript of those in first draft. — ED.

of clothing they have for a fiew of those beeds,   those beeds
the[y] trafick with Indians Still higher up this river for roabs,
Skins, cha-pel-el bread,[1] beargrass &c. who in their turn trafick
with those under the rockey mountains for Beargrass, *quarmash*
[*Pashîco*] roots & robes &c.

The nativs of the waters of the Columbia appear helthy,
Some have tumers on different parts of their bodies, and Sore
and weak Eyes are common,   maney have lost their Sight
entirely, great numbers with one eye out and frequently the
other verry weak,   This misfortune I must again ascribe to
the water &c.   They have bad teeth, which is not common
with indians, maney have worn their teeth down and Some
quite into their gums, this I cannot satisfactorily account for
it,   do ascribe it in some measure to their method of eateing,
their food, roots pert[i]cularly, which they make use of as they
are taken out of the earth frequently nearly covered with sand,
I have not Seen any of their long roots offered for Sale clear
of sand.   They are rether below the Common Size high cheeks
womin Small and homely, and have Swelled legs and thighs,
and their knees remarkably large which I ascribe to the method
in which they sit on their hams   go nearly necked wareing
only a piece of leather tied about their breast which falls down
nearly as low as the waste, a small roabe about 3 feet square,
and a piece of leather tied about their breach,   They [*womin*]
have all flat heads in this quarter both men and women.   They
are dirty in the extream, both in their person and cookery.
.ware their hare loose hanging in every direction.   They ask
high prices for what they Sell and Say that the white people
below give great prices for every thing &c.

The noses are all pierced and when they are dressed they

---

1 Elsewhere spelled "shappellel" and "shappalell"; the word is a corruption
of the Chinook *tsâ-po-lil*, meaning "bread" or "flour."   Gass says (p. 289) : "A
kind of bread the natives make of roots, and bake in the sun; and which is strong
and palatable."   In the Lewis and Clark collection of dried plants which is deposited
in the Philadelphia Academy of Natural Sciences is a specimen of "an umbelliferous
plant of the root of which the Wallowallows make a kind of bread.   The natives call
it Shappalell."   This Meehan identifies as *Cymopterus campestris*; but C. V. Piper,
of the Washington Agricultural experiment station, regards it as a species of *Loma-
tium.* — ED.

have a long tapered piece of white shell or wampum put through the nose, those Shells are about 2 inches in length.   I observed in maney of the villeages which I have passed, the heads of the female children in the press for the purpose of compressing their heads in their infancy into a certain form, between two boards[1]

---

[1] This custom is described by Gass (pp. 224–225). — ED.

CHAPTER XX

FROM THE RAPIDS TO THE SEA

Clark's Journal, November 2–21, 1805

[Clark, first draft :]   *Nov.* 2ᵈ *Saturday* 1805

MERIDIAN altitude 59° – 45′ – 45″. Made a portage of about 1½ miles with half of the Baggage, and run the rapid with the canoes without much damage, one struck a rock & split a little, and 3 others took in some water 7 squars came over the portage loaded with Dried fish & *Bear-grass,* Soon after 4 men came down in a canoe after takeing brackfast, & after taking a meridian altitude we set out Passed 2 bad rapids one at 2 & the other at 4 mile below the Isᵈ on Larᵈ and upper end of Strawberry Island on the Starᵈ Side   from the Creek end of last Course

S. 50° W.   5 miles to a timbered bottom on the Larᵈ Side, passed the Lower point of Strawbery Isᵈ at 3 miles, a Isᵈ covᵈ with wood below on Starᵈ Side   a remarkable high rock on Starᵈ Side about 800 feet high & 400 yds round, the *Beaten* Rock.   The mountains and bottoms thickly timbered with Pine Spruce Cotton and a kind of maple   Passed 2 small wooded Islands on Stᵈ side, below the lower Island on the Stard Side at 4 miles an Indian village of 9 Houses,   The river wider and bottoms more extencive.

S. 47° W.   12 miles to a Starᵈ point of rocks of a high clift of black rocks.   passed a Starᵈ Point at 4 miles.   here the mountains are low on each side & thickly timbered with pine.   river about 2 miles wide,   passed a rock at 10 miles in the middle of the river   this rock is 100 feet high & 80 feet Diameter, a deep bend to Starᵈ Side.

[188]

CAPE HORN, COLUMBIA RIVER

Labiech killed 14 Geese & a Brant   Collins one   Jos. Fields
& R[euben] 3   those gees are much smaller than common,
and have white under their rumps & around the tale,   The
tide rises here a fiew 9[1] Inches,   I cannot assertain the presise
hite it rises at the last rapid or at this place of camp.   The
Indians we left at the portage passed us this evening one other
canoe come up

S. 58° W. 4 miles to a Star.ᵈ point of a large bottom.   Encamped on
the Lar.ᵈ Side   river about 2 miles wide   country
thickly timbered   we Encamped behind a large rock
in the Lar.ᵈ Bend   A canoe with 7 Ind.ˢ came down &
encamped with us

November 2ⁿᵈ Saturday 1805

Examined the rapid below us more pert[i]celarly[2]   the
danger appearing too great to Hazzard our Canoes loaded,
dispatched all the men who could not Swim with loads to the
end of the portage below,   I also walked to the end of the
portage with the carriers where I delayed untill everry articles
was brought over and canoes arrived Safe.   here we brackfast
and took a Merid.ⁿ altitude *59° – 45′ – 45″*.   about the time
we were Setting out 7 Squars came over loaded with Dried
fish, and bear grass neetly buldled up,   Soon after 4 Indian
men came down over the rapid in a large canoe.   passed a
rapid at 2 miles & 1 at 4 miles opposit the lower point of a
high Island on the Lar.ᵈ Side, and a little below 4 Houses on
the Star.ᵈ Bank,   a Small creek on the Lar.ᵈ Side opposit Strawberry Island, which heads below the last rapid,   opposit the
lower point of this Island passed three Islands covered with
tall timber opposit the Beaten rock,   Those Islands are nearest
the Starboard Side; imediately below on the Star.ᵈ Side passed
a village of *nine* houses, which is Situated between 2 Small
creeks, and are of the Same construction of those above;   here
the river widens to near a mile, and the bottoms are more
extensive and thickly timbered, as also the high mountains on

---

[1] The figure 9 was inserted later. — ED.

[2] At this place the expedition is close by the town of Cascades, Wash. — ED.

each Side, with Pine, Spruce pine, cotton wood, a Species of ash, and alder.   at 17 miles passed a rock near the middle of the river, about 100 feet high and 80 feet Diameeter,   proceed on down a smoth gentle Stream of about 2 miles wide, in which the tide has its effect as high as the Beaten rock or the Last rapids at Strawberry Island,   saw great numbers of waterfowl of Different kinds, such as Swan, Geese, white & grey brants, ducks of various kinds, Guls, & Pleaver.   Labiesh killed 14 brant Joseph Fields 3 & Collins one.   we encamped under a high projecting rock on the Lar.ᵈ Side,   here the mountains leave the river on each Side, which from the great Shute to this place is high and rugid; thickly covered with timber principalley of the Pine Species.   The bottoms below appear extensive and thickly covered with wood.   river here about 2-½ miles wide. Seven Indians in a canoe on their way down to trade with the nativs below, encamp with us,   those we left at the portage passed us this evening and proceeded on down.   The ebb tide rose here about 9 Inches, the flood tide must rise here much higher.   we made 29 miles to day from the Great Shute.

[Clark, first draft:]   *November 3ʳᵈ Sunday 1805*

 The fog so thick this morning we did not think it prudent to set out untill 10 oClock   we set out and proceeded on verry well, accompanied by our Indian friends.   This morning *Labich* killed 3 Geese flying Collins killed a Buck.   The water rose [figure erased] Inches last night the effects of *tide*.   The Countrey has a handsome appearance in advance   no mountains extensive bottoms.   the water shallow for a great distance from shore.   The fog continued thick untill 12 oClock, we coasted and halted at the mouth of a large river on the Lar.ᵈ Side,   this river throws out emence quantitys of sand and is verry shallow, the narrowest part 200 yards wide   bold current, much resembling the river Plat,[1]   several Islands about 1 mile up and has a sand bar of 3 miles in extent imedeately in its mouth,   dischargeing it[s] waters by 2 mouths, and crowding its corse sands so as to throw the Columbian waters on its

---

[1] Now Sandy River, draining the western slope of Mount Hood. — ED.

Nothern banks, & conf.^d it to ½ m^l in width   Passed a small
Prarie on the Star.^d Side above, a large creek opposit *Qk Sand
River* on the Star.^d Side, extensive bottoms and low hilley
Countrey on each side (*good wintering Place*) a high peeked
mountain suppose to be Mt Hood is on the Lar^d Side S. 85° E.
40 miles distant from the mouth of quick Sand river.

Course Nov. 3.^d

West   3 miles to the upper mouth of quick Sand river, countrey
            low on each side riseing to a hilley countrey   passed a
            large creek opposit St.^d Side & 2 sand bars

S. 70.° W. 7 miles to the upper point of a large Island covered with
            [blank space in MS.]   passed the Lower Mouth of
            Sandy river at 3 Miles opposit the head of a large
            Island St^d Side faced with rocks and the side is pine &
            cotton   a large creek falls in opposit to the head of
            this Island — Isl^d of Fowls as I saw some 1000 pass
            over — on the Star^d Side   passed some ruged rocks in
            the middle of the river opposit the Island.   river wide
            The Countrey below quick Sand river on the Lard.
            Side is low, Piney Countrey.   Passed the lower point
            of the Island at 3½ miles long & 1½ wide.   emence
            quantity of Geese, Brants, Ducks & sea otters, some
            of the large & small kind of Swan & Sand hill cranes,
            also Luns & white gulls

S. 87.° W. 3 miles on the North Side of the Island and Encamped we
            met 2 canoes of Indians 15 in number who informed
            us they had seen 3 Vestles 2 days below us, we
            camped on the Island, and sent out hunters on it and
            Capt Lewis walked out, after Dark Capt Lewis with
   ____   3 men went into a large Pond on this Island & killed
    13   a swan & several ducks.   The Party killed this day 3
            swan 8 Brant, & 5 Ducks.   The canoe was borrowed
            of the Ind.^s here & taken over by 4 men into the pond.
            I gave the Indians a Brant to eate.

November 3.^d Sunday 1805

The Fog so thick this morning that we could not see a man
50 Steps off, this fog detained us untill 10 oClock at which

time we Set out, accompanied by our Indian friends who are
from a village near the great falls,   previous to our Setting out
Collins killed a large Buck, and Labiech killed 3 Geese flying.
I walked on the Sand beech Lar.d Side, opposit the canoes as
they passed along.   The under groth rushes, vines &c. in the
bottoms too thick to pass through,   at 3 miles I arrived at the
enterance of a river which appeared to scatter over a Sand bar,
the bottom of which I could See quit[e] across and did not
appear to be 4 Inches deep in any part ;   I attempted to wade
this Stream and to my astonishment found the bottom a quick
Sand, and impassable.   I called to the Canoes to put to Shore,
I got into the Canoe and landed below the mouth, & Cap.t Lewis
and my Self walked up this river about 1-½ mile to examine
this river which we found to be a verry considerable Stream
Dischargeing its waters through 2 chanels which forms an Island
of about 3 miles in length on the river and 1-½ miles wide, composed of corse sand which is thrown out of this quick sand river
compressing the waters of the Columbia and throwing the
whole current of its waters against its Northern banks, within
a chanel of ½ a mile wide,   Several Small Islands 1 mile up
this river,   This Stream has much the appearance of the *River
Platt.* roleing its quick sands into the bottoms with great
velocity after which it is divided into 2 chanels by a large sand
bar before mentioned,   the narrowest part of this River is 120
yards   on the Opposit Side of the Columbia a large Creek
[*small river called Seal river*] [1] falls in   above this creek on the
Same Side is a Small prarie.   extensive low country on each
Side, thickly timbered.

The Quick Sand river appears to pass through the low
countrey at the foot of those high range of mountains in a
Southerly direction.   The large Creek which falls into the
Columbia on the Star.d Side rise in the Same range of mountains to the N. N. E. and pass through some ridgey land.
A Mountain which we Suppose to be M.t Hood, is S. 85° E
about 47 miles distant from the mouth of quick sand river.
This Mt.n is covered with Snow and in the range of mountains
which we have passed through and is of a conical form but

---

1 Seal River is now known as Washougal in Clarke County, Washington. — ED.

rugid.[1]   after takeing dinner at the mouth of this river we proceeded on passed the head of a Island near the lar[d] Side back
of which on the Same Side and near the head a large Creek
falls in, and nearly opposit & 3 miles below the upper mouth
of quick Sand river, is the lower mouth,   This Island is 3-½
miles long, has rocks at the upper point, Some timber on the
borders of this Island, in the middle open and ponney [*pondy*
— *i. e.*, containing ponds].   Some rugid rocks in the middle of
the Stream opposit this Island.   proceeded on to the center
of a large Island in the middle of the river which we call
Dimond Island from its appearance,   here we met 15 Ind[n] men
in 2 canoes from below,   they informed us they Saw 3 vestles
below &c. &c.   we landed on the North side of this Dimond
Island and Encamped,[2] Cap[t] L walked out with his gun on the
Island, sent out hunters & fowlers.   below quick Sand River
the Countrey is low rich and thickly timbered on each Side of
the river, the Islands open & some ponds   river wide and
emence numbers of fow!s flying in every direction, Such as
Swan, geese, Brants, Cranes, Stalks [*Storks*], white guls, comerants & plevers &c.   also great numbers of Sea Otter in the
river.   a canoe arrived from the village below the last rapid
with a man his wife and 3 children, and a woman whome had
been taken prisoner from the Snake Ind[s] on Clarks River [*on
a river from the South which we found to be Mulknoma*[3]]   I sent
the Interpreters wife who is a *So so ne* or Snake Indian of the
Missouri, to Speake to this squar,   they could not understand
each other Sufficiently to converse.   This family and the Ind[s]
we met from below continued with us.   Cap[t] Lewis borrowed
a Small canoe of those Indians & 4 men took her across to a
Small lake in the Isl[d]   Cap[t] L. and 3 men set out after night
in this canoe in serch of the Swans, Brants Ducks &c. &c.

---

[1] Mount Hood (11,225 feet) was first sighted by Lieutenant Broughton of Vancouver's expedition, October 29th, 1792.   He named it for an English admiral, who
was later Lord Bridport.— ED.

[2] Now Government Island ; nearly opposite whose lower end is East Portland,
Oregon. — ED.

[3] The Multnomah River, which name has been applied, sometimes to the entire
course of the Willamette, sometimes to the lower part only, from its junction (at
Oregon City) with the Clackamas. — ED.

which appeared in great numbers in the Lake,   he killed a
Swan and Several Ducks, which made our number of fowls
this evening 3 Swan, 8 brant and 5 Ducks, on which we made
a Sumpteous supper.   We gave the Indian who lent the Canoe
a brant, and some meat to the others.   one of those Indians,
the man from the village near the Lower Rapids has a gun
with a brass barrel & cock of which he prises highly — Note
the mountain we saw from near the forks proves to be Mount
Hood

[Clark, first draft:]   *Nov.* 4*th Monday* 1805

a cloudy cool morning, wind West,   we set out at ½ past 8
oClock haveing dispatched 4 men in the small canoe to hunt

Course

West   6 miles to the North side & lower point of a large Island,
           passed the lower point of dimon[d] Island at 3 miles,
           a little below the head of a large Island on the
           Lar^d Side (river wide and Countrey low on both Sides
           & thickly covered with pine)   this Island is seperated
           from one on its Lar^d by a narrow chan! in which there
           is only water in high tide.   which rises here 18 Inches.
           high tide at 6 oClock P M

We landed at a village 200 men of Flatheads of 25 houses
50 canoes built of straw,   we were treated very kindly by them,
they gave us round root near the size of a hens egg roasted
which they call *Wap-to* to eat.

N. 88° W. 6 miles to Point on the Star^d Side passed a village [of] 25
          Houses on the Lar^d mane shore,   those houses are
          differently built from those above all except one verry
          large house covered with bark & Thached with straw.
          verry worm
N. 80° W. 3 miles on the Star^d Side,   a Pon[d] and a small plain on
          St^d Side   passed the head of an Island at 1 mile near
          the middle of the river to a 2^d Island ops^d the end of
          this course

N. 76° W. 4 miles on the Star^d Side passed a Island near the large
Island L^d a range of high hills on the Lar^d Side running S E. & N W. leaveing a large bottom on the
river.

I walked out on the Star^d Side found the country
fine,   an open Prarie for 1 mile back of which the
wood land comence riseing back,   the timber on the
edge of the Prarie is white oke,   back is spruce pine &
other species of Pine mixed   some under groth of a
wild crab & a species of wood I'm not acquainted
[with],   a species of maple & cotton wood grow near
this river, some low bushes

Indians continue to be with us, several canoes continue with
us,   The Indians at the last village have more cloth and Uro-
pean trinkets than above   I saw some Guns, a sword, maney
Powder flasks, salers Jackets, overalls, hats & shirts, Copper
and Brass trinkets with few Beeds only.   dureing the time I
was at Dinner the Indians stole my tomahawk which I made
use of to smoke   I serched but could not find it,   a Pond on
the Star^d Side off from the river.   Raspberries and [blank
space in MS.] are also in the bottoms   met a large and small
canoe with 12 men from below   the men were dressed with a
variety of articles of European manufactory   the large canoe
had emiges on the bow & stern handsomly carved in wood &
painted with the figure of a Bear in front & man in a stern.
Saw white geese with black wings.   Saw a small crab-apple
with all the taste & flavor of the common.   Those Indians
were all armed with Pistols or bows and arrows ready sprung
war axes &c.

N W.   3 miles on the Star^d Side passed the Lower point of Immage
canoe Island and 4 small Islands at its lower point all
on the Lar^d Side.
N. 35° W. 1 mile on the Star^d Side, bottoms low and extensive not
subject to over flow,   river about 1½ miles wide
North   3 miles to a white tree on the Star^d Side.   high tide here at
5 oClock P. M.

Mount Hellen bears N. 25° E about 80 miles,   this is the
mountain we saw near the forks of this river.   it is emensely

high and covered with snow, riseing in a kind of cone   perhaps the highest pinecal from the common leavel in America passed a village of 4 h: on the Star^d Side at 2 mi[l]es, one at 3m^ls.

N. 28° W. 3 miles to a stard bend & camped near a village on the
St^d Side   passed one on each side.   proceded on untill
after dark to get clere of Indians   we could not   2
___   canoes pursued us and 2 others came to us, and were
29   about us all night   we bought a fiew roots &c.

One deer 2 Ducks & Brant killed

November 4th Monday 1805

A cloudy cool morning wind from the West   we Set out at ½ past 8 oClock,   one man Shannon set out early to walk on the Island to kill something, he joined us at the lower point with a Buck.   This Island is 6 miles long and near 3 miles wide thinly timbered   (Tide rose last night 18 inches perpendicular at Camp)   near the lower point of this dimond Island is the head of a large Island Seperated from a Small one by a narrow chanel, and both Situated nearest the Lar^d. Side, those Islands as also the bottoms are thickly covered with Pine &c.   river wide, country low on both Sides;   on the Main Lar^d. Shore a Short distance below the last Island we landed at a village of *25 houses* : 24 of those houses we[re] thached with Straw, and covered with bark, the other House is built of boards in the form of those above, except that it is above ground and about 50 feet in length [*and covered with broad split boards*]   This village contains about 200 Men of the *Skilloot*[1] nation   I counted 52 canoes on the bank in front of this village maney of them verry large and raised in bow.   we recognized the man who over took us last night, (*our pilot who came in his canoe*)   he invited us to a lodge in which he had Some part and gave us a roundish roots about the Size of a Small Irish potato which they roasted in the embers until they became Soft,   This root they call *Wap-pa-to* the *Bulb* of

---

[1] This was the tribe known to later travellers as Kreluit.   They were of lower Chinookan origin, and acted as middlemen between the Indians of the coast and those higher up the river. — ED.

which the Chinese cultivate in great quantities called the *Sa-git ti folia* or common arrow head,[1] (*we believe it to be the Same*) it has an agreeable taste and answers verry well in place of bread.   we purchased about 4 bushels of this root and divided it to our party,

at 7 miles below this village passed the upper point of a large Island nearest the Lar.ᵈ Side, a Small Prarie in which there is a pond opposit on the Star.ᵈ   here I landed and walked on Shore, about 3 miles   a fine open Prarie for about 1 mile, back of which the countrey rises gradually and wood land comencies Such as white oake, pine of different kinds, wild crabs [*with the taste and flavour of the common crab*] and Several Species of undergroth of which I am not acquainted,   a few cotton wood trees & the Ash of this countrey [2] grow scattered on the river bank,   Saw Some Elk and Deer Sign, and joined Cap.ᵗ Lewis at a place he had landed with the party for Diner.   Soon after Several canoes of Indians from the village above came down, dressed for the purpose as I supposed of Paying us a friendly visit,   they had scarlet & blue blankets Salor Jackets, overalls, Shirts and hats independant of their usial dress ;   the most of them had either [*war axes Spears or Bows Sprung with quivers of arrows,*] Muskets or pistols and tin flasks to hold their powder,   Those fellows we found assumeing and disagreeable, however we Smoked with them and treated them with every attention & friendship.

dureing the time we were at dinner those fellows Stold my pipe Tomahawk which they were Smoking with,   I imediately serched every man and the canoes, but could find nothing of my Tomahawk,   while Serching for the Tomahawk one of those Scoundals Stole a cappoe [*Capotte (gr: coat)*] of one of our interperters, which was found Stufed under the root of a tree,

---

[1] The roots of the common arrowhead (*Sagittaria latifolia*), also common through-out the Northern States ; the species cultivated in China is *S. sinensis*.   Until a recent revision of the American genus by J. G. Smith several species were confused.   These tubers form an important article of food among many Northwestern tribes.   It is some-times called "swamp potato." — ED.

[2] The white oak of the Columbia is *Quercus garryana*; the wild crab is *Pyrus rivularis* Dougl. ; the cotton wood is *Populus trichocarpa* T. & Gr. ; the ash is *Fraxinus oregana* Nutt. — C. V. PIPER.

near the place they Sat, we became much displeased with
those fellows, which they discovered and moved off on their
return home to their village, except 2 canoes which had passed
on down. we proceeded on met a large & a Small canoe from
below with 12 men the large canoe was orninented with
Images carved in wood the figures of a Bear in front & a man
in Stern, Painted & fixed verry netely on the canoe, rising to near
the hight of a man two Indians verry finely Dressed & with
hats on was in this canoe passed the lower point of the
Island¹ which is *nine* miles in length haveing passed 2 Islands
on the Star.ᵈ Side of this large Island, three Small Islands at its
lower point. the Indians make Signs that a village is Situated
back of those Islands on the Lar.ᵈ Side. and I believe that
a chanel is Still on the Lrᵈ. Side as a canoe passed in between the Small Islands, and made Signs that way, probably to traffick with some of the nativs liveing on another
chanel, at 3 miles lower, and 12 Leagues below quick sand
river passed a village of four large houses (*Mulknomans*) on the
Lar.ᵈ Side, near which we had a full view of M.ᵗ *Helien* [St.
Helens] which is perhaps the highest pinical in America
[*from their base*] it bears N. 25°. E. about 90 miles. This
is the mountain I saw from the Muscle Shell rapid on the
19ᵗʰ of October last covered with Snow, it rises Something in
the form of a Sugar lofe² about a mile lower passed a Single
house on the Lar.ᵈ Side, and one on the Star.ᵈ Side, passed
a village on each side and camped near a house on the Star.ᵈ Side
we proceeded on untill one hour after dark with a view to get
clear of the nativs who was constantly about us, and troublesom, finding that we could not get Shut of those people for
one night, we landed and Encamped on the Star.ᵈ Side³ Soon

---

¹ Named by the explorers Image-canoe, and later Wappatoo ; now known as
Sauvies Island. As it lies across the entrance to the Multnomah, that river was not
seen by Lewis and Clark in passing it ; but, hearing of it on the return trip, Clark
ascended it for a short distance (April 3, 1806). — ED.

² This was probably the explorers' first view of Mount St. Helens, which rises to
an altitude of 9,750 feet in Skamania County, Washington. This peak was first
sighted by Vancouver in May, 1792, and named the following October, in honor of
Lord St. Helens, then British ambassador at Madrid. — ED.

³ Probably near Knapp's Landing, Washington, a few miles below the mouth of
the Multnomah. — ED.

after 2 canoes came to us loaded with Indians, we purchased a fiew roots of them.

This evening we saw vines much resembling the raspberry which is verry thick in the bottoms.   A range of high hills at about 5 miles on the Lar.ᵈ side which runs S. E. & N. W. covered with tall timber   the bottoms below in this range of hills and the river is rich and leavel,   Saw white geese with a part of their wings black.   the river here is 1-½ miles wide, and current jentle.   opposit to our camp on a Small Sandy Island the brant & geese make such a noise that it will be impossible for me to sleap.   we *made 29 miles* to day

Killed a Deer and Several brant and ducks.   [*I saw a Brarow tamed at the 1.ˢᵗ village to day*]   The Indians which we have pass.ᵈ to day (*in their boats were of*) of the *Scil-loot* nation (*going up to the falls — differ a little*) in their language from those near & about the long narrows of the *Che-luc-it-te-quar* or *E-chee-lute,*   their dress differ but little, except they have more of the articles precured from the white traders,   they all have flatened heads both men and women, live principally on fish and *Wap pa too* roots,   they also kill some fiew Elk and Deer,   dureing the short time I remained in their village they brought in three Deer which they had killed with their Bow & arrows.   They are thievishly inclined as we have experienced.

.

[Clark, first draft:]   *Nov.ʳ 5ᵗʰ Tuesday* 1805

a cloudy morning   some rain the after part of last night & this morning.   I could not sleep for the noise kept [up] by the Swans, Geese, White & black brants Duck &.ᶜ on a opposit base, & sand hill Crane, they were emencly numerous and their noise horrid.   We set out at sun rise & course

N. 35.° W   3 miles to a Star.ᵈ point   river about ¾ of a mile wide   a small prarie on the St.ᵈ

N. 30.° W.   3 miles to the South West Side of an Island seperated from the Star.ᵈ Side by a narrow chanel   river widens to about 1 ½ miles   *Green bryor* Is.ᵈ

N. 12° W. 3 miles to a Lar⁴ point of rocks opposit the upper p⁴ of an
  Is⁴ on St⁴ Side ps⁴ 2 houses on the Lar⁴ Side, passed
  the lower p⁴ of the Island St⁴ at 2 miles. behind this
  Island a little above the lower point on the St⁴ side is a
  large village of ¼ of a mile in extent. I counted 14
  large houses in front next the slew [slough] 7 canoes
  loaded with Indians came of [f] to see us. low rock

N. 22° W. 6 miles to a Star⁴ point passed a large slew ¼ of a mile
  wide or at a ½ of a mile on the Lar⁴ Side some low
  rockey clifts below. The language of those people
  have a great similarity to those above. Met 3 canoes
  of Indians

N. 30. W. 5 miles to a point of woodland Star⁴ side. a range of high
  hills here forms the Star⁴ bank of the river, the shore
  bold and rocky covered with a thick growth of pine
  timber an extensive low Island & bottom on the
  Lar⁴ side[1] passed 2 Islands on St⁴ & the Low⁴ p⁴ of 3⁴

N. 40. W. 7 m. to a point of woodland St⁴ passed the Lower point
  of the Island close under the Lar⁴ Side at 5 miles a
  small Island in the middle of the river. passed an old
  village on the Island at 3 miles. The high hills leave
  the river on the Star⁴ at 3 miles a high bottom below
  met 4 canoes of Indians one of those canoes had
  emiges bow & stern & 26 Indians in them all

N. 40° W. 5 miles to a point of high piney land on the Lar⁴ Side the
  Star⁴ Shore bold and rockey passed a Creek at 2 miles
  on the Star⁴ Side. below which is an old village. rained
  _32_ all the evening and some fine rain at intervals all day
  river wide & Deep

our hunters killed 10 Brant 4 of which were white with
black wings 2 Ducks, and a Swan which were divided. We
came too and Encamped on the Lar⁴ Side under a high ridgey
land, the high land come to the river on each side. the river
about 1½ mile wide the high lands rise gradually from the
river & bottoms. we are all wet cold and disagreeable, rain
continues & encreases. I killed a Pheasent which is very fat.
my feet and legs cold. I saw 17 Snakes to day on a Island
but little appearance of Frost in this place.

---

[1] This course to the word " side " is entered in Lewis's handwriting. — ED.

November 5ᵗʰ Tuesday 1805

Rained all the after part of last night, rain continues this morning, I [s]lept but verry little last night for the noise Kept [up] dureing the whole of the night by the Swans, Geese, white & Grey Brant Ducks &c. on a Small Sand Island close under the Larᵈ Side; they were emensely noumerous, and their noise horid. we Set out early here the river is not more than ¾ of a mile in width, passed a Small Prarie on the starᵈ Side, passed 2 houses about ½ a mile from each other on the Larᵈ Side a canoe came from the upper house, with 3 men in it mearly to view us, passed an Islᵈ covered with tall trees & green briers Seperated from the Starᵈ Shore by a narrow chanel at 9 miles, I observed on the Chanel which passes on the Starᵈ Side of this Island a short distance above its lower point is Situated a large village, the front of which occupies nearly ¼ of a mile fronting the Chanel, and closely connected, I counted 14 houses (*Quathlapotle*[1] *nation*) in front here the river widens to about 1-½ miles. Seven canoes of Indians came out from this large village to view and trade with us, they appeared orderly and well disposed, they accompanied us a fiew miles and returned back. about 1-½ miles below this village on the Larᵈ Side behind a rockey Sharp point, we passed a chanel ¼ of a mile wide [Willamette slough], which I take to be the one the Indian canoe entered yesterday from the lower point of *Immaged Canoe* Island so named Some low clifts of rocks below this chanel, a large Island close under the Starᵈ Side opposit, and 2 Small Islands, below, here we met 2 canoes from below, below those Islands a range of high hills form the Starᵈ Bank of the river, the shore bold and rockey, covered with a groth of Pine, an extensive low Island, Seperated from the Larᵈ side by a narrow chanel, on this Island we Stoped to Dine I walked out, found it open & covered with grass interspersed with small ponds, in which was great numbᵣˢ of foul, the remains of an old village on the lower part of this Island, I saw Several deer, our hunters killed on this Island a Swan, 4 white 6 grey brant & 2 Ducks

---

[1] The Cathlapotle tribe of the Chinookan family ; of that stock but few remnants now exist. —POWELL (*U. S. Bur. Ethnol. Rep.*,1886, pp. 65, 66).

all of them were divided, below the lower point of this Island a range of high hills which runs S. E. forms the Lar.ᵈ bank of the river the Shores bold and rockey & hills covered with pine. The high hills leave the river on the Star.ᵈ Side, a high bottom between the hill & river. We met 4 Canoes of Indians from below, in which there is 26 Indians, one of those canoes is large, and ornimented with *Images* on the bow & Stern. That in the Bow [is] the likeness of a Bear, and in Stern the picture of a man. we landed on the Lar.ᵈ Side & camped a little below the mouth of a creek[1] on the Star.ᵈ Side a little below the mouth of which is an Old village which is now abandaned ; here the river is about one and a half miles wide, and deep, The high Hills which run in a N. W. & S. E. derection form both banks of the river the Shore boald and rockey, the hills rise gradually & are Covered with a thick groth of pine &c. The valley which is from above the mouth of Quick Sand River to this place may be computed at 60 miles wide on a Derect line, & extends a great Distance to the right & left, rich thickly covered with tall timber, with a fiew Small Praries bordering on the river and on the Islands ; Some fiew standing Ponds & Several Small Streams of running water on either Side of the river ; This is certainly a fertill and a handsom valley, at this time crouded with Indians. The day proved cloudy with rain the greater part of it, we are all wet cold and disagreeable — I saw but little appearance of frost in this valley which we call Columbia [or] Wap-pa-too Valley (*Columbian valley*) from that root or plants growing Spontaniously in this valley only In my walk of to Day I saw 17 Striped Snakes I killed a grouse which was verry fat, and larger than common. This is the first night which we have been entirely clear of Indians since our arrival on the waters of the Columbia River. we made 32 miles to day by estimation.

---

[1] The Creek was the present Kalama River, Washington. — ED.

[Clark, first draft:]   *November 6.ᵗʰ Wednesday*

a cold wet morning   rain cont.ᵈ untill [blank space in MS.]
oClock   we set out early & proceeded on the course of last
night &.ᶜ

N. 50.° W.   1 mile on the Larᵈ Side under some high land.   bold
rockey shores

N. 60.° W.   1 mile under a bold rockey shore on the Larᵈ Side ops.ᵈ the
upper point of a Island close under the Starᵈ Side the
high lands closeing the river on that side   above river
wide

N. 75.° W.   12 miles to a point of high land on the Larᵈ Side, passed
two Lodges on the Larᵈ Side at 2 miles in a bottom,
The high land leave the river on the Star.ᵈ Side.
passed a remarkable knob of high land on the Star.ᵈ
Side at 3 miles Close on the waters edge.   we purchased of the Indians who came in their canoes to us
with salmon trout and *Wap-to* roots. Some of their
salmon [t]rout roots & 2 Dressed Beaver skins for
which I gave 5 small fishing hooks.   passed a Island
nearest the Larᵈ Side   at 10 mile the head of a
Is.ᵈ on St.ᵈ opposit High Cliffs, with several species
of Pine Cedars &.ᶜ arbor vitae & different species of
undergroth

N. 80.° W.   2 miles under a high clift on the Larᵈ Side the lower
point of the Island on Starᵈ opposit those hills are
covered thickly with spruce pine *arber vita* Hackme-
tack as called a kind of alder red wood &.ᶜ &.ᶜ rain
continue[s]

N. 88.° W.   5 miles to a high clift a little below an old village in the
Star.ᵈ bend and opposit an old village on a Lar.ᵈ point
of a handsom & extensive bottom.   passed a Island in
the middle of the river 3 miles long and one wide,
passed a small Island close on the Starᵈ Side & a
lower point of a former Isl.ᵈ below which the lands
high & with clifts to the river Star.ᵈ Side.

S. 45.° W.   5 miles under a clift of verry high land on the Star.ᵈ side
wind high a head.   we overtook 2 Indian canoes
going down to trade

S. 50.° W.   1 mile under a high rockey Hill of pine.   The Indians
leave us, steep assent, some clifts

S. 75° W.   1 mile under a high hill with a bold rockey shore, high
            steep assent   river about 1 mile wide

West   1 mile under a high steep hill bold rockey shore.   En-
            camped under the hill on stones scercely land suffi-
            cent between the hills and river clear of the tide for
            us to lie.   Cloudy & rain all wet and disagreeable.
            this evening made large fires on the stones and dried
            our bedding.   The flees are verry troublesome which
       ___ colect in our blankets at every old village we encamp
       29   at.   we killed nothing to day,   we halted to dine
            and the bushes so thick that our hunters could not get
            through, red wood, green bryors, a kind of Burch,
            alder, red holley a kind of maple &c &c   The species
            of Pine is Spruce Pine fir arber vitia &c red Loril,
            the bottoms have rushes grass & nettles,   the Slashes
            long grass bulrushes flags &c some willow on the
            waters edge

November 6th Wednesday 1805

A cool wet raney morning   we Set out early   at 4 miles
pass 2 Lodges of Indians in a Small bottom on the Lar.d Side
I believe those Indians to be travelers,   opposit is the head of
a long narrow Island close under the Starboard Side, back
of this Island two Creeks fall in about 6 miles apart, and
appear to head in the high hilley countrey to the N. E.   opposit
this long Island is 2 others one Small and about the middle of
the river (*an Island in the mouth of the large river Cow e liskee*[1]
*150 yds wide.   9 miles lower a large creek same side   between the
mouths of these rivers are 3 small islands one on the L.d shore one
near the middle*) the other larger and nearly opposit its lower
point, and opposit a high clift of Black rocks on the Lar.d Side
at 14 miles (*from our camp*):   here the Indians of the 2 Lodges
we passed to day came in their canoes with Sundery articles to
Sell,   we purchased of them *Wap-pa-too roots, salmon-trout*, and

---

[1] The Cowlitz River; at its mouth are Freeport and Monticello, Wash.   It
drains a large valley in a county of the same name, and through it the Northern
Pacific Railway now runs. — ED.

I purchased 2 beaver Skins for which I gave 5 small fish
hooks.   here the hills leave the river on the Lar.^d Side, a
butifull open and extensive bottom in which there is an old
Village, one also on the Star.^d Side a little above both of
which are abandened by all their inhabitents except Two
Small dogs nearly starved, and an unreasonable portion of
flees.   The Hills and Mountains are covered with Sever[al]
kinds of Pine, *Arber Vitea* or white cedar, *red Loril* [laurel],
alder and Several Species of under groth, the bottoms have
common rushes, nettles, & grass the Slashey parts have Bull
rushes & flags Some willow on the waters edge, passed an
Island (*near L.^d shore*) 3 miles long and one mile wide, (*& 2
sm. isl both*) one close under the Star.^d Side below the (*large
creek*) long narrow Island below which the Star.^d Hills are
verry [high] from the river bank and continues high and
rugid on that Side all day (*called Fanny's Island the large one.*)
we over took two Canoes of Indians going down to trade,[1]
one of the Indians Spoke a fiew words of english and Said
that the principal man who traded with them was Mr Haley,
and that he had a woman in his Canoe who Mr Haley was
fond of &c. he Showed us a Bow of Iron and Several other
things which he Said' Mr Haley gave him. we came too to
Dine on the long narrow Island found the woods so thick
with under groth that the hunters could not get any distance
into the Isl.^d the red wood, and Green bryers interwoven, and
mixed with pine, alder, a Speci[e]s of Beech, ash &c. we
killed nothing to day. The Indians leave us in the evening,
river about one mile wide hills high and Steep on the St.^d No
place for Several Miles suff[i]cently large and leavil for our
camp, we at length Landed at a place which by moveing the
stones we made a place Sufficently large for the party to lie
leavil on the Smaller Stones clear of the *Tide.* Cloudy with
rain all day we are all wet and disagreeable, had large fires
made on the Stone and dried our bedding and kill the flees,
which collected in our blankets at every old village we encamped near I had like to have forgotten a verry remarkable

---

1 The Indians in this part of the country have but few horses, their intercourse
and business being chiefly by water. — GASS (p. 232).

Knob[1] riseing from the edge of the water to about 80 feet high, and about 200 paces around at its Base and Situated on the long narrow Island above (*below the mouth of Cow e liske riv.*) and nearly opposit to the 2 Lodges we passed to day, it is some distance from the high land & in a low part of the Island.

(*camped opposite to the upper point of an Isl. aft.ª called Sturgeon Island*)[2]

[Clark, first draft :]   *November 7ᵗʰ Thursday* 1805

a cloudy fogey morning, a little rain. Set out at 8 oClock proceeded on

N. 82° W.	2½	miles on the Sta Side under a high hill steep assent
N. 45° W.	1½	miles and the high land on the Starᵈ Side steep assent
N. 60° W.	1	mile on the Stᵈ Side high hills a thick fog can't see across the River opposit the lower pᵗ of an Isᵈ
West	2	miles on the Starᵈ Side under a hill high and rockey
N W.	1	mile to the head of an Island close under the Starᵈ Side, sep. by a narrow chanel. 2 canoes of Indians met us, and return with us, a Island in the middle of the river, we followed those Indˢ on the North Side of the Island thro' a narrow chanel to their village on the Starᵈ Side of 4 houses, they gave us fish to eate and sold us fish salmon trout, some *Wap-to* roots and 3 Dogs, the language of those people have a similarrity with those above.

The women ware a kind of s[t]rand made of the cedar bark but soft in place of a tite pice of leather as worn by the women above. the men have nothing except a robe about them, they are badly made and use but fiew ornements. The womens peticoat is about 15 Inches long made of *arber-vita* or the white Cedar bark wove to a string and hanging down in tossles and [t]ied so as to cover from their hips as low as the peticoat will reach and only covers them when standing, as in any other

---

[1] Mount Coffin, a high isolated rock just below the mouth of Cowlitz River. It is a well-known landmark on the Columbia, so named because at its base were deposited the Indian dead, surrounded by their trophies. — ED.

[2] "Sturgeon Island" is now Puget's Island, named for Vancouver's lieutenant (1792). — ED.

position the Tosels seperate.   Those people sold us otter skins for fish hooks of which they were fond.

We delayed 1½ hours & set out the tide being in & the river so cut with Islands   we got an Indian to pilot us into the main chanel.   one of our canoes seperated from us this morning in the fog   great numbers of water fowls of every description common to this river

N. 10° W.   15 miles to a white tree in a Star.ᵈ bend under a high hill passed several marshey Islᵈ on the Star.ᵈ Side opposit to which & on the Star.ᵈ Side is a village of 4 houses. passed several marshey Islands on the Lar.ᵈ Sᵈ an Indian village on one of those Islands.   they came and traded 2 beaver skins for fishing hooks, and a fiew *Wapto* roots.   The river verry wide.   The beaver skins I wish for to make a robe as the one I have is worn out.   to an old village of 7 houses under the hill Star.ᵈ Side.   Several slashey Islᵈ on Stard Side,   we called and bought a Dog & some fish.

S W.   3 miles to a point of high land on the Star.ᵈ Side passed a small Island on Star.ᵈ Side the head of a large low marshy Island on the middle river about from 5 to 7 miles wide

S. 62° W.   5 miles to a Point Star.ᵈ Side a Deep bend to the Starᵈ Side under a high mountain.   pine

S. 70° W   3 miles to a point on the Star.ᵈ Side high mountains some high mountains on the Larᵈ Side off the river.   We encamped on the Starᵈ Side under a high hill steep and mountainous we with dificulty found leavel rocks

34   sufficent to lie on,   Three Indians followed us they could speake a little English, they were detected in stealing a knife & returned late to their village.   The rain continued untill 9 oClock moderately.   We are in view of the opening of the Ocian, which creates great joy.[1] a remarkable rock of about 50 feet high and about 20 feet Diameter is situated opposit our Camp about ½ a mile from shore   several marshey Islands towards the Larᵈ Side the shape of them I can't see as the river is wide and day foggy

---

[1] In the Courses and Distances given in Codex H, pp. 132–148, Clark writes, " *Ocian in view !* O ! the joy." — Ed.

November 7th Thursday 1805

A cloudy foggey morning Some rain.   we Set out early proceeded under the Star.d Side under a high rugid hills with Steep assent the Shore boalt and rockey, the fog so thick we could not See across the river,   two cano[e]s of Indians met and returned with us to their village which is Situated on the Star.d Side behind a cluster of Marshey Islands, on a narrow chan.l of the river through which we passed to the *village* of 4 Houses,   they gave us to eate Some fish, and Sold us, fish, *Wap pa to* roots three *dogs* and 2 otter skins for which we gave fish hooks principally of which they were verry fond.

Those people call themselves *War-ci-â-cum* (*War-ki-a-cum*)[1] and Speake a language different from the nativs above with whome they trade for the *Wapato* roots of which they make great use of as food.   their houses differently built, raised entirely above ground eaves about 5 feet from the ground Supported and covered in the same way of those above,   dores about the Same size but in the Side of the house in one corner, one fire place and that near the opposit end, around which they have their beads raised about 4 feet from the flore which is of earth,   under their beads they Store away baskets of dried fish Berries & *Wappato*, over the fire they hang the fiesh as they take them and [of] which they do not make immediate use. Their Canoes are of the Same form of those above.   The Dress of the men differ verry little from those above, The womin altogether different, their robes are Smaller only covering their Sholders & falling down to near the hip.   and Sometims when it is cold a piec of fur curiously plated[2] and connected so as to meet around the body from the arms to the hips.   "The garment which occupies the Waist and thence as low as the knee before and mid leg behind, cannot properly be called a petticoat, in the common accep[ta]tion of the word; it is a *Tissue* formed of white cedar bark bruised or broken into Small Strans, which are interwoven in their center by means of Several cords of the same Materials which Serves as well for

---

[1] A Chinookan tribe, apparently now extinct. — ED.

[2] Made out of small skins cut into thongs, and wove somewhat like carpeting. — GASS (p. 232).

a girdle as to hold in place the Strans of bark which forms the
tissue, and which Strans, confined in the middle, hang with
their ends pendulous from the waist, the whole being of Suff[i]
cent thickness when the female Stands erect to conceal those
parts useally covered from familiar view, but when she stoops
or places herself in any other attitude this battery of Venus is
not altogether impervious to the penetrating eye of the amorite.
This tissue is Sometims formed of little Strings of the Silk
grass twisted and knoted at their ends " &c. [*Those Indians
are low and ill Shaped all flat heads*]

after delaying at this village one hour and a half we Set out
piloted by an Indian dressed in a Salors dress, to the Main
Chanel of the river, the tide being in we should have found
much dificuelty in passing into the main Chanel from behind
those islands, without a pilot, a large marshey Island near the
middle of the river[1] near which several Canoes came allong
Side with Skins, roots fish &c. to Sell, and had a temporey
residence on this Island, here we see great numbers of water
fowls about those Marshey Islands; here the high mountan-
ious Countrey approaches the river on the Lard Side, a high
Mount? to the S. W. about 20 miles, the high mountan?
countrey continue on the Star? Side, about 14 miles below
the last village and 18 miles of this day we landed at a village
of the same nation. This village is at the foot of the high
hills on the Star? Side back of 2 small Islands it contains 7
indifferent houses built in the same form of those above, here
we purchased a Dog some fish, *wap pa to*, roots and I purchased
2 beaver Skins for the purpose of makeing me a *roab*, as the
robe I have is rotten and good for nothing. opposit to this
village the high mountaneous countrey leave[s] the river on
the Lar? Side below which the river widens into a kind of Bay
& is crouded with low Islands Subject to be covered by the
tides. We proceeded on about 12 miles below the Village
under a high mountaneous Countrey on the Star? Side, Shore
boald and rockey and Encamped under a high hill on the

---

[1] Now Tenasillihee Island. The high mountain to the southwest was Saddle
Mountain, a prominent landmark. — ED.

Star.ᵈ Side opposit to a rock¹ Situated half a mile from the
shore, about 50 feet high and 20 feet Deamieter; we with
dificuelty found a place clear of the tide and Sufficiently large
to lie on and the only place we could get was on round stones
on which we lay our mats   rain continu.ᵈ moderately all day &
Two Indians accompanied us from the last village,   they we
detected in Stealing a knife and returned,   our Small Canoe
which got Seperated in the fog this morning joined us this
evening from a large Island situated nearest the Lard Side
below the high hills on that Side, the river being too wide to
See either the form Shape or Size of the Islands on the Lard
Side.

Great joy in camp   we are in *view* of the *Ocian*,² (*in the
morning when fog cleared off just below last village (first on leaving
this village) of Warkiacum*) this great Pacific Octean which we
been so long anxious to See. and the roreing or noise made by
the waves brakeing on the rockey Shores (as I suppose) may
be heard disti[n]ctly

We made 34 miles to day as computed.

[Clark, first draft:]   *Nov.ʳ 8ᵗʰ Friday 1805*

   a cloudy morning some rain and wind   we changed our
clothes and set out at 9 oClock   proceeded on close under the
Star.ᵈ Side

S. 63.° W. 2 miles to a point on the Star.ᵈ Side passing under high
            mountainious country.   some low Islands opposit at
            about 3 miles   3 Inds in a canoe over took us
S. 60.° W. 6 miles to Cape swells³ on the Starᵈ Side, a Deep bend to
            the Star.ᵈ Side   high country on both sides,   passed an
            old village 2 H.ˢ at 1 mile on Stᵈ 4 houses at 3 miles and
            halted to dine at an old village of several in a deep bay
            on the Star.ᵈ Side of 5 miles Deep.   several arms still
            further into the land   saw great numbers of Swan
            Geese and Ducks in this shallow bay,

---

¹ This is the present Pillar Rock. — Eᴅ.
² The ocean could not possibly be seen from this point, although during a storm the
breakers might be heard.   The explorers probably mistook the great bay of the river,
which just below this point widens to fifteen miles, for the expanse of the ocean. — Eᴅ.
³ Cape Swells was the upper boundary of Gray's Bay. — Eᴅ.

Cloudy and disagreeable all the Day. Great maney flees at this old village, R. Fields killed a goose & 2 canvis back Ducks in this bay   after Dinner we took the advantage of the returning tide & proceeded on to the 2ᵈ point, at which place we found the Swells too high to proceed   we landed and drew our canoes up so as to let the tide leave them.   The three Indians [left] after selling us 4 fish for which we gave seven small fishing hooks, and a pice of red cloth.   Some fine rain at intervals all this day.   the swells continued high all the evening & we are compelled to form an Encampment on a Point scercely room sufficent for us all to lie cleare of the tide water.   hills high & with a steep assent, river wide & at this place too salt to be used for Drink.   we are all wet and dis-agreeable, as we have been continually for several days past, we are at a loss & cannot find out if any settlement is near the mouth of this river.   The swells were so high and the canoes roled in such a manner as to cause several to be verry sick. Reuben fields, Wiser McNeal & the Squar wer of the number

November 8ᵗʰ Friday 1805

A cloudy morning Some rain,   we did not Set out untill 9 oClock, haveing changed our Clothing.   proceeded on close under the Starᵈ Side, the hills high with steep assent, Shore boald and rockey   Several low Islands in a Deep bend or Bay to the Larᵈ Side, river about 5 or 7 miles wide,   three Indians in a Canoe overtook us, with salmon to Sell,   passed 2 old villages on the Starᵈ Side and at 3 miles entered a nitch of about 6 miles wide and 5 miles deep with Several Creeks makeing into the Starᵈ Hill,   this nitch we found verry Shallow water and call it the Shallow nitch, (*Bay*)[1]   we came too at the remains of an old village at the bottom of this nitch and dined, here we Saw great numbers of fowl,   Sent out 2 men and they killed a Goose and two *canves back* Ducks   here we found great numbers of flees which we treated with the greatest caution

---

[1] Now Gray's Bay in Wahkiakum County, Washington.   This was named for Capt. Robert Gray of Boston, who in 1792 discovered the mouth of Columbia River and named it for his ship.   It was upon his discovery that the United States based its claims to the Oregon country. — ED.

and distance; after Diner the Indians left us and we took the advantage of a returning tide and proceeded on to the Second point on the St.ᵈ here we found the Swells or Waves so high that we thought it imprudent to proceed; we landed unloaded and drew up our Canoes.[1] Some rain all day at intervales, we are all wet and disagreeable, as we have been for Several days past, and our present Situation a verry disagreeable one in as much, as we have not leavel land Sufficient for an encampment and for our baggage to lie cleare of the tide, the High hills jutting in so close and steep that we cannot retreat back, and the water of the river too Salt to be used, added to this the waves are increasing to Such a hight that we cannot move from this place, in this Situation we are compelled to form our camp between the hite of the Ebb and flood tides, and rase our baggage on logs. We are not certain as yet if the white people who trade with those people or from whome they pre-cure their goods are Stationary at the mouth, or visit this quarter at stated times for the purpose of trafick &c. I believe the latter to be the most probable conjecture. The Seas roled and tossed the Canoes in such a manner this evening that Several of our party were Sea sick.

[Clark, first draft:]   *Nov.ʳ 9ᵗʰ Saturday 1805*

The tide of last night obliged us to unload all the canoes one of which sunk before she was unloaded by the high waves or swells which accompanied the returning tide, The others we unloaded, and 3 others was filled with water soon after by the swells or high sees which broke against the shore imediately where we lay, rained hard all the fore part of the day, the [tide] which rose untill 2 oClock P M to day brought with it such emence swells or waves, aded to a hard wind from the south which loosened the drift trees which is verry thick on the shore, and tossed them about in such a manner, as to en-danger our canoes very much, with every exertion and the strictest attention by the party was scercely sufficent to defend our canoes from being crushed to pieces between those emencly

---

[1] This was Gray's Point, the western boundary of the bay of that name. — ED.

large trees maney of them 200 feet long and 4 feet through.
The tide of this day rose about [blank space in MS.] feet &
15 Inches higher than yesterday this is owing to the wind
which sets in from the Ocian, we are compelled to move our
camp from the water, as also the loading every man as wet
all the last night and this day as the rain could make them
which contin.ᵈ all day. at 4 oClock the wind shifted about to
the S. W imediately from the Ocian and blew a storm for about
2 hours, raised the tide verry high all wet & cold Labiech
killed 4 Ducks very fat & R. Fields saw Elk sign. not withstanding the disagreeable time of the party for several days past
they are all chearfull and full of anxiety to see further into the
Ocian, the water is too salt to drink, we use rain water. The
salt water has acted on some of the party already as à Pergitive.
rain continues.

November 9ᵗʰ Saturday 1805

The tide of last night did not rise Sufficiently high to come
into our camp, but the Canoes which was exposed to the mercy
of the waves &c. which accompanied the returning tide, they
all filled, and with great attention we Saved them untill the
tide left them dry. wind Hard from the South, and rained
hard all the fore part of the day, at 2 oClock P M the flood
tide came in accompanied with emence waves and heavy winds,
floated the trees and Drift which was on the point on which
we Camped and tosed them about in such a manner as to en-
danger the canoes verry much, with every exertion and the
Strictest attention by every individual of the party was scercely
sufficient to Save our Canoes from being crushed by those
monsterous trees maney of them nearly 200 feet long and from
4 to 7 feet through. our camp entirely under water dureing
the hight of the *tide*, every man as wet as water could make them
all the last night and to day all day as the rain continued all
day, at 4 oClock P M the wind Shifted about to the S. W.
and blew with great violence imediately from the Ocean for
about two hours, notwithstanding the disagreeable Situation
of our party all wet and cold (and one which they have ex-

perienced for Several days past) they are chearfull and anxious to See further into the Ocian, The water of the river being too Salt to use we are obliged to make use of rain water. Some of the party not accustomed to Salt water has made too free a use of it on them it acts as a pergitive.

At this dismal point we must Spend another night as the wind & waves are too high to proceed.

[Clark, first draft:] *November 10th Sunday 1805*

rained verry hard the greater part of the last night & continues this morning, the wind has layed and the swells are fallen. we loaded our canoes and proceeded on, passed a Deep Bay on the Star.d Side I call [blank space in MS.]

S. W. 8 miles to point on the Star.d Side passed a deep Bay and 6 points on the Star.d Side rained hard saw enoumurable quantites of sea guls. and Ducks.

The wind rose from the N W. and the swells became so high, we were compelled to return about 2 miles to a place where we could unl.d our canoes, which was in a small Bay on Driftwood on which we had also to make our fires to dry our selves as well as we could, the shore being either a clift of Purpendicular rocks or steep assents to the hight of 4 or 500 feet, we continued on this drift wood untill about 3 oClock when the evening appearing favourable we loaded & set out in hopes to turn the Point below and get into a better harber, but finding the *waves & swells* continue to rage with great fury below, we got a safe place for our stores & a much beter one for the canoes to lie and formed a campment on Drift logs in the same little Bay under a high hill at the enterence of a small drean, which we found very conv.t on account of its water, as that of the river is Brackish. The logs on which we lie is all on flote every high tide. The rain continues all day. we are all wet also our bedding and maney other articles. we are all employed untill late drying our bedding. nothing to eate but Pounded fish

Rained verry hard the greater part of last night and continues this morning,   the wind has luled and the waves are not high; we loaded our canoes and proceeded on passed Several Small and deep nitch[es] on the Stard. Side,   we proceeded on about 10 miles saw great numbers of Sea Guls,   the wind rose from the N. W. and the waves became So high that we were compelled to return about 2 miles to a place we could unload our canoes, which we did in a Small nitch at the mouth of a Small run on a pile of drift logs where we continued untill low water, when the river appeared calm   we loaded and Set out, but was obliged to return finding the waves too high for our canoes to ride,   we again unloaded the canoes, and sto[w]ed the loading on a rock above the tide water, and formed a camp on the Drift Logs which appeared to be the only situation we could find to lee, the hills being either a perpendicular clift, or Steep assent, riseing to about 500 feet.[1]   our canoes we Secured as well as we could.   we are all wet the rain haveing continued all day, our beding and maney other articles,   employ our Selves drying our blankets.   nothing to eate but dried fish pounded which we brought from the falls.   we made 10 miles to day

[Clark, first draft:]   *November* 11*th*. *Monday* 1805

   a hard rain all the last night   we again get wet   the rain continue[s] at intervales all day.   Wind verry high from S W and blew a storm all day   sent out Jo. Fields & Collins to hunt,   at 12 oClock at a time the wind was verry high and waves trimendeous, five Indians came down in a canoe loaded with fish of salmon spe. called *Red Charr*,   we purchased of those Indians 13 of these fish, for which we gave fishing hooks & some trifling things.   We had seen those Indians at a village behind some marshey Islands a few days ago,   they are on their way to trade those fish with white people which they make signs live below round a point,   those people are badly clad, one is dressd in an old Salors Jawket & Trouses, the

---

1 This camp was on the lee side of Point Ellice, which Gass thought should be called "Blustry Point."— ED.

others Elk skin robes.   we are truly unfortunate to be compelled to be 4 days nearly in the same place at a time that our day[s] are precious to us,   The wind shifted to [blank space in MS.]   the Indians left us and crossed the river which is about 5 miles wide through the highest sees I ever saw a small vestle ride,   Their canoe is small, maney times they were out of sight before the[y] were 2 miles off   certain it is they are the best canoe navigators I ever saw.   The tide was 3 hours later to day than yesterday and rose much higher,   the trees we camped on was all on flote for above 2 hours from 3 untill 5 oClock PM,   the great quantites of rain which has fallen losens the stones on the side of the hill & the small ones fall on us,   our situation is truly a disagreeable one   our canoes in one place at the mercy of the waves our baggage in another and our selves & party scattered on drift trees of emence size, & are on what dry land they can find in the crevices of the rocks & hill sides

November 11ᵗʰ Monday 1805

A hard rain all the last night,   dureing the last tide the logs on which we lay was all on float,   Sent out Jo Fields to hunt, he Soon returned and informed us that the hills was So high & Steep, & thick with undergroth and fallen Timber that he could not get out any distance;   about 12 oClock 5 Indians came down in a canoe,   the wind verry high from the S. W. with most tremendious waves brakeing with great violence against the Shores, rain falling in torrents,   we are all wet as usial — and our Situation is truly a disagreeable one;   the great quantites of rain which has loosened the Stones on the hill Sides; and the Small stones fall down upon us, our canoes at one place at the mercy of the waves, our baggage in another; and our selves and party Scattered on floating logs and Such dry Spots as can be found on the hill sides, and crivicies of the rocks.   we purchased of the Indians 13 red charr which we found to be an excellent fish.   we have seen those Indians above and are of a nation who reside above and on the opposit

Side who call themselves *Calt har mar*. [*Cath lah ma*][1] they are badly clad & illy made, Small and Speak a language much resembling the last nation,   one of those men had on a Salors Jacket and Pantiloons.   and made Signs that he got those clothes from the white people who lived below the point &c. those people left us and crossed the river (which is about 5 miles wide at this place) through the highest waves I ever Saw a Small vestles ride.   Those Indians are certainly the best Canoe navigaters I ever Saw.   rained all day.

[Clark, first draft :]   *November 12*th *Tuesday 1805.*

a tremendious thunder storm abt 3 oClock this morning accompanied by wind from the S W. and Hail,   this Storm of hard clap's of thunder Light[n]ing and hail untill about 6 oClock at intervales   It then became light for a short time when the heavens became darkened by a black cloud from the S. W. & a hard rain suckceeded which lasted untill 12 oClock with a hard wind which raised the seas tremendiously high braking with great force and fury against the rocks & trees on which we lie,   as our situation became seriously dangerous, we took the advantage of a low tide & moved our camp around a point a short distance to a small wet bottom at the mouth of a small creek, which we had not observed when we first came to this cove, from its being very thick and obscured by drift trees & thick bushes,   send out men to hunt they found the woods so thick with Pine & decay[ed] timber and under groth that they could not get through,   saw some Elk tracks, I walked up this Creek & killed 2 salmon trout,   the men killd 13 of the Salmon species,   The Pine of fur [fir] speces, or spruce Pine grow here to an emence size & hight maney of them 6 & 7 feet through and upwards of 200 feet high.   It would be distressing to a feeling person to see our situation at this time all wet and cold with our bedding &c also wet, in a cove scercely large [e]nough to contains us, our Baggage in

---

1 Another extinct Chinookan tribe ; their name and that of the Warkiacum are perpetuated in the present Wahkiakum County, Wash., and its county seat Cathlamet (located opposit Puget Island). — ED.

a small holler about ½ a mile from us, and canoes at the mercy of the waves & drift wood, we have secured them as well as it is possible by sinking and wateing them down with stones to prevent the emence [waves] dashing them to pices against the rocks. one got loose last night & was left on a rock by the tide some distance below, without receving much damage. fortunately for us our men are helthy. It was clear at 12 for a short time. I observed the mountains on the opposit side was covered with snow. our party has been wet for 8 days and is truly disagreeable, their robes & leather clothes are rotten from being continually wet, and they are not in a situation to get others, and we are not in a situation to restore them. I observe great numbers of sea guls, flying in every derection. Three men Gibson Bratten & Willard attempted to decend in a canoe built in the Indian fashion and ab.̈ the size of the one the Indians visited us in yesterday, they could not proceed, as the waves tossed them about at will, they returned after proceeding about 1 mile we got our selves tolerable comfortable by drying our selves & bedding. Cought 3 salmon td.̈ evining in a small branch above about 1 mile

November 12.ᵗʰ Tuesday 1805

A Tremendious wind from the S. W. about 3 oClock this morning with Lightineng and hard claps of Thunder, and Hail which Continued untill 6 oClock a. m. when it became light for a Short time, then the heavens became sudenly darkened by a black cloud from the S. W. and rained with great violence untill 12 oClock, the waves tremendious brakeing with great fury against the rocks and trees on which we were encamped. our Situation is dangerous. we took the advantage of a low *tide* and moved our camp around a point to a Small wet bottom, at the Mouth of a Brook, which we had not observed when we came to this cove; from its being verry thick and obscured by drift trees and thick bushes. It would be distressing to See our Situation, all wet and colde our bedding also wet, (and the robes of the party which compose half the bedding is rotten and we are not in a Situation to supply their places) in a wet bottom scercely large enough to contain us our baggage half a mile from us, and Canoes at the mercy of the waves, altho Secured as well as possible, Sunk with emence parcels of Stone to wate them down to prevent their dashing to pecies against the rocks; one got loose last night and was left on a rock a Short distance below, without rec[ei]ving more damage than a Split in her bottom. Fortunately for us our men are healthy. 3 men Gibson Bratten & Willard attempted to go arou[n]d the point below in our Indian Canoe, much Such a canoe as the Indians visited us in yesterday, they proceeded to the point from which they were oblige[d] to return, the waves tossing them about at will. I walked up the branch and giged 3 Salmon trout. the party killed 13 Salmon to day in the branch about 2 miles above. rain continued

[Clark, first draft:]   *November 13th Wednesday 1805*

Some intervales of fair weather last night, rain and wind Continue this morning, as we are in a cove & the mountains verry high & Pine species verry high & thick cannot deturmine the procise course of the winds. I walked to the top of the first part of the mountain with much fatigue as the distance was about 3 miles thro' intolerable thickets of small Pine, arrowwood a groth much resembling arrow wood with briers, growing to 10 & 15 feet high interlocking with each other & Furn, aded to this dificulty the hill was so steep that I was obliged to drawing myself up in many places by the bowes, the Countrey continues thick and hilley as far back a[s] I could see. Some Elk sign, rained all day moderately. I am wet &c. &c. The Haile which fell 2 night past, is yet to be seen on the mountain on which I was to day. I saw a small red Berry which grows on a stem of about 6 or 8 Inches from the Ground, in bunches and in great quantity on the Mountains, the taste insiped. I saw a number of verry large spruce Pine one of which I measured 14 feet around and verry tall. My princupal object in assd⁵ this mountain was to view the river below, the weather being so cloudey & thick that I could not see any distance down, discovered the wind high from the N. W. and waves high at a short distance below (squar displeased with me for not [blank space in MS.]. *Wap-to* a excellent root which is rosted and tastes like a potato I cue my hare) our Encampment. despatched 3 men in a Indian canoe (which is calculated to ride high swells) down to examine if they can find the Bay at the mouth & good harbers below for us to proceed in safty. The Tides at every flud come in with great swells & Breake against the rocks & Drift trees with great fury the rain continued all the evening nothing to eate but Pounded fish which we have as a reserve see store, and what Pore fish we can kill up the branch on which we are encamped. our canoe and the three men did not return this evening. if we were to have cold weather to accompany the rain which we have had for 6 or 8 days passed we must eneviatebly suffer verry much as Clothes are scerce with us

November 13ᵗʰ Wednesday 1805

Some intervales of fair weather last night, rain continue[d] this morning. I walked up the Brook & assended the first Spur of the mountain with much fatigue, the distance about 3 miles, through an intolerable thickets of Small pine, a groth much resembling arrow wood on the Stem of which there is thorns, this groth about 12 or 15 feet high interlockᵈ into each other and scattered over the high fern & fallen timber, added to this the hills were so steep that I was compelled to draw my Self up by the assistance of those bushes. The Timber on those hills are of the pine species large and tall maney of them more than 200 feet high & from 8 to 10 feet through at the Stump those hills &c. as far back as I could See, I saw Some *Elk* Sign, on the Spur of the mountain tho' not fresh. I killed a Salmon trout on my return. The Hail which fell 2 nights past is yet to be Seen on the mountains; I Saw in my ramble to day a red berry resembling Solomons Seal berry

which the nativs call *Sol-me* and use it to eate.[1] my principal
object in assending this mountain was to view the countrey
below, the rain continuing and weather proved So cloudy that
I could not See any distance. on my return we dispatched
3 men Colter, Willard and Shannon in the Indian canoe to get
around the point if possible and examine the river, and the
Bay below for a go[o]d harber for our canoes to lie in Safty &c.
The tide at every floot tide came in [*with great swells braking
against the rocks and Drift trees*] with great fury. The rain
continue all day. nothing to eate but pounded fish which we
Keep as a reserve and use in Situations of this kind.

[Clark, first draft :]   *Novr 14.th Thursday 1805*

   Rained last night without intermission and this morning the
wind blew hard from the [blank space in MS.] we could not
move, one canoe was broken last night against the rocks, by
the waves dashing her against them in high *tide* about 10
oClock 5 Indians came up in a canoe thro emence waves &
swells, they landed and informed us they saw the 3 men we
sent down yesterday, at some distance below   Soon after those
people come Colter one of the 3 men returned and informed
us that he had proceeded with his canoe as far as they could,
for the waves and could find no white people, or Bay, he saw
a good Canoe harber & 2 camps of Indians at no great
distance below and that those with us had taken his gig &
knife &c which he forcably took from them & they left us,
after our treateing them well. The rain continue all day   all
wet as usial, killed only 2 fish to day for the whole Party,
at 3 oClock Cap.t Lewis, Drewyer Jo & R. Fields, & Frasure
set out down on the shore to examine if any white men were
below within our reach, they took a empty canoe & 5 men
to set them around the Point on a Gravelley Beech which
Colter informed was at no great distance below. The canoe

---

1 This berry is identified by Coues (*L. and C.*, iii, p. 826) as *Smilacina sessilifolia*;
but Silas B. Smith of Astoria (a grandson of the Clatsop chief Comowool, or Coboway, to whom Lewis and Clark gave their Fort Clatsop) says (*Wonderland*, 1900,
p. 61) that the *solme* is simply the wild cranberry. — ED.

returned at dusk half full of water, from the waves which dashed over in passing the point   Capt Lewisis object is also to find a small Bey as laid down by Vancouver just out of the mouth if the Columbia River.   rained as usial all the evening, all wet and disagreeable situation.

November 14th Thursday 1805

rained all the last night without intermition, and this morning.   wind blows verry hard,   but our situation is Such that we cannot tell from what point it comes.   one of our canoes is much broken by the waves dashing it against the rocks.   5 Indians came up in a canoe, thro' the waves, which is verry high and role with great fury.   They made Signs to us that they saw the 3 men we Sent down yesterday.   only 3 of those Indians landed, the other 2 which was women played off in the waves, which induced me to Suspect that they had taken Something from our men below,   at this time one of the men Colter return^d by land and informed us that those Indians had taken his Gigg & basket,   I called to the Squars to land and give back the gigg, which they would not doe untill a man run with a gun, as if he intended to Shute them when they landed, and Colter got his gig & basket   I then ordered those fellows off, and they verry readily cleared out   they are of the *War-ci-a-cum* N.

Colter informed us that " it was but a Short distance from where we lay around the point to a butifull Sand beech, which continued for a long ways, that he had found a good harber in the mouth of a creek near 2 Indian Lodges — that he had proceeded in the canoe as far as he could for the waves, the other two men Willard & Shannon had proceeded on down ["]

Capt Lewis concluded to proceed on by land & find if possible the white people the Indians say is below and examine if a Bay is Situated near the mouth of this river as laid down by Vancouver in which we expect, if there is white traders to find them &c.   at 3 oClock he Set out with 4 men Drewyer Jos. & Ru. Fields & R. Frasure, in one of our large canoes and 5 men to set them around the point on the Sand beech.   this canoe returned nearly filled with water at Dark which it receved by the waves dashing into it on its return, haveing landed Capt Lewis & his party Safe on the Sand beech. The rain continues all day. all wet. The rain &c. which has continued without a longer intermition than 2 hours at a time for ten days past has distroy.^d the robes and rotted nearly one half of the fiew clothes the party has, perticularley the leather clothes fortunately for us we have no very cold weather as yet. and if we have cold weather before we can kill & Dress Skins for clothing the bulk of the party will Suffer verry much.

[Clark, first draft:]   *November 15.th Friday 1805*

Rained all the last night at intervales of sometimes of 2 hours, This morning it became cold & fair, I prepared to set out at which time the wind sprung up from the S. E. and blew down the River & in a fiew minits raised such swells and waves brakeing on the Rocks at the Point as to render it unsafe to proceed. I went to the point in an empty canoe and found it would be dangerous to proceed even in an empty *canoe* The sun shown untill 1 oClock P. M. which gave an oppertunity for us to dry some of our bedding & examine our baggage, the greater Part of which I found wet. some of our Pounded fish spoiled I had all the arms put in order & amunition examined.

The rainey weather continued without a longer intermition than 2 hours at a time, from the 5.th in the morn.^g untill the 16.th is *eleven* days rain, and the most disagreeable time I have experenced confined on a tempiest coast wet, where I can neither git out to hunt, return to a better situation, or proceed on: in this situation have we been for Six days past. fortunately the wind lay about 3 oClock we loaded I in great haste and set out passed the blustering Point below which is a sand beech, with a small marshey bottom for 3 miles on the Star.^d Side, on which is a large village of 36 houses deserted by the Inds & in full possession of the flees, a small creek fall[s] in at this village, which waters the Country for a few miles

[223]

back ; Shannon & 5 Indians met me here,   Shannon informed
me he met Cap.! Lewis some distance below & he took Willard
with him & sent him to meet me,   the Ind.ᵃ with him wer
rogues, they had the night before stold both his and Willards
guns from under their heads,   Cap.! Lewis & party arrived at
the camp of those Indians at so timely a period that the Ind.ᵃ
were allarmed & delivered up the guns &.ᶜ   The tide meeting
of me and the emence swells from the Main Ocian (imedeately
in front of us) raised to such a hite that I concluded to form a
camp on the highest spot I could find in the marshey bottom,
and proceed no further by water as the Coaste becomes verry
[dangerous] for crafts of the size of our Canoes,   and as the
Ocian is imedeately in front and gives us an extensive view of
it from Cape disapointment to Point addams, except 3 small
Islands off the mouth and S W of us.   my situation is in the
upper part of Haleys Bay S. 86.° W. course miles to Cape Disap.!
and S. 35.° W. course miles from Point Addams.

The River here at its mouth from Point addams to the enterance of Haley Bay above is [blank space in MS.] miles or
thereabouts, a large Is.ᵈ the lower point of which is immediately
in the mouth above

4 Indians in a canoe came down with *papto* [wapatoo] roots
to sell, for which they asked blankets or robes, both of which
we could not spare   I informed those Indians all of which
understood some English that if they stole our guns &.ᶜ the
men would certainly shute them,   I treated them with great
distance, & the sentinal which was over our Baggage allarmed
them verry much,   they all Promised not to take any thing,
and if any thing was taken by the squars & bad boys to return
them &.ᶜ the waves became verry high   Evening fare &
pleasent,   our men all comfortable in the camps they have
made of the boards they found at the Town above

November 15ᵗʰ Friday 1805

Rained all the last night,   this morning it became calm and
fair, I preposed Setting out, and ordered the canoes Repared

and loaded; before we could load our canoes the wind Sudenly
Sprung up from the S. E. and blew with Such violence, that
we could not proceed in Safty with the loading.   I proceeded
to the point in an empty canoe, and found that the waves
dashed against the rocks with such Violence that I thought it
unsave to Set out with the loaded canoes.   The Sun Shown
untill 1 oClock P. M. which afford[ed] us time to Dry our
bedding and examine the baggage which I found nearly all wet,
Some of our pounded fish Spoiled in the wet,   I examined the
amunition and caused all the arms to be put in order.

about 3 oClock the wind luled, and the river became calm,
I had the canoes loaded in great haste and Set Out, from this
dismal nitich where we have been confined for 6 days passed,
without the possibility of proceeding on, returning to a better
Situation, or get out to hunt; Scerce of Provisions, and torents
of rain poreing on us all the time.   proceeded on passed the
blustering point below which I found a butifull Sand beech
thro which runs a Small river from the hills,   below the mouth
of this Stream is a *village* of 36 houses uninhabited by anything except flees,   here I met G. Shannon and 5 Indians.
Shannon informed me that he met Cap.̱ Lewis at an Indian
Hut about 10 miles below who had sent him back to meet me,
he also told me the Indians were thievish, as the night before
they had Stolen both his and Willards rifles from under their
heads [*they threatened them with a large party from above
which Cap.̱ Lewis's arrival confirmed*] that they Set out on
their return and had not proceeded far up the beech before
they met Cap.̱ Lewis, whose arival was at a timely moment and
alarmed the Indians So that they instantly produced the Guns.
I told those Indians who accompanied Shannon that they
should not come near us, and if any one of their nation Stold
anything from us, I would have him Shot, which they under-
stoot verry well.   as the tide was comeing in and the Seas
became verry high imediately from the *ocian* (imediately faceing us) I landed and formed a camp on the highest Spot I
could find between the hight of the tides, and the Slashers in
a small bottom   this I could plainly See would be the extent
of our journey by water, as the waves were too high at any

stage for our Canoes to proceed any further down. in full view of the *Ocian* from *Point Adams or Rond* (*see La Payrouse*) to Cape Disapointment, I could not see any Island in the mouth of this river as laid down by Vancouver. the Bay which he laies down in the mouth is imediately below me.[1] This Bay we call Haley's bay[2] from a favourite trader with the Indians which they Say comes into this Bay and trades with them course to Point adams is S. 35°. W. about 8 miles to Cape Disapointment is S. 86° W. about 14 miles 4 Indians of the *War-ki-a-cum* nation came down with *pap-pa-too* (*Wappatoo*) to Sell &c. The Indians who accompanied Shannon from the Village below Speake a Different language from those above, and reside to the north of this place The[y] Call themselves *Chinnooks*,[3] I told those people that they had attempted to Steal 2 guns &c. that if any one of their nation stole any thing that the Senten! whome they Saw near our baggage with his gun would most certainly Shute them, they all promised not to tuch a thing, and if any of their womin or bad boys took any thing to return it imediately and chastise them for it. I treated those people with great distance. our men all comfort-

---

1 This bay is now known as Baker's Bay (sometimes called Rogue's Harbor). George Vancouver was commissioned by the English government to explore the N. W. coast of America; he did this during 1792–94, but in the first of these voyages (1792) he failed to find the Columbia, although he was in the above-named bay. One of his officers, however, Lieut. W. R. Broughton, discovered it in the autumn of that year, ascended the river to the Cascades, and took possession of the country for Great Britain.

In 1786 a French expedition for scientific research and commercial information, headed by La Pérouse, made some explorations along the Alaska coast and for some distance southward. The report of his voyage was not published until 1798; the most important part of it is that which records his scientific observations. — ED.

2 The Haley's Bay of Lewis and Clark is now Baker's Bay. It was named in 1792 by Lieutenant Broughton, for the Captain of an American brig which he encountered in this bay. Point Adams was the name given by Captain Gray to the southern cape at the mouth of the Columbia. He named the northern cape Point Hancock; but Capt. John Meares, who in 1788 explored this coast, and failed to recognize the entrance of the Columbia as the mouth of a great river, called the bay Deception, and the northern headland, Cape Disappointment. Vancouver retained this nomenclature, which consequently persisted. — ED.

3 Sometimes known as Chinooks (or Tsinuks) proper; they are almost extinct now. From them is named the Chinookan family, embracing many of the tribes encountered by Lewis and Clark on the lower Columbia. — ED.

able in their Camps[1] which they have made of boards from the old village above. we made 3 miles to day.

[Clark, first draft:]   *November 16th Satturday* 1805

a fine morning   cool the latter part of the night,   I had all our articles of every discription examined, and found much wet, had all put out & dried.   The 5 Indians Thieves left me.   I took a meridean alt.d with Sext. *50° – 36' – 15* the shakeing emige below.   I sent out several hunters some to kill fowl others to hunt deer or Elk.   The Sea is fomeing and looks truly dismal to day, from the wind which blew to day from the S.W.   an Indian canoe passed down to day, loaded with roots &c.   Three Indians came up from below I gave them smoke but allowed them no kind of Priveleges whatever,   they camped with the 4 which came down yesterday, near us,   The evening prov.d cloudy & I could make no luner observations.   one man sick with a violent cold cought by lying in his wet clothes, several nights.   Course from Stormey point to Cape Disapointment is [blank space in MS.] miles, passed a small creek and an old village at 2 miles on the Star.d Side a small creek at 1 mile   we Encamped just above a Point in a Deep bay to the Star.d Side into which falls 2 small rivers St.d   Grat maney Indians liveing on the Bay & those two rivers,   the lower End of a large Island in the mouth of the Columbia ops.d to us,   we see Islands at some distance from Land S.W.   the Countrey on the Star.d Side high broken & thickly timbered, that on the Lar.d at some distance from Point Ad.ms high and mountains on a Pinecal of which is snow. at this time.   near the Point is Low bottom land.

our hunters and fowlers killed 2 Deer 1 Crane & 2 ducks, my Serv.t york killed 2 Geese & 8 white, black and Speckle Brants, The white Brant with part of their wings black is much the largest, the black brant is verry small, a little larger than a large duck   the deer pore but large

---

1 Fort Columbia, opposite Astoria — a new fort, equipped with heavy ordnance — is probably upon or near the site of the old camp of Lewis and Clark (Nov. 15-25, 1805), as well as that of the Chinook village of their friend Concomly. — O. D. WHEELER.

November 16th Saturday 1805

Cool the latter part of the last night this morning clear and butifull; I had all our articles of every discription examined and put out to Dry. The 5 *Chin nooks* left us   I took a meridenal altitude with the Sext! 50°. 35'. 15. which gave for Lattitude 46°. 19'. 11"1/10 North.   I sent out Several hunters and fowlers in pursute [of] Elk, Deer, or fowls of any kind. wind hard from the S. W. the Waves high & look dismal indeed breaking with great fury on our beech   an Indian canoe pass down to day loaded with *Wap-pa-ta-* roots; Several Indians came up to day from below, I gave them Smoke but allowed them no kind of privilage whatever in the camp,   they with the 4 which came down yesterday encamped a Short distance from us.   The evening proved cloudy and I could not take any Luner observations.   One man Sick with a violent cold, caught by laying in his wet leather clothes for maney nights past.

The Countrey on the Star.d Side above Haleys Bay is high broken and thickley timbered   on the Lar.d Side from Point Adams the countrey appears low for 15 or 20 miles back to the mountains, a pinical of which now is covered with Snow or hail,   as the Opposit [shore] is too far distant to be distinguished well, I shall not attempt to describe any thing on that side at present.   our hunters and fowlers killed 2 Deer 1 Crain & 2 Ducks, and my man York killed 2 geese and 8 Brant, 3 of them white with a part of their wings black and much larger than the Grey brant which is a sise larger than a Duck.[1]

[Clark, first draft:]   *November 17th Sunday 1805*

a fair cool windey morning   wind from the *East*. every tide which rises 8 feet 6 Inches at this place, comes in with high swells which brake on the sand shore with great fury.   I sent out 6 men to kill deer & fowls this morning.

---

[1] Clark here gives (Codex H, pp. 132–148) the "courses and distances" on the waters of the Columbia, from the mouth of Snake River to the ocean ; these cover the voyage from October 18 to November 16.   This matter is here omitted, as transcripts of those in the first draft. — ED.

Took Equal altitude with Sext!

	h	m	s			h	m	s
A. M.	8	47	7	P M.		2	34	49
"	8	50	29	"		2	37	10
"	8	53	56	"		2	39	35

Altitude produced 27°. 58′ 00

at half past 1 oClock Cap! Lewis and his Party returned haveing around passed Point Disapointment and some distance on the Main Ocian to the N W. several Indians followed him & soon after a canoe with *Wapto* roots, & Liquorice boiled, which they gave as presents, in return for which we gave more than the worth to satisfy them   a bad practice to receive a present of Indians, as they are never satisfied in return.   our hunters killed 3 Deer & the fowlers 2 Ducks & 4 brant   I surveyed a little on the corse & made some observ^{ns}.   The Chief of the nation below us came up to see us   the name of the nation is *Chin-nook* and is noumerous   live principally on fish roots a fiew Elk and fowls.   they are well armed with good Fusees.   I directed all the men who wished to see more of the Ocean to Get ready to set out with me on tomorrow day light.   the following men expressed a wish to accompany me i.e. Serj. Nat Pryor Serj! J. Ordway, Jo: Fields R. Fields, Jo. Shannon, Jo. Colter, William Bratten, Peter Wiser, Shabono & my servant York.   all others being well contented with what part of the Ocean & its curiosities which could be seen from the vicinity of our Camp.

November 17th Sunday 1805

A fair cool morning wind from the East.   The tide rises at this place 8 feet 6 inches and comes in with great waves brakeing on the Sand beech on which we lay with great fury Six hunters out this morning in serch of Deer & fowl.[1]

At half past 10 Clock Cap! Lewis returned haveing travesed Haley Bay to Cape Disapointment and the *Sea* coast to the North for Some distance.   Several *Chinnook* Indians followed

[1] The astronomical data are here omitted, being a transcript of those given in first draft. — ED.

Cap! L—, and a Canoe came up with roots mats &c. to Sell. those Chinnooks made us a present of a rute boiled much resembling the common liquorice in taste and Size : [*They call cul-wha-mo*] [1] in return for this root we gave more than double the value to Satisfy their craveing dispost". It is a bad practice to receive a present from those Indians as they are never satisfied for what they recive in return if ten time the value of the articles they gave. This *Chinnook* Nation is about 400 Souls inhabid the countrey on the Small rivers which run into the bay below us and on the Ponds to the N. W. of us, live principally on fish and roots, they are well armed with fusees and Sometimes kill Elk Deer and fowl. our hunters killed to day 3 Deer, 4 brant and 2 Ducks, and inform me they Saw Some Elk Sign. I directed all the men who wished to see more of the main *Ocian* to prepare themselves to Set out with me early on tomorrow morning. The principal chief of the Chinnooks & his family came up to See us this evening.

[Clark, first draft :]   *Nov!* 18*th Monday 1805*

a little cloudy this morning   I set out at day light with 10 men & my servent. Shabono, Serj! Pryor Odderway Jos & R. Fields Shannon Colter, Wiser, Lebiech & york   proceeded on Down the shore from the 1ˢ.ᵗ point N. W. 6 miles to a lodge at the enterance of a river on the St.ᵈ in the middle of a boggey Bay S. 79°. W. 7 miles to the mouth of a River (old cabins open bogs abound for 2 m.ˢ back) we call after the nation *Chin-nook* River   from this river to camp Point is S. 64°. E to Bluff Point (a small Island in a nitch of the Bay in the same ground) is S. 20°. W. 1½ miles   to *Cape Disap!* is South   To point *adams* is S. 22°. E about 25 miles.   passed a part of a fish about 1 mile above   I supposed to be a Grampass   The men killed 4 brants & Leb. killed 48 plover of 2 different

---

1 Silas B. Smith says of this plant (*Wonderland*, 1900, p. 61) : " ' culhoma ' should be ' culwhayma.'   It is the root of what is popularly known as the wild blue *lupine* . . . it tastes something like a sweet potato."   Douglas identifies it as *Lupinus littoralis*; the licorice (*Glycyrrhiza lepidata*) does not grow at the mouth of the Columbia. — ED.

kinds yellow & black legs   had them picked cooked and we Dined on them.

S.   80.° W. 1 mile to the bottom of a nitch at a branch from a pond
South 8.° W. to an Is.ᵈ in the 2ᵈ nitch   from this passed 2 points in the
        course   To the center of the 1.ˢᵗ nitch a run is 1 mile
        To the d° of the 2 d° is 1 mile

At a run & Island near the shore   here the Traders ancher & trade.   we passed at each point a soft clifts of yellow brown & dark soft stones   here Cap.ᵗ Lewis myself & seve.ˡ of the men marked our names day of the month & by Land &.ᶜ &.ᶜ from this S. W. 3 miles to the Iner p.ᵗ of Cape Disapointm.ᵗ passed a point & 2 small nitches (Reuben Fields killed a Vulter)   we found a curious flat fish shaped like a turtle, with fins on each side, and a tale notched like a fish, the Internals on one side and tale & fins flat wise   This fish (Flownder)[1] has a white belly on one side & lies flat to the Ground   passed from last nitch across to the ocean ½ a mile   low land   the Cape is a high Partly bald hill, founded on rock,   I assended a high seperate bald hill covered with long corse grass & seperated from the hight of countrey by a slashey bottom 2 miles N. 60 W of the Cape. thence to a 2ᵈ Grassey p.ᵗ is N. 50.° W. 2 miles   Those hills are founded on rocks & the waves brake with great fury against them,   the Coast is sholey for several miles of[f] this Cape & for some distance off to the N W   a Sand bar in the mouth, sholey some distance out from the mouth   The coast from the Cape N W is open for a short distance back then it becomes thick piney countrey intersperced with points

Point addams is S. 20° W about 20 miles the course on that side bears S. 45.° W.   I cannot assertain the prosise course of the Deep water in the mouth of the river,   the channel is but narrow.   I proceeded on up above the 2ᵈ point and Encamped on the shore above the high tide,   evening clear, for a short time Sup.ᵈ on Brant and pounded fish   men all chearfull, express a Desire to winter near the falls this winter

---

[1] This word " Flownder " was written in later. — ED.

November 18ᵗʰ *Monday* 1805

A little cloudy this morning I set out with 10 men and my man York to the Ocian by land.   i. e. Serjᵗ Ordway & Pryor, Jos. & Ru Fields, Go. Shannon, W. Brattin, J. Colter, P. Wiser, W. Labieche & P. Shabono one of our interpreters & York.   I set out at Day light and proceeded on a Sandy beech

N. 80°. W. 1 Mile to a point of rocks about 40 feet high, from the top of which the hill Side is open and assend with a Steep assent to the tops of the mountains,   a Deep nitch and two Small Streams above this point,   then my course was

N. W. 7 Mile[s] to the enterance of a creek at a lodge or cabin of Chinnooks passing on a wide Sand bar the bay to my left and Several Small ponds containing great numbers of water fowls to my right; with a narrow bottom of alder & Small balsam between the Ponds and the Mountⁿ at the Cabin I saw 4 womin and Some children one of the women in a desperate Situation, covered with sores scabs & ulsers no doubt the effects of venereal disorders which Several of this nation which I have Seen appears to have.

This creek appears to be nothing more than the conveyance of Several Small dreans from the high hills and the ponds on each side near its mouth.   here we were set across all in one canoe by 2 squars.   to each I gave a small hook

S. 79°. W. 5 Miles to the mouth of *Chin nook* river,[1]   passed a low bluff [*of a small hite*] at 2 miles below which is the remains of huts near which place is also the remains of a whale on the sand,   the countrey low open and Slashey, with elivated lands interspersed covered with (*Some*) pine & thick under groth.   This river is 40 yards wide at low tide.   here we made a fire and dined on 4 brant and 48 Plever which was killed by Labiech on the coast as we came on.   Rubin Fields Killed a Buzzard [*Vulture*] of the large Kind near the [*meat of the*] whale we Saw [*W. 25ˡᵇ*] measured from the tips of the wings across 9½ feet, from the point of the Bill to the end of the tail 3 feet 10-¼ inches, middle toe 5-½ inches, toe nale 1 inch & 3-½ lines, wing feather 2-½ feet long & 1 inch 5

---

[1] Wallacut River, on the U. S. Coast survey chart. — Eᴅ.

lines diamiter, tale feathers 14-½ inches, and the *head* is 6-½ inches including the beak. [*head in Peale's Mus.*] [1] after dine-ing we crossed the river in an old canoe which I found on the sand near Some old houses and proceeded on

S. 20° W. 4 Miles to a Small rock island in a deep nitch passed a nitch at 2 miles in which there is a dreen from Some ponds back; the land low opposite this nitch a bluff of yellow clay and Soft Stone from the river to the commencement of this nitch. below the countrey rises to high hills of about 80 or 90 feet above the water. at 3 miles passed a nitch. this rock Island is Small and at the South of a deep bend in which the nativs inform us the Ships anchor, and from whence they receive their goods in return for their peltries and Elk skins &c. this appears to be a very good harber for large Ships. here I found Cap! Lewis name on a tree. I also engraved my name, & by land the day of the month and year, as also Several of the men.

S. 46° E. 2 Miles to the iner extremity of *Cape Disapoint-ment* passing a nitch in which there is a Small rock island, a Small Stream falls into this nitch from a pond which is ime-diately on the Sea coast passing through a low isthmus. this Cape is an ellivated circlier [circular] point covered with thick timber on the iner Side and open grassey exposur next to the Sea and rises with a Steep assent to the hight of about 150 or 160 feet above the leavel of the water this cape as also the Shore both on the Bay & Sea coast is a dark brown rock.[2] I crossed the neck of Land low and ½ of a mile wide to the main Ocian, at the foot of a high open hill projecting into the ocian, and about one mile in Si[r]cumfrance. I assended this hill which is covered with high corse grass.[3] decended to the N. of it and camped. [walked] 19 Miles [to-day]. I picked up a flounder on the beech this evening

---

[1] This was the Californian condor (*Pseudogryphus californianus*), as large as the condor of the Andes. — ED.

[2] In the Courses and Distances (Codex H, p. 148) which here end, Clark entered "*Ocian* 165 Miles from *quick sand river*. Ocian 190 Miles from the first rapid. Ocian 4162 Miles from the Mouth of *Missouri R.*" — EP.

[3] Clark climbed to the top of Cape Disappointment, where the old light house stands, not far from Fort Canby. — O. D. WHEELER.

from Cape Disapointment to a high point of a Mount.ᵃ which
we shall call [*Clarke's Point of View*]¹ beares S. 20° W. about
40 [*25*] miles,   point adams is verry low and is Situated within
the derection between those two high points of land, the water
appears verry Shole from off the mouth of the river for a great
distance, and I cannot assertain the direction of the deepest
chanel, the Indians point nearest the opposit Side. the
waves appear to brake with tremendious force in every direction quite across a large Sand bar lies within the mouth
nearest to point Adams which is nearly covered at high tide.
I suped on brant this evening with a little pounded fish.
Some rain in the after part of the night. men appear much
Satisfied with their trip beholding with estonishment the high
waves dashing against the rocks & this emence Ocian

[Clark, first draft:]   *November 19ᵗʰ Tuesday* 1805

    began to rain a little before day and continued raining untill
11 oClock   I proceeded on thro emencely bad thickets & hills,
crossing 2 points to a 3.ʳᵈ on which we built a fire and cooked
a Deer which Jos. Field killed   from this point I can see into
a Deep bend in the coast to the N. E. for 10 miles. after
Brackfast I proceeded on N. 20° E 5 miles to commencement
[of] a large sand bar at a low part   ponds a little off from the
coast here the high rockey hills end and a low Marshey
Countrey suckceeds. I proceeded up the course N. 10° W.
4 miles & marked my name & the Day of the Month on a
pine tree, the waters which Wash this sand beach is tinged
with a deep brown colour for some distance out. The course
cont.ᵈ is N. 20° W. low coast and sand beech, saw a Dead
Sturgen 10 feet long on the sand & the back bone of a whale
as I conceived   raind   I then returned to the Clift & dined,
some curious Deer on this course, darker large bodi[e]d short
legs pronged horns & the top of the tale black under part
white as usial   passed a nitch in the rocks below into which
falls a stream, after Dinner I set out on my return S. E.
passed over a low ridge & thro a piney countrey 2½ miles to

¹ Now known as False Tillamook Head. — Ed.

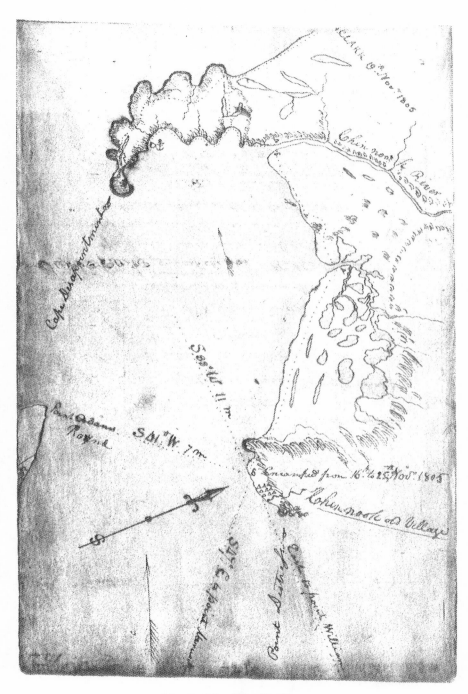

Mouth of the Columbia River,
sketch-map by Clark.

the Bay, thence up the Bay to the mouth of the *Chinnook* River crossed in the canoe we had left there & Encamped on the upper side   The Hills in the·point of this bay are not high, & imedeately below this River the[y] present yellow Bluffs

Above the River and up for about 2 miles the land is low slashey and contains much drift wood, the countrey up this creek is low with Copse of high land or as I may say elevated. The Buzzard which Ruben Fields killed from the top of one to the top of the other wing is 9 feet 0 Inches, from the point of the Bill to the tale is 3 feet 10¼ In⁎ middle Toe 5½ Inches, Toe nale 1 Inches 3½ wing feather 2 feet ½ In. Tale feathers 14¼ In. diameter of one feather is 1¼ & 1 line Head is 6¼ Inch long including the back

November 19ᵗʰ Tuesday 180

a cloudy rainey day proceeded up the coast which runs from my camp 1-¼ miles west of the iner extʸ of the cape N. 20° W. 5 miles through a rugged hilley countrey thickly timbered off the Sea coast to the Comencment of an extencive Sand beech which runs N. 10° W. to point Lewis about 20 miles distance. I proceeded up this coast 4 miles and marked my name on a low pine. and returned 3 miles back (the countrey opsᵈ this Sand coast is low and Slashey, crossed the point 2 miles to the bay and encamped on Chinnook river   See another book for perticulars[1]

Cape Disapointment at the Enterance of the Columbia River into the Great South Sea or Pacific Ocean.

Tuesday November the 19ᵗʰ 1805.[2]

I arose early this morning from under a Wet blanket caused by a Shower of rain which fell in the latter part of the last night, and Sent two men on a head with directions to proceed

[1] Here ends Codex H, which is immediately succeeded by Codex I (also in Clark's handwriting), covering the time from Nov. 19, 1805, to Jan. 29, 1806. — ED.

[2] The journal proper begins on p. 34 of Codex I, the preceding pages being occupied with a list of distances in their journey from Fort Mandan to the ocean, and observations on weather, natural history, etc., — all which we have transferred to "Scientific Data." — ED.

on near the Sea Coast and Kill Something for brackfast and that
I should follow my self in about half an hour. after drying
our blankets a little I set out with a view to proceed near the
Coast the direction of which induced me to conclude that at the
distance of 8 or 10 miles, the Bay was at no great distance
across. I overtook the hunters at about 3 miles, they had
killed a Small Deer on which we brackfast[ed], it Comen[c]ed
raining and continud moderately untill 11 oClock A M.

after takeing a Sumptious brackfast of Venison which was
rosted on Stiks exposed to the fire, I proceeded on through
ruged Country of high hills and Steep hollers on a course from
the Cape N 20° W. 5 [1] miles on a Direct line to the commencement of a Sandy coast which extended N. 10° W. from the top
of the hill above the Sand Shore to a Point of high land distant
near 20 miles. this point I have taken the Liberty of Calling
after my particular friend Lewis. [2] at the commencement of
this Sand beech the high lands leave the Sea Coast in a Direction to Chinnook river, and does not touch the Sea Coast
again below point Lewis leaveing a low pondey Countrey,
maney places open with small ponds in which there is great
numb: of fowl I am informed that the *Chinnook* Nation inhabit this low countrey and live in large wood houses on a
river which passes through this bottom Parrilal to the Sea
coast and falls into the Bay

I proceeded on the sandy coast 4 miles, and marked my
name on a Small pine, the Day of the month & year, &c and
returned to the foot of the hill, from which place I intended to
Strike across to the Bay, I saw a Sturgeon which had been
thrown on Shore and left by the tide 10 feet in length, and
Several joints of the back bone of a Whale, which must have
foundered on this part of the Coast. after Dineing on the
remains of our Small Deer I proceeded through over a land
S E with Some Ponds to the bay distance about 2 miles, thence

---

[1] Regarding these figures, Coues says (*L. and C.*, ii, p. 715): "Adjust all Clark's
compass-bearings about the mouth of the Columbia for a magnetic variation of
21° 30' E." — ED.

[2] This promontory is now known as North Head, where a new and modern lighthouse stands. North of it is Long Beach, a well-known summer resort, extending
for several miles along the coast. — ED.

up to the mouth of Chinnook river 2 miles, crossed this little
river in the Canoe we left at its mouth and Encamped on the
upper Side in an open sandy bottom.   The hills next to the
bay [on] Cape disapointment to a Short distance up the Chinnook river is not verry high thickly Cover.ᵈ with different
Species of pine &c. maney of which are large,   I observed in
maney places pine of 3 or 4 feet through growing on the bodies
of large trees which had fallen down, and covered with moss
and yet part Sound.   The Deer¹ of this Coast differ materially
from our Common deer in as muech as they are much darker,
deeper bodied, Shorter ledged [legged] horns equally branched
from the beem the top of the tail black from the rute [root] to
the end.   Eyes larger and do not lope but jump.²

[Clark, first draft:]   Nov.ʳ 20.ᵗʰ Wednesday 1805

Some rain last night   dispatch.ᵈ 3 men to hunt   Jo Fields
& Colter to hunt Elk & Labich to kill some Brant for our
brackfast   The Morning cleared up fare and we proceeded on
by the same route we went out,   at the River we found no
Indians,   made a raft & Ruben Fields crossed and took over
a small canoe which lay at the Indian cabin.   This Creek is
at this time of high tide 300 yards wide & the marshes for
some distance up the creek covered with water.   not an
Indian to be seen near the creek,   I proceeded on to camp &
on my way was over taken by 3 Indians one gave us sturgeon
& *Wapto roots* to eate   I met several parties on [the] way   all
of them appeared to know me & was distant,   found all well
at camp,   maney Indians about one of which had on a robe
made of 2 sea orters skins.   Cap.ᵗ Lewis offered him many
things for his skins with others a blanket a coat all of which
he refused   we at length purchased it for a belt of Blue Beeds
which the Squar had.   The tide being out we walked home on
the beech.

¹ This Coues calls "the original description of the Columbian black-tailed deer
(*Cariacus columbianus*)," a distinct species from that found on the Missouri. — ED.
² Like a sheep frightened. — BIDDLE (ii, p. 80).

Wednesday November the 20ᵗʰ 1805

Some rain last night dispatched Labeech to kill some fowl for our brackfast he returned in about 2 hours with 8 large Ducks on which we brackfast I proceeded on to the enterance of a Creek near a Cabin. No person being at this Cabin and 2 Canoes laying on the opposit Shore from us, I deturmined to have a raft made and Send a man over for a canoe, a Small raft was Soon made, and Reuben Fields crossed and brought over a Canoe. This Creek which is the outlet of a number of ponds, is at this time (high tide) 300 yᵈˢ wide. I proceeded on up the Beech and was overtaken by three Indians one of them gave me Some dried Sturgeon and a fiew Wappato roots, I employ[e]d those Indians to take up one of our Canoes which had been left by the first party that Came down, for which Service I gave them each a fishing hook of a large Size. on my way up I met Several parties of Chinnooks which I had not before Seen, they were on their return from our Camp. all those people appeared to know my deturmonation of keeping every individual of their nation at a proper distance, as they were guarded and resurved in my presence &c. found maney of the *Chin nooks* with Capᵗ Lewis of whome there was 2 Cheifs *Com com mo ly*[1] & *Chil-lar-la-wil* to whome we gave Medals and to one a flag. one of the Indians had on a roab made of 2 Sea Otter Skins the fur of them were more butifull than any fur I had ever Seen both Capᵗ Lewis & my self endeavored to purchase the *roab* with differant articles[2] at length we precured it for a belt of blue beeds which the Squar-wife of our interpreter Shabono wore around her waste. in my absence the hunters had killed Several Deer and fowl of different kinds.

[Clark, first draft:]   *November 21ˢᵗ Thursday 1805*

a cloudy morning, most of the Indians left us, The nation on the opposit side is small & called *Clap-sott*, Their great

---

[1] A daughter of this chief became the wife (1813) of Duncan M'Dougal, one of the associates of John Jacob Astor. See Irving's *Astoria* (Phila., 1841), ii, pp. 219–221. — ED.

[2] Several of the men have robes made of brant-skins ; one of them had a hat made of the bark of white cedar and bear-grass, very handsomely wrought and waterproof. One of our party purchased it for an old razor. — GASS (p. 242).

chief name *Stil-la-sha*. The nation liveing to the North is
called *Chieltz*. The chief is name[d] *Mâ-laugh* not large
nation and wore his beards as informed by the Ind? In my
absence the hunters killed 7 Deer, 4 brants & a crane. Great
numbers of the dark brant passing Southerley, the white yet
stationary, no Gees & swan to be seen. The wind blew hard
from the S. E. which with the addition of the flood tide raised
emence swells & waves which almost entered our Encampment. morn? dark & Disagreeable, a supriseing climat. We
have not had one cold day since we passed below the last falls
or great Shute & some time before the climent is temperate,
and the only change we have experienced is from fair weather
to rainey windey weather, I made a chief & gave a medel
this man is name[d] *Tow-wâle* and appears to have some influence with the nation and tells me he lives at the great shute.
we gave the squar a coate of Blue Cloth for the belt of Blue
Beeds we gave for the Sea otter skins purchased of an Indian.
at 12 oClock it began to rain, and continued moderately all
day, some wind from the S.E. waves too high for us to
proceed on our homeward bound journey. (Lattitude of this
place is 46° – 19′ – 11″ ¹/₁₀ North) Several Indians and squars
came this evening I beleave for the purpose of gratifying the
passions of our men, Those people appear to view sensuality
as a necessary evill, and do not appear to abhore this as crime
in the unmarried females. The young women sport openly
with our men, and appear to receve the approbation of theer
friends & relations for so doing maney of the women are
handsom. They are all low both men and womin, I saw the
name of J. Bowmon marked or picked on a young squars left
arm. The women of this nation Pick their legs in different
figures as an orniment the[y] ware their hair loose, some
trinkets in their ears, none in the nose as those above, their
Dress is as follows, i. e. the men were a roabe of either the skins
of [blank space in MS.] a small fured animal, & which is most
common, or the Skins of the Sea orter, Loon, Swan, Beaver,
Deer, Elk, or blankets either red, blu, or white, which roabes
cover the sholders arms & body, all other parts are nak?

The women were a short peticoat of the iner bark of the

white Ceder or *arber vita*, which hang down loose in strings
nearly as low as the knee, with a short Robe which falls half
way down the Thigh. no other part is covered The orniments are beeds, Blue principally, large Brass wire around their
rists some rings, and maney men have salors clothes, maney
have good fusees & Ball & Powder. The women ware a string
of something curious tied tight above the anckle, all have large
swelled legs & thighs The men [have] small legs & thighs
and generally badly made. They live on Elk, Deer, fowls,
but principally fish and roots of 3 kinds. Lickorish, Wapto
&c. The women have more privalages than is common among
Indians. Pocks & venereal is common amongst them. I saw
one man & one woman who appeared to be all in scabs & several men with the venereal their other Disorders and the
remides for them I could not lern we divided some ribin
between the men of our party to bestow on their favourite
Lasses, this plan to save the knives & more valueable articles.

Those people gave me Sturgion Salmon & wapto roots, &
we bought roots, some mats &c. &c. for which we were obliged
to give emence prices. we also purchased a kind of Cramberry
which the Indians say the[y] geather in the low lands, off of
small either vines or bushes just above the ground. we also
purchased hats made of Grass &c. of those Indians, some very
handsom mats made of flags some fiew curious baskets made
of a strong weed & willow or [blank space in MS.] splits, also
a sweet soft black root, about the sise & shape of a carrot,
this root they value verry highly. The *Wapto* root is scerce,
and highly valued by those people, this root they roste in hot
ashes like a potato and the outer skin peals off, tho this is a
trouble they seldom perform.

Thursday November 21st 1805.

A cloudy morning most of the Chinnooks leave our camp
and return home, great numbers of the dark brant passing to
the South, the white Brant have not yet commenced their
flight. the Wind blew hard from the S. E. which with the
addition of the flood tide raised verry high waves which broke

with great violence against the shore throwing water into our
camp   the forepart of this day Cloudy at 12 oClock it began
to rain and continud all day moderately,   Several Indians
Visit us to day of differant nations or Bands Some of the
Chiltz Nation who reside on the Sea Coast near Point Lewis,
Several of the *Clatsops*[1] who reside on the Opposit Side of the
Columbia imediately opposit to us, and a Cheif from the Grand
rapid to whome we gave a Medal.

An old woman & Wife to a Cheif of the *Chunnooks* came
and made a Camp near ours.   She brought with her 6 young
Squars (*her daughters & nieces*) I believe for the purpose of
Gratifying the passions of the men of our party and receving
for those indulgiences Such Small [presents] as She (the old
woman) thought proper to accept of.

Those people appear to View Sensuality as a Necessary evel,
and do not appear to abhor it as a Crime in the unmarried
State.   The young females are fond of the attention of our
men and appear to meet the sincere approbation of their friends
and connections, for thus obtaining their favours,   the Womin
of the Chinnook Nation have handsom faces low and badly
made with large legs & thighs which are generally Swelled
from a Stopage of the circulation in the feet (which are Small)
by maney Strands of Beeds or curious Strings which are drawn
tight around the leg above the ankle,   their legs are also
picked [i.e., tattooed] with defferent figures,   I saw on the
left arm of a Squar the following letters *J. Bowman*,   all those
are considered by the natives of this quarter as handsom deck-
erations, and a woman without those deckorations is Considered
as among the lower Class   they ware their hair lose hanging
over their back and Sholders   maney have blue beeds threaded
& hung from different parts of their *ears* and about ther neck
and around their wrists,   their dress otherwise is prosisely like
that of the Nation of *War ci a cum* as already discribed.   a
Short roab, and *tissue* or kind of peticoat of the bark of Cedar
which fall down in strings as low as the knee behind and not

---

[1] The Chehalis (Tsihalis), here called Chiltz, are a Salishan tribe; the name has
often been used collectively to include several tribes of that family.   The Clatsops
belong to the Chinookan stock. — ED.

so low before. Maney of the men have blankets of red blue or Spotted Cloth or the common three & 2½ point blankets, and Salors old Clothes which they appear to prise highly, they also have robes of *SeaOtter*, Beaver, Elk, Deer, fox and cat common to this Countrey, which I have never Seen in the U States. they also precure a roabe from the nativs above, which is made of the Skins of a Small animal about the Size of a cat, which is light and dureable and highly prized by those people. the greater numbers of the men of the Chinnooks have Guns and powder and Ball. The Men are low homely and badly made, Small crooked legs large feet, and all of both Sects have flattened heads. The food of this nation is principally fish & roots the fish they precure from the river by the means of nets and gigs, and the Salmon which run up the Small branches together with what they collect drifted up on the Shores of the Sea coast near to where they live. The roots which they use are Several different kinds, the *Wap pa to* which they precure from the nativs above, a black root which they call *Shaw-na-tâh-que*[1] & the Wild licquorish is the most Common, they also kill a fiew Elk Deer & fowl. maney of the Chinnooks appear to have Venerious and pustelus disorders. one woman whome I saw at the Creek appeared all over in Scabs and ulsers &c.

We gave to the men each a pece of ribin. We purchased cramberies Mats verry netely made of flags and rushes, Some roots, Salmon and I purchased a hat made of Splits & Strong grass, which is made in the fashion which was common in the U States two years ago also small baskets to hold Water made of Split and Straw, for those articles we gave high prices.

---

[1] This should be shanatawhee. It is the root of the edible thistle [*Cnicus edulis*] ; the first year's growth of the thistle, that has one straight root something like a parsnip, it is tender, sweet, and palatable. — S. B. SMITH (*Wonderland*, 1900, p. 61).

CHAPTER XXI

AT FORT CLATSOP

Clark's Journal, November 22, 1805—January 6, 1806
Lewis's Journal, November 29—December 1, 1805, and January 1-6, 1806
Orderly Book, January 1, 1806.

[Clark, first draft:]   *Nov.* 22*nd* *Friday* 1805

SOME little rain all the last night with wind, before day the wind increased to a storm from the S.S.E. and blew with violence throwing the water of the river with emence waves out of its banks almost over whelming us in water, O! how horriable is the day. This storm continued all day with equal violence accompanied with rain, several Indians about us, nothing killed   the waves & brakers flew over our camp, one canoe split by the Tossing of those waves   we are all confined to our Camp and wet.   purchased some *Wap to* roots for which was given brass arm ban[d]s & rings of which the squars were fond.   we find the Indians easy ruled and kept in order by a stricter indifference towards them

Friday November 22*nd* 1805.

a moderate rain all the last night with wind,   a little before Day light the wind which was from the S.S.E. blew with Such Violence that we wer almost overwhelmned with water blown from the river,   this Storm did not sease at day but blew with nearly equal violence throughout the whole day accompan[i]ed with rain. O! how horriable is the day   waves brakeing with great violence against the Shore throwing the Water into our Camp &c.   all wet and confind to our Shelters,   Several Indian men and women crouding about the mens shelters to day, we purchased a fiew Wappato roots for which we gave Arm-

ban[d]s, & rings to the old Squar,   those roots are equal to
the Irish potato, and is a tolerable substitute for bread

The threat which I made to the men of this nation whome I
first Saw, and an indifference towards them, is : I am fulley convinced the cause of their conducting themselves with great propriety towards ourselves & Party.

[Clark, first draft:]   *November 23ʳᵈ Saturday 1805*

The [day] cloudy and calm,   a moderate rain the greater
part of the last night,   sent out men to hunt this morning and
they killed 3 Bucks   rained at intervales all day.   I marked
my name the Day of the Month & year on a Beech tree & (By
Land) Capᵗ Lewis Branded his and the men all marked their
nams on trees about the camp.   one Indian came up from
their village on some lakes near Haleys bay.   In the Evening
7 Indians of the *Clatt-sopp* nation, opposit came over,   they
brought with them 2 Sea orter skins, for which the[y] asked
such high prices we were uneabled to purchase, with[out] re-
duceing our small stock of merchindize on which we have to
depend in part for a subsistance on our return home,   kiled 4
brant & 3 Ducks to day

Saturday November 22 [3]ʳᵈ 1805.

A calm Cloudy morning,   a moderate rain the greater part
of the last night,   Capᵗ Lewis Branded a tree with his name
Date &c.   I marked my name the Day & year on a alder
tree, the party all Cut the first letters of their names on different trees in the bottom.   our hunters killed 3 Bucks, 4 Brant
& 3 Ducks to day.

in the evening Seven indians of the *Clot sop* Nation came
over in a Canoe, they brought with them 2 Sea otter Skins for
which they asked blue beads &ᶜ and Such high pricies that we
were unable to purchase them without reducing our Small
Stock of Merchendize, on which we depended for Subcistance
on our return up this river.   mearly to try the Indian who

had one of those Skins, I offered him my Watch, handkerchief a bunch of red beads and a dollar of the American coin, all of which he refused and demanded "*ti-â-co-mo-shack*"[1] which is *Chief beads* and the most common blue beads, but fiew of which we have at this time

This nation is the remains of a large nation destroyed by the Small pox or Some other [disease] which those people were not acquainted with, they Speak the Same language of the Chinnooks and resemble them in every respect except that of Stealing, which we have not cought them at as yet.

[Clark, first draft:]   *November 24th Sunday 1805*

a fare morning. sent out 6 hunters and Detained to make the following observations i. e.

Took time dis. & azomith of the Sun A M.

Time			Dist			azmth
h.	m.	s.				
8	33	20	22°	16′	30″	S 64° E.
8	37	48	23	19	45	S 63° E.
8	41	35	24	13	0	S 62° E

Equal altitudes with Sextant

	H.	m	s		h	m	s
A. M.	8	53	5.5	P. M.			
	"	55	33		(lost)		
	"	58	3				

Altitude produced [blank space in MS.]

observed Time & Distance of Sun & Moons nearest Limbs Sun West P M

---

[1] A word still in use among the coast Indians, in the "Chinook jargon" or "trade-language"; it is given by Horatio Hale as *tyee-kamosuk*, in *Oregon Trade Language* (London, 1890), pp. 52, 53. A dictionary of this jargon is also given by Granville Stuart, in *Montana as It Is* (N. Y. 1865), pp. 99–127. Cf. Boas's *Chinook Texts* (Washington, 1894). — ED.

Time			distance		
h.	m.	s.			
2	42	11	40°	32'	45"
"	43	38	40	33	15
"	44	53	"	33	30
"	46	9	"	34	15
"	47	29	"	34	30
"	48	53	"	34	45
"	51	29	"	35	15
"	52	50	"	35	30
"	54	00	"	36	00
"	55	38	"	36	15

Several of the *Chennook* N. came, one of them brought an Sea otter skin for which we gave some blue Beeds. This day proved to be fair and we dried our wet articles bedding &.^{c} The hunters killed only 1 brant no Deer or any thing else

Observed time and Distance of Moons [blank space in MS.] Limb an *a pegasi* Star East P. M.

Time			distance		
h	m	s			
6	16	46	67°	56'	30"
"	19	29	"	54	15
"	25	39	"	50	45
"	28	20	"	50	15
"	31	53	"	48	30

The old chief of Chinn-nook nation and several men & women came to our camp this evening & smoked the pipe

[A vote of the men, as to location of winter quarters. — ED.][1]

Serg^t J. Ordway	cross & examine		S
Serj^t N. Pryor	d°	d°	S
Sg^t P. Gass	d°	d°	S
Jo. Shields	proceed to Sandy R		
G. Shannon	exam^n	cross	falls
T. P. Howard	d°	d°	falls

[1] Gass tells us (p. 245) that the commanders held a consultation with their men as to the location of their quarters. The present statement is apparently the vote taken on this occasion. — ED.

P. Wiser	d°	d°	S.R.
J. Collins	d°	d°	S. R
Jo. Fields	d°	d°	up
A! Willard	d°	d°	up
R. Willard	d°	d°	up
J. Potts	d°	d°	falls
R. Frasure	d°	d°	up
Wᵐ Bratten	d°	d°	up
R. Fields	d°	d°	falls
J : B : Thompson	d°	d°	up
J. Colter	d°	d°	up
H. Hall	d°	d°	S. R.
Labeech	d°	d°	S. R.
Peter Crusatte	d°	d°	S R
J. P. Depage	d°	d°	up
Shabono	—	—	—
S. Guterich	d°	d°	falls
W. Werner	d°	d°	up
Go : Gibson	d°	d°	up
Jo. Whitehouse	d°	d°	up
Geo Drewyer	Exam other side		falls
Mc Neal	d°	d°	up
York	''	''	lookout

falls	Sandy River	lookout up
5	10	12

Janey [Sacajawea ? — ED.] in favour of a place where there is plenty of Pota:

Cp. L & F   Proceed on to morrow & examine The other side if good hunting to winter there, as salt is an obj: if not to proceed on to Sandy   it is probable that a vestle will come in this winter, & that by proceeding on at any distance would not inhance our journey in passing the Rockey Mountains, &c

W C. In favour of proceding on without delay to the opposit shore & there examine, and find out both the disposition of the Indians, & probibilaty of precureing subsistance, and also enquire if the Tradeing vestles will arrive before the time we should depart in the spring, and if the Traders, comonly arive in a seasonable time, and we can subsist without a depend: on our stores of goods, to continue as the climent would be more favourable on the Sea Coast for our naked men than higher up the countrey where the climate must be more severe. The advantage of the arival of a vestle from whome we can precure goods will be more than an over ballance, for the bad liveing we shall have in liveing on Pore deer & Elk we may get in this neighbourhood.[1] If we cannot subsist on the above terms to proceed on, and make station camps, to neighbourhood of the Frendly village near the long narrows & delay untill we can proceed up the river. Salt water I view as an evil in as much as it is not helthy. I am also of opinion that one two or three weeks Exemination on the oppo[site] side if the propects are any wise favourable, would not be too long

Variation of the Compass is 16′ East

Sunday November 24ᵗʰ 1805.

A fair morning Sent out 6 hunters, and we proceeded to make the following observations[2] a Chief and Several men of the *Chinnook* nation came to Smoke with us this evening one of the men brought a Small Sea otter Skin for Which we gave Some blue beads. this day proved fair Which gave us an oppertunity of drying our wet articles, bedding &ᶜ &ᶜ nothing killed to day except one Brant. the variation of the Compass is 16°. East.

being now determined to go into Winter quarters as soon as possible, as a convenient Situation to precure the Wild animals of the forest which must be our dependance for Subsisting this Winter, we have every reason to believe that the Nativs have not provisions Suffi[ci]ent for our consumption, and if they had, their prices are So high that it would take ten times as much to purchase their *roots & Dried fish* as we have in our possesion, encluding our Small remains of Merchindize and Clothes &ᶜ This certinly enduces every individual of the party to make diligient enquiries of the nativs [for] the part of the Countrey in which the Wild animals are most plenty. They generaly agree that the Most *Elk* is on the Opposit Shore, and that the

---

[1] Coues thinks (*L. and C.,* ii, pp. 720, 721) that Jefferson might have been expected, in ordinary circumstances, to send a ship to the Columbia River, to meet the expedition ; but that he preferred not to risk giving possible offence to Spain by such action. — ED.

[2] The astronomical data, being transcripts of those given in the first draft, are here omitted. — ED.

greatest Numbers of *Deer* is up the river at Some distance above. The Elk being an animal much larger than Deer, easier to Kill, & better meat (in the Winter when pore) and Skins better for the Clothes of our party : added to [this] a convenient Situation to the Sea coast where We Could make Salt, and a probibility of Vessels comeing into the Mouth of Columbia (" which the Indians inform us would return to trade with them in 3 months ") from whome we might precure a fresh Supply of Indian trinkets to purchase provisions on our return home : together with the Solicitations of every individual, except one of our party induced us [to] Conclude to Cross the river and examine the opposit Side, and if a Sufficent quantity of Elk could probebly be precured to fix on a Situation as convenient to the Elk & Sea Coast as we could find. added to the above advantagies in being near the Sea Coast one most Strikeing one occurs to me i. e, the Climate which must be from every appearance much milder than that above the 1ˢᵗ range of Mountains, The Indians are Slightly Clothed and give an account of but little Snow, and the weather which we have experienced since we arrived in the neighbourhood of the Sea coast has been verry warm, and maney of the fiew days past disagreeably so. if this Should be the case it will most Certainly be the best Situation of our Naked party dressed as they are altogether in leather.

[Clark, first draft :]   *November 25ᵗʰ Munday 1805*

a fine day   several Indians come up from below,   we loaded and set out up the river, and proceeded on to the Shallow Bay, landed to dine,   The swells too high to cross the river, agreeabley to our wish which is to examine if game can be precured sufficent for us to winter on that side,   after dinner which was on Drid pounded fish we proceeded on up on the North Side to near the place of our Encampment of the 7ᵗʰ Instant and encamped after night   The evening cloudy   wind of to day Generally from the E.S.E.   Saw from near of [our] last campment Mount Ranier bearing [blank space in MS.]

[249]

Monday 25ᵗʰ November 1805

The Wind being high rendered it impossible for us to cross the river from our Camp, we deturmind to proceed on up where it was narrow, we Set out early accompanied by 7 *Clât-sops* for a fiew miles, they left us and crossed the river through emence high waves ; we Dined in the Shallow Bay on Dried pounded fish, after which we proceeded on near the North Side of the Columbia, and encamp[ed] a little after night near our Encampment of the 7ᵗʰ instant near a rock at Some distance in the river.[1] evening Cloudy the Winds of to day is generally E. S. E. which was a verry favourable point for us as the highlands kept it from us Mᵗ Sᵗ Hilians Can be Seen from the Mouth of this river.

[Clark, first draft:]   *November 26ᵗʰ Tuesday 1805*

Cloudy and some rain this morning at day light wind blew from the E.N.E. we set out and proceeded on up on the North Side of this great river to a rock in the river from thence we crossed to the lower point of an [blank space in MS.] Island passed between 2 Islands to the main shore, and proceeded down the South Side, passed 2 Inlets & halted below the 2ᵈ at a Indian village of 9 large houses those Indians live on an emenence behind a Island or a Channel of the river not more than 300 yds wide, they live on fish & Elk and Wapto roots, of which we bought a few at a high price they call them selves *Cat-tar-bets* (description)

We proceeded on about 8 miles and Encamped in a deep bend to the South, we had not been encamped long ere 3 Indians came in a canoe to trade the Wapto roots we had rain all the day all wet and disagreeable a bad place to camp all around this great bend is high land thickly timbered brushey & almost impossible to penetrate we saw on an Island below the village a place of deposit for the dead in canoes Great numbers of Swan Geese Brant Ducks & Gulls in this great bend which is crouded with low Islands covered with weeds

---

[1] Pillar Rock, mentioned above. — ED.

grass &c: and overflowed every flood tide   The people of the
last village is [blank space in MS.]   they ask emence prices for
what they have to sel   Blue Beeds is their great trade   they
are fond of clothes or blankits of Blue red or brown

   We are now decending to see if a favourable place should
offer on the So Side to winter &c:

from a high Point ops.ᵈ a high Isl.ᵈ down the South Side is S. 30.° W 6
m.ˡˢ to a point of low land ops.ᵈ up.ʳ p.ᵗ of Is.ᵈ passed low.ʳ p.ᵗ 1.ˢᵗ Is.ᵈ marshey.
at the up.ʳ p.ᵗ of 2 low Is.ᵈ opsd each other at 4 miles

S. 12.° E	2	miles to an Ind.ⁿ *Cat-tar-bet* vilg of 9 houses passed an inlet 300 yds wide on St.ᵈ at ½ a mile
S. 60.° W	1	mile to high land on the South
S. 70.° W	1	d° to a South point Low land a low Is.ᵈ ops.ᵈ pass the former
S. 50.° W	6	miles to a high point S.
South	2	miles to a bend camped
N. 70.° W.	6	miles to a point N.° 1 a deep bend to the left
S. 50.° W	8	miles to Point N.° 2 passing a deep bend to the South
S. 50 W	1½	miles
S. 40 W	1½	miles to p.ᵗ in Bay
		From the *Peninsolu* to the upper point is
N. 65.° E		To Point [blank space in MS.] miles across the river is N. 25.° W 4 miles
		from P.ᵗ N.° 2 to Cape Disapointm.ᵗ N. 70.° W.
		To point Adams is West
		To 1.ˢᵗ Creek small above Adams S. 60 W
		To 2.ᵈ Creek d° d° S. 40 W
		to 3.ᵈ d° d° d° S. 20 W.
		To Fort River is imedeately cross S 10° E
		To the opening of the mouth of River S. 50 E
		The bay turns to the N of East & receves 2 other small Brooks

Tuesday 26.ᵗʰ November 1805

Cloudy and Some rain this Morning from 6 oClock.   Wind
from the E.N.E.   we Set out out early and crossed a Short
distance above the rock, out in the river, & between Some low
Marshey Islands to the South Side of the Columbia at a low

bottom about 3 miles below Point *Samuel*[1] and proceeded [on]
near the South Side leaveing the Seal Islands to our right and
a marshey bottom to the left 5 Miles to the *Calt-har-mar*
[*Cathlahma*] Village of 9 large wood houses on a handsom
elivated Situation near the foot of a Spur of the high land behind a large low Island Seperated from the Southerly Shore
by a Chanel of about 200 yards Wide, This Nation appear
to differ verry little either in language, Customs dress or appearance from the *Chinnooks & War. ci a cum* live principally
on fish and *pappato* they have also other roots, and Some *Elk*
meat.

We purchased Some green fish & *Wap pá to* for which we
gave imoderate pricies. after dining on the fresh fish which
we purchased, we proceeded on through a Deep bend to the
South and encamped under a high hill, where we found much
difficuelty in precuring wood to burn, as it was raining hard,
as it had been the greater part of the day. Soon after we encamped 3 Indians of the last town Came in a Canoe with *Wap.
pa to* roots to sell to us, Some of which we purchased with
fish hooks. from the Village quite around this bend to the
West the land is high and thickly timbered with pine balsom
&c. a Short distance below the *Calt har mer* Village on the
Island which is Opposit I observed Several Canoes Scaffold[ed]
in which [were] contained their dead, as I did not examine
this mode of depos[it]ing the dead, must refer it to a discription hereafter.

---

[1] Point Samuel must be that cape now known as Cathlamet Head. On the explorers' return (see March 24, 1806) they mention a Cathlamet village just below this
point. Confusion has arisen because the present town of Cathlamet is on the north
side of the river. Thomas U. Strong of Portland, Oregon, writes that "Some time
after the expedition of Lewis and Clark the Cathlamet Tribe of Indians, very much
reduced by some pestilence that prevailed, moved over to the north bank of the Columbia River and settled somewhere near the present town of Cathlamet where some
kinsfolk of theirs, the Wahkiakums, had already a village." The old village of the
time of Lewis and Clark was on the south bank near the present town of Knappa,
on the Columbia River Railway. — ED.

[Clark, first draft :]   *November 27th Wednesday* 1805

Some rain all the last night & this morning at day light 3 canoes and 11 men came down with roots meat, skins &c. to sell, they asked such high prices we were unable to purchase any thing, and as we were about setting out, discovered that one of those Indians had stole an ax, we serched and found it under the roabe of one man whome we shamed verry much we proceeded on, around Point William[1] the swells became high and rained so hard we concluded to halt and dry our selves, soon after our landing the wind rose from the East and blew hard accompanied with rain, this rain obliged us to unload & draw up our canoes, one of which was split t[w]o feet before we got her out of the river, this place the Peninsoley is about 50 yards and 3 miles around this point of Land. water salt below not salt above

Wednesday 27th November 1805

Rained all the last night, and this morning it Continues moderately. at day light 3 Canoes and 11 Indians Came from the Village with roots mats, Skins &c. to sell, they asked such high prices that we were unable to purchase any thing of them, as we were about to Set out missed one of our axes which was found under an Indians roab. I smamed (*Shamed*) this fellow verry much and told them they should not proceed with us. we proceded on between maney Small Islands passing a Small river of [blank space in MS.] yds wide which the Indians Call Kekemarke[2] and around a verry remarkable point which projects about 1½ Miles directly towards the Shallow bay the isthmus which joins it to the main land is not exceding 50 yards and about 4 Miles around. we call this Point William below this point the waves became So high we were compelled to land unload and traw [draw] up the Canoes, here we formed a camp on the neck of Land Which joins Point William to the

---

[1] Now Tongue Point, so named by Broughton in 1792 from a fancied resemblance to that member. —ED.

[2] This river is now known as the John Day River. —ED.

main at an old indian hut.[1]   The rain Continued hard all day we are all Wet and disagreeable.   one Canoe Split before we Got her out of the Water 2 feet.   The water at our camp Salt that above the isthmus fresh and fine — [2]

[Clark, first draft :]   *November 28ᵗʰₙ Thursday 1805*

Wind shifted about to the S. W. and blew hard accompanied with hard rain all last night,   we are all wet bedding and stores, haveing nothing to keep our selves or stores dry,   our Lodge nearly worn out, and the pieces of sales & tents so full of holes & rotten that they will not keep any thing dry,   we sent out the most of the men to drive the point for deer,   they scattered through the point some stood on the *pen[in]solu*,   we could find no deer, several hunters attempted to penetrate the thick woods to the main South Side without suckcess   the swan & gees wild and cannot be approached,   and wind to high to go either back or forward, and we have nothing to eate but a little Pounded fish which we purchas.ᵈ at the Great falls, This is our present situation! truly disagreeable.   aded to this the robes of our selves and men are all rotten from being continually wet, and we cannot precure others, or blankets in these places.   about 12 oClock the wind shifted about to the N.W. and blew with great violence for the remainder of the day   at maney times it blew for 15 or 20 minits with such violence that I expected every moment to see trees taken up by the roots,   some were blown down.   Those squals were suckceeded by rain   O ! how Tremendious is the day.   This dredfull wind and rain continued with intervales of fair weather, the greater part of the evening and night

Thursday 28ᵗʰ November 1805

Wind shifted about to the S.W. and blew hard accompanied with hard rain.   rained all the last night   we are all wet our

---

[1] The camp was facing the site of Astoria, near the spot where the government now has a hydrographic station. — ED.

[2] The width of the Columbia just above Astoria and Tongue Point is between twelve and fifteen miles ; and at the bar, between Point Adams and Cape Disappointment, it is six or seven miles wide. — ED.

bedding and Stores are also wet, we haveing nothing which is
Sufficient to keep ourselves bedding or Stores dry,   Several
men in the point hunting deer without suckcess,   the Swan
and brant which are abundant Cannot be approached sufficently
near to be killed, and the wind and waves too high to proceed
on to the place we expect to find Elk, & we have nothing to
eate except pounded fish which we brought from the Great
falls,   this is our present situation ; truly disagreeable.   about
12 oClock the wind shifted around to the N.W. and blew with
Such violence that I expected every moment to See trees taken
up by the roots, maney were blown down.   This wind and
rain Continued with short intervales all the latter part of the
night.   O ! how disagreeable is our Situation dureing this
dreadfull weather.

[Lewis:]   *November 29ᵗʰ 1805* [1]

the wind being so high the party were unable to proceed
with the perogues.   I determined therefore to proceed down
the river on it's E. side in surch of an eligible place for our
winters residence and accordingly set out early this morning
in the small canoe accompanyed by 5 men. Drewyer R. Fields,
Shannon, Colter & labiesh,   proceeded along the coast.

S. 40. W. 5 M. to a point of land [2] passing two points one at 3 M.
                    bearing S 10. W. and the 2ⁿᵈ at 1½ further a little
                    retreating from the 1ˢᵗ land high and woods thick.
S. 35. W. 2. M! along the point,   land still high and thickly timbered
                    here a deep bay commences. runing
S. 40. E. 2. M! along the bay.   the land more open,   pass a small
                    prarie at 1 M.

---

[1] Here we insert (alternating with Clark's record) the entries made by Lewis during Nov. 29–Dec. 1, while on a reconnaissance on the Netul River for a site for their
winter-quarters.   They are found in a fragment called by Coues Codex Ia. — ED.

[2] This was Point George, later the site of Astoria (founded in 1811).   When
Fort Astoria was surrendered to the British (Dec., 1813), it was rechristened Fort
George.   In 1818 the United States took formal repossession of the place ; but it
remained a British fur-trade post, until abandoned, 1824, in favor of a site higher up
the river.   The point is now called Smith Point, and on it is the modern town of
Astoria. —ED.

send out the hunters they killed 4. deer 2 brant a goat and seven ducks,

it rained up on us by showers all day. left three of these deer and took with us one encamped at an old Indian hunting lodge which afforded us a tolerable shelter from the rain. which continued by intervales throughout the night.

[Clark, first draft:]   *November 29ᵗʰ Friday 1805*

Blew hard and rained the greater part of the last night and this morning, Capᵗ Lewis and 5 men set out in our small Indian canoe (which is made in the Indian fashion calculated to ride the waves) down the South Side of the river to the place the Indians informed us by signs that numbers of Elk were to be found near the river. The swells and waves being too high for us to proceed down in our large canoes in safety. I sent out two hunters to hunt deer, & one to hunt fowl, all the others employed in drying their leather and prepareing it for use, as but fiew of them have many other clothes to boste of at this time, we are smoked verry much in this camp The shore on the side next the sea is covered with butifull pebble of various colours our diat at this time and for several days past is the dried pounded fish we purchased at the falls boiled in a little salt water.

Friday 29ᵗʰ of November 1805°

The wind and rain Continued all the last night, this morning much more moderate. the waves Still high and rain continues. Capᵗ Lewis and 5 hunters Set out in our Indian Canoe (which is calculated to ride wave[s]) dow[n] to the place we expected to find Elk [and] from the Indⁿ information, the[y] pointed to a Small Bay which is yet below us. I sent out 2 men to hunt Deer which I expected might be on the open hill Sides below, another to hunt fowl in the deep bend above the point, all the others engaged drying their leather before the fire, and prepareing it for use — they haveing but fiew other Species of Clothing to ware at this time

The winds are from Such points that we cannot form our

Camp So as to prevent the Smoke which is emencely disagreeable, and painfull to the eyes. The Shore below the point at
our camp is formed of butifull pebble of various colours. I
observe but fiew birds of the Small kind, great numbers of wild
fowls of Various kinds, the large Buzzard with white wings,
grey and bald eagle's, large red tailed Hawks, ravens & crows
in abundance, the blue Magpie, a Small brown bird which
frequents logs & about the roots of trees,[1] Snakes, Lizards,
Small bugs, worms, Spiders, flyes & insects of different kinds
are to be Seen in abundance at this time.

[Lewis :]   *November 30*[th] *1805*

    cloudy morning   set out before sun rise and continued our
rout up the bey

S. 60. E. 1½ to a point. land not very high and open woods a
                little back from the bay.

S. 80. E. 3   M to the center of a bend passing a point at 1. M.
                land the same from the commenc? of this course.

S. 35. W. 2½ M across the bay to a point of marshey ground which
                for three miles in width borders this coast

S. 60. W. 2   m. to a point of marshey ground

S. 50. W. ¾ M. to a marshey point at arm of the bay. from this
                point a point of highland bore S. 25 E. 3 miles
                distant

N. 80. W. 2½ to a marshey point passing the arm of the bey ¼ of a
                mile wide the country to the S. E. appears to be
                low for a great distance and is marshey and un-
                timbered for three miles back, from this point, the
                eastern point or commencement of the bay bore
                N. 15 E. 3 miles. —

N. 60. W. 5   M. passing an inlet of 100 y[ds] wide at 4. M. to a
                point of marshey ground, here an inlet of from 40
                to 60 y[ds] in width comes in just opposite to the upper
                point of a shore which we have heretofore thought
                and Island but which I am now convinced is the
                main land. we asscended this stream about 2 M.
                it's course being S. 15 E. we halted near a small
                cops of timbered land to which we walked and dined

---

[1] Coues thinks this probably the winter wren, a variety of *Anothura hiemalis*. — ED.

Sent out three men to examin the country to the S. & W. they returned after about 2 hours and informed me that the wood was so thick and obstructed by marrasses & lakes that they were unable to proceed to the Ocean which could not be at any considerable distance f[r]om the apparent sound of the waves breaking on the Coast. we now returned and asscended the inlet which we had last passed no fresh appearance of Elek or deer in our rout so far. asscend the inlet as we intended about 1. M. found it became much smaller and that it did not keep it's direction to the high land which boar S. 10. W. but inclined [MS. torn] West. therefore returned to the large arm of the bay [1] which we passed this morning. here we expect to meet with the Clât-sop Indians, who have tantilized us with there being much game in their neighbourhood. this information in fact was the cause of my present resurch, for where there is most game is for us the most eliguble winter station. continued our rout up the large arm of the bay about 6 miles and encamped on the Star.ᵈ side on the highland. the water was quite sweet. therefore concluded that it must be supplyed from a large crick. at our camp it is 120 y.ᵈˢ wide, tho' it gets narrower above. it rained but little on us today tho' it was cloudy generally. Wind from N.E. saw a great abundance of fowls, brant, large geese, white brant sandhill Cranes, common blue crains, cormarants, haulks, ravens, crows, gulls and a great variety of ducks, the canvas back, duckinmallard, black and white diver, brown duck – &c &c

[Clark, first draft:] *November 30ᵗʰ Saturday 1805*

Some rain and hail with intervales of fair weather for 1 and 2 hours dureing the night and untill 9 oClock this morning at which time it cleared up fair and the sun shown, I send 5 men in a canoe in the Deep bend above the Peninsulear to hunt fowls, & 2 men in the thick woods to hunt Elk had all our

---

[1] This was the bay later called by the explorers Meriwether. Broughton (1792) named this large inlet in Clatsop County, Ore., Young's, for a British naval officer — a name it retains to this day. — ED.

wet articles dried & the men all employed dressing their skins,
I observe but few birds in this countrey of the small kinds
great numbers of wild fowl,　The large Buzzard with white
under their wings Grey & Bald eagle large red tailed hawk
ravins, crows, & a small brown bird which is found about logs
&.ᶜ but fiew small hawks or other smaller birds to be seen at
this time　Snakes, Lizzards, Small bugs worms spiders, flies,
& insects of different kinds are to be seen in plenty at this
time.　The squar gave me a piece of Bread to day made of
some flower she had cearfully kept for her child, and had unfortunately got wet.　The hunters killed only 3 hawks, saw 3
Elk but could not git a shot at them,　The fowlers, killed
3 black ducks, with white sharp bills, a brown spot in their
foward, some white under the tail, which is short, and a fiew
of the tips of the wing feathers white,　Their toes are long
seperated and flaped, no craw,　keep in emence large flocks in
the shallow waters & feed on Grass &.ᶜ　Several men complaining of being unwell to day.　a Broock comes in to the bend
above the 1ˢͭ point above.　and a river falls in the next nitch
above　this river is small.　I observe rose bushes Pine, a kind
of ash a species of Beech and a species of Maple, in addition to
the pine Lorrel and under groth common to the woods in this
Lower Countrey　the hills are not high & slope to the river

Saturday 30.ᵗʰ of November 1805

Some rain and hail with intervales of fair weather for the
Space of one or two hours at a time dureing the night untill
9 oClock this morning, at which time it cleared away and the
Sun Shewn for [blank space in MS.] hours,　Several men out
hunting　I send 5 men in the bend above to hunt fowl &c.
in a Canoe,　employ all the others in drying our wet articles
by the fire.　Several men Complain of a looseness and griping
which I contribute to the diet, pounded fish mixed with Salt
water,　I derect that in future that the party mix the pounded
fish with fresh water.　The squar gave me a piece of bread
made of flour which She had reserved for her child and care-

fully Kept untill this time, which has unfortunately got wet, and a little Sour. this bread I eate with great satisfaction, it being the only mouthfull I had tasted for Several months past. my hunters killed *three* Hawks, which we found fat and delicious, they Saw 3 Elk but could not get a Shot at them. The fowlers killed 3 black Ducks with Sharp White beeks Keep in large flocks & feed on Grass, they have no Craw and their toes are seperate, Common in the U. States [1]

The Chinnooks *Cath lâh mâh* & others in this neighbourhood bury their dead in their Canoes. for this purpose 4 pieces of Split timber are Set erect on end, and sunk a fiew feet in the ground, each brace having their flat Sides opposit to each other and sufficiently far assunder to admit the width of the Canoe in which the dead are to be deposited; through each of those perpindicular posts, at the hight of 6 feet a mortice is cut, through which two bars of wood are incerted; on those cross bars a Small canoe is placed, in which the body is laid after beaing Carefully roled in a robe of Some dressed Skins; a paddle is also deposited with them; a larger Canoe is now reversed, overlaying and imbracing the Small one, and resting with its gunnals on the cross bars; one or more large mats of flags or rushes are then rol⁴ around the Canoe and the whole securely lashed with a long cord usially made of the bark of the *arbar. vita* or white cedar. on the cross bars which support the Canoes is frequently hung or laid various articles of Clothing culinary utensils &⁑ we cannot understand them Sufficiently to make any enquiries relitive to their religious opinions, from their depositing Various articles with their dead, [they] beleve in a State of future ixistance.

(*Copy for Dr. Barton*) I walked on the point and observed rose bushes different Species of pine, a Sp[e]cies of ash, alder, a Species of wild Crab Loral.[2] and Several Species of under groth common to this lower part of the Columbia river. The hills on this coast rise high and are thickly covered with lofty pine maney of which are 10 & 12 feet through and more than 200 feet high. hills have a Steep assent.

---

[1] This is the coot (*Fulica americana*). — ED.

[2] Laurel is probably the Madrona (*Arbutus menziesii*). — C. V. PIPER.

Cloudy morning wind from the S.E. sent out the men to hunt and examin the country, they soon returned all except Drewyer and informed me that the wood was so thick it was almost impenetrable and that there was but little appearance of game; they had seen the track of one deer only and a few small grey squirrels. these s[q]uirrels are about the size of the red squirrel of the lakes and eastern Atlantic States, their bellies are of a redish yellow, or tanners ooze colour the tale flat and as long as the body eyes black and moderately large back and sides of a greyish brown

the brier with a brown bark and three l[e]aves which put-forth at the extremety of the twigs like the leaves of the blackbury brier, tho' it is a kind of shrub and rises sometimes to the hight of 10 fe[et] the green brier yet in leaf; the ash with a remarkable large leaf; the large black alder. the large elder with sky blue buries. the broad leave shrub which grows something like the quill wood but has no joints, the leaf broad and deeply indented. the bark p[e]als and hangs on the stem and is of a yelowish brown colour. the seven bark is also found here as is the common low cramburry there is a wild crab apple which the natives eat this growth differs but little in appearance from that of the wild crab of the Atlantic States. but the fruit consists of little oval burries which grow in clusters at the extremities of the twigs like the black haws. the

fruit is of a brown colour, oval form and about double as large
as the black haw; the rind is smoth and tough somewhat
hard ; the seed is like that of the wild crab and nearly as large ;
the pulp is soft of a pale yellow coulour; and when the fruit
has been touched by the frost is not unpleasant, being an
agreeable assed.   the tree which bears a red burry in clusters
of a round form and size of a red haw.   the leaf like that of
the small magnolia, and bark smoth and of a brickdust red
coulour it appears to be of the evergreen kind.   half after one
oclock Drewyer not yet arrived.   heard him shoot 5 times just
above us and am in hopes he has fallen in with a gang of elk.

[In Clark's handwriting :] Cap⸌ Lewis rough notes when he
left Cap⸌ Clark near the mouth of Columbia for a few days to
examine the S.W. side.

[Clark, first draft :]   *December 1ˢᵗ Sunday 1805*

Cloudy windey morning wind from the East,   sent out 2
hunters in the woods,   I intended to take 5 men in a canoe
and hunt the marshey Islands above, found the wind too high
& returned to partake of the dried fish,   The day some what
cooler than usial, but scercely perceveable.   began to rain at
sun set and continued half the night.   my hunters returned
without any thing saw 2 gang of *Elk* a disagreeable situation,
men all employed in mending their leather clothes, socks
&⸳ and Dressing some Leather.   The sea which is imedeately
in front roars like a repeeted roling thunder and have rored in
that way ever since our arrival in its borders which is now 24
days since we arrived in sight of the Great Western Ocian, I
cant say Pasific as since I have seen it, it has been the reverse
Elegant canoes.

                          Sunday December 1ˢᵗ 1805.

A cloudy windey morning wind from the East,   dispatched
two hunters,   I deturmined to take a canoe & a fiew men and
hunt the Marshey Islands above Point William,   the Wind
rose so high that I could not proceed, and returned to partake

[of] the dried fish, which is our standing friend, began to rain hard at Sun set and Continud. My hunters returned without any thing haveing Seen 2 parcels of elk men all employed to day in mending their leather Clothes, Shoes &c and Dressing leather.

The emence Seas and waves which breake on the rocks & Coasts to the S.W. & N W roars like an emence fall at a distance, and this roaring has continued ever Since our arrival in the neighbourhod of the Sea Coast which has been 24 days Since we arrived in Sight of the Great Western; (for I cannot Say Pacific) Ocian as I have not Seen one pacific day Since my arrival in its vicinity, and its waters are forming and petially [perpetually] breake with emenc waves on the Sands and rockey coasts, tempestous and horiable. I have no account of Cap! Lewis Since he left me.

[Clark, first draft :]   *December* 2$^{nd}_{11}$ *Monday* 1805.

Cloudy and some little rain this morning I despatched 3 men to hunt and 2 and my servent in a canoe to a creek above to try & catch some fish I am verry unwell the dried fish which is my only diet does not agree with me and several of the men complain of a lax, and weakness. I expect Cap! Lewis will return to day with the hunters and let us know if Elk or deer can be found sufficent for us to winter on. If he does not come I shall move from this place to one of better prospects for game &c Joseph Fields come home with the marrow bones of an Elk which he had killed 6 miles distant, I sent out 6 men in a canoe for the meat, the evening being late they did not return this night which proved fair moon shineing night. This is the first Elk we have killed on this side the rockey mount? a great deal of Elk sign in the neighbourhood.

Monday 2nd *December* 1805

Cloudy with Some rain this morning I Send out three men to hunt & 2 & my man York in a Canoe up the *Ke-ke-mar-que* Creek in serch of fish and fowl. I feel verry unwell, and have

entirely lost my appetite for the Dried pounded fish which is
in fact the cause of my disorder at present.   The men are
generally complaining of a lax and gripeing.   In the evening
Joseph Field came in with the Marrow bones of a elk which
he killed at 6 miles distant,   this welcome news to us.   I dispatched Six men in a empty Canoe with Jo: imediately for the
elk which he Said was about 3 miles from the Water   this is
the first Elk which has been killd on this Side of the rockey
mountains   Jo. Fields givs me an account of a great deel of
Elk Sign & says he Saw 2 Gangs of those animals in his rout,
but it rained So hard that he could not Shoot them.   The
party up the Creek returned without any thing and informs me
they could not See any fish in the Creek to kill and the fowls
were too wild to be killed,   this must be owing to their being
much hunted and pursued by the Indians in their Canoes.

[Clark, first draft :]   *December* 3$^{rd}_{\,\parallel}$ *Tuesday* 1805

   a fair windey morning wind from the East,   the men sent
after an Elk yesterday return.^{d} with an Elk which revived the
sperits of my men verry much,   I am unwell and cannot eate,
the flesh   O ! how disagreeable my situation, a plenty of meat
and incap[ab]le of eateing any.   an Indian canoe came down
with 8 Indians in it from the upper village,   I gave a fish hook
for a fiew *Wap-e-to* roots, which I eate in a little Elk supe,
The Indians proceeded on down.   wind continues to blow, and
Serj.^{t} Pryor & Gibson who went to hunt yesterday has not
return.^{d} as yet   I marked my name & the day of the month
and year on a large Pine tree on this peninsella & by land
" Capt William Clark December 3rd 1805.   By Land.   U. States
in 1804–1805 "   The squar Broke the two shank bones of
the Elk after the marrow was taken out, boiled them & extracted a Pint of Greese or tallow from them.   Serj.^{t} Pryor &
Gibson returned after night and informed me they had been
lost the greater part of the time they were out, and had killed
6 Elk which they left lying haveing taken out their intrals.
Some rain this afternoon

Tuesday 3ᵈ December 1805

a fair windey morning wind from the East　the men returned with the Elk which revived the Spirits of my party
verry much.　I am still unwell and can't eate even the flesh of
the Elk.　an Indian Canoe of 8 Indians Came too,　those
Indˢ are on their way down to the *Clât-sops* with *Wap pa to* to
barter with that Nation,　I purchasᵈ a fiew of those roots for
which I gave Small fish hooks,　those roots I eate with a little
Elks Soupe which I found gave me great relief　I found the
roots both nurishing and as a check to my disorder.　The Indians proceeded on down through emence high waves　maney
times their Canoe was entirely out of Sight before they were ½
a mile distant.　Serjᵗ Pryor & Gibson who went hunting
yesterday has not returned untill after night,　they informed
me that they had killed 6 Elk at a great distance which they
left lying, haveing taken out their interals, that they had been
lost and in their ramble saw a great deel of Elk Sign.　after eateing the marrow out of two shank bones of an Elk, the Squar
choped the bones fine boiled them and extracted a pint of
Grease, which is Superior to the tallow of the animal.　Some
rain this evening　I marked my name on a large pine tree imediately on the isthmus　William Clark December 3ʳᵈ 1805.
By Land from the U.States in 1804 & 1805.

[Clark, first draft:]　　　　　　　*December 4ᵗʰⁱⁱ Wednesday 1805*

Some little rain all the last night and this morning after day
the rain increased and continued.

I despatched Serjᵗ Pryer & 6 men to the Elk which he had
killed yesterday, with directions to save the meet and take
loads to the River below in the next great bend.　a spring tide
which rose 2 feet higher than common flud tides, and high
water at 11 oClock to day.　wind from the S.E　in the after
noon hard wind from South.　rained all day, moderately　the
swells too high for me to proceed down, as I intended.　I
feel my self something better and have an appetite to eate
something

Wednesday 4ᵗʰ December 1805

Some rain all the last night, this morning it increased with the wind from the S.E. I Se[n]t out Sergiant Pryor and 6 men to the Elk he had killed with directions to carry the meat to a bay which he informed me was below and as he believed at no great distance from the Elk, and I Should proceed on to that bay as soon as the wind would lay a little and the tide went out in the evening. the Smoke is exceedingly disagreeable and painfull to my eyes, my appetite has returned and I feel much better of my late complaint. a Spring tide to day rose 2 feet higher than common flood tides and high water at 11 oClock. Hard wind from the South this evening, rained moderately all day and the waves too high for me to proceed in Safty to the bay as I intended, in Some part of which I expected would be convenient for us to make winter quarters, the reports of seven hunte[r]s agreeing that elke were in great abundance about the Bay below. no account of Capt Lewis. I fear Some accident has taken place in his craft or party.

[Clark, first draft:]   *December 5ᵗʰ Thursday 1805*

Som hard showers of rain last night, this morn cloudy and drisley rain, in the bay above the showers appear harder. High water to day at 12 oClock this tide is 2 Inˢ higher than that of yesterday all our stores again wet by the hard showers of last night Capt Lewis's long delay below has been the cause of no little uneasiness on my part for him, a 1000 conjectures has crouded into my mind respecting his probable situation & safty. rained hard. Capt Lewis returned haveing found a good situation and Elk sufficent to winter on, his party killed 6 Elk & 5 Deer in their absence in serch of a situation and game Rain continued all the after pt of the day accompanied with hard wind from the S W. which prevented our moveing from this Camp.

Thursday 5ᵗʰ of December 1805

Some hard Showers of rain last night, this morning cloudy and drisley at Some little distance above the isthmus the rain is much harder.   high water to day at 12.   this tide is 2 inches higher than that of yesterday,   all our Stores and bedding are again wet by the hard rain of last night.   Cap! Lewis's long delay below, has been the Sorce of no little uneas[i]ness on my part of his probable Situation and Safty,   the repeeted rains [1] and hard winds which blows from the S.W. renders it impossible for me to move with loaded Canoes along an un-known coast   we are all wet and disagreeable, the party much better of indispositions.   Cap! Lewis returned with 3 men in the Canoe and informs me that he thinks that a Sufficient number of Elk may be pr[o]cured convenient to a Situation on a Small river which falls into a Small bay a Short distance below,   that his party had Killed 6 Elk & 5 Deer in his rout, two men of his party left behind to secure the Elk.

this was verry Satisfactory information to all the party.   we accordingly deturmined to proceed on to the Situation which Cap! Lewis had Viewed as Soon as the wind and weather should permit and Comence building huts &c?

[Clark, first draft :]   *December 6*[th.] *Friday* 1805

Wind blew hard all the last night, and a moderate rain,   the waves verry high,   This morning the wind which is still from the S W increased and rained continued all day   at Dusk wind shifted to the North and it cleared up and became fare.   High water to day at 12 oClock & 13 Inches higher than yesterday we were obliged to move our camp out of the water on high grown[d]   all wet.

Friday 6[th.] *of December* 1805

The wind blew hard all the last night with a moderate rain, the waves verry high,   the wind increased & from the S.W. and the rain Continued all day,   about Dark the wind Shifted to the North cleared away and became fair weather.

---

1 There is more wet weather on this coast than I ever knew in any other place ; during a month, we have had but three fair days, and there is no prospect of a change. — GASS (p. 249).

The high tide of today is 13 inches higher than yesterday, and obliged us to move our Camp which was in a low Situation, on higher ground   Smoke exceedingly disagreeable.

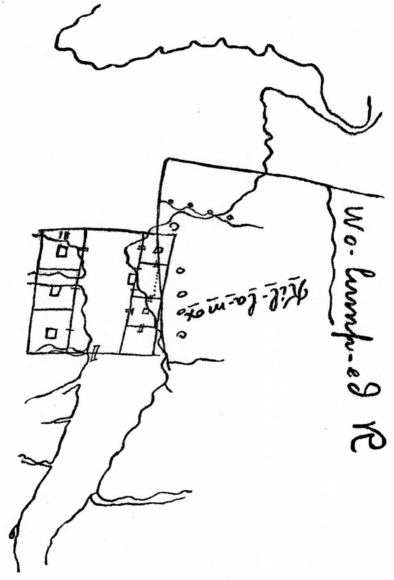

CLARK'S PLAN OF FORT CLATSOP

Here given, should be compared with his larger plan, under date of December 30th, *post*

Some rain from 10 to 12 last night   this morning fair   we set out at 8 oClock down to the place Capᵗ Lewis pitched on for winter quarters when he was down   proceeded on against the tide at the point N° 2 we met our men sent down after meat

To point Adams is West

To pᵗ Disapointment N. 75 W.

They informed me that they found the Elk after being lost in the woods for one Day and part of another   the most of the meat was spoiled,   they distance was so great and uncertain and the way bad, they brought only the skins,   york was left behind by some accident which detained us some time eer he came up   after passing round the pᵗ N° 2 in verry high swells, we stopᵈ & Dined in the commencement of a bay, after which proceeded on around the bay to S E & assended a creek 8 miles to a high pᵗ & camped haveing passed arm makeing up to our left into the countrey

(*Mᵗ Sᵗ Helens* is the mountain we mistook for *Mᵗ Reeaneer*)

receved 2 small Brooks on the East, extencive marshes at this place of Encampment We propose to build & pass the winter   The situation is in the center of as we conceve a hunting countrey.   This day is fair except about 12 oClock at which time some rain and a hard wind imedeately after we passed the point from the N.E which continued for a about 2 hours and cleared up   no meat

Saturday 7ᵗʰ of December 1805

Some rain from 10 to 12 last night,   this morning fair, have every thing put on board the Canoes and Set out to the place Capᵗ Lewis had viewed and thought well Situated for winter quarters.   we proceeded on against the tide to a point about [blank space in MS] miles   here we met Sergᵗ Pryor and his party returning to the Camp we had left without any meat,   the waves verry verry high, as much as our Canoes could bear rendered it impossible to land for the party,   we proceeded on around the point into the bay and

[269]

landed to take brackfast on 2 Deer which had been killed &
hung up, one of which we found the other had been taken
off by [s]ome wild animal probably Panthors or the Wild [cat?]
of this Countrey hère all the party of Serg' Pryors joined us
except my man York, who had stoped to rite his load and
missed his way, Serg' Pryor informed us that he had found
the Elk, which was much further from the bay than he expected,
that they missed the way for one day and a half, & when he
found the Elk they were mostly spoiled, and they only brought
the Skins of 4 of the Elk. after brackfast I delayed about
half an hour before York Came up, and then proceeded around
this Bay which I call [*have taken the liberty of calling*] Meriwethers Bay the Cristian name of Cap' Lewis who no doubt
was the 1ˢᵗ white man who ever Surveyed this Bay, we assended a river which falls in on the South Side of this Bay 3
miles to the first point of high land on the West Side, the
place Cap' Lewis had viewed and formed in a thick groth of
pine about 200 yards from the river, this situation is on a
rise about *30 feet higher than the high tides leavel* and thickly
Covered with lofty pine. this is certainly the most eligable
Situation for our purposes of any in its neighbourhood. Meriwethers Bay is about 4 miles across deep & receves 2 rivers
the *Kil-how-â-nah-kle* and the *Ne tul* and Several Small Creeks.[1]
we had a hard wind from the N E and Some rain about 12
oClock to day which lasted 2 hours and Cleared away. From
the Point above Meriwethers Bay to Point Adams is *West* to
point Disapointment is N. 75° W. (*camped on the Ne tul*)

[Clark, first draft:]   *December 8ᵗʰ Sunday* 1805

a cloudy morning, I took 5 men and set out to the *See* to
find the nearest place & make a way to prevent our men getting
lost and find a place to make salt, steered S. 62° W at 2
miles passed the head of a Brook runing to the right, the lands
good roleing much falling timber, lofty Pine of the Spruce kind,
& some fur, passed over a high hill & to a creek which we kept

---

[1] The rivers here mentioned are now called Klaskanine, and Lewis and Clark's
(formerly Netul) — ED

down 1½ miles and left it to our right, saw fish in this creek & Elk Bear tracks on it, passed over a ridge to a low marshey bottom which we crossed thro water & thick brush for ½ a mile to the commencement of a Prarie which wavers, covered with grass & Sackay commis, at ½ crossed a marsh 200 yds wide, boggey and arrived at a creek which runs to the right. Saw a gange of Elk on the opposit side below, rafted the creek, with much dificulty & followed the Elk thro emence bogs, & over 4 small knobs in the bogs about 4 miles to the South & killed an Elk, and formed a camp, covered our selves with the Elk skins, the left of us Bogs & a lake or pond those bogs shake, much cramberry growing amongst the moss. Some rain this evening we made a harty supper of the Elk & hung up the bal^e

Sunday 8th December 1805   Fort Clatsop [1]

We haveing fixed on this Situation as the one best Calculated for our Winter quarters I determin'd to go as direct a Course as I could to the Sea Coast which we could here roar and appeared to be at no great distance from us, my principal object is to look out a place to make Salt, blaze the road or rout that they men out hunting might find the direction to the fort if they Should get lost in cloudy weather — and See the probability of game in that direction, for the Support of the Men, we Shall Send to make Salt, I took with me five men and Set out on a Course S 60 W proceeded on a dividing ridge through lofty piney land much falling timber. passed the heads of 2 brooks one of them had wide bottoms which was over flown & we waded to our knees crossed 2 Slashes [2] (*Swamps*) and arrived at a Creek in a open ridgey prarie covered with Sackacomma (*Sac de Commis*) this Creek we were obliged to raft, which is about 60 yards over and runs in a direction to Point adams, we discovered a large gange of

---

[1] The exact site of Fort Clatsop has recently been determined by the Oregon Historical Society See *Proceedings*, 1900, pp 13–23 — ED

[2] The *Century Dictionary* defines "slashes" (adj slashey) as a wet or swampy place overgrown with bushes It is common parlance in Virginia and Kentucky, where Clay was known as the "mill boy of the slashes" — ED

Elk in the open lands, and we prosued them through verry bad Slashes and Small ponds about 3 miles, Killed one and camped on a spot Scercely large enough to lie Clear of the Water. it is almost incredeable to assurt the bogs which those animals can pass through, I prosue'd this gang of Elk through bogs which the wate of a man would Shake for ½ an Acre, and maney places I Sunk into the Mud and water up to my hips without finding any bottom on the trale of those Elk. Those bogs are covered with a kind of Moss among' which I observe an ebundance of Cramberries. in those Slashes Small Knobs are promisquisly scattered about which are Steep and thickly Covered with pine Common to the Countrey & Lorel. we made a camp of the Elk skin to keep off the rain which continued to fall, the Small Knob on which we camped did not afford a Sufficiency of dry wood for our fire, we collected what dry wood we could and what Sticks we could Cut down with the Tomahawks, which made us a tolerable fire.

[Clark, first draft:]   *December 9ᵗʰ Monday 1805*

    rained all the last night   we are all wet,   send 2 men in pursute of the Elk & with the other 3 I set out with a view to find the Ocian in our first direction, which can be at no great Distance, I crossed 3 Slashes by wadeing to my knees & was prevented proceeding by the 4ᵗʰ which was a pond of 200 yᵈˢ wᵉ I went around, and was stoped by a 5ᵗʰ which apᵈ to be a runᵍ stream to the right   I then returned to the raft and recrossᵈ & proceeded down the stream I first struck about 2 miles & met 3 Indians, who informed me they lived on the see cost at a short distance, I determᵈ to accompany them to their vilˢ & we set out crossed the stream, and 2 of the Indians took the canoe over the wavering open rich plains for ½ a mile and we crossed the same stream which run to the left, we then left the canoe and proceeded to the same stream which runs to the right and empties its self into the see here I found their vilˢ 4 Lodges on the west bank of this little river which is here 70 yards wide, crossed in a canoe & was

THE SITE OF FORT CLATSOP

invited to a lodge by a young Chief was treated [with] great Politeness, we had new mats to set on, and himself and wife produced for us to eate, fish, Lickorish, & black roots, on neet small mats, and cramberries & Sackacomey berries, in bowls made of horn, supe made of a kind of bread made of berries common to this countrey which they gave me in a neet wooden trencher, with a Cockle shell to eate it with It began to rain and with a tremendous storm from the S.W. which lasted untill 10 oClock P M. when I was dispos⁴ to go to sleep 2 neet mats was produced & I lay on them but the flees were so troublesom that I slept but little Those people has 2 plays which they are fond of one is with a Been which they pass from one hand into the other, and the oponent guess on this game the resquiset numbʳ of the white Beeds which is the principal property. they other game is with round Pices of wood much the shape of the [blank space in MS.] Back-gammon which they role thro between 2 pins.

Monday 9ᵗʰ December, 1805

rained all the last night we are all wet, I directed 2 hunters Drewyer & Shannon to go in pursute of the Elk, with the other 3 men I deturmined to proceed on to the Ocian, & Set out on a Westerley direction crossed 3 Slashes and arived at a Creek which I could not cross as it was deep and no wood to make a raft, I proceeded down this Creek a Short distance and found that I was in a fork of the creek, I then returned to (*the*) raft on which we had crossed the day (*before*). crossed and kept down about one mile and met 3 Indians loaded with fresh Salmon which they had Giged in the creek I crossed yesterday in the hills, those indians made Signs that they had a town on the Seacoast at no great distance, and envited me to go to their town which envitation I axcepted and accom-panᵈ them, they had a Canoe hid in the Creek which I had just before rafted which I had not observed, we crossed in this little Canoe just large enough to carry 3 men an[d] their loads after Crossing 2 of the Indians took the Canoe on theire Sholders and Carried it across to the other Creek about

¼ of a mile, we Crossed the 2ᵈ Creek and proceeded on to the mouth of the creek which makes a great bend above the mouth of this Creek or to the S. is 3 houses and about 12 families of the Clatsop Nation, we crossed to those houses, which were built on the S exposur of the hill, Sunk into the ground about 4 feet the walls roof & gable ends are of Split pine boards, the dores Small with a ladder to decend to the iner part of the house, the fires are 2 in the middle of the house their beads ar all around raised about 2½ feet from the bottom flore all covered with mats and under those beads was Stored their bags baskets and useless mats, those people treated me with extrodeanary friendship, one man attached himself to me as Soon as I entered the hut, Spred down new mats for me to Set on, gave me fish berries rutes &c on Small neet platters of rushes to eate which was repeated, all the Men of the other houses came and Smoked with me Those people appeared much Neeter in their diat than Indians are Comonly, and frequently wash theer faces and hands. in the eve[ni]ng an old woman presented [in] a bowl made of a light coloured horn a kind of Surup made of Dried berries which is common to this Countrey which the natives Call Shele wele (*She-well*)[1] this Surup I though[t] was pleasent, they Gave me Cockle Shells to eate a kind of Seuip (*Soup*) made of bread of the *Shele well* berries Mixed with roots in which they presented in Neet trenchers Made of wood. a flock of Brant lit in the Creek which was 70 yds wide I took up my Small rifle and Shot one which astonished those people verry much, they plunged into the Creek and brought the brant on Shore. in the evening it began to rain and Continud accompanied with a Violent wind from the S W. untill 10 oClock P M those people have a Singular game which they are verry fond of and is performed with Something (*a piece of bone*) about the Size of a large been (*bean*) which they pass from, one hand into the other with great dexterity dureing which time they Sing, and ocasionally, hold out their hands for those who Chuse to risque their property to guess which hand the been is in ; the

---

[1] Usually written salal or sallal, sometimes shallun ; the fruit of *Gaulthieria shallon*, a small evergreen shrub allied to the common wintergreen (*G procumbens*) — ED

individual who has the been is a banker & opposed to all in the room.   on this game they risque their beeds & other parts of their most valuable effects.   this amusement has occupied about 3 hours of this evening,   Several of the lodge in which I am in have lost all the beeds which they had about them they have one other game which a man attempted to Show me, I do not properly understand it,   they make use of maney peces about the Shape and size of Backgammon Pices (*Men*) which they role (*on the floor*) through between two pins Stuck up at certain distancies &c[1]   when I was Disposed to go to Sleep the man who' had been most attentive named *Cus-ka lah* producd 2 new mats and Spred them near the fire, and derected his wife to go to his bead which was the Signal for all to retire which they did emediately.   I had not been long on my mats before I was attacked most Violently by the flees and they kept up a close Siege dureing the night

[Clark, first draft :]   *December* 10th 1805 *Tuesday*

   a cloudey rainy morning   those people was some what astonished, at three shot I made with my little riffle to day, a gangue of Brant lit in the little river, I kill[d] 2 of them as they lit, and on my return saw a duck which I took the head off of,   the men plunged into the water like Spaniards Dogs after those fowls,   after eateing a brackfast which was similar to my suppar, I attempted to purchase some fiew roots which I offered red beeds for,   they would give scercely any thing for Beeds of that colour, I then offered small fish hooks which they were fond of and gave me some roots for them,   I then set out on my return by the same road I had went out accomp[d] by my young Chief by name *Cus-ca-lar* who crossed me over the 3 Creek[s], and returned   I proceeded on to my camp thro a heavy cold rain,   saw no game   at the Sea Cost

   [1] These games are described by George Gibbs, in the U S Geological Survey s *Contributions to American Ethnology*, i (Washington, 1877), p 206   They are called, in the jargon, *it-lu-kam* and *tsil-tsil,* respectively.   They are, as might be expected, accompanied with much betting, and success in them is thought to depend on certain charms or incantations   The Biddle text mentions (ii, p 94) the passion of the Indians for gambling — E<small>D</small>

near those Indins I found various kinds of shells, a kind of Bay ops^d those people with a high p^t about 4 miles below, out from which at some distance I saw large rocks, as the day was cloudy I could not see distinctly found Capt Lewis with all hands felling trees, to build with, rained nearly all day, in my absence they men had b^t in the 6 Elk which was killed some days past 4 men complaining of being unwell from various causes

Tuesday 10th December 1805

a Cloudy rainey morning verry early I rose and walked on the Shore of the Sea coast and picked up Several curious Shells I saw Indians Walking up and down the beech which I did not at first understand the cause of, one man came to where I was and told me that he was in Serch of fish which is frequently thrown up on Shore and left by the tide, and told me (*in English*) the "Sturgion was verry good" and that the water when it retired left fish which they eate this was Conclusive evedance to me that this Small band depended in Some Measure for their winters Subsistance on the fish which is thrown on Shore and left by the tide after amuseing my self for about an hour on the edge of the rageing Seas I returned to the houses, one of the Indians pointed to a flock of Brant Sitting in the creek at Short distance below and requested me to Shute one, I walked down with my Small rifle and killed two at about 40 yds distance, on my return to the houses two Small ducks Set at about 30 Steps from me the Indians pointed at the ducks they were near together, I Shot at the ducks and accidently Shot the head of one off, this Duck and brant was Carried to the house and every man came around examined the Duck looked at the gun the Size of the ball which was 100 to the pound and Said in their own language *Clouch Musket, (English word Musket) wake, com ma-tax, Musket*[1] which is, a good Musket do not under Stand this kind of Musket &c. I entered the Same house I slept in, they

---

[1] Uttered in the trade jargon; it would be written, according to Hale (*Oregon Trade Language*, pp 45, 48, 52), as *Kloshe musket, wake kumtuks musket* — ED

imediately Set before me their best roots, fish and Surup,   I
attempted to purchase a Small Sea otter Skin for read [red]
beeds which I had in my pockets, they would not trade for
those beeds not priseing any other Colour than Blue or White,
I purchased a little of the berry bread and a fiew of their roots
for which I gave Small fish hooks, which they appeared fond
of   I then Set out on my return by the Same rout I had
Come out accompanied by *Cus-ka-lah* and his brother as far as
the Second [3ᵈ] Creek, for the purpose of Setting me across,
from which place they returned, and I pıoceeded on through
a heavy rain to the Camp at our intended fort,   Saw a bears
track & the tracks of 2 Elk in the thick woods   found Capᵗ
Lewis with all the men out Cutting down trees for our huts
&c.   in my absence the Men brought in the six Elk which
was killed Several days ago,   4 men complaining of Violent
Coalds.   three Indians in a canoe came up from the *Clat sop*
Village yesterday and returned to day.   The Sea Coast is
about 7 Miles distant Nearly West about 5 miles of the distance through a thick wood with reveens hills and Swamps
the land, rich black moald 2 miles in a open wavering Sandy
prarie, ridge runing parrelal to the river, covered with Green
Grass.

[Clark, first draft :]   *December 11ᵗʰ Wednesday*

    rained all last night moderately,   we are all employed put-
ting up the huts,   rained at intervales all day moderately
employed in putting up cabins for our winter quarters,   one
man with Tumers, one with a Strained Knee, one sick with
Disentary & Serjᵗ Pryor unwell from haveing his sholder out
of place

                                    Wednesday 11ᵗʰ December 1805

    rained all the last night moderately   we are all employed
putting up huts or Cabins for our winters quarters,   Sergeant
Pryor unwell from a dislocation of his sholder, Gibson with
the disentary, Jo. Fields with biles on his legs, & Werner with
a Strained Knee.   The rain Continued moderately all day.

[Clark, first draft:] *December* 12*th* *Thursday* 1805

Some moderate showers last night and this morning all hands who are well employed in building cabins, despatched 2 men to get board timber, The flees so bad last night that I made but a broken nights rest we can't get them out of our robes & skins, which we are obliged to make use of for bedding Some rain to day at Intervales all at work, in the evening 2 canoes of Indians came from the 2 villages of *Clotsop* below, & brought Wapitoo roots a black root they call *Si-ni-tor* and a small sea orter skin all of which we purchased for a fiew fishing hooks & some Snake Indian Tobacco. Those Indians appear well disposed, I made a Chief of one & gave him a small *medel*, his name is *Con-year* we treated those people well, they are tite Deelers, value Blu & white beeds verry highly, and sell their roots also highly as they purchase them from the Indians above for a high price

Thursday 12*th* *December* 1805

All hands that are well employ'd in cutting logs and raising our winter Cabins, detached two men to Split boards. Some rain at intervales all last night and to day The flees were so troublesom last night that I made but a broken nights rest, we find great dificuelty in getting those trouble[some] insects out of our robes and blankets. in the evening two Canoes of *Clât Sops* Visit us they brought with them *Wappato*, a black Sweet root they Call *Sha-na toe qua*, and a Small Sea Otter Skin, all of which we purchased for a fiew fishing hooks and a Small Sack of Indian tobacco which was given [us] by the Snake Ind[a]

Those Indians appear well disposed we gave a Medal to the principal Chief named *Con-ny-au* or *Com mo-wol*[1] and treated those with him with as much attention as we could. I can readily discover that they are close deelers, & Stickle for a verry little, never close a bargin except they think they have the advantage Value Blue beeds highly, white they also prise

---

1 The real name of this chief was Coboway; his grandson, Silas B Smith, attributed the mistake in the explorers orthography to the uncertainty of the liquid sounds in the Clatsop language — ED

but no other Colour do they Value in the least　the *Wap pa to* they Sell high, this root the[y] purchase at·a high price from the nativs above.

[Clark, first draft :]　　　　　　　*December* 13*ᵗʰ Friday* 1805

　The Indians left us to day after brackfast, haveing sold us 2 of the robes of a small animal for which I intend makeing a Capot, and sold Capᵗ Lewis 2 Loucirvia Skins for the same purpose.[1]　Drewyer & Shannon returned from hunting havᵍ killed 18 Elk and butchered all except 2 which they could not get as night prevented ther finding them & they spoilᵈ　3 Indians in a canoe came and offered us for sale *Sinutor* roots, fish & 2 Sea otter skins for sale none of which we could purchase　Some rain last night and this day at several times, light showers　we continue building our houses of the streightest & most butifullest logs,　sent out 2 men to split timber to cover the cabins, and I am glad to find the timber splits butifully, and of any width

　　　　　　　　　　　　　　　　　Friday 13*ᵗʰ December* 1805

　The *Clatsops* leave us to day after a brackfast on Elk which they appeared to be very fond of　before they left us they Sold me two robes of the skins of a Small animal about the size of a cat, and to Captain Lewis 2 Cat or Loucirva Skins for the purpose of makeing a Coat　Drewyer & Shannon returned from hunting　haveing killed 18 Elk & left them boochered in the woods near the right fork of the river about 6 miles above this place.　in the evining 3 Indians came in a canoe, and offered to us for Sale roots & and 2 Sea otter Skins, neither of which we could purchase this evening,　Some Showers of rain last night, and to day Several verry hard Showers. we Continue to put up the Streight butifull balsom pine[2] on our houses　and we are much pleased to find that the timber Splits most butifully and to the width of 2 feet or more

----

　[1] Loup cervier (loucirva) was the name for the Canadian lynx; this was *L rufus fasciatus,* common to Oregon and Washington　The small animal was the sewellel (*Haplodon rufus*) — Eᴅ

　[2] Which makes the finest puncheons I have ever seen　They can be split ten feet long and two broad, not more than an inch and a half thick — Gᴀss (p 252)

[Clark, first draft:] *December 14th Saturday 1805*

a cloudy day & rained moderately all day we finish the log works of our building, the Indians leave us to day after selling a small sea otter skin and a roabe, send 4 men to stay at the Elk which is out in the woods &c

Saturday 14th December 1805

The Day Cloudy and rained moderately all day we finish the log work of our building, the Indians leave us to day after Selling a Small Sea otter skin and a roab, dispatch 4 men to the Elk out in the woods with derections to delay untill the party goes up tomorrow all employd in finishing a house to put meat into. all our last Supply of Elk has Spoiled in the repeeted rains which has been fallen ever Since our arrival at this place, and for a long time before, Scerce one man in camp can bost of being one day dry Since we landed at this point, the Sick getting better, my man York Sick with Cholick & gripeing.

[Clark, first draft:] *December 15th Sunday 1805*

I set out with 16 men in 3 canoes for the Elk proced up the 1st right hand fork 4 miles & pack the meat from the woods to the canoes from 4 mile to 3 miles distance all hands pack not one man exempted from this labour I also pack my self some of this meat, and cook for those out in packing Some rain in the evening cloudy all day, the last load of meat all the party got out of the road or Direction and did not get to the canoe untill after night, 5 did not join to night

Sunday the 15th December 1805

I set out early with 16 men and 3 canoes for the Elk, proceed up the River three Miles and thence up a large Creek from the right about 3 miles [to] the hite of the tide water drew up the canoes and all hands went out in three different parties and brought in to the Canoe each Man a quarter of Elk, I sent them out for a Second load and had Some of the first Cooked against their return, after eateing a harty diner dispatched the party for a third and last load, about half the men missed their way and did not get to the Canoes untill after Dark, and Serg^t Ordway Colter, Colins Whitehouse d McNeal Staid out all night without fire and in the rain. Cloudy all day Some rain in the evening

[Clark, first draft :]   *December 16th Monday 1805*

rained all the last night we covered our selves as well as we could with Elk skin, & set up the greater part of the night, all wet I lay in the wet verry cold, the 5 men who stayed out all night joined me this morning Cold & wet, Ordway Colter Collens, Jo Whitehouse J Mc Neal, I had the two canoes loaded with the 11 Elk which was brought to the canoes, despatched 12 men to meet me below with 2 Elk, The rain continues, with Tremendious gusts of wind, which is Tremend^s I proceeded on and took in the 2 Elk which was brought to the creek, & send back 7 men to carrey to the canoe & take down to camp 3 Elk which was left in the woods, and I proceeded on to camp thro the same chanel I had ass^d The winds violent Trees falling in every derection, whorl winds, with gusts of rain Hail & Thunder, this kind of weather lasted all day, Certainly one of the worst days that ever was ! I found 3 Indeans with Capt Lewis in camp they had brought fish to sell, we had a house covered with Punchens & our meat hung up Several men complaining of hurting themselves carry[ing] meat, &^c

Monday 16th December 1805

I as also the party with me experiencd a most dreadfull night rain and wet without any couvering, indeed we Set up the greater part of the Night, when we lay down the water soon Came under us and obliged us to rise the five men who Stayed out all night join^d me this morning wet and Cold, haveing Stayed out without fire or Shelter and the rain poreing down upon them all night their appearance was truly distressing they had left all their loads near the place they Spent the night. I dispatched 12 men for 2 Elk which was reathei

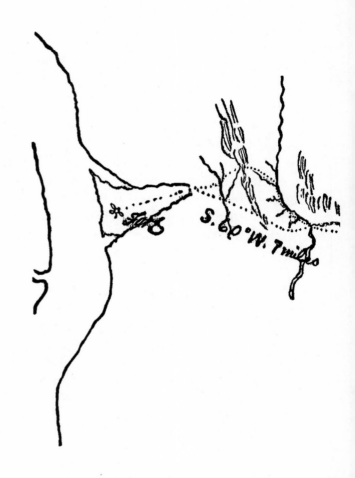

MAP SHOWING LOCATION OF FORT CLATSOP,

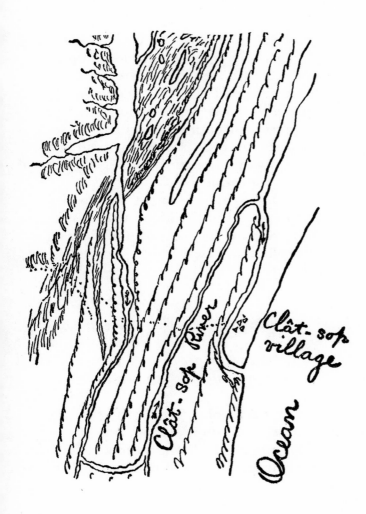

Clát-sop River

Clát-sop village

Ocean

AND TRAIL TO THE INDIAN VILLAGE

below on the opposit Side of the Creak, with directions to
meet me at the 2ᵈ bend in the creek below,   had all the meat
which had been brought in yesterday put into 2 canoes and proceeded down to the 2ᵈ bend where I met the 12 men with the
2 Elk,   dispatchᵈ 6 men with one of those who Staid out last
night for the meet left in the woods & the remainder [of] an
elk at Some distance and proceeded on my Self with 3 canoes
to the fort.   wind violent from the S E trees falling, rain and
hail,   we with Some risque proceeded on thro the high waves
in the river,   a tempestious disagreeable day.

I found 3 indians at our camp, they brought fish to Sell
which were pore & not fit for use,   had the Meet house coverᵈ
and the Meat all hung up,   Several men complain of haveing
hurt themselves [with] heavy loads of meat.¹

[Clark, first draft:]   *December 17ᵗʰ Tuesday 1805*

rained some last night and this morning,   all hands at work
about the huts Chinking them,   The 7 men left to bring in
the Elk left in the woods come with 2   the 3ʳᵈ they could
not find, as it was that left by the party that got lost night before last

The after part of the Day fair & Cool,   fore part of the Day
rain hailed & blew hard,   The mountain which lies S E of this
is covered with snow to day   we fleece all the meat and hang
it up over a small smoke   The trees are hard to split for Punchens to cover our houses &ᶜ

Tuesday 17ᵗʰ of December 1805

Some rain last night and a continuation of it this morning.
all the men at work about the houses, Some Chinking, Dobbing Cutting out dores &ᶜ &ᶜ   The 7 men left to bring in the
Elk arrived and informed that they could not find the meat
that the party who Stayed out all night had left.   the forepart
of this day rained hailed and blew hard, the after part is fair and
cool   a Mountain which is S [blank space in MS for insertion

───────────────

¹ In the weather diary for this date (Codex I, p 28) Clark wrote: "returned with
16 Elk" — ED

of degrees] ° E about 10 miles distant, has got snow on its top which is ruged and uneavin [1]

cause a Small fire & Smoke to be made under the meat which is hung up in Small peaces: The trees which our men have fallen latterly Split verry badly into boards. The most of our Stores are wet   our Leather Lodge has become So rotten that the Smallest thing tares it into holes and it is now Sc[a]rcely Sufficent to keep off the rain off a Spot Sufficiently large for our bead.

[Clark, first draft:]   *December 18.ᵗʰ Wednesday 1805*

rained and snowed alturnetely all the last night and the gusts of snow and hail continue untill 12 oClock,   cold and a dreadfull day wind hard and unseatled,   we continue at work at our huts,   the men being but thinly dressed, and no shoes causes us to doe but little   at 12 the snow & hail seased & the after part of the day was cloudy with some rain.

Wednesday 18.ᵗʰ December 1805

rained and Snowed alternetly all the last night, and Spurts of Snow and Hail Continued untill 12 oClock, which has chilled the air which is cool and disagreeable,   the wind hard & unsettled.   The men being thinly Dressed and mockersons without Socks is the reason that but little can be done at the Houses to day.   at 12 the Hail & Snow seased, and rain Suckceeded for the latter part of the day

[Clark, first draft:]   *December 19.ᵗʰ Thursday 1805*

Some rain with intervales of fair weather last night,   The morning clear and wind from S W   I despatched Sjᵗ Pryer with 8 men in 2 canoes across the bay for the boa[r]ds of an Indian house which is abandoned,   the other part of the men continue to doe a little at the huts,   the after part of the day cloudy with hail & rain,   Sgᵗ Pryer and party returned with 2 canoe loads of Boards,   two Indians came & stayed but a short time

---

[1] A reference to Saddle Mountain, from the vicinity of which descends the river on which the party had encamped — ED

Thursday 19ᵗʰ December 1805

Some rain with intervales of fair weather last night, this morning Clear & the wind from the S W. we dispatched Sjᵗ Pryor with 8 men in 2 Canoes across Meriwethers Bay for the boards of an old Indian house which is vacant, the residue of the men at work at their huts the after part of the Day cloudy with Hail and rain, Serjᵗ Pryor & party returned in the evening with a load of old boards which was found to be verry indifferent 2 Indians Cam[e] and Stayed a Short time to day.

[Clark, first draft:]   *December 20ᵗʰ Friday 1805*

Some rain and hail last night and this morning it rained hard untill 10 oClock, men all employd carrying Punchens and covering cabins 4 of which we had covered, & set some to Dobing the after part of the day cloudy and some showers of rain 3 Indians came with Lickorish Sackacomie berries & mats to sell, for which they asked such high prices that we did not purchase any of them. Those people ask double & tribble the value of everry thing they have to sell, and never take less than the full value of any thing, they prise only Blue & white beeds, files fish hooks and Tobacco. Tobacco and Blue beeds principally

Friday 20ᵗʰ of December 1805

Some rain and hail last night and the rained continued untill 10 oClock A.M. Men all employd in carrying punchens or boards & covering the houses, 4 of which were covered to day, the after part of the day cloudy with Several showers of rain 3 Indians arrive in a Canoe. they brought with them mats, roots & Sackacome [*sac à commis*] berries to Sell for which they asked Such high prices that we did not purchase any of them Those people ask generally double and tribble the value of what they have to Sell, and never take less than the real value of the article in Such things as is calculated to do them Service. Such as Blue & white beeds, with which they trade with the nativs above; files which they make use of to Sharpen their tools, fish hooks of different Sises and tobacco Tobacco and blue beeds they do prefur to every thing.

[Clark, first draft:]   *December 21ˢᵗ Saturday 1805*

rain as usial last night and all day to day moderately. we continued at the cabins dobbing & shink[l]ing of them, fall several trees which would not split into punchins the Indians were detected in stealing a spoon & a Bone, and left us, our sackey commy out send 2 men to gather some at the ocian saw Elk sign

Saturday 21ˢᵗ December 1805

rained as useal all the last night, and cont⁴ moderately all day to day without any intermition, men employd at the houses one of the indians was detected Stealing a horn Spoon, and leave (*turned from*) the camp dispatched two men to the open lands near the Ocian for Sackacome, which we make use of to mix with our tobacco to Smoke which has an agreeable flavour.

[Clark, first draft :]   *December 22ⁿᵈ Sunday 1805*

rained all the last night & to day without much intermition we finish dobbing 4 huts which is all we have covered, the Punchin floor & Bunks finished Drewyer go out to trap. Sjᵗ J. Ordway, Gibson & my servent sick several with Biles on them & bruses of different kinds, much of our meat spoiled.

Sunday 22ⁿᵈ December 1805

rained continued all the last night and to day without much intermition, men employd doeing what they can at the houses. Drewyer set out up the Creek to Set his traps for beaver, Sergᵗ Ordway, Gibson & my servent Sick, Several men complain of biles, and bruses of differant kinds

We discover that part of our last Supply of meat is Spoiling from the womph [warmth] of the weather notwithstanding a constant Smoke kept under it day and night.

[287]

[Clark, first draft:]   *December 23rd Monday 1805*

rained without intermition all last night, and this day much Thunder in the morning and evening with rain and some hail to day, we are all employd about our huts have ours covered and dobed & we move into it, 2 canoes of Indians came up to day I purchased 3 mats verry neetly made, 2 bags made with Flags verry neetly made, those the *Clotsops* carry ther fish in also a Panthor Skin and some Lickorish roots, for which I gave a worn out file, 6 fish hooks & some Pounded fish which to us was spoiled, but those people were fond of in the evining those people left us I also gave a string of wompom to a chief, and sent a small pice of Sinimon to a sick Indian in the Town who had attached himself to me

Monday 23rd December 1805

Rained without intermition all the last night and to day with Thunder and Hail the fore and after part of this day. Cap.t Lewis and my self move into our hut to day unfinished. two canoes with Indians of the *Clât sop* nation came up to day I purchased 3 mats and bags all neetly made of flags and rushes, those bags are nearly square of different sizes open on one Side, I also purchased a panthor Skin 7½ feet long including the tail, [for] all of which I gave 6 Small fish hooks, a Small worn out file & Some pounded fish which we could not use as it was So long wet that it was Soft and molded, the Indians of this neighbourhood prize the pound'd fish verry highly, I have not observed this method of Secureing fish on any other part of the Columbian Waters then that about the Great falls I gave a 2.d Chief a String of wampom, and Sent a little pounded fish to *Cus-ca-lah* who was Sick in the village & could not come to see us

[Clark, first draft:]   *December 24th Tuesday —5*

Some hard rain at different times last night, and moderately this morning without intermition all hands employed in carrying Punchens & finishing covering the huts, and the greater part of the men move into them a hard rain in the evening *Cuscalar* the young *Clotsop* Chief came with a young brother and 2 young squar, they gave or laid before Capt Lewis and my self a mat and each a large Parsel of roots, some time after he demanded 2 files for his Present we returned the present as we had no files to spear which displeased them a little they then offered a woman to each which we also declined axcepting which also displeased them. Jo Fields finish for Capt Lewis and my self each a wide slab hued to write on,   I gave a handkerchief &^c

Tuesday 24.th December 1805

hard rain at Different times last night and all this day without intermition.   men all employ^d in finishing their huts and moveing into them.[1]

Cuscalah the Indian who had treated me so politely when I was at the Clâtsops Village, come up in a canoe with his young brother & 2 Squars   he laid before Capt Lewis and my self each a mat and a parcel of roots   Some time in the evening two files was demanded for the presents of mats and roots,   as we had no files to part with, we each returned the present which we had received, which displeased Cuscalah a little.   He then offered a woman to each of us which we also declined axcepting of, which displeased the whole party verry much — the female part appeared to be highly disgusted at our refuseing to axcept of their favours &^c

our Store of Meat entirely Spoiled,   we are obliged to make use of it as we have nothing else except a little pounded fish, the remains of what we purchased near the Great falls of the Columbia, and which we have ever found to be a convenient resort, and a portable method of curing fish.

---

1 The spot on which Lewis and Clark's winter encampment was fixed is still discernible, and the foundation logs remained till within a year or two   The trail by which they used to reach the coast can also be traced — GIBBS (*Contrib N Amer Ethnology*, p 238)

It is not certain what date Gibbs meant here, regarding these remains of Fort Clatsop ; he resided in Oregon and Washington during 1854–60   On the present appearance of the site of Fort Clatsop, see Wheeler, *Trail of Lewis and Clark*, ii, p 196   Clark's two maps of the neighborhood of the fort, with trail to the coast, are given herewith, pp 268, 282, 283 *ante*   See also his larger sketch-plan of the fort, under date of December 30th, *post* — ED

[Clark, first draft :]   *December 25ᵗʰ Christmas 1805 Wednesday*

Some rain at different times last night and showers of hail with intervales of fair starr light   This morning at day we were saluted by all our party under our winders,   a Shout and a Song. after brackfast we divided our tobacco which amounted to 2 Carrots, one half we gave to the party who used Tobacco those who did not we gave a Handkerchief as a present,   The day proved showery all day,   the Indˢ left us this evening all our party moved into their huts. we dried some of our wet goods.   I rcved a present of a Fleeshe Hoserey [fleece hosiery] vest draws & socks of Capᵗ Lewis, pʳ Mockersons of Whitehouse, a small Indian basket of Guterich, & 2 Doz weasels tales of the Squar of Shabono, & some black roots of the Indians   G. D. saw a Snake passing across the parth   Our Diner to day consisted of pore Elk boiled, spilt [spoiled] fish & some roots, a bad Christmass diner   worm day

Christmas Wednesday 25ᵗʰ December 1805

at day light this morning we we[re] awoke by the discharge of the fire arm[s] of all our party & a Selute, Shouts and a Song which the whole party joined in under our windows, after which they retired to their rooms   were chearfull all the morning.   after brackfast we divided our Tobacco which amounted to 12 carrots one half of which we gave to the men of the party who used tobacco, and to those who doe not use it we make a present of a handkerchief,   The Indians leave us in the evening   all the party Snugly fixed in their huts.   I recved a pres[e]nt of Capᵗ L of a fleece hosrie [hosiery] Shirt Draws and Socks, a pʳ Mockersons of Whitehouse a Small Indian basket of Gutherich, two Dozen white weazils tails of the Indian woman, & some black root of the Indians before their departure.   Drewyer informs me that he saw a Snake pass across the parth to day.   The day proved Showerey wet and disagreeable

we would have Spent this day the nativity of Christ in feasting, had we any thing either to raise our Sperits or even gratify our appetites, our Diner concisted of pore Elk, so much

Christmas
Wednesday 25th December 1805

at day light this morning we we awoke by
the discharge of the fire arm of all our party &
a Selute, Shout and a Song, which the whole
party joined in under our windows, after which
they retired to their rooms were Chearfull
all the morning— after brackfast we divided our tobacco which amounted to 12 carots,
one half of which we gave to the men of the
party who used tobacco, and to those who
doe not use it we make a present of a handkerchief, The Indians leave us in the evening
all the party Snugly fixed in their hutts—. I
recved a present of Capt. L. of a fleece hosiery shirt
Draws and Socks,— a pr. Mockersons of Whitehouse
a Small Indian basket of Guthergill, two Dozen
white weazils tails of the Indian woman, &
Some black root of the Indians before their
departure. Drewyer informs me that he Saw
a Snake pass across the parth to day— The
day proved Showerey wet and disagreeable.

we would have Spent this day the nativity of Christ in feasting, had we any thing
either to raise our Spirits or even gratify
our appetites, our Diner consisted of poar
Elk, so much Spoiled that we eate it thro
mear necessity, Some Spoiled pounded fish and
a few roots.

MS. page by Clark, dated December 25, 1805.

Spoiled that we eate it thro' mear necessity,[1] Some Spoiled pounded fish and a fiew roots.

[Clark, first draft:]　　　　　　　*December 26ᵗʰ Thursday* 1805

rained and blew hard last night, some hard Thunder, The rain continued as usial all day and wind blew hard from the S E　Joseph Fields finish a Table & 2 seats for us　we dry our wet articles and have the blankets fleed,　The flees are so troublesom that I have slept but little for 2 night past and we have regularly to kill them out of our blankets every day for several past　maney of the men have ther Powder wet by the horns being repeatedly wet,　hut smoke[s] verry bad.

Thursday 26ᵗʰ of December 1805

rained and blew with great Violence S E all the last night, Some hard claps of Thunder, the rain as usial continued all day. we dry our wet articles before the fire, and have our blankets fleed,　great numbers were Caught out of the blankets, those trouble[some] insects are so abundant that we have to have them kill⁴ out of our blankets every day or get no Sleep at night. The powder in maney of the mens horns are wet from their being so long exposed to the rain &c

[Clark, first draft:]　　　　　　　*December 27ᵗʰ Friday* 1805

rained last night as usial and the greater part of this day, the men complete Chimneys & Bunks to day,　in the evening a Chief and 4 men come of the *Clotsop* nation chief *Co-ma-wool* we sent out R Fields & Collins to hunt and order Drewyer, Shannon & Labiach to set out early to morrow to hunt, Jo Fields, Bratten, & Gibson to make salt at Point Addams, Willard & Wiser, to assist them in carrying the Kittles &ᶜ to the Ocian, and all the others to finish the Pickets and gates. worm weather I saw a Musquetor which I showed Capᵗ Lewis　Those Indians gave is [us], a black root they call *Shan-na-tâh-que* a kind of Licquirish which they rost in embers

---

[1] And we are without salt to season that — GASS (p 254)

and call *Cul-ho-mo*, a black berry the size of a Cherry & Dried which they call *Shel-well*— all of which they prise highly and make use of as food to live on, for which Cap.ᵗ Lewis gave the chief a cap of sheep skin and I his Son, ear bobs, Pice of riben, a pice of brass, and 2 small fishing hooks, of which they were much pleased, Those roots & berres, are greatfull to our Stomcks as we have nothing to eate but Pore Elk meet, nearly spoiled; & this accident of spoiled meet, is owing to warmth & the repeeted rains, which cause the meet to tante before we can get it from the woods. Musquetors troublesom

Friday 27 ᵗʰ *December* 1805

rained last night as usial and the greater part of this day. In the evening *Co-ma wool* the Chief and 4 men of the *Clatsop* nation [came] the[y] presented us a root which resembles the licquirish in Size and taste, which they roste like a potato which they Call *Cul ho-mo*, also a black root which is cured in a kill like the *pash-a-co* above; this root has a Sweet taste and the nativs are verry fond of it   they call this root *Shaw-na-tâh-que*. also a dried berry about the size of a Chery which they Call *Shell well* all those roots those Indians value highly and give them Verry Spearingly. in return for the above roots, Cap.ᵗ Lewis gave the Cheif a Small peice of Sheap Skin to Ware on his head, I gave his Son a par of ear bobs and a pece of ribon, and a Small piece of brass for which they were much pleased.

Those roots and berries are timely and extreamly greatfull to our Stomachs, as we have nothing to eate but Spoiled Elk meat, I Showed Cap.ᵗ L 2 Musquetors to day, or an insect So much the size shape and appearance of a Musquetor that we could observe no kind of differance.

[Clark, first draft :]   *December* 28 ᵗʰ *Saturday* 1805

rained as usial, a great part of the last night, and this morn-ing rained and the wind blew hard from the S.E. sent out the hunters and salt makers, & employd the baleanc of the men carrying the Pickets &.ᶜ &.ᶜ The 2 hunters sent out yesterday returned, haveing killed one deer near the Sea cost, my boy york verry unwell from violent colds & strains carrying in meet and lifting logs on the huts to build them   This day is worm, and rained all day moderately without intermition.

Saturday the 28ᵗʰ of December 1805

rained as usial the greater part of the last night and a continuation this morning accompanied with wind from the S East Derected Drewyer, Shannon, Labeash, Reuben Field, and Collins to hunt; Jos. Fields, Bratton, Gibson to proceed to the Ocean at some conveneint place form a Camp and Commence makeing Salt with 5 of the largest Kittles, and Willard and Wiser to assist them in carrying the Kittles to the Sea Coast   all the other men to be employed about putting up pickets & makeing the gates of the *fort*.   My Man Y. verry unwell from a violent coald and Strain by carrying meet from the woods and lifting the heavy logs on the works &ᶜ   rained all Day without intermition.   the Weather verry worm.

[Clark, first draft :]   *December 29ᵗʰ Sunday 1805*

rained last night as usial,   this morning cloudy without rain a hard wind from the S E.   the Indˢ left us this morning and returned to their village, after begging for maney things which they did not secure as we could not spare them   I gave the Chief *Canio* a razor,   sent out 3 men across the river to hunt,   all others employd putting up pickets   Pete Crusat sick with a violent cold   My servent better.   we are told by the Indians that a whale has foundered on the Coast to the N W and their nations is collecting fat of him.   the wind is too high for us to see it,   Capᵗ Lewis is been in readiness 2 days to go and collect some of the whale oyle   the wind has proved too high as yet for him to set out in safty   In the evening a young Chief 4 men and 2 womin of the War-ci-a-cum tribe came in a large canoe with *Wapto* roots, Dressed Elk skins &ᶜ to sell, the Chief made me a present of about a half a bushel of those roots   we gave him a medal of a small size and a piece of red

[293]

ribin to tie around the top of his Hat which was made with a
double cone, the diameter of the upper about 3 Inches
the lower a about 1 foot   We purchased about 1½
bushels of those roots for which we gave some few red beeds,
small pices of brass wire and old check   those roots proved
greatfull to us as we are now liveing on spoiled Elk which
is extreamly disagreeable to the smel. as well as the taste,

I can plainly discover that a considerable exchange of property is continually carried on between the Tribes and villages
of those people   they all dress litely ware nothing below the
waste, a pice of fur abᵗ around the body, and a short robe
which composes the total of their dress, except a few split hats,
and beeds around ther necks wrists and anckles, and a few in
their ears   They are small and not handsom generally speaking women perticularly.

The *Chin-nook* womin are lude and carry on sport publickly
the Clotsop and others appear deffident, and reserved

A List of the Tribes near the mouth of the Columbia river
as given by the Indians, the Places they reside, the names of
the Tribes and principal Chiefs of each all of which speak the
same language[1]

1ˢᵗ *Clot-sop* Tribe in several small villages on the Sea Co[a]st
to the S E of the Mouth & on the S.E. bank of the Columbia
river — not noumerous

     1ˢᵗ Chief *Con-ni â Co-mo-wool*
     2.   dᵒ   *Sha-no-ma*
     3   dᵒ   *War-ho-lott*

2ⁿᵈ *Chin-nook* Tribe reside opposit on the N.W. Side & in
small villages & single houses made of split boards on a creek
of Haleys bay, and on small lakes or ponds, at no great distance from the river or bay.   Tolerably noumerous — so said

     1ˢᵗ Chief is *Stock-home*
     2ᵈ   dᵒ   *Com-com-mo-ley*
     3   dᵒ   *Shil-lar-la-wit*
     4   dᵒ   *Nor-car-te*
     5   dᵒ   *Chin-ni-ni*

[1] The following list of the neighboring tribes is found on four pages towards the
end of the Clark-Voorhis field-book — ED

3rd *Chiltch* Tribe reside near the Sea Coast & North of the *Chin-nooks* live in houses and is said to be noumerous Speak same Language

1st Chief *Mar-lock-ke*
2^{d} d^{o} *Col-chote*
3rd do *Ci-in-twar*

4th *Ca-la-mox* Tribe reside on the Sea coast to the S.E of the Columbia River and on a Small river, and as I am informed by the *Clot-sops* inhabit 10 Villages 6 of them on the ocian & 4 on the Little river, Those Ca-la-mox are said not to be noumerous Speake the Clotsop language

1st Chief *O-co-no.*

5th *Calt-har-mar* Tribe reside in one village of large Houses built of split boards and neetly made, on the S E Side of the Columbia River, behind a Island in a Deep bend of the River to the S E. they are not noumerous, and live as the others do on fish, black roots Lickuerish berries, and *Wap-pe-to* roots, and is as low as those Wapeto roots grow, which is about 15 miles on a Direct line from the Sea.

1st Chief *Clax-ter* { at war against the Snake Ind^{s} to the S of the falls

2^{d} d^{o} *Cul-te-ell*
3 do [blank space in MS] at war

6th *Clax-ter* Nation This nation reside on [blank space in MS] Side of the Columbia River in [blank space in MS] villages above about

[full line blank in MS]

and are noumerous they latterly floged the Chinnooks, and are a Dasterly Set

1st and great Chief *Qui-oo*

7th *War-ci-a-cum* Tribe reside on the N W Side of the Columbia in the great bend behind some Islands, this tribe is not noumerous reside in 2 village[s] of Houses

The Chief *Scum ar-qua-up*

The flees are so noumerous in this countrey and difficult to get cleare of that the Indians have diff^{t} houses & villages to

which they remove frequently to get rid of them, and not withstanding all their precautions, they never step into our hut
without leaveing sworms of those troublecom insects.   Indeed
I scercely get to sleep half the night clear of the torments of
those flees, with the precaution of haveing my blankets serched
and the flees killed every day.   The 1ˢᵗ of those insects we saw
on the Collumbia River was at the 1ˢᵗ Great falls.   I have the
satisfaction to say that we had but little rain in the course of
this day, not as much as would wet a person   but hard wind
and cloudy all day.

Sunday 29ᵗʰ December 1805

　rained all the last night a[s] usial,   this morning cloudy
without rain, a hard wind from the S E   I gave the Cheif a
razor, and himself and party left us after begging us for maney
articles none of which they recevied as we Could not Spare the
articles they were most in want of   Peter Crusat Sick with a
violent Cold, my Man Y. better;   all hands employed about
the Pickets & gates of the fort.   we were informed day before
yesterday that a whale had foundered on the coast to the S W.
near the *Kil a mox* N. and that the greater part of the *Clatsops*
were gorn for the oile & blubber,   the wind proves too high for
us to proceed by water to See this Monster, Capᵗ Lewis has
been in readiness Since we first heard of the whale to go and
see it and collect Some of its Oil,   the wind has proved too
high as yet for him to proceed.   this evining a young Chief 4
Men and 2 womin of the *Warciacum* nation arrived, and offered
for Sale Dressed Elk Skins and *Wappato*,   the Chief made us
a preasent of about $\frac{1}{2}$ a bushel of those roots. and we purchased
about 1$\frac{1}{2}$ bushels of those roots for which we gave Some fiew
red beeds Small peaces of brass wire & old Check   those roots
proved a greatfull addition to our Spoiled Elk, which has become verry disagreeable both to the taste & smell   we gave
this Chief a Medal of a Small size and a piece of red riben to
tie around the ⎰ ⎱ top of his hat which was of a Singular
Construction ⎱　　　⎰ (*in Peales Museum*)   Those people
will not sell ⎰　　　⎱ all their *Wappato* to us   they inform us that they are on their way to trade with the *Clâtsops*.

The Nations above carry on a verry considerable interchange
of property with those in this neighbourhood   they pass altogether by water, they have no roads or pathes through the
Countrey which we have observed, except across portages from
one creek to another,   all go litely dressed ware nothing below the waste in the Coaldest of weather, a piece of fur around
their bodies and a Short roabe composes the sum total of their
dress, except a few hats, and beeds about their necks arms and
legs   Small badly made and homely generally.   The flees are
So noumerous and hard to get rid of; that the Indians have
different houses which they resort to occasionally, not withstanding all their precautions, they never Step into our house
without leaveing Sworms of those tormenting insects; and they
torment us in such a manner as to deprive us of half the nights
Sleep frequently.   the first of those insects which we saw on
the Columbian waters was at the Canoe portage at the great
falls.   Hard winds & cloudy all day but verry little rain to
day.

[Clark, first draft:]   *December* 30.*th* *Monday* 1805

    Hard wind and some rain last night,   this morning fair and
the sun shown for a short time   4 Indians came from the
upper Villages they offered us roots which we did not chuse
to axcept of, as their expectations for those presents of a fiew
roots is 3 or 4 times their real worth,   those Indians with those
of yesterday continued all day.   Drewyer & party of hunters
returned and informed they had killed 4 Elk,   a party of 6
men was imediately sent for the meet, they returned at Dusk,
with the 4 Elk, of which we had a sumptious supper of Elk
Tongues & marrow bones which was truly gratifying
    The fort was completed this evening and at sun set we let
The Indians know that, our custom will be to shut the gates
at sun set, at which time they must all go out of the fort [1]   those

---

[1] The sketch-plan here given of the fort on the Pacific Coast, wherein the Lewis
and Clark expedition spent the winter of 1805–06 was traced by Clark upon the
rough elk-skin cover of his field-book   In the original it is much faded, and the
lines have been pulled out of shape by a fold in the skin ; no doubt, when drawn,

people who are verry foward and disegreeable, left the huts with reluctiance. This day proved the best we have had since at this place, only 3 Showers of rain to day, cloudy nearly all day, in the evening the wind luled and the fore part of the night fair and clear. I saw flies & different kinds of insects in motion to day Snakes are yet to be seen, and Snales without cover is common and large, fowls of every kind common to this quarter abound in the Creek & Bay near us

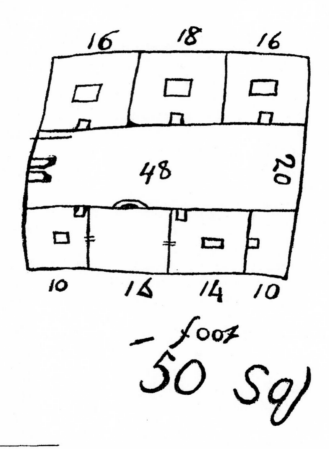

the walls of the fort were straight   Apparently the stockade was 50 feet square, with a long cabin of three rooms ranged along the upper wall, each with what seems to be a central fire-place ; and along the lower wall four cabins, two of them with fire-places and one with an outside chimney ; the gates are to the left and the parade ground is 20 × 48 feet   In this connection, see also the plan in the map given on p 268, *ante*   From that it would appear that the gates opened to the south — ED

Monday 30*th* *December* 1805

Hard wind and Some rain last night   this morning the Sun Shown for a Short time   four Indians came down from the *Warciacum* village,   they offered us roots which we did not think proper to accept of as in return they expect 3 or 4 times as much as the roots as we could purchase the Roots for, and are never satisfied with what they receive,   those 4 Indians & these that came yesterday Stayed all day   Drewyer returned and informed that he had killed 4 Elk at no great distance off, a party of 6 men was imediately dispatched for the meat, and returned at Dusk with the 4 Elk.   we had a Sumptious Supper of Elks tongues & marrow bones which was truly gratifying   our fortification is completed this evening   and at Sun set we let the nativs know that our Custom will be in futuie, to Shut the gates at Sun Set at which time all Indians must go out of the fort and not return into it untill next morning after Sunrise at which time the gates will be opened,   those of the *Warciacum* Nation who are very fo[r]ward left the houses with reluctianc[e]   this day proved to be the fairest and best which we have had since our arrival at this place, only thiee Showers dureing this whole day,   wind the fore part of the day.

[Clark, first draft:]   *December* 31*st* *Tuesday* 1805

A Cloudy night & some rain,   this day proved cloudy and some showers of rain to day   all the Indians continued at their camp near us,   2 others canoes came one from the War-ci-a-cum Village, with three Indians, and the other from higher up the river of the *Skil-lute* nation with three men and a Squar ; Those people brought with them some *Wap to* roots, mats made of flags, & rushes, dried fish and some fiew *She-ne-tock-we* (or black) roots & Dressed Elk skins, all of which they asked enormous prices for, particularly the Dressed Elk Skins ;   I purchased of those people some *Wapto* roots, two mats and a small pouch of Tobacco of their own manufactory, for which I gave large fish hooks, [of] which they were verry fond,   those Indians are much more reserved and better be-

[299]

haved to day than yesterday the sight of our Sentinal who walks on his post, has made this reform in those people who but yesterday was verry impertenant and disagreeable to all This evening they all cleared out before the time to shut the gates, without being derected to doe So I derected sinks to be dug and a Sentinal Box which was accomplished

One of those Indeans brought a Musquet to be repared, which only wanted a Screw flattened, for which he gave me a Peck of Wapto roots, I gave him a flint and a pice of Sheep Skin of which he was pleased. January 1st Wednesday 1806 in another book [1]

Tuesday 31st December 1805

last night was cloudy and Some rain, this day prove Cloudy and Showerry all day, all the Indians continue at their camp near us, two other canoes arrived, one from the *Warciâcum* Village with 3 indians and the other [*of 3 men & a squar*] from higher up the river and are of the *Skil-lute* Nation, those people brought with them Some *Wappato* roots, mats made of flags and rushes dried fish, and fiew *Shaw-na-tâh-que* and Dressed Elk Skins, all of which they asked enormous prices for, perticularly the dressed Elk Skins, I purchased of those people Some *Wappato* two mats and about 3 pipes of their tobacco in a neet little bag made of rushes This tobacco was much like what we had Seen before with the *Sosone* or Snake indians, for those articles I gave a large fishing hook and Seveial other Small articles, the fishinghooks they were verry fond of Those *Skillutes* are much better behaved than the *Warciacum* indeed we found a great alteration in the conduct of them all this morning, the Sight of our Sentinal on his post at the gate, together with our deturmined proseedure of putting all out at Sun set has made this reform in those *Warciacoms* who is fo[r]ward impertinant an[d] thieveish.

---

[1] Here end the entries in the Clark-Voorhis field-book On the last fly-leaf is written : "Presented to J. J Audubon at St Louis, April 19th 1843, by D D Mitchell, Supt Indian Affairs " It is not known how this field-book was returned to the custody of the Clark heirs See Introduction for description of this MS — ED

The nativs all leave the fort this evening before Sun set without being told or desired to do So   we had Sinks dug & a Sentinal box made.   a *Skillute* brought a gun which he requested me to have repared, it only wanted a Screw flattened so as to catch, I put a flint into his gun & he presented me in return a peck of *Wappato* for payment,   I gave him piece of a Sheap Skin and a Small piece of blue Cloth to cover his lock for which he was much pleased and gave me in return Some roots &ᶜ

I saw flies and different kinds of insects in motion to day. Snakes are yet to be Seen and Snales without covers is common and verry large   water fowls of various kinds are in great numbers in the rivers and Creeks and the sides of Meriwethers Bay near us but excessively wild.   the fore part of this night fair and clear

With the party of *Clâtsops* who visited us last was a man of much lighter Coloured than the nativs are generaly,   he was freckled with long duskey red hair, about 25 years of age, and must Certainly be half white at least,   this man appeared to understand more of the English language than the others of his party, but did not Speak a word of English,   he possessed all the habits of the indians [1]

[Lewis:]   *Fort Clatsop* 1806
                              January 1ˢᵗ *Tuesday* [*Wednesday*] [2]

This morning I was awoke at an early hour by the discharge of a volley of small arms, which were fired by our party in front of our quarters to usher in the new year ; this was the only mark of rispect which we had it in our power to pay this

---

[1] Ross Cox, in his *Adventures on the Columbia* (New York, 1832) describes this man as a *lusus naturæ*   " His skin was fair, his face partially freckled, and his hair quite red   He was about five feet ten inches high, was slender, but remarkably well made ; his head had not undergone the flattening process   His father was a sailor who had deserted from an English ship, his name, Jack Ramsay, was tattooed on the son's arm   Poor Jack was fond of his father's countrymen, and had the decency to wear trousers whenever he came to the fort (Astoria)   We therefore made a collection of old clothes for his use ; sufficient to last him many years " — Eᴅ

[2] Here begins Codex Ɉ, written by Lewis ; it contains the journal of the expedition from Jan 1 to March 20, 1806 — Eᴅ

celebrated day. our repast of this day tho' better than that of Christmass, consisted principally in the anticipation of the 1ˢᵗ day of January 1807, when in the bosom of our friends we hope to participate in the mirth and hilarity of the day, and when with the zest given by the recollection of the present, we shall completely, both mentally and corporally, enjoy the repast which the hand of civilization has prepared for us. at present we were content with eating our boiled Elk and wappe-toe, and solacing our thirst with our only beverage *pure water*. two of our hunters who set out this morning reterned in the evening having killed two bucks elk; they presented Capᵗ Clark and myself each a marrow-bone and tonge, on which we suped visited today by a few of the Clatsops who brought some roots and burries for the purpose of trading with us. we were uneasy with rispect to two of our men, Willard and Wiser, who were dispatched on the 28ᵗʰ ultᵒ with the salt-makers, and were directed to return immediately; their not having returned induces us to believe it probable that they have missed their way. our fourtification being now com-pleted we issued an order for the more exact and uniform discipline and government of the garrison.

[Orderly Book; Lewis:] *Fort Clatsop, January* 1ˢᵗ 1806

The fort being now completed, the Commanding officers think proper to direct: that the guard shall as usual consist of one Sergeant and three privates, and that the same be regularly relieved each morning at sunrise The post of the new guard shall be in the room of the Sergeants rispectivly commanding the same the centinel shall be posted, both day and night, on the parade in front of the commanding offercers quarters; tho' should he at any time think proper to remove himself to any other part of the fort, in order the better to inform himself of the desighns or approach of any party of savages, he is not only at liberty, but is hereby required to do so It shall be the duty of the centinel also to announce the arrival of all parties of Indians to the Sergeant of the Guard, who shall immediately report the same to the Commanding officers

The Commanding Officers require and charge the Garrison to treat the natives in a friendly manner; nor will they be permitted at any time, to abuse, assault or strike them; unless such abuse assault or stroke be first given by the natives. nevertheless it shall be right for any individual, in a peaceable manner, to refuse admittance to, or put out of his room, any native who may become troublesome to him; and should such native refuse to go when requested, or attempt to enter their rooms after being forbidden to do so; it shall be the duty of the Sergeant of the guard on information of the same, to put such native out of the fort and see that he is not again admitted during that day unless specially permitted; and the Sergeant of the guard may for this purpose imploy such coercive measures (not extending to the taking of life) as shall at his discretion be deemed necessary to effect the same.

When any native shall be detected in theft, the Serg^t of the guard shall immediately inform the Commanding offercers of the same, to the end that such measures may be pursued with rispect to the culprit as they shall think most expedient

At sunset on each day, the Serg^t attended by the interpreter Charbono and two of his guard, will collect and put out of the fort, all Indians except such as may specially be permitted to remain by the Commanding offercers, nor shall they be again admitted untill the main gate be opened the ensuing morning

At Sunset, or immediately after the Indians have been dismissed, both gates shall be shut, and secured, and the main gate locked and continue so untill sunrise the next morning: the water-gate may be used freely by the Garrison for the purpose of passing and repassing at all times, tho' from sunset, untill sunrise, it shall be the duty of the centinel, to open the gate for, and shut it after all persons passing and repassing, suffering the same never to remain unfixed long[er] than is absolutely necessary.

It shall be the duty of the Serg^t of the guard to keep the kee of the Meat house, and to cause the guard to keep regular fires therein when the same may be necessary; and also once at least in 24 hours to visit the canoes and see that they are safely secured; and shall further on each morning after he is relieved, make his report verbally to the Command[in]g officers.

Each of the old guard will every morning after being relieved furnish two loads of wood for the commanding offercers fire.

No man is to be particularly exempt from the duty of bringing meat from the woods, nor none except the Cooks and Interpreters from that of mounting guard.

Each mess being furnished with an ax, they are directed to deposit in the room of the commanding offercers all other public tools of which they are possessed; nor shall the same at any time hereafter be taken from the said deposit without the knoledge and permission of the commanding officers; and any individual so borrowing the tools are strictly required to bring the same back the moment he has ceased to use them, and [in] no case shall they be permited to keep them out all night

Any individual selling or disposing of any tool or iron or steel instrument, arms, accoutrements or ammunicion, shall be deemed guilty of a breach of this order, and shall be tryed and punished accordingly. the tools loaned to John Shields are excepted from the restrictions of this order.

MERIWETHER LEWIS
Capt 1st U. S. Reg^t
Wm CLARK Capt &^c

[Clark, first draft:] [1]   *January 1st Wednesday 1806*

This morning proved cloudy with moderate rain, after a pleasent worm night during which there fell but little rain This morning at Day we wer Saluted from the party without, wishing us a " hapy new Year " a Shout and discharge of their arms. no Indians to be Seen this morning they left the place of their encampment dureing the last night. The work of our houses and fort being now complete, we Ishued an order in

---

[1] Clark made entries for Jan 1–3 on what are pp 146, 147 of the Philadelphia Codex I; then apparently reversed the book, and rewrote these entries — following Lewis's journal so closely that Clark's is, during Jan. 1–29, almost a verbatim copy of the latter — ED

which we pointed out the rules & regulations for the government of the Party in respect to the Indians as also for the Safty and protection of our Selves &c two Clotsops Came with a mat and Some fiew roots of Cut-wha-mo, for which they asked a file   they did not trade but continued all night

Sent out 2 hunters this morning who returned, haveing killed 2 Elk about 3 miles distant, Some fiew Showers of rain in the Course of this day.   Cloudy all the day.

Fort Clatsop 1806 *Wednesday the 1st of January*

This morning I was awoke at an early hour by the discharge of a Volley of Small arms, which were fired by our party in front of our quarters to usher in the new year,   this was the only mark of respect which we had it in our power to pay this Selibrated day.   our repast of this day tho' better than that of Christmas consisted principally in the anticipation of the 1st day of January 1807, when in the bosom of our friends we hope to participate in the mirth and hilarity of the day, and when with the relish given by the recollection of the present, we Shall completely, both mentally and corporally, [enjoy] the repast which the hand of civilization has produced for us   at present we were content with eating our boiled Elk and *Wappato*, and Solacing our thirst with our only beverage *pure water*   two of our hunters who Set out this morning returned in the evening haveing killed two Buck Elks; they presented Capt Lewis and my self each a marrow bone and tongue on which we Suped. we are Visited to day by a fiew of the Clatsops by water they brought some roots and berries for the purpose of tradeing with us   our fortification being now complete we issue an order for the more exact and uniform dicipline and government of the garrison.

January 1st 1806[1]

A List of the names of Sundery persons, who visit this part of the Coast for the purpose of trade &c &c in large Vestles;

---

[1] This list is found on three pages toward the end of the Clark-Voorhis field-book — Ed

all of which speake the English language &ᶜ as the Indians inform us

Moore	Visit them in a large 4 masted ship, they expect him in 2 moons to trade
1 Eyᵈ [one-eyed] Skellie	in a large ship, long time gorn
Youin	In a large Ship, and they expect him in 1 moon to trade with them.
Swepeton	In a Ship, they expect him in 3 month back to trade
Mackey	In a Ship, they expect him back in 1 or 2 Moons to trade with them
Meship	In a Ship, the[y] expect him 2 moons to trade.
Jackson	Visit them in a Ship and they expect him back in 3 months to trade
Balch	In a Ship and they expect him in 3 months to trade.
Mʳ Haley	Visits them in a Ship & they expect him back to trade with them in 3 Moons to trade he is the favourite of the Indians (from the number of Presents he gives) and has the trade principally with all the tribes
Washilton	In a Skooner, they expect him in 3 months to return and trade with them — a favourite
Lemon	In a Slupe, and they expect him in 3 moons to trade with them
Davidson	Visits this part of the coast and river in a Brig for the purpose of Hunting the Elk returns when he pleases he does not trade any, kills a great many Elk &ᶜ &ᶜ
Fallawan	In a Ship with guns he fired on & killed several Indians, he does not trade now and they doe not know when he will return, well done

[Another draft of the above by Clark, found in Codex I — Eᴅ]

A List of the Names as given by the India[n]s of the Traders Names and the quallity of their Vessels which they Say Visit the mouth of the Columbia 2 [times] a year for the purpose of Tradeing with the nativs, and from their accounts Spring and autum

Mr Haley their favourite Trader visits them in a 3 Masted Vessel
Youens   Visits in a 3 Masted Vessle

Tallamon	do	3	do	do	no trade
Swipton	do	3	do	do	Trader
Moore	do	4	do	do	do
Mackey	do	3	do	do	do
Washington	do	3	do	do	do
Meship	do	3	do	do	do
Davidson	do	2	do	do	Hunts Elk
Jackson	do	3	do	do	Trader
Bolch	do	3	do	do	do
Skelley has been along time gorn					one Eye
Callallamet	do	3			Trader has a wooden Leg

[Lewis:]   *Thursday, January 2nd 1806*

Sent out a party of men and brought in the two Elk which
were killed yesterday. Willard and Wiser have not yet returned nor have a party of hunters returned who set out on the
26th Ulto   the Indians who visited yesterday left us at 1. P M
today after having disposed of their roots and berries for a few
fishinghooks and some other small articles. we are infested
with swarms of flees already in our new habitations; the presumption is therefore strong that we shall not devest ourselves
of this intolerably troublesome vermin during our residence
here   The large, and small or whistling swan, sand hill Crane,
laige and small gees, brown and white brant, Cormorant,
duckan mallard, Canvisback duck, and several other species of
ducks, still remain with us; tho' I do not think that they are
as plenty as on our first arrival in the neighbourhood   Drewyer
visited his traps and took an otter. the fur of both the beaver
and otter in this country are extreemly good; those annamals
are tolerably plenty near the sea coast, and on the small Creeks
and rivers as high as the grand rappids, but are by no means as
much so as on the upper part of the Missouri

[Clark, first draft:]   *January 2nd Thursday 1806*

A Cloudy rainey morning after a wet night   Dispatched
12 Men for the two Elk Killed yesterday which they brought

in at 11 oClock. the day proved cloudy and wet, the Indians left us at 1 oClock P.M. Drewyer visited his traps which had one otter in one of them. The flees are verry troublesom, our huts have alreadey Sworms of those disagreeable insects in them, and I fear we Shall not get rid of them dureing our delay at this place.

Thursday 2ⁿᵈ of January 1806

Sent out a party of men and brought in the two Elk which was killed yesterday. Willard & Wiser have not yet returned nor have a party of hunters who Set out on the 26ᵗʰ ulto: the Indians who visited us yesterday left us at 1 P.M. to day after haveing disposed of their roots and berries for a fiew fishing hooks and Some other small articles. we are infestᵈ with sworms of flees already in our new habitations; the presumption is therefore Strong that we shall not devest our selves of this intolerably troublesom vermin dureing our residence here. The large, & small or whistling swan, Sand hill crane, large & Small Gees, brown and white brant, Comorant, Duckanmallard, canvis back duck, and Several other species of Ducks Still remain with us; tho' I doe not think they are as plenty as on our first arrival in this neighbourhood Drewyer visit his traps at [and] took out an otter. the fur of both the beaver and otter as also the rackoon in this countrey are extreemly good; those animals are tolerably plenty near the Sea coast, on the Small creeks and rivers as high as the grand Rapids.

[Lewis:]   *Friday January 3ᵈ* 1806

At 11. A M. we were visited by our near neighbours, Cheif or Tiá. Co-mo-wool, alias Conia and six Clatsops. the[y] brought for sale some roots buries and three dogs also a small quantity of fresh blubber. this blubber they informed us they had obtained from their neighbours the Callamucks[1] who inhabit the coast to the S.E. near whose vilage a whale had

[1] A variant of Tillamook — once a large Salishan tribe on the Oregon coast; now almost extinct — Eᴅ

recently perished. this blubber the Indians eat and esteeme
it excellent food. our party from necessaty having been
obliged to subsist some lenth of time on dogs have now become extreemly fond of their flesh; it is worthy of remark
that while we lived principally on the flesh of this anamal we
were much more healthy strong and more fleshey than we had
been since we left the Buffaloe country. for my own part I
have become so perfectly reconciled to the dog that I think
it an agreeable food and would prefer it vastly to lean Venison
or Elk. a small Crow, the blue crested Corvus and the smaller
corvus with a white brest, the little brown ren, a large brown
sparrow, the bald Eagle and the beatifull Buzzard of the columbia still continue with us. Sent Serg^t Gass and George
shannon to the saltmakers who are somewhere on the coast
to the S W. of us,[1] to enquire after Willard and Wiser who
have not yet returned. Reubin Fields Collins and Pots the
hunters who set out on the 26th [28th] Ult° returned this evening after dark. they reported that they had been about 15
Miles up the river at the head of the bay just below us and
had hunted the country from thence down on the East side
of the river, even to a considerable distance from it and had
proved unsuccessfull having killed one deer and a few fowls,
barely as much as subsisted them. this reminded us of the
necessity of taking time by the forelock, and keep out several
parties while we have yet a little meat beforehand. I gave
the Chief Comowooll a pare of sattin breechies with which he
appeared much pleased.

[Clark, first draft:]   *January* 3rd *Friday* 1806

The Sun rose fair this morning for the first time for Six
weeks past, the Clouds soon obscure it from our view, and
a Shower of rain Suckceeded. last night we had Sharp lighten-
ing a hard thunder Suckceeded with heavy Showers of hail,

---

[1] The site of the salt-makers' cairns was located June 9, 1900, by a committee
of the Oregon Historical Society (see *Proceedings*, 1900, pp 16–23), who had the
testimony of a pioneer and an Indian, that had known contemporaries of the explorers
It was upon what is known as Clatsop Beach, near the mouth of Necanicum River,
a little north of a summer resort called Seaside — ED

and rain, which Continud with intervales of fair Moon Shine dureing the night   Sent out Serg^t Gass & 2 men to the Salt makers with a v[i]ew to know what is the cause of the delay of 2 of our party *Willard* & *Wiser* who we are uneasy about, as they were to have been back 6 days ago.

Friday the 3rd January 1806

At 11 A M. we were visited by our near neighbour Chief or *tiá Co mo wool* alias *Conia* (*Cŏŏnê*) and six Clatsops   they brought for Sale Some roots berries and 3 Dogs also a Small quantity of fresh blubber.   this blubber they informed us they had obtained from their neighbours the *Cal lá mox* who inhabit the coast to the S E.   near one of their Villages a Whale had recently perished   this blubber the Indians eat and esteem it excellent food.   our party from necescity have been obliged to Subsist some length of time on dogs have now become extreamly fond of their flesh ; it is worthey of remark that while we lived principally on the flesh of this animal we wer much more helthy strong and more fleshey then we have been Sence we left the Buffalow Country.   as for my own part I have not become reconsiled to the taste of this animal as yet   a Small crow, the blue crested Corvus and the smaller corvus with a white breast, the little brown ren, and a large brown Sparrow, the bald Eagle, and the butifull Buzzard of the Columbia Still continue with us,   Send Sarj^t Gass and G Shannon to the Salt makers who are on the Sea Coast to the S W of us, to enquire after Willard & Wiser who have not yet returned.   R Field, potts & Collins the hunters who Set out on the 28th ult°, retu1ned this evening after dark   they reported that they had been about 15 miles up the river which falls into Merewethers Bay to the East of us, and had hunted the Country a considerable distance to East, and had proved unsucksesfull haveing killed one Deer and a fiew fowls, bearly as much as Subsisted them   this reminded us of the necessity of takeing time by the forelock, and keep out Several parties while we have yet a little meat beforehand   Capt Lewis gave the Cheif Cania a par of Sattin breechies with which he appeared much pleased

Comowooll and the Clatsops who visited us yesterday left us in the evening   These people the Chinnooks and others residing in this neighbourhood and speaking the same language have been very friendly to us; they appear to be a mild inoffensive people but will pilfer if they have an opportunity to do so where they conceive themselves not liable to detection they are great higlers in trade and if they conceive you anxious to purchase will be a whole day bargaining for a handfull of roots; this I should have thought proceeded from their want of knowledge of the comparitive value of articles of merchandize and the fear of being cheated, did I not find that they invariably refuse the price first offered them and afterwards very frequently accept a smaller quantity of the same article; in order to satisfy myself on this subject I once offered a Chinnook my watch two knives and a considerable quantity of beads for a small inferior sea Otter's skin which I did not much want,   he immediately conceived it of great value, and refused to barter except I would double the quantity of beads; the next day with a great deal of importunity on his part I received the skin in exchange for a few strans of the same beads he had refused the day before.   I therefore believe this trait in their character proceeds from an avaricious all grasping disposition   in this rispect they differ from all Indians I ever became acquainted with, for their dispositions invariably lead them to give whatever they are possessed off no matter how usefull or valuable, for a bauble which pleases their fancy, without consulting it's usefullness or value.   nothing interesting occurred today, or more so, than our wappetoe being all exhausted

Comowool and the Clatsops who visited us yesterday left us in the morning.   Those people the *Chinnooks* and others resideing in this neighbourhood and Speaking the Same language have been verry friendly to us; they appear to be a Mild inoffensive people, but will pilfer if they have an oppertunity to do so when they conceive themselves not liable to detection. they are great higlers in trade and if they conceive you anxious to purchase will be a whole day bargaining for a hand full of roots; this I should have thought proceeded from their want of Knowledge of the comparitive value of articles of Merchindize and the fear of being Cheated, did I not find that they invariably refuse the price first offered them and afterwards very frequently accept a smaller quantity of the Same article; in order to satisfy myself on this point, I onc[e] offered a Clatsop man my watch a knife, a Dollar of the coin of U States and a hand full of beeds, for a Small Sea otter Skin, which I did not much want, he imediately Conceived it of great value, and refused to Sell unless I would give as maney more blue beeds; the next day with a great deel of importunity on his part we received the Skin in exchange for a fiew Strans of the Same beeds he had refused the day before. I therefore beleive this treat [trait] in their Charector proceeds from an avericious all grasping disposition. in this respect they differ from all Indians I ever became acquainted with, for their dispositions invariably lead them to give whatever they are possessed off no matter how usefull or valueable, for a bauble which pleases their fancy, without consulting its usefullness or value. nothing occured to day, or more So, than our *Wappato* being all exhausted.

[Lewis:]   *Sunday January 5th. 1806*

At 5 P.M. Willard and Wiser returned, they had not been lost as we apprehended. they informed us that it was not untill the fifth day after leaving the Fort that they could find a convenient place for making salt; that they had at length established themselves on the coast about 15 Miles S W from this, near the lodge of some Killamuck families; that the Indians were very friendly and had given them a considerable quantity of the blubber of a whale which perished on the coast some distance S E. of them; part of this blubber they brought with them, it was white & not unlike the fat of Poork, tho' the texture was more spongey and somewhat coaiser. I had a part of it cooked and found it very pallitable and tender, it resembled the beaver or the dog in flavour. it may appear somewhat extraordinary tho' it is a fact that the flesh of the beaver and dog possess a very great affinity in point of flavour. These lads also informed us that J. Fields, Bratton and Gibson (the Salt Makers) had with their assistance erected a comfortable camp killed an Elk and several deer and secured a good stock of meat; they commenced the making of salt and found that they could obtain from 3 quarts to a gallon a day; they brought with them a specemine of the salt of about a gallon, we found it excellent, fine, strong, & white; this was a great treat to myself and most of the party, having not had any since the 20ᵗʰ Ultᵐᵒ; I say most of the party, for my friend Capᵗ Clark. declares it to be a mear matter of indifference with him whether he uses it or not; for myself I must confess I felt a considerable inconvenience from the want of it; the want of bread I consider as trivial provided, I get fat meat, for as to the species of meat I am not very particular, the flesh of the dog the horse and the wolf, having from habit become equally formiliar with any other, and I have learned to think that if the chord be sufficiently strong, which binds the soul and boddy together, it dose not so much matter about the materials which compose it. Colter also returned this evening unsuccessfull from the chase, having been absent since the 1ˢᵗ Insᵗ Capᵗ Clark determined this evening to set out early tomorrow with two canoes and 12 men in quest of the whale, or at all events to purchase from the Indians a parcel of the blubber, for this purpose he prepared a small assortment of merchandize to take with him.

[Clark:]   *Sunday 5ᵗʰ of January 1806*

At 5 P.M. Willard and Wiser returned, they had not been lost as we expected they informᵈ us that it was not untill the 5ᵗʰ day after leaveing the fort, that they could find a convenient place for makeing Salt; that they had at length established themselves on the Sea Coast about 15 miles S W from this, near the houses of Some Clat-sop & Kilamox families; that

the Indians were very friendly and had given them a considerable quantity of the blubber of the whale which perished on
the coast Some distance S.E of them, it was white and not unlike the fat of Pork, tho' the texture was more Spungey and
Somewhat Coarser. we had part of it cooked and found it
very pallitable and tender, it resembles the Beaver in flavour.
those men also informed us that the Salt makers with their assistance had erected a comfortable camp, had killed an Elk and
Several Deer and secured a good Stock of Meat; they commenced the makeing of Salt and found that they could make
from 3 quarts to a gallon a day; they brought with them a
specimen of the Salt, of about a gallon,   we found it excellent
white & fine, but not so strong as the rock salt or that made in
Kentucky or the Western parts of the U, States.   this salt was
a great treat to most of the party, haveing not had any Since
the 20th ult^o as to my self I care but little whether I have any
with my meat or not; provided the meat [is] fat, haveing from
habit become entirely cearless about my diat, and I have learned
to think that if the cord be Sufficiently Strong which binds the
Soul and boddy together, it does not so much matter about the
materials which compose it

Colter returned this evening unsecksessfull from the chase,
haveing been absent since the 1st inst^t

I determine to Set out early tomorrow with two canoes & 12
men in quest of the whale, or at all events to purchase from
the indians a parcel of the blubber,   for this purpose I made
up a Small assortment of merchindize, and directed the men to
hold themselves in readiness &^{c}

[Lewis:]   *Monday January 6th 1806*

Capt Clark set out after an early breakfast with the party
in two canoes as had been concerted the last evening;   Charbono and his Indian woman were also of the party; the Indian
woman was very impo[r]tunate to be permited to go, and was
therefore indulged; she observed that she had traveled a long
way with us to see the great waters, and that now that monstrous fish was also to be seen, she thought it very hard she

could not be permitted to see either (she had never yet been to the Ocean).

The Clatsops, Chinnooks, Killamucks &c. are very loquacious and inquisitive; they possess good memories and have repeated to us the names capasities of the vessels &c of many traders and others who have visited the mouth of this river; they are generally low in stature, proportionably small, reather lighter complected and much more illy formed than the Indians of the Missouri and those of our frontier; they are generally cheerfull but never gay. with us their conversation generally turns upon the subjects of trade, smoking, eating or their women; about the latter they speak without reserve in their presents, of their every part, and of the most formiliar connection. they do not hold the virtue of their women in high estimation, and will even prostitute their wives and daughters for a fishinghook or a stran of beads. in common with other savage nations they make their women perform every species of domestic drudgery. but in almost every species of this drudgery the men also participate, their women are also compelled to geather roots, and assist them in taking fish, which articles form much the greatest part of their subsistance; notwithstanding the survile manner in which they treat their women they pay much more rispect to their judgment and oppinions in many rispects than most indian nations; their women are permitted to speak freely before them, and sometimes appear to command with a tone of authority; they generally consult them in their traffic and act in conformity to their opinions.

I think it may be established as a general maxim that those nations treat their old people and women with most differrence [deference] and rispect where they subsist principally on such articles that these can participate with the men in obtaining them; and that, that part of the community are treated with least attention, when the act of procuring subsistence devolves entirely on the men in the vigor of life   It appears to me that nature has been much more deficient in her filial tie than in any other of the strong affections of the human heart, and therefore think, our old men equally with our women indebted to

[315]

civilization for their ease and comfort. Among the Siouxs, Assinniboins and others on the Missouri who subsist by hunting it is a custom when a person of either sex becomes so old and infurm that they are unable to travel on foot from camp to camp as they rome in surch of subsistance, for the children or near relations of such person to leave them without compunction or remo[r]se; on those occasions they usually place within their reach a small peace of meat and a platter of water, telling the poor old superannuated wretch for his consolation, that he or she had lived long enough, that it was time they should dye and go to their relations who can afford to take care of them much better than they could. I am informed that this custom prevails even among the Minetares Arwaharmays and Recares when attended by their old people on their hunting excurtions; but in justice to these people I must observe that it appeared to me at their vilages, that they provided tolerably well for their aged persons, and several of their feasts appear to have principally for their object a contribution for their aged and infirm persons.

This day I overhalled our merchandize and dryed it by the fire, found it all damp; we have not been able to keep anything dry for many days together since we arrived in this neighbourhood, the humidity of the air has been so excessively great. our merchandize is reduced to a mear handfull, and our comfort during our return the next year much depends on it, it is therefore almost unnecessary to add that we much regret the reduced state of this fund

[Clark:]   *Monday 6th of January 1806*

The last evening Shabono and his Indian woman was very impatient to be permitted to go with me, and was therefore indulged; She observed that She had traveled a long way with us to See the great waters, and that now that monstrous fish was also to be Seen, She thought it verry hard that She could not be permitted to See either (She had never yet been to the Ocian). after an early brackfast I Set out with two Canoes down the *Netel* R into Meriwether Bay with a view to proced

on to the Clatsop town, and hire a guide to conduct me through
the creeks which I had every reason to beleeve Comunicated
both with the Bay and a Small river near to which our men
were making Salt   Soon after I arrived in the Bay the wind
Sprung up from the N. W. and blew So hard and raised the
waves so high that we were obliged to put into a Small creek
Short of the Village.   finding I could not proceed on to the
Village in safety, I deturmined to assend this Creek as high as
the canoes would go; which from its directions must be near
the open lands in which I had been on the 10th ult°, and leave
the Canoes and proceed on by land.   at the distance of about
3 miles up this creek I observed Some high open land, at
which place a road set out and had every appearance of a portage,   here I landed drew up the canoes and Set out by land,
proceeded on through 3 deep Slashes to a pond about a mile
in length and 200 yards wide, kept up this pond leaving it to
the right, and passing the head to a creek which we could not
cross,   this Creek is the one which I rafted on the 8th & 9
ultimo: and at no great distance from where I crossed in
Cus ca lars Canoe on the 10th ult° to which place I expected a
find a canoe,   we proceeded on and found a Small Canoe at the
place I expected, calculated to carry 3 men, we crossed and from
the top of a ridge in the Prarie we Saw a large gange of Elk
feeding about 2 miles below on our direction   I divided the
party So as to be certain of an elk, Several Shot[s] were fired
only one Elk fell.   I had this Elk butchered and carried to a
Creak in advance at which place I intended to encamp,   two
other Elk were badly Shot, but as it was nearly dark we could
not pursue them,   we proceeded on to the forks of the Creek
which we had just crossed turning around to the S. W. and
meeting one of equal Size from the South, the two makeing a
little river 70 yards wide which falls into the Ocian near the
3 Clat Sop houses which I visited on the 9th ult°   in the forks
of this Creek we found Some drift pine which had been left on
the Shore by the tide of which we made fires.   the evening a
butifull Clear moon Shiney night, and the 1st fair night which
we have had for 2 months

Chapter XXII

AT FORT CLATSOP

Lewis's Journal, January 7–20, 1806
Clark's Journal, January 7–20

[Lewis:]   *Monday (Tuesday) January 7th 1806*

LAST evening Drewyer visited his traps and caught a beaver and an otter; the beaver was large and fat we have therefore fared sumptuously today; this we consider a great prize for another reason, it being a full grown beaver was well supplyed with the materials for making bate with which to catch others   this bate when properly prepared will intice the beaver to visit it as far as he can smell it, and this I think may be safely stated at a mile, their sense of smelling being very accute.   To prepare beaver bate, the castor or bark stone is taken as the base, this is gently pressed out of the bladderlike bag which contains it, into a phiol of 4 ounces with a wide mouth; if you have them you will put from four to six stone in a phiol of that capacity,   to this you will add half a nutmeg, a douzen or 15 grains of cloves and thirty grains of cinimon finely pulverized, stir them well together and then add as much ardent sperits to the composition as will reduce it the consistency [of] mustard prepared for the table; when thus prepared it resembles mustard precisely to all appearance. when you cannot procure a phiol a bottle made of horn or a tight earthen vessel will answer, in all cases it must be excluded from the air or it will soon loose it's virtue;   it is fit for uce immediately it is prepared but becomes much stronger and better in about four or five days and will keep for months provided it be perfectly secluded from the air   when cloves are not to be had use double the quantity of Allspice, and when no spice can be obtained use the bark of the root of

sausafras; when sperits can not be had use oil stone of the
beaver adding mearly a sufficient quantity to moisten the other
materials, or reduce it to a stif past[e.]   it appears to me that
the principal uce of the spices is only to give a variety to the
scent of the bark stone and if so the mace vineller [vanilla]
and other sweetsmelling spices might be employed with equal
advantage.   The male beaver has six stones, two [of] which
contain a substance much like finely pulvarized bark of a pale
yellow colour and not unlike tanner's ooz in smell, these are
called the *bark stones* or castors;[1] two others, which like the
bark stone resemble small bladders, contain a pure oil of a
strong rank disagreeable smell, and not unlike train oil, these
are called the *oil stones;* and 2 others of generation.   the Bark-
stones are about two inc[h]es in length, the others somewhat
smaller   all are of a long oval form, and lye in a bunch together between the skin and the root of the tail, beneath or
behind the fundament with which they are closely connected
and seem to communicate.   the pride of the female lyes on
the inner side much like those of the hog.   they have no
further parts of generation that 1 can perceive and therefore
beleive that like the birds they copulate with the extremity of
the gut.   The female have from two to four young ones at a
birth and bring fourth once a year only, which usually happens
about the latter end of may and begining of June.   at this
stage she is said to drive the male from the lodge, who would
otherwise destroy the young   dryed our lodge and had it put
away under shelter; this is the first day during which we have
had no rain since we arrived at this place.   nothing extraordinary happened today.

[Clark:]   *Tuesday 7ᵗʰ of January* 1806

Some frost this morning.   I[t] may appear somewhat incrediable, but So it is that the Elk which was killed last evening was eaten except about 8 pounds, which I directed to be

¹ The preputial glands, containing the substance called castoreum (which once had
much vogue as an efficacious medicine)   See H T Maitin's monograph on the
beaver, *Castorologia* (Montreal, 1892), pp 90-98 — *Jesuit Relations,* lxix, p 291

taken along with the Skin, I proceded up the South fork of the Creek about 2 miles and crossed on a pine tree which had been fallen by the Saltmakers on their first going out, on this tree we crossed the deepest of the Water and waded on the opposit Side for 30 yards,[1] from thence to the Ocian ¾ of a mile through a Continuation of open ridgey Prarie, here the Coast is Sandy, we proceeded on the Sandy beech nearly South for 3 miles to the mouth of [a] butifull river with bold and rapid current of 85 yards wide and 3 feet deep in the Shallowest place, a Short distance up this river on the N E side is the remains of an old village of Clatsops   I entered a house where I found a Man 2 Wom[e]n & 3 Children, they appeared retchedly pore & dirty, I hired the man to Set us across the River which I call after the Nation *Clatsop* river [2] for which I gave 2 fishing hooks. at this place the Creek over which I crossed on a tree passes within 100 yards of the *Clatsop* river over which the nativs have a portage which affords them an easy communication with the villages near point adams, and at the mouth of the creek, on which we lay last night. in walking on the Sand after crossing the river I saw a Singular Species of fish which I had never before Seen   one of the men Call this fish a Skaite, it is properly a Thornback. I proceeded on about 2 miles to near the base of [a] high Mountain where I found our Salt makers, and with them Serg[t] Gass, Geo. Shannon was out in the woods assisting Jo Field and gibson to kill Some Meat, the Salt Makers had made a Neet close camp, convenient to wood Salt water and the fresh water of the Clâtsop river which at this place was within 100 paces of the Ocian   they wer also Situated near 4 houses of Clatsops & Killamox, who they informed me had been verry kind and attentive to them. I hired a young Indian to pilot me to the whale for which Service I gave him a file in hand and promised Several other small articles on my return, left Serg[t] gass and one man of my party Werner to make Salt & permited Bratten to accompany me, we proceeded on the round Slipery Stones under a high hill which projected into the ocian about 4 miles

---

[1] A branch of Skipanon Creek in the northwest corner of Clatsop County — ED
[2] Now the Necanicum, falling into the ocean north of Tillamook Head — ED

further than the direction of the Coast.[1]   after walking for 2½ miles on the Stones, my guide made a Sudin halt, pointed to the top of the mountain and uttered the word *Pe shack* which means bad, and made signs that we could not proceed any further on the rocks, but must pass over that mountain,   I hesitated a moment & view this emence mountain the top of which was obscured in the clouds, and the assent appear[d] to be almost perpindecular ; as the small Indian parth allong which they had brought emence loads but a fiew hours before, led up this mountain and appeared to assend in a Sideling direction, I thought more than probable that the assent might be torerably easy and therefore proceeded on,   I soon found that the [path] become much worst as I assended, and at one place we were obliged to Support and draw our selves up by the bushes & roots for near 100 feet, and after about 2 hours labour and fatigue we reached the top of this high mountain, from the top of which I looked down with estonishment to behold the hight which we had assended, which appeared to be 10 or 12 hundred feet up a mountain which appeared to be almost perpindicular,   here we met 14 Indians men and women loaded with the Oil & Blubber of the whale   In the face of this tremendeous precipic[e] imediately below us, there is a Stra (*tar*) of white earth (which my guide informed me) the neighbouring indians use to paint themselves, and which appears to me to resemble the earth of which the French Porcelain is made ; I am confident that this earth contains argile,[2] but whether it also contains silex or magnesia, or either of those earths in a proper perpotion I am unable to deturmine   we left the top of the precipice and proceeded on a bad road and encamped on a small run passing to the left : all much fatiagued

[Lewis :]   *Tuesday (Wednesday) January 8th 1806*

Our meat is begining to become scarse ; sent Drewyer and Collins to hunt this morning.   the guard duty being hard on

---

[1] Tillamook Head, a high forest-covered point, upon which an important coast lighthouse now stands — ED

[2] The word argil was first used as synonomous with alumina   It is now confined to potter's clay   This earth was doubtless some form of kaolinite — ED

the men who now remain in the fort I have for their relief since the departure of Capt Clark made the Cooks mount guard. Serg^t Gass and Shannon have not yet returned, nor can I immajen what is the cause of their detention.   In consequence of the clouds this evening I lost my P.M observation for Equal Altitudes, and from the same cause have not been able to take a single observation since we have been at this place.   nothing extraordinary happened today.

The Clatsops Chinnooks and others inhabiting the coast and country in this neighbourhood, are excessively fond of smoking tobacco. in the act of smoking they appear to swallow it as they draw it from the pipe, and for many draughts together you will not perceive the smoke which they take from the pipe; in the same manner also they inhale it in their lungs untill they become surcharged with this vapour when they puff it out to a great distance through their nost[r]ils and mouth; I have no doubt the smoke of the tobacco in this manner becomes much more intoxicating and that they do possess themselves of all it's virtues in their fullest extent; they freequently give us sounding proofs of it's creating a dismorallity of order in the abdomen,   nor are those light matters thought indelicate in either sex, but all take the liberty of obeying the dictates of nature without reserve.   these people do not appear to know the uce of sperituous liquors, they never having once asked us for it; I presume therefore that the traders who visit them have never indulged them with the uce of it; from what ever cause this may proceede, it is a very fortunate occurrence, as well for the natives themselves, as for the quiet and safety of thos whites who visit them.

[Clark:]   *Wednesday 8th January* 1806

The last night proved fair and cold   wind hard from the S. E   we Set out early and proceeded to the top of the mountain next to the [former?] which   is much the highest part and that part faceing the sea is open,   from this point I beheld the grandest and most pleasing prospects which my eyes ever surveyed,   in my frount a boundless Ocean; to the

N. and N.E. the coast as as far as my sight could be extended,
the Seas rageing with emence wave[s] and brakeing with great
force from the rocks of Cape Disapointment as far as I could
See to the N.W.   The Clatsops Chinnooks and other villagers
on each Side of the Columbia river and in the Praries below
me, the meanderings of 3 handsom Streams heading in Small
lakes at the foot [of] the high Country; The Columbia
River for some distance up, with its Bays and Small rivers:
and on the other side I have a view of the coast for an emence
distance to the S E by S.   the nitches and points of high
land which forms this corse for a long ways aded to the in-
oumerable rocks of emence Sise out at a great distance from
the shore and against which the Seas brak with great foice
gives this coast a most romantic appearance.   from this point
of View[1] My guide pointed to a Village at the mouth of a
Small river near which place he Said the whale was,   he also
pointed to 4 other places where the princ[i]pal Villages of the
Killamox were Situated,   I could plainly See the houses of 2
of those Villeges & the Smoke of a 3ʳᵈ which was two far of[f],
for me to disern with my naked eye.   after taking the courses
and computed the Distances in my own mind, I proceeded on
down a Steep decent to a Single house the remains of an old
Kil a mox Town in a nitch imediately on the Sea coast, at
which place great Nᵒ of eregular rocks are out and the waves
comes in with great force.   Near this old Town I observed
large Canoes of the neetest kind on the ground, Some of which
appeared nearly decayed others quit[e] Sound, I examoned
those canoes and found that [they] were the repository of
the dead   This Custom of Secureing the Dead differs a
little from the Chinnooks   the Kilamox Secure the dead
bodies in an oblong box of Plank, which is placed in an
open canoe resting on the ground, in which is put a paddle
and Sundery other articles the property of the disceased.   The
Coast in the neighbourhood of this old village is slipping from
the Sides of the high hills, in emence masses; fifty or a hun-

---

1 Called by the explorers, Clark's Point of View   It is now known as False
Tillamook Head, or Cape Falcon, and was the headland seen from Cape Disappointment, Nov 18, 1805 — Ed

dred acres at a time give way and a great proportion of [in] an instant precipitated into the Ocean. those hills and mountains are principally composed of a yellow clay; their Slipping off or Spliting assunder at this time is no doubt caused by the incessant rains which has fallen within the last two months the mountans covered with a verry heavy c[g]roth of pine & furr, also the white cedar or *arbor vita* and a Small proportion of the black alder, this alder grows to the hight of Sixty or Seventy feet and from 2 to 3 feet in diamiter Some Species of pine (*or fur*) on the top of the Point of View rise to the emmence hight of 210 feet and from 8 to 12 feet in diameter, and are perfectly Sound and Solid Wind hard from the S E and See looked [wild] in the after part of the Day breaking with great force against the Scattering rocks at some distance from Shore, and the ruged rockey points under which we wer obleged to pass and if we had unfortunately made one false Step we Should eneviateably have fallen into the Sea and dashed against the rocks in an instant, fortunately we passed over 3 of those dismal points and arived on a butifull Sand Shore on which we continued for 2 miles, crossed a Cıeek 80 yards near 5 Cabins, and proceeded to the place the whale had perished, found only the Skelleton of this Monster on the Sand between (*2 of*) the Villages of the *Kil a mox* nation; the Whale was already pillaged of every Valuable part by the Kilamox Ind* in the Vecinity of whose village's it lay on the Strand where the waves and tide had driven up & left it. this Skeleton (*of the Whale Cap' Clark*) measured 105 feet.[1] I returned to the Village of 5 Cabins on the creek which I shall call *E co-la* or Whale Creek,[2] found the nativs busily engaged boiling the blubber, which they performed in a large Squar wooden trought by means of hot stones; the oil when extracted was secured in bladders and the Guts of the whale; the blubber from which the oil was only partially extracted by this

[1] Gass says the head alone measured twelve feet   Coues thinks this was probably the great gray whale of the Pacific (*Rhachianectes glaucus*), but that the length must have been exaggerated — ED

[2] The Nehalem River, a considerable stream in Tillamook County emptying into a bay of the same name — ED

process, was laid by in their cabins in large flickes [flitches] for use; those flickes they usially expose to the fire on a wooden Spit untill it is prutty well wormed through and then eate it either alone or with roots of the rush, *Shaw na tâk-we* or Diped in the oil. The *Kil a mox* although they possessed large quantities of this blubber and oil were so prenurious that they disposed of it with great reluctiance and in small quantities only; insomuch that my utmost exertion aided by the party with the Small Stock of merchindize I had taken with me were not able to precure more blubber than about 300ᵇ and a fiew gallons of oil; Small as this stock is I prise it highly; and thank providence for directing the whale to us; and think him much more kind to us than he was to jonah, having Sent this Monster to be *Swallowed by us* in Sted of *Swallowing of us* as jonah's did   I recrossed *Ecola* Creek and encamped on the bank at which place we observed an ebundance of fine wood the Indian men followed me for the purpose of Smokeing   I enquired of those people as well as I could by Signs the Situation, mode of liveing & Strength of their nation   They informed me that the bulk of their nation lived in 3 large villages Still further along the Sea coast to the S S W at the enterence of 3 Creek[s] which fell into a bay, and that other houses were scattered about on the coast, Bay and on a Small river which fell into the Bay in which they cought Salmon, and from this Creek (which I call *Kil a mox* River)[1] they crossed over to the (*Wap pato I*) on the *Shock.ah lil com* (which is the Indian name for the Columbia river)[2] and purchased Wappato &c   that the nation was verry large and that they had a great maney houses,   In Salmon Season they cought great numbers of that fish in the Small creeks, when the Salmon was Scerce they found Sturgion and a variety of other fish thrown up by

---

[1] The Indians were speaking here of Tillamook Bay, into which several rivers and creeks run   The largest of these (doubtless the one Clark named Kilamox from hearsay) is now Wilson River, from whose upper waters a portage to Sauvie (Wappato) Island would not be difficult — Ed

[2] Silas B Smith says that Clark misunderstood the Indians at this point   They never name a river, only localities, so that there was no Indian word for the Columbia Shocatilcum (Shockahlilcom) was a chief of the tribe from whom the Tillamook purchased wappato — Ed

the waves and left by the tide which was verry fine, Elk was plenty in the mountains, but they could not Kill maney of them with their arrows. The *Kil â mox* in their habits customs manners dress & language differ but little from the Clatsops, Chinnooks and others in the neighbourhood, [their houses] are of the Same form of those of the Clatsops with a Dore at each end & two fire places i, e the house is double as long as wide and divided into 2 equal parts with a post in the middle Supporting the ridge pole, and in the middle of each of those divisions they make their fir's, dores Small & houses Sunk 5 feet.

[Lewis:]   *Friday (Thursday) January 9ᵗʰ 1806*

Our men are now very much engaged in dressing Elk and Deer skins for mockersons and cloathing   the deer are extreemly scarce in this neighbourhood, some are to be found near the praries and open grounds along the coast   this evening we heard seven guns in quick succession after each other, they appeared to be on the Creek to the South of us and several miles distant; I expect that the hunters Drewyer and Collins have fallen in with a gang of Elk.   some marrow bones and a little fresh meat would be exceptable ; I have been living for two days past on poor dryed Elk, or *jurk* as the hunters term it.

The Clatsops Chinnooks &c bury their dead in their canoes for this purpose four pieces of split timber are set erect on end, and sunk a few feet in the grown[d], each brace having their flat sides opposite to each other and sufficiently far assunder to admit the width of the canoes in which the dead are to be deposited ; through each of these perpendicular posts, at the hight of six feet a mortice is cut, through which two bars of wood are incerted; on these cross bars a small canoe is placed in which the body is laid after being carefully roled in a robe of some dressed skins ; a paddle is also deposited with them ; a larger canoe is now reversed, overlaying and imbracing the small one, and resting with it's gunwals on the cross bars ; one or more large mats of rushes or flags are then

Two swords, a bludgeon and a paddle,
apparently drawn by Lewis.

roled around the canoes and the whole securely lashed with a long cord, usually made of the bark of the *Arbor vita* or white cedar. on the cross bars which support the canoes is frequently hung or laid various articles of cloathing culinary eutensels &c. I cannot understand them sufficiently to make any enquiries relitive to their religeous opinions, but presume from their depositing various articles with their dead that they believe in a state of future existence.

The persons who usually visit the entrance of this river for the purpose of traffic or hunting I believe are either English or Americans; the Indians inform us that they speak the same language with ourselves, and give us proofs of their varacity by repeating many words of English, as musquit, powder, shot, [k]nife, file, damned rascal, sun of a bitch &c whether these traders are from Nootka sound, from some other late establishement on this coast, or immediately from the U'States or Great Brittain, I am at a loss to determine, nor can the Indians inform us the Indians whom I have asked in what direction the traders go when they depart from hence, or arrive here, always point to the S W from which it is presumeable that Nootka cannot be their destination; and as from Indian information a majority of these traders annually visit them about the beginning of April and remain with them six or seven Months, they cannot come immediately from Great Britain or the U'States, the distance being too great for them to go and return in the ballance of the year. from this circumstance I am sometimes induced to believe that there is some other establishment on the coast of America south West of this place of which little is but yet known to the world, or it may be perhaps on some Island in the pacific ocean between the Continents of Asia and America to the South West of us.[1]

---

[1] In 1788 the English trader Meares established a post at Nootka Sound, and built and launched the first vessel ever constructed on the Northwest Coast; and American traders erected, three years later, a post at Clayoquot, and built and launched a schooner Americans and British were trading on that coast thereafter For accounts of their early voyages thereto, see Bancroft, *N W Coast*, ii, pp 320-326 Most ships, whether traders or whalers, then sailed by way of the Sandwich Islands These facts will sufficiently explain our text The brig "Lydia," from Boston, Captain Hill commanding, was in Columbia River in November, 1805, a fortnight

This traffic on the part of the whites consists in vending, guns, (principally old british or American musquits) powder, balls and shot, Copper and brass kettles, brass teakettles and coffee pots, blankets from two to three point, scarlet and blue Cloth (coarse), plates and strips of sheet copper and brass, large brass wire, knives, beads and tobacco with fishinghooks buttons and some other small articles; also a considerable quantity of Sailor's cloaths, as hats coats, trowsers and shirts for these they receive in return from the natives, dressed and undressed Elk-skins, skins of the sea Otter, common Otter, beaver, common fox, spuck,[1] and tiger cat; also dryed and pounded sammon in baskets, and a kind of buisquit, which the natives make of roots called by them shappelell The natives are extravegantly fond of the most common cheap blue and white beads, of moderate size, or such that from 50 to 70. will weigh one penneyweight the blue is usually p[r]efered to the white; these beads constitute the principal circulating medium with all the indian tribes on this river; for these beads they will dispose [of] any article they possess the beads are strung on strans of a fathom in length and in that manner sold by the bredth or yard

[Clark:]   *Thursday 9ᵗʰ of January* 1806

a fine morning wind from the N E. last night about 10 oClock while Smokeing with the nativ's I was alarmed by a loud Srill voice from the cabins on the opposite side, the

after Lewis and Clark had passed down the river, possibly while they lay encamped in Gray's Bay, or upon Point Ellice See Jewitt, *Journal kept at Nootka Sound* (New York, 1812), and later editions under title of *Adventures and Sufferings of John R Jewitt* This author says, " We proceeded about ten miles up the river to a small Indian village, where we heard from the inhabitants that Captains Clark and Lewis, from the United States of America, had been there about a fortnight before on their journey overland, and had left several medals with them, which they showed us " The " Lydia ' remained upon the Northwest coast until August of the next year The ignorance of the explorers as to the vicinity of this ship is to be assigned to either the stupidity or the cunning of the Indians Possibly the crafty Chinook Concomly resented the explorers' treatment of his nation, and took his revenge by keeping them in ignorance of a fact that would have been of great value to the expedition — ED

    1 A term applied by the natives to the young of the sea-otter — ED

Indians all run immediately across to the village, my guide who continued with me made Signs that Some one's throat was Cut, by enquiry I found that one man McNeal was absent, I imediately Sent off Serg^t N. Pryor & 4 men in quest of McNeal who' they met comeing across the Creak in great hast, and informed me that the people were alarmed on the opposit side at Something but what he could not tell, a Man had verry friendly envited him to go and eate in his lodge, that the Indian had locked armes with him and went to a lodge in which a woman gave him Some blubber, that the man envited him to another lodge to get Something better, and the woman [*Knowing his design*] held him [*McNeal*] by the blanket which he had around him (*He not knowing her object freed himself & was going off, when* [*This woman a Chinnook an old friend of McNeals*] and another ran out and hollow'd and his pretended friend disapeared   I emediately ordered every man to hold themselves in a State of rediness and Sent Serg^t Pryor & 4 men to know the cause of the alarm which was found to be a premeditated plan of the pretended friend of McNeal to ass[ass]anate [him] for his Blanket and what fiew articles he had about him, which was found out by a Chinnook woman who allarmed the men of the village who were with me in time to prevent the horred act   this man was of another band at Some distance and ran off as soon as he was discovered. we have now to look back and Shudder at the dreadfull road on which we have to return of 45 miles S E of Point adams & 35 miles from Fort *Clatsop*. I had the blubber & oil divided among' the party and set out about Sunrise and returned by the Same rout we had went out, met Several parties of men & women of the Chinnook and Clatsops nations, on their way to trade with the *Kil a mox* for blubber and oil ; on the Steep decent of the Mountain I overtook five men and Six women with emence loads of the Oil and blubber of the Whale, those Indians had passed by Some rout by which we missed them as we went out yesterday ; one of the women in the act of getting down a Steep part of the Mountain her load by Some means had Sliped off her back, and She was holding the load by a Strap which was fastened to the mat bag in which it was in, in one hand and holding a bush by the other, as I was in front of my party, I endeavoured to relieve this woman by takeing her load untill She could get to a better place a little below, & to my estonishment found the load as much as I could lift and must exceed 100^{lbs} the husband of this woman who was below Soon came to her releif, those people proceeded on with us to the Salt works, at which place we arrived late in the evening, found them without meat, and 3 of the Party J Field Gibson & Shannon out hunting as I was excessively fatigued and my party appeared verry much so, I deturmined to Stay untill the morning and rest our selves a little. The Clatsops proceeded on with their lodes. The Clatsops, Chinnooks Kilámox &c are verry loquacious and inquisitive; they possess good memories and have repeeted to us the names capasities of the Vessels &c of maney traders and others who have visited the mouth of this river; they are generally low in Statu[r]e, proportionably Small, reather lighter complected and much more illy formed than the Indians of the Missouri and those of our fronteers; they are generally Chearfull but never gay with us their conversation generally turns upon the subject of trade, Smokeing, eating or their women; about the latter, they Speak without reserve in their presence, of their every part, and of the most farmiliar Connection they do not hold the virtue of their women in high estimation, and will even prostitute their wives and Daughters for a fishing-hook or a Stran of beeds. in Common with other Savage nations they make their womin perform every Species of domestic drugery; but in almost every Species of this drugery the men also participate. their woman are compelled to gather roots, and assist them in takeing fish; which articles form much the greater part of their Subsistance; notwithstanding the Survile manner in which they treat their womin they pay much more respect to their judgement and oppinion in maney respects than most indian nations; their womin are permited to Speak freely before them, and Sometimes appear to command with a tone of authority; they generally consult them in their traffic and act conformably to their opinions.

I think it may be established as a general maxim that those

nations treat their old people and women with most defference
and respect where they Subsist principally . on Such articles
that these can participate with the men in obtaining them ;
and that, that part of the Community are treated with least
attention, when the act of precureing subsistance devolves
entirely on the men in the vigor of life.   It appears to me
that nature has been much more deficient in her filial ties than
in any others of the Strong effections of the humane heart, and
therefore think our old men equally with our woman indebted
to sivilization for their ease and comfort.   I am told among
the Sioux's, Assinniboins and others on the *Missouri* who Subsist by hunting it is a Custom when a person of either Sex
becoms So old and infirm that they are unable to travel on
foot, from Camp to Camp as they rove in serch of subsistance,
for the Children or near relations of such person to leave them
without compunction or remorse ;   on those occasions they
usially place within their reach a Small piece of meat and a
platter of water, telling the poor old Superannuated retch for
their Consolation, that he or She had lived long enough, and
that it was time they Should die and go to their relations who
can afford to take care of them, much better than they Could
I am informed that the Menetares Arwarharmays and Ricares
when attended by their old people on their hunting expedition[s] prosued the Same Custom ; but in justice to those
people I must observe that it appeared to me at their villages,
that they provided tolerably well for their aged persons, and
Several of their *feasts* appear to have principally for their object a contribution for their aged and infirm persons   In one
of the Mandan villages I Saw an old man to whome I gave a
knife and enquired his age,   he Said he had Seen more than
100 winters, and that he Should Soon go down the river to
their old village.   he requested I would give him Something
to prevent the pain in his back   his grand Son a Young man
rebuked the old man and Said it was not worth while, that it
was time for the old man to die   the old man occupied one
Side of the fire and was furnished with plenty of covouring
and food, and every attention appeared to be paid to him. &c
Jo Field in my absence had killed an Elk and a Deer, brought

in the Deer and half of the Elk on a part of which we Suped,
Some rain a little after dark   I visited a house near the Salt
boilers found it inhabited by 2 families,   they were pore dirty
and their house Sworming with flees.

[Lewis:]   *Saturday (Friday) January 10ᵗʰ 1806*

About 10.A M I was visited by Tia *Shâh-hâr-wâr-cap* and
eleven of his nation in one large canoe; these are the Cuth'-
lâh-mâh' nation who reside first above us on the South side of
the Columbia river; this is the first time that I have seen the
Chief, he was hunting when we past his vilage on our way to
this place   I gave him a medal of the smallest size; he presented me with some indian tobacco and a basquit of woppetoe,
in return for which I gave him some thread for making a
skiming-net and a small piece of tobacco   these people speak
the same language with the Chinnooks and C[l]atsops whom
they also resemble in their dress customs manners &c.   they
brought some dryed salmon, wappetoe, dogs, and mats made
of rushes and flags, to barter;   their dogs and a part of their
wappetoe they disposed off, an[d] remained all night near the
fort   This morning Drewyer and Collins returned having
killed two Elk only, and one of those had died in their view
over a small lake which they had not the means of passing it
being late in the evening and has of course spoiled, as it laid
with the entrals in it all night;   as the tide was going out we
could not send for the elk today, therefore ordered a party to
go for it early in the morning and George and Collins to continue their hunt; meat has now become scarce with us. —
Capt Clark returned at 10 P M this evening with the majority of the party who accompanyed him; having left some men
to assist the saltmakers to bring in the meat of two Elk which
they had killed, and sent 2 others through by land to hunt.
Capt. Clark found the whale on the Coast about 45 Miles S E.
of Point Adams [Round], and about 35 Miles from Fort Clatsop by the rout he took; The whale was already pillaged of
every valuable part by the Killamucks, in the vicinity of one

of whose villages it lay on the strand where the waves and tide had driven [it] up and left it. this skelleton measured one hundred and five feet.   Cap' C. found the natives busily engaged in boiling the blubber, which they performed in a large wooden trought by means of hot stones ;   the oil when extracted was secured in bladders and the guts of the whale ; the blubber, from which the oil was only partially extracted by this process, was laid by in their lodges in large fliches for uce ; this they usually expose to the fire on a wooden spit untill it is pretty well warmed through and then eat it either alone or with the roots of the rush, squawmash, fern[1] wappetoe &c. The natives although they possessed large quantities of this blubber and oil were so penurious that they disposed of it with great reluctance and in small quantities only ; insomuch that the utmost exertions of Cap' C. and the whole party aided by the little stock of merchandize he had taken with him and some small articles which the men had, were not able to procure more blubber than about 300 lb and a few gallons of the oil ; this they have brought with them, and small as the store is, we prize it highly, and thank providence for directing the whale to us, and think him much more kind to us than he was [to] jonah, having sent this monster to be *swallowed by us* in stead of *swallowing of us* as jona's did   Cap' C found the road along the coast extreemly difficult of axcess, lying over some high rough and stoney hills, one of which he discribes as being much higher than the others ; having it's base washed by the Ocea[n] over which it rares it's towering summit perpendicularly to the hight of 1500 feet ;   from this summit Cap' C. informed me that there was a delightfull and most extensive view of the ocean, the coast and adjacent country ; this Mou' I have taken the liberty of naming *Clark's Mountain and point of view;* it is situated about 30 M. S E of Point Adams (*Disapointment*) and projects about 2½ miles into the Ocean ; *Killamucks* [*Qu. Clatsop*] river falls in a little to the N.W.

---

[1] A species of brake (*Pteris aquilina lanuguinosa*) the root of which is edible and nutritious   " Squawmash " is only a corruption of camass (*Camassia esculenta*) The "rush " is one of the horsetails (*Equisetum telmateia*) ; its root is edible, although insipid to the taste — ED

[333]

of this mountain; in the face of this tremendious precepice
there is a stra[tum] of white earth (see specimen N° [blank
space in MS.]) which the neighbouring Indians use to paint
themselves, and which appears to me to resemble the earth of
which the French Porcelain is made; I am confident this earth
contains Argill, but w[h]ether it also contains Silex or magnesia, or either of those earths in a proper proportion I am
unable to determine   Shannon and Gass were found with the
Salt makers and ordered to return   M⟨c⟩Neal was near being
assassinated by a Killamuck Indian, but fortunately escaped in
consequence of a Chinnook woman giving information to Cap⟨t⟩
C , the party and Indians with them before the villain had prepared himself to execute his purposes   The party returned
excessively fortiegued and tired of their jaunt.   Killamucks
[*Clatsop*] river is 85 yards wide, rappid and 3 feet deep in the
shallowest part.   The Killamucks in their habits customs
manners dress and language differ but little from the Clatsoops
& Chinnooks.   they place their dead in canoes and [*resting on
the ground*] uncovered, having previously secured the dead
bodies in an oblong box of plank.

The coast in the neighbourhood of Clarks Mountain is sliping off & falling into the Ocean in immence masses; fifty or a
hundred acres at a time give way and a great proportion in an
instant [is] precipitated into the Ocean   these hills and mountains are principally composed of a yellow clay; there sliping
off or spliting assunder at this time is no doubt caused by the
incessant rains which have fallen within the last two months
the country in general as about Fort Clatsop is covered with
a very heavy growth of several species of pine & furr, also the
arbor vita or white cedar and a small proportion of the black
Alder which last sometimes grows to the hight of sixty or
seventy feet, and from two to four feet in diameter   some
species of the pine rise to the immence hight of 210 feet and
are from 7 to 12 feet in diameter, and are perfectly sound and
solid

[Clark:]   *Friday the 10th of January 1806*

I derected Serg^t Gass to continue with the salt makers untill Shannon return from hunting, and then himself and Shannon to return to the Fort, I set out at Sunrise with the party waded the Clatsop river which I found to be 85 Steps across and 3 feet deep, on the opposite Side a Kilamox Indian Came to [me] and offered to Sell Some roots of which I did not want [any], he had a robe made of 2 large Sea otter Skins which I offered to purchase, but he would not part with them, we returned by nearly the Same rout which I had come out, at four miles, I met Gibson & Shannon each with a load of meat, they informed me that they had killed Elk about 2 miles off, I directed 3 men to go with the hunters and help them pack the meat to the place they were makeing Salt, and return to the fort with Serg^t Gass, the balance of the party took the load of the 3 men, after crossing the 2^d Creek frasure informed me that he had lost his big knife, here we Dined I put frasurs load on my guide who is yet with me, and Sent him back in Serch of his knife with directions to join the other men who were out packing meat & return to the fort all together. I arrived at the Canoes about Sunset, the tides was Comeing in I thought it a favourable time to go on to the fort at which place we arrived at 10 oClock P M, found Several inidians of the Cath'lâh-mâh nation the great Chief *Shâh-hâr-wâh cop* who reside not far above us on the South Side of the Columbia River, this is the first time I have Seen the Chief, he was hunting when we passed his village on our way to this place, we gave him a medal of the Smallest Size, he presented me with a basquet of Wappato, in return for which I gave him a fish hook of a large Size and Some wire, those people Speak the Same language with the Chinnooks and Clatsops, whome they all resemble in Dress, Custom, manners &c they brought Some Dried Salmon, Wappato, Dogs, and mats made of rushes & flags to barter; their Dogs and part of their Wappato they disposed of, and remained in their Camp near the fort all night.

In my absence the hunters from the fort killed only two Elk which is yet out in the woods Capt Lewis examined our Small

Stock of merchendize found Some of it wet and Dried it by the fire   Our Merchindize is reduced to a mear handfull, and our comfort, dureing our return next year, much depends on it,   it is therefore almost unnecessary to add that it is much reduced   T[he] nativs in this neighbourhood are excessively fond of Smokeing tobacco.   in the act of Smokeing they appear to swallow it as they draw it from the pipe, and for maney draughts together you will not perceive the Smoke they take from the pipe,   in the Same manner they inhale it in their longs untill they become Surcharged with the Vapour when they puff it out to a great distance through their noistils and mouth; I have no doubt that tobacco Smoked in this manner becomes much more intoxicating, and that they do possess themselves of all its virtues to the fullest extent;   they frequently give us Sounding proofs of its createing a dismorallity of order in the abdomen,   nor are those light matters thought indelicate in either Sex, but all take the liberty of obeying the dicktates of nature without reserve   Those people do not appear to know the use of Speritious licquors, they never haveing once asked us for it; I prosume therefore that the traders who visit them have never indulged them with the use of it; of whatever cause this may proceed, it is a verry fortunate occurrence, as well for the nativs themselves, as for the quiet and Safty of those whites who visit them.   George Drewyer visited this [his] traps in my absence and caught a Beaver & a otter; the beaver was large and fat, and Cap¹ L has feested Sumptiously on it yesterday; this we consider as a great prize, it being a full grown beaver was Well Supplyed with the materials for makeing bate with which to catch others   this bate when properly prepared will entice the beaver to visit it as far as he can Smell it, and this I think may be Safely Stated at ½ a mile, their sence of Smelling being verry accute   To prepare beaver bate, the Caster or bark Stone is taken as the base, this is generally pressed out of the bladder like bag which contains it, into a phiol of 4 ounces with a wide mouth; if you have them you will put from 4 to 6 Stone in a phial of that capacity, to this you will add half a Nutmeg, a Dozen or 15 grains of Cloves and 30 grains of Sinimon finely pulverised, stur them well together, and then add as much ardent Sperits to the composition as will reduce it to the Consistancey of Mustard prepared for the table, when thus prepared it resembles mustard precisely to all appearance   When you cannot precure a phial a bottle made of horn or a light earthern vessel will answer, in all cases it must be excluded from the air or it will Soon lose its Virtue; it is fit for use imediately it is prepared but becoms much stronger and better in 4 or 5 days and will keep for months provided it be purfectly Secluded from the air.   when cloves are not to be had use double the quantity of allspice, and when no spices can be obtained use the bark of the root of the Sausafras; when Sperits cannot be had use oil Stone of the beaver adding mearly a Sufficent quantity to moisten the other materials, or reduce it to a Stiff paste.   it appears to me that the principal use of the Spices is only to give a variety to the Scent of the bark Stone and if So the mace` vineller, and other Sweet Smelling Spices might be employd with equal advantage.   The Male Beaver has Six stones, two[of] which contanes a substance much like finely pulverised bark of a pale yellow Colour and not unlike tanner's ooz in smell,   these are Called the *bark stones* or castors;   two others, which like the bark stone resemble Small blatters, contain a pure oil of a Strong rank disagreable Smell, and not unlike train Oil,   these are Called the *Oil Stones*,   and two others of Generation.   The bark stones are about 2 inches in length, the others somewhat Smaller, all are of a long Oval form, and lye in a bunch together between the skin and the root of the tail beneath or behind the fundiment with which they are closely connected and Seam to communicate,   the pride of the female lye on the inner Side much like those of the hog they have no further parts of Generation that I can proceive, and therefore believe that like the birds they Coperate [copulate] with the extremity of the gut   The female have from 2 to 4 young ones at a birth and bring forth once a year only which usially happins about the latter end of May and beginning of June.   at this Stage She is said to drive the Mail from the lodge, who would otherwise distroy the young.

[Lewis:]   *Sunday (Saturday) January 11ᵗʰ 1806*

Sent a party early this morning for the Elk which was killed on the 9ᵗʰ they returned with it in the evening; Drewyer and Collins also returned without having killed anything   this morning the Sergᵗ of the guard reported the absence of our Indian Canoe, on enquiry we found that those who came in it last evening had been negligent in securing her and the tide in the couɪse of the night had taken her off; we sent a party down to the bay in surch of her, they returned unsuccessfull, the party also who went up the river and Creek in quest of the meat were ordered to lookout for her but were equally unsuccessfull; we ordered a party to resume their resurches for her, early tomorrow; this will be a very considerable loss to us if we do not recover her; she is so light that four men can carry her on their sholders a mile or more without resting; and will carry three men and from 12 to 15 hundred lbˢ the Cuthlâhmâhs left us this evening on their way to the C[l]atsops, to whom they purpose bartering their wappetoe for the blubber and oil of the whale, which the latter purchase for beads &c. from the Killamucks;   in this manner there is a trade continually carryed on by the natives of the river each trading some article or other with their neighbours above and below them; and thus articles which are vended by the whites at the entrance of this river, find their way to the most distant nations enhabiting it's waters.

[Clark:]   *Saturday 11ᵗʰ of January 1806*

Sent a party early this morning for the Elk which was killed on the 9ᵗʰ they returned with it in the evining;   This morning the Sergᵗ of the guard reported that our Indian Canoe had gone a Drift, on enquiry we found that those who came in it last evening had been negligent in Secureing her, and the tide in corse of the night had taken her off; we Sent a party down to the bay in Serch of her, they returned unsecksessfull,   the party who went up the river and creek after meat were derected to look out for her but were equally unsecksessfull; this will be a verry considerable loss to us if we do not recover her, She is so light that 4 men can carry her on their Sholders a mile or more without resting, and will carry four men and fiom 10 to 12 hundred pounds. The Cathlâmâhs left us this evening on their way to the Clatsops, to whome they perpose bartering their Wappato for the blubber & Oil of the whale, which the latter purchased for Beeds &ᶜ from the Kilámox; in this Manner there is a trade continually carried on by the nativs of the river each tradeing Some articles or other with their neighbours above and below them, and those articles which are Vended by the Whites at their enterance of this river, find their way to the most distant nations inhabiting its waters.

[Lewis:]   *Monday (Sunday) January 12ᵗʰ 1806*

The men who were sent in surch of the canoe returned without being able to find her, we therefore give her over as lost This morning sent out Drewyer and one man to hunt, they returned in the evening, Drewyer having killed seven Elk; I scarcely know how we should subsist were it not for the exertions of this excellent hunter. At 2 P M. the ballance of the party who had been left by Capᵗ C arrived; about the same time the two hunters [*also arrived*] who had been dispatched by Capt C for the purpose of hunting, [*on the 9ᵗʰ inst*] they had killed nothing We have heretofore usually divided the meat when first killed among the four messes into which we have divided our party leaving to each the care of preserving and the discretion of using it, but we find that they make such prodigal use of it when they hapen to have a tolerable stock on hand that we have determined to adapt a different system with our present stock of seven Elk; this is to jirk it & issue to them in small quantities

[Clark:]   *Sunday the 12ᵗʰ January 1806*

This morning Sent out Drewyer and one man to hunt, they returned in the evening Drewyer haveing killed 7 Elk; I scercely know how we Should Subsist, I beleive but badly if it was not for the exertions of this excellent hunter; maney

[339]

others also exert themselves, but not being accquainted with the best method of finding and killing the elk and no other wild animals is to be found in this quarter, they are unsucksessfull in their exertions.   at 2 P M. Serg˙ Gass and the men I left to assist the salt makers in carrying in their meat arrived also the hunters which I directed to hunt in the point, they killed nothing   We have heretofore devided the Meat when first killed among the four messes, into which we have divided our party, leaveing to each the care of preserving and distribution of useing it; but we find that they make such prodigal use of it when they happen to have a tolerable Stock on hand, that we are determined to adopt a Different System with our present stock of Seven Elk; this is to jurk it and issue it to them in Small quantities

[Lewis:]   *Tuesday (Monday) January 13ᵗʰ 1806*

This morning I took all the men who could be spared from the Fort and set out in quest of the flesh of the seven Elk that were killed yesterday,   we found it in good order being un- touched by the wolves, of which indeed there are but few in this country; at 1 P M. we returned having gotten all the meat to the fort.   this evening we exhausted the last of our candles, but fortunately had taken the precaution to bring with us moulds and wick, by means of which and some Elk's tallow in our possession we do not yet consider oursleves destitute of this necessary article; the Elk we have killed have a very small portion of tallow

The traders usually arrive in this quarter, as has been before observed, in the month of April, and remain untill October; when here they lay at anchor in a bay within Cape Disappoint- ment on the N side of the river;   here they are visited by the natives in their canoes who run along side and barter their comodities with them, their being no houses or fortification on shore for that purpose   the nations who repare thither are fi[r]st, those of the sea coast S E of the entrance of the river, who reside in the order in which their names are mentioned, begining at the entrance of the river (viz) The Clatsop, Killa-

muck, Ne-cost, Nat-ti, Nat-chies, Tarl-che, E-slitch, You-cone
and So-see   secondly those inhabiting the N.W. coast begining at the entrance of the river and mentioned in the same
order; the Chinnook and Chiltch the latter very numerous;
and thirdly the Cath-lâh-mah, and Skil-lutes, the latter numerous and inhabiting the river from a few miles above the
marshey Islands, where the Cuth-lâh-mâhs cease, to the grand
rappids.   These last may be esteemed the principal carryers or
intermediate traders betwen the whites and the Indians of the
sea Coast, and the E-ne-shurs, the E-chee-lutes, and the Chil-
luck-kit-te quaws, who inhabit the river above, to the grand falls
inclusive, and who prepare most of the pounded fish which is
brought to market[1]   The bay in which this trade is carryed
on is spacious and commodious, and perfectly secure from all
except the S and S E winds, these however are the most
prevalent and strong winds in the Winter season.   fresh water
and wood are very convenient and excellent timber for refiting
and reparing vessels. —

[Clark:]   *Monday 13ᵗʰ January* 1806

Capᵗ Lewis took all the men which could be speared from
the Fort and Set out in quest of the flesh of the Seven Elk
which were killed yesterday   they found the meat all Secure
untouched by the Wolves, of which indeed there are but fiew
in this countrey; at 1 P M the party returned with the 2ᵈ and
Last load of meat to the fort.   this evening we finished all
[the] last of our candles, we brought with us, but fortunately
had taken the precaution to bring with us moulds and wick,
by means of which and Some Elk tallow in our possession we
do not think our Selves distitute of this necessary article,   the
Elk which have been killed have a verry Small portion of
tallow   The Traders usially arrive in this quarter, in the

---

[1] In the Biddle text (ii, pp 116–120) is given an enumeration of the tribes, with
their population, located on the seacoast near the Columbia, on both sides of the
river   The explicit statement is made that "our personal observation has not
extended beyond the Killamucks;" and, at the close, that details of the characters
and customs of those tribes "must be left to future adventurers"   The tribes whom
they mention belong mainly to the Salishan, Chinookan, and Yakonan families — ED

month of april, and remain until october; when here they lay
at anchor in a Bay within Cape Disapointment on the N. side
of the river; here they are visited by the nativs in their Canoes
who run along Side and barter their comodities with them,
their being no houses or fortification on Shore for that purpose

The nations who repare thither ar[e] first those of the Sea
Coast S E. & N W of the enterance of the river, who reside
in the order in which their names are mentioned to the S E
the Clatsops, Kil á mox, and those to the N W the Chinnooks, and Chiltch; (*Ch on the coast to the N. W*) and Secondly the Cath-lâh-mâh, War-ki-a-cum, and Skil-lutes, the
latter noumerous and inhabiting (*the river Cowe lis kee*) those
last may be considered or [as] intermedeate traders between
the whites and nations on the Sea Coast, and the E-ne-churs,
the E-chee-lutes, and the Chil-luck-kit-te-quaws, who inhabit
the river up to the great falls inclusive, and who prepare most
of the pounded fish which is brought to Market

The Bay in which the trade is Carried on is Spacious and
Commodious, and perfectly Secure from all except the S &
S E. Winds and those blow but Seldom the most prevalent
& strong winds are from the S W. & N W in the Winter
Season   fish water and wood are very convenient and excel-
lent timber for refitting and repareing vessels.

[Lewis:]   *Wednesday (Tuesday) January 14ᵗʰ 1806*

This morning the Serg^t of the Guard reported the absence
of one of the large perogues, it had broken the chord by which
it was attatched and the tide had taken it off; we sent a party
immediately in surch of her, they returned in about 3 hours
having fortunately found her. we now directed three of the
perogues to be drawn up out of reach of the tide and the
fourth to be mored in the small branch just above the landing
and confined with a strong rope of Elk-skin. had we lost
this perogue also we should have been obliged to make three
small ones, which with the few tools we have now left would
be a serious undertaking. a fatiegue of 6 men employed in
jerking the Elk beaf.

From the best estimate we were able to make as we d[e]-scended the Columbia we conceived that the natives inhabiting that noble stream, for some miles above the great falls to the grand rappids inclusive annually prepare about 30,000 lb⁸ of pounded sammon for market   but whether this fish is an article of commerce with the whites or is exclusively sold to, and consumed by the natives of the sea Coast, we are at a loss to determine.   the first of those positions I am disposed to credit most, but, still I must confess that I cannot imagine what the white merchant's object can be in purchasing this fish, or where they dispose of it   and on the other hand the Indians in this neighbourhood as well as the Skillutes have an abundance of dryed sammon which they take in the creeks and inlets, and I have never seen any of this pounded fish in their lodges, which I presume would have been the case if they purchased this pounded fish for their own consumption.   the Indians who prepared this dryed and pounded fish, informed us that it was to trade with the whites, and shewed us many articles of European manufacture which they obtained for it it is true they obtain those articles principally for their fish but they trade with the Skillutes for them and not immediately with the whites; the intermediate merchants and carryers, the Skillutes, may possibly consume a part of this fish themselves and dispose of the ballance of it [to] the natives of the sea coast, and from them obtain such articles as they again trade with the whites.

[Clark:]   *Tuesday 14ᵗʰ January 1806*

This morning the Serjᵗ of the guard reported the absence of one of our canoes it had broken the cord by which it was at-tached and the tide had taken her off; We Sent a party im-ediately in Serch of her, they returned in about 3 hours haveing fortunately found her   We now derect that 3 of the [canoes] be drawed up out of reach of the tide and the 4ᵗʰ to be tied with a long Strong Cord of Elk Skins, ready for use. had we lost this large Canoe We Should have been obliged to make 3 other Small ones, which with the fiew tools we have now left would be a Serious undertakeing. a fatiege of six men employd in jurking the Elk beef   From the best estermate we were enabled to make as we decended the columbia we conceived that the nativs inhabiting that noble Stream (from the enterance of Lewis's iiver to the neighbourhood of the falls the nativs consume all the fish they Catch either for food or fuel) From Towarnehiooks River or a fiew mil[e]s above the Great falls to the grand rapids inclusive anually prepare about 30,000 lb⁸ of pounded fish (Chiefly Salmon) for Market, but whether this fish is an article of Commerce with their neighbours or is exclusively Sold to, and Consumed by the nativs of the sea coast, we are at a loss to determine the latter of those positions I am dispose[d] to credit most, as I cannot imagine what the white merchants obje[c]ts could be in purchaseing fish, or where they could dispose of it   on the other hand the Indians in this neighbourhood as well as the Skillutes and those above have an abundance of Dryed Salmon which they take in the creeks and inlets, they are excessively fond of the pounded fish haveing frequently asked us for Some of it   the Indians who prepared this pounded fish made signs that they traded it with people below them for Beeds and trinkets &ᶜ and Showed us maney articles of European Manufacture which they obtained for it; the Skillutes and Indians about the great rapids are the intermediate merchants and Carryers, and no doubt consume a part of this fish themselves and dispose of the ballance of it to the nativs of the Sea coast, and from this obtain Such articles as they again trade with the whites

The persons who usially visit the enterence of this river for the purpose of traffic or hunting, I believe is either English or Americans; the Indians inform us that they Speak the Same language with ourselves, and gave us proofs of their varacity by repeating maney words of English, *Sun of a pitch &ᶜ (heave the lead & maney blackguard phrasses)*. Whether those traders are from Nootka Sound, from Some other late establishment on this Coast, or imediately from the U. States or Great Brittain, I am at a loss to determine, nor can the Indians inform us   the Indians whome I have asked in what direction the

traders go when they depart from hence, allways point to the
S. W. from which it is prosumeable that Nootka cannot be
their distination; and from Indian information a Majority of
those traders annually visit them about the beginning of April
and remain Some time and either remain or revisit them in
the fall of which I cannot properly understand, from this
circumstance they canot come directly from the U States or
Great Brittain, the distance being to great for them to go and
return in the ballance of a year　I am Sometimes induced to
believe that there is Some other Establishment on the Coast
of America *South* of this place of which little is but yet
known to the world, or it may be perhaps on Some Island in
the Pacific Ocian between the Continant of America & Asia
to the S.W. of us　This traffic on the part of the whites consist in vending, guns, principally old British or American
Musquets, powder, balls and shote, brass tea kittles, Blankets
from two to three points, scarlet and blue Cloth (Coarse), plates
and Strips of Sheet Copper and brass, large brass wire Knives
Beeds & Tobacco with fishing hook buttons and Some other
Small articles; also a considerable quantity of Salors Clothes,
as hats, Coats, Trouse[r]s and Shirts. for those they receive
in return from the nativs Dressed and undressed Elk Skins,
Skins of the Sea otter, Common otter, beaver, common fox,
Speck, and [*Spotted or*] tiger Cat, also Some Salmon dried or
pounded and a kind of buisket, [*the native dispose of some of*
these biscuits not a great article of trade] which the nativs make
of roots called by them Shappelell　The nativs are extravi-
gantly fond of the most common cheap Blue and white beeds,
of moderate size, or Such that from 50 to 70 will way one
pennyweight, the blue is usially preferred to the white; those
beeds constitute the principal Circulating medium with all the
Indian tribes on the river; for those beeds they will dispose
of any article they possess. the beeds are Strung on Strans
of a fathom in length & in that manner Sold by the bre[d]th
[*arms length or double arms length*] or yard

[Lewis:]   *Thursday (Wednesday) January 15th 1806*

Had a large coat completed out of the skins of the Tiger
Cat and those also of a small animal about the size of a squirrel not known to me; these skins I procured from the Indians
who had previously dressed them and formed them into robes;
it took seven of these robes to complete the coat. we had
determined to send out two hunting parties today but it rained
so incessantly that we posponed it. no occurrence worthy of
relation took place today.

The implyments used by the Chinnooks Clatsops Cuthlah-
mahs &c in hunting are the gun the bow & arrow, deadfalls,
pitts, snares, and spears or gigs; their guns are usually of an
inferior quality being oald refuse American & brittish Musquits which have been repared for this trade. there are some
very good peices among them, but they are invariably in bad
order; they apear not to have been long enou[g]h accustomed
to fire arms to understand the management of them. they
have no rifles. Their guns and amunition they reserve for
the Elk, deer and bear, of the two last however there are but
few in their neighbourhood   they keep their powder in small
japaned tin flasks which they obtain with their amunition from
the traders; when they happen to have no ball or shot, they
substitute gravel or peices of potmettal, and are insensible of
the damage done thereby to their guns. The bow and arrow
is the most common instrument among them, every man being
furnished with them whether he has a gun or not; this instrument is employed indiscriminately in hunting every species of
anamal on which they subsist. Their bows are extreamly neat
and very elastic, they are about two and a half feet in length,
and two inches in width in the center, thence tapering graduly
to the extremities where they are half an inch wide   they are
very flat and thin, formed of the heart of the arbor-vita or
white cedar, the back of the bow being thickly covered with
sinews of the Elk laid on with a Gleue which they make from
the sturgeon; the string is made of sinues of the Elk also
the arrow is formed of two parts usually tho' sometimes entire;
those formed of two parts are unequally divided that part on
which the feathers are placed occupyes four fifths of it's length

and is formed of light white pine reather larger than a swan's quill, the lower extremity of this is a circular mortice secured by sinues roled around it; this mortice receives the one end of the 2nd part which is of a smaller size than the first and about five inches long, in the end of this the barb is fixed and confined with sinue, this barb is either stone, iron or copper, if metal in this form forming at it's point a greater angle than those of any other Indians I have observed, the shorter part of the arrow is of harder wood as are also the whole of the arrow when it is of one piece only as these people live in a country abounding in ponds lakes &c and frequently hunt in their canoes and shoot at fowl and other anamals where the arrow missing its object would be lost in the water they are constructed in the manner just discribed in order to make them float should they fall in the water, and consequently can again be recovered by the hunter; the quiver is usually the skin of a young bear or that of a wolf invariably open at the side in stead of the end as the quivers of other Indians generally are; this construction appears to answer better for the canoe than if they were open at the end only maney of the Elk we have killed since we have been here, have been wounded with these arrows, the short piece with the barb remaining in the animal and grown up in the flesh. the deadfalls and snares are employed in taking the wolf the raccoon and fox of which there are a few only. the spear or gig is used to take the sea otter, the common otter, spuck, and beaver. their gig consists of two points or barbs and are the same in their construction as those discribed before as being common among the Indians on the upper part of this river their pits are employed in taking the Elk, and of course are large and deep, some of them a cube of 12 or 14 feet these are usually placed by the side of a large fallen tree which as well as the pit lye across the roads frequented by the Elk these pitts are disguised with the slender boughs of trees and moss; the unwary Elk in passing the tree precipiates himself into the pitt which is sufficiently deep to prevent his escape, and is thus taken.

Capt Lewis had a large coat finished made of the Skins of
the tiger Cat, and those of the Small animal about the Size
of Small cat not known to me; those Skins were precured
from the Indians who had previously dressed them and formed
them into robes; it took Seven of those robes to Complete
the coat.   no occurrence worthey of remark took place.
rained hard all day.   The imployments used by the Chinnooks Clatsops, Cath-lah-mahs Kil-a-mox &^{c} in hunting are
the gun the bow & arrow, dead falls, Pitts, Snares, and Spears
or gigs;   their guns are usially of an inferior quallity being
old refuse american or brittish muskets which have been repared for this trade   there are Some verry good pieces among
them, but they are invariably in bad order   they appear not
to be long enough acquainted with fire arms to understand the
management of them.   They have no rifles.   Their guns and
amunition they reserve for the Elk, Deer, and Bear, of the
two last however there are but fiew in their neighbourhoods.
they keep their powder in Small japaned tin flasks which they
obtain with their amunition from the traders; when they
happen to have no Ball or Shot they Substitute Gravel and
are insenceable of the dammage done thereby to their Guns.

The Bow and arrow is the most common instrument among
them, every man being furnished with them whether he has a
gun or not, this instrement is imployed indiscreminately in
hunting every Species of animal on which they Subsist,   Their
bows are extreemly meet [neat] and very elastic, they are about
two feet six inches long and two inches wide in the Center,
thence tapering gradually to the extremities, where they ar $\frac{3}{4}$
of an Inch wide,   they are very flat and thin, formed of the
heart of the arbor vita or white cedar, the back of the Bow
being thickly covered with Sinues of the Elk laid on with a
Gleue which they make from the Sturgeon; the String is made
of the Sinues of the Elk also,   the arrow is formed of two parts
usually tho' Sometimes entire; those formed of 2 parts are
uneaquilly devided, the part on which the feathers are placed
occupie $^4/_5$ of it's length and is formed of light white pine rather
larger than a Swans quill, in the lower extremity of this is a

circular mortice Secured by sinues raped around it; this mortice
rec[e]ives the one end of the 2ᵈ part which is of Smaller Size
than the first and about five inches long, in the end of this the
barb is fixed and Confined with Sinues, the berb is either Iron
Copper or Stone — in this form   forming at its point a greater angle than
those of any other Indians I   have
observed.   The Shorter part of the arrow is of harder wood,
as are also the whole of the arrow where it is of one piece only.
as these people live in a Countrey abounding in Ponds lakes
&c. and frequently hunt in their Canoes and Shoot at fowls
and other animals where the arrow missing its object would be
lost in the water they are constructed in the Manner just
discribed in order to make them flote Should they fall in the
water, and consequently can again be recovered by the hunter;
the quiver is useally the Skin of a young bear or that of a wolf
invariably open at the Side in Sted of the end, as the quiver
of other Indians generally are,   this Construction appears to
answer better for the Canoe, than if they were open at the end
only.   maney of the Elk which our hunters have killᵈ Sence
we have been here have been wounded with those arrows, the
Short piece with the barbe remaining in the Animal and grown
up in the flesh.   the Deadfalls & snares are employd in takeing the Wolf, the racoon and fox of which there are a fiew.
the Spear or gig is used to take the Sea otter, [or] *Spuck*,
[*Ind. name*] & Beaver   The gig consists of two points or birbs
and are the Same in their construction as those which are
common among the Indians on the upper part of this river and
before discribed   Their pitt are employed in takeing the Elk,
and of Course are large and Deep, Some of them a Cube of
12 or 14 feet, those ar commonly placed by the Side of a
large fallen tree which as well as the pitt lie across the roads
frequented by the Elk,   these pitts are disguised with the
Slender bows of trees & moss: the unwarry Elk in passing
the tree precipates himself into the pitt which is Sufficiently
deep to prevent his escape.

[Lewis:]   *Friday (Thursday) January 16ᵗʰ 1806*

This evening we finished curing the meat   no occurrence worthy of relation took place today   we have plenty of Elk beef for the present and a little salt, our houses dry and comfortable, and having made up our minds to remain until the 1ˢᵗ of April, every one appears content with his situation and his fare.   it is true that we could even travel now on our return as far as the timbered country reaches, or to the falls of the river ; but further it would be madness for us to attempt to proceede untill April, as the indians inform us that the snows lye knee deep in the plains of Columbia during the winter, and in these plains we could scarcely get as much fuel of any kind as would cook our provision as we descended the river; and even were we happyly over these plains and again in the woody country at the foot of the Rocky Mountains we could not possibly pass that immence barrier of mountains on which the snows ly in winter to the debth in many places of 20 feet ;   in short the Indians inform us that they are impracticable untill about the 1ˢᵗ of June, at which time even there is an abundance of snow but a scanty subsistence may be obtained for the horses. we should not therefore forward ourselves on our homeward journey by reaching the rocky mountains. early than the 1ˢᵗ of June, which we can easily effect by seting out from hence on the 1ˢᵗ of April.

The Clatsops Chinnooks &c in fishing employ the common streight net, the scooping or diping net with a long handle, the gig, and the hook and line   the common net is of different lengths and debths usually employed in taking the sammon, Carr [cherr] and trout in the inlets among the marshey grounds and the mouths of deep creeks   the skiming or [s]cooping net to take small fish in the spring and summer season ; the gig and hook are employed indiscriminately at all seasons in taking such fish as they can procure by their means   their nets and fishing lines are made of the silk-grass or white cedar bark ; and their hooks are generally of European manufactory, tho' before the whites visited them they   made hooks of bone and other substances   formed in the following manner A C, and   C.B are two small pieces of bone about the size of a strong twine, these are flattened and leveled off of their extremities near C. where they are firmly attatched together with sinues and covered with rosin   CA. is reduced to a sharp point at A where it is also bent in a little; C B. is attatched to the line, for about half it's length at the upper extremity B the whole forming two sides of an accute angled triangle.

[Clark:]   *Saturday [Thursday] 16th January 1806*

This evening we finished cureing the meat   no occurrence worthey of relation took place to day   we have a plenty of Elk beef for the present and a little salt, our houses dry and comfortable,   haveing made up our minds to Stay untill the 1st of April every one appears contented with his Situation, and his fare   it is true we could travel even now on our return as far as the timbered Country reaches, or to the falls of the river, but further it would be madness for us to attempt to proceed untill april, as the indians inform us that the Snows lyes Knee deep in the Columbian Plains dureing the winter, and in those planes we could not git as much wood as would cook our provisions untill the drift wood comes down in the Spring and lodges on the Shore &c   and even were we happily over those plains and in the woodey Countrey at the foot of the *rockey Mountains*, we could not possibly pass that emence bearier of Mountains on which the snow lyes in winter to the debth in maney plac[e]s of 20 feet;   in Short the Indians tell us they [are] impassable untill about the 1st of June, at which time even then is an abundance of snow but a Scanty Subsistance may be had for the horses.   We Should [not] fo[r]ward our homeward journey any by reaching the Rocky Mountains earlier than the 1st of June which we can effect by Setting out from hence by the 1st of April

The Clatsops, Chinnooks &c. in fishing employ the common Streight net, the scooping or dipping net with a long handle, the gig, and the hook and line   the common nets are of different lengths and debths usually employd in takeing the Salmon, Carr and trout in the inlets among the marshey

[351]

grounds and the mouths of deep Creeks, the Skiming or [s]cooping nets to take Smaller fish in the Spring and Summer Season; the gig and hook are employed indiscreminately at all Seasons in takeing Such fish as they can precure by these means. their nets and fishing lines are made of the Silk Grass or White Cedar bark; and their hooks are generally of European Manufactory, tho' before the whites visited them they made their Hooks of bone and other Substances formed in the following Manner   AC and BC are two Small pieces of bone about the Size of a Strong twine, these   are flattened & beaveled off to their extremites at C. where they are firmley attached together and Covered with rozin   CA is reduced to a Sharp point at A where it is also bent in a little; CB is attached to the line, at the upper extremity B. the whole forming two Sides of an accute angled triangle.   the [line] has a loop at D [by] which it is anexed to a longer line and taken off at pleasure Those Hooks are yet common among' the nativs on the upper parts of the Columbia river for to Catch fish in Deep places.

[Lewis:]   *Saturday (Friday) January 17th 1806*

This morning we were visited by Comowool and 7 of the Clatsops our nearest neighbours, who left us again in the evening   They brought with them some roots and buries for sale, of which however they disposed of but very few as they asked for them such prices as our stock in trade would not license us in giving   the Chief Comowool gave us some roots and buries for which we gave him in return a mockerson awl and some thread; the latter he wished for the purpose of making a skiming net   one of the party was dressed in t[h]ree very eligant Sea Otter skins which we much wanted; for these we offered him many articles but he would not dispose of them for any other consideration but blue beads, of these we had only six fathoms left, which being 4 less than his price for each skin he would not exchange nor would a knife or an equivalent in beads of any other colour answer his purposes, these coarse blue beads are their f[av]orite merchandize, and are called by them *tia Commáshuck'* or Chiefs beads. the best wampum is not so much esteemed by them as the most inferior beads. Sent Coalter out to hunt this morning, he shortly after returned with a deer, venison is a rarity with us we have had none for some weeks. Drewyer also set out on a hunting excertion and took one man with him. he intends both to hunt the Elk and trap the beaver.

The Culinary articles of the Indians in our neighbourhood consist of wooden bowls or throughs, baskets, wooden spoons and woden scures or spits. Their wooden bowls and troughs are of different forms and sizes, and most generally dug out of a solid piece; they are ither round or semi-globular, in the form of a canoe, cubic, and cubic at top terminating in a globe at bottom; these are extreemly well executed and many of them neatly carved, the larger vessels with hand-holes to them; in these vessels they boil their fish or flesh by means of hot stones which they immerce in the water with the article to be boiled. they also render the oil of fish or other anamals in the same manner. their baskets are formed of cedar bark and beargrass so closely interwoven with the fingers that they are watertight without the aid of gum or rosin; some of these are highly ornamented with strans of beargrass which they dye of several colours and interweave in a great variety of figures; this serves them the double perpuse of holding their water or wearing on their heads; and are of different capacities from that of the smallest cup to five or six gallons; they are generally of a conic form or reather the segment of a cone of which the smaller end forms the base or bottom of the basket. these they make very expediciously and dispose off for a mear trifle. it is for the construction of these baskets that the beargrass becomes an article of traffic among the natives this grass grows only on their high mountains near the snowey region; the blade is about ⅜ of an inch wide and 2 feet long, smoth pliant and strong; the young blades which are white from not being exposed to the sun or air, are those most commonly employed, particularly in their neatest work Their spoons are not remarkable nor abundant, they are generally large and the bole brawd. their meat is roasted with a sharp scure, one end of which is incerted in the meale with the other is set erect in the ground   the spit for roasting fish has it's upper extremity split, and between it's limbs the center of the fish is inscerted with it's head downwards and the tale and extremities of the scure secured with a string,   the sides of the fish, which was in the first instance split on the back, are expanded by means of small splinters of wood which extend crosswise the fish   a small mat of rushes or flags is the usual plate or dish on which their fish, flesh, roots or burries are served   they make a number of bags and baskets not watertight of cedar bark, silk-grass, rushes, flags and common coarse sedge.   in these they secure their dryed fish, roots, buries. &c.

[Clark:]   *Sunday [Friday] 17ᵗʰ January 1806*

This morning we were visited by Comowool and 7 of the Clatsops our nearest neighbours, who left us again in the evening   They brought with them Some roots and beries for Sale, of which however they disposed of very fiew as they asked for them Such prices as our Stock in trade would not licence us in giveing   The chief Comowool gave us some roots and berries, for which we gave him in return a Mockerson awl and some thread ; the latter he wished for the purpose of makeing a Skiming net   one of the party was dressed in three verry elegant Sea otter Skins which we much wanted ; for these we offered him maney articles but he would not dispose of them for aney other Consideration but Blue beeds, of those we had only Six fathoms left, which being 4 less than his price for each Skin he would not exchange nor would a Knife or any other equivalent in beeds of aney other Colour answer his purpose,   these Coarse blue beeds are their favourite Merchandize and are Called by them *Tia com ma shuck* or chief beeds,   the best Wampom is not as much esteemed by them as the most indifferent beeds.   Sent Colter out to hunt he Shortly after returned with a Deer, Venison is a rarity with us we have had none for Some weeks.   Drewyer Set out on a hunting expedition one man went with him.   he intends to hunt the Elk and trap the beaver.

The Culinary articles of the Indians in our neighbourhood consists of wooden bowls or troughs, Baskets, Shell and wooden Spoons and wooden Scures or Spits, their wooden Bowles and troughs are of different forms and Sizes, and most generally dug out of Solid piecies; they are either round, Square or in the form of a canoe; those are extreemly well executed and maney of them neetly covered, the larger vessels with hand-holes to them; in these vessels they boil their fish or flesh by means of hot Stones which they immerce in the water with the articles to be boiled. They also render the Oil of the fish, or other animals in the same manner. Their baskets are formed of Cedar bark and bargrass So closely interwoven withe hands or fingers that they are watertight without the aid of gum or rozin; Some of those are highly orniminted with the Strans of bargrass which they dye of Several Colours and interweave in a great variety of figures; this Serves a double purpose of holding the Water or wareing on their heads; and are of different capacities, from that of a Smallest cup to five or Six gallons, they are generally of a Conic form or reather the Segment of a Cone of which the Smaller end forms the base or bottom of the basket. these they make verry expediciously and dispose of for a mear trifle it is for the construction of those baskets that Bargrass becoms an article of traffic among the nativs of the Columbia this grass grows only on their mountains near the Snowey region; the blade is about $\frac{3}{8}$ of an inch wide and 2 feet long Smothe plient and strong; the young blades which are white from not being exposed to the Sun or air, are those which are most Commonly employ'd, particularly in their neatest work. Their wooden Spoons are not remarkable nor abundant, they are large & the bowls broad. their meat is roasted with a Sharp Scure, one end of which is incerted in the meat while' the other is Set erect in the ground The Spit for roasting fish has its upper extremity Split, and between its limbs the Center of the fish is incerted with its head downwards, and the tale and the extremities of the Scure Secured with a String, the Side[s] of the fish, which was in the first instance Split in the back, are expanded by means of Small Splinters of wood which extend Crosswise the fish. a Small

mat of rushes or flags is the usual plate, or Dish on which
their fish, flesh, roots & berries are served. they make a
number of Bags and Baskets not water tight of Cedar bark
Silk Grass, rushes, flags, and common corse Sedge. in those
they Secure their dried fish, roots berries &c

[Lewis:]   *Sunday (Saturday) January 18th. 1806*

Two of the Clatsops who were here yesterday returned today
for a dog they had left; they remained with us a few hours and
departed   no further occurrence worthy of relation took place.
the men are still much engaged in dressing skins in order to
cloath themselves and prepare for our homeward journey.
The Clatsops Chinnooks &c construct their houses of timber
altogether   they are from 14 to 20 feet wide and from 20 to
60 feet in length, and acommodate one or more families sometimes three or four families reside in the same room. thes[e]
houses a[re] also divided by a partition of boards, but this
happens only in the largest houses as the rooms are always
large compared with the number of inhabitants   these houses
are constructed in the following manner; two or more posts
of split timber agreeably to the number of divisions or partitions are furst provided, these are sunk in the ground at one
end and rise perpendicularly to the hight of 14 or 18 feet, the
tops of them are hollowed in such manner as to receive the
ends of a round beam of timber which reaches from one to
the other, most commonly the whole length of the building,
and forming the upper part of the roof; two other sets of
posts and poles are now placed at proper distances on either
side of the first, formed in a similar manner and parrallel to it;
these last rise to the intended hight of the eves, which is usually
about 5 feet   smaller sticks of timber are now provided and
are placed by pares in the form of rafters, resting on, and
reaching from the lower to the upper horizontal beam, to both
of which they are attatched at either end with the cedar bark;
two or three ranges of small poles are now placed horizontally
on these rafters on each side of the roof and are secured likewise with strings of the Cedar bark. the ends sides and par-

titions are then formed with one range of wide boards of ab[o]ut two inches thick, which are sunk in the ground a small distance at their lower ends and stand erect with their upper ends laping on the outside of the eve poles and end rafters to which they are secured by an outer pole lying parallel with the eve poles and rafters being secured to them by chords of cedar bark which pass through wholes made in the boards at certain distances for that purpose; the rough [roof] is then covered with a double range of thin boards, and an aperture of 2 by 3 feet is left in the center of the roof to permit the smoke to pass. these houses are sometimes sunk to the debth of 4 or 5 feet in which cace the eve of the house comes nearly to the surface of the earth. in the center of each room a space of six by eight feet square is sunk about twelve inches lower than the floor having it's sides secured with four sticks of squar timber, in this space they make their fire, their fuel being generally pine bark. mats are spread arround the fire on all sides, on these they set in the day and frequently sleep at night. on the inner side of the ho[u]se on two sides and sometimes on three, there is a range of upright peices about 4 feet removed from the wall; these are also sunk in the ground at their lower ends, and secured at top to the rafters, from these other peices ar extended horizontally to the wall and are secured in the usual method by bark to the upright peices which support the eve poles on these short horizontal pieces of which there are sometimes two ranges one above the other, boards are laid, which either form ther beads, or shelves on which to put their goods and chattles of almost every discription. their uncured fish is hung on sticks in the smoke of their fires as is also the flesh of the Elk when they happen to be fortunate enough to procure it which is but seldom.

[Clark:]   *Monday [Saturday]* 18th *January* 1806

Two of the Clatsops that were here yesterday returned to day for a Dog they had left; they remained with us a fiew hours and departed. no further accounts worthey of relation took place the men are much engaged dressing Skins in order to Cloath themselves and prepare for the homeward journey

The Clatsops Chinnooks &c construct their *Houses* of timber altogether. they are from 14 to 20 feet wide, and from 20 to 60 feet in length, and accomodate one or more families   sometimes three or four families reside in the Same room. this house is also devided by petitions of Boards, but this happens only in the largest houses, as the rooms are always large compared with the number of inhabitents. those houses are constructed in the following manner; two or more posts of Split timber agreeably to the number of devisions or partitions are fiist provided,   these are Sunk in the ground at one end and raised pirpindicular to the hight of 12 or 14 feet,   the top of them are hollowed So as to recive the end of a round beem of timber which reaches from one to the other or the entire length of the house; and forming the ridge pole;   two other Sets of posts and poles are then placed at proper distancies on either Side of the first, formed in a Similar manner and parrelal to it; those last rise to the intended hight of the eves, which is usially about 5 feet,   Smaller Sticks of timber is then previded and are placed by pears in the form of rafters, resting on, and reaching from the lower to the upper horizontial beam, to both of which they are atached at either end with the Cedar bark; two or 3 ranges of Small poles are then placed Horizontially on these rafters on each Side of the roof & are Secured likewise with Cedar bark   the ends, sides, and partitions are then formed, with one range of wide boards of about 2 inches thick, which are Sunk in the ground a Small distance at their lower ends & stands erect with their upper ends lapping on the out side of the eve poles and end rafters to which they are secured by a outerpole lyeing parrelal with the eve pole and rafters being Secured to them by cords of Cedar baik which pass through wholes made in the bods at certain distances for that purpose;   the rough [roof] is then Covered with a double range of thin boards, and an aperture of 2 by 3 feet left in the center of the roof to admit the Smoke to pass   These houses are commonly Sunk to the debth of 4 or 5 feet in which case the eve of the house comes nearly to the surface of the earth.   in the center of each room a Space of from 6 by 8 feet is Sunk about 12 inches lower than the floar haveing its Sides Secured by four thick boards or Squar pieces of timber,   in this Space they make their fire, their fuel being generally dry pine Split Small which they perform with a peice of an Elks horn Sharpened at one end diove into the wood with a Stone   Mats are Spred around the fire on all Sides, on these they Sit in the day and frequently Sleep at night   on the inner Side of the house on two Sides and Some-times on three, there is a range of upright pieces about 4 feet removed from the wall; these are also Sunk in the ground a[t] their lower end, and Secured at top to the rafters, from those, other pieces are extended horozontially to the wall and are Secured in the usial manner with bark to the upright pieces which Support the eve pole   on these Short horizon-tial peic[e]s of which there are Sometimes two ranges one above the other, boards are laid, which either form their beads, or Shelves on which to put their goods and Chattles, of almost every discription   their uncured fish is hung on Sticks in the Smoke of their fires as is also the flesh of the Elk when they happen to be fortunate enough to precure it which is but seldom

[Lewis:]   *Monday (Sunday) January 19ᵗʰ 1806*

   This morning sent out two parties of hunters, consisting of Collins and Willard whom we sent down the bay towards point Adams, and Labuish and Shannon whom we sent up Fort River;[1] the fi[r]st by land and the latter by water   we were visited today by two Clatsop men and a woman who brought for sale some Sea Otter skins of which we purchased one, giv-ing in exchange the remainder of our blue beads consisting of 6 fathoms and about the same quantity of small white beads and a knife.   we also purchased a small quantity of train oil for a pair of Brass armbands and a hat for some fishinghooks.   these hats are of their own manufactory and are composed of Cedar bark and bear grass interwoven with the fingers and ornimented

---

1 The Netul, or Lewis and Clark River — ED

with various colours and figures,   they are nearly waterproof, light, and I am convinced are much more durable than either chip or straw.   These hats form a small article of traffic with the Clatsops and Chinnooks who dispose of them to the whites.   the form of the hat is that which was in vogue in the U^{ed} States and great Britain in the years 1800 & 1801 with a high crown reather larger at the top than where it joins the brim ; the brim narrow or about 2 or 2½ inches.

Several families of these people usually reside together in the same room ; they appear to be the father & mother and their sons with their son's wives and children ; their provision seems to be in common and the greatest harmoney appears to exist among them.   The old man is not always rispected as the head of the family, that duty most commonly devolves on one of the young men   They have seldom more than one wife, yet the plurality of wives is not denied them by their customs These families when asociated form nations or bands of nations each acknowledging the authority of it's own chieftain who dose not appear to be heriditary, nor his power to extend further than a mear repremand for any improper act of an individual ;   the creation of a chief depends upon the upright deportment of the individual & his ability and disposition to render service to the community ; and his authority or the deference paid him is in exact equilibrio with the popularity or voluntary esteem he has acquired among the individuals of his band or nation.   Their laws like those of all uncivilized Indians consist of a set of customs which have grown out of their local situations.   not being able to speak their language we have not been able to inform ourselves of the existence of any peculiar customs among them,

[Clark:]   *Tuesday* [Sunday] 19th *of January* 1806

This morning Sent out two parties of hunters, one party towards Point adams and the other party up *Ne tel* River by water. We were visited to day by two Clatsop men and a woman who brought for Sale Some Sea Otter Skins of which we purchased one gave in exchange the remainder of our blue beeds Consisting of 6 fathoms, and the same quantity of small white beids and a knife.   we also purchased a Small quantity of train oil for a par of Brass arm bands, and a hat for Some fishinghooks   these hats are of their own manufactory and are composed of Cedar bark and bear grass interwoven with the fingers and ornimented with various colours and figures,   they are nearly water proof, light, and I am Convinced are much more dureable than either Chip or Straw,   These hats form a article of traffic with Clatsops an[d] Chinnooks who dispose of them to the Whites,   the form of the Hats is that which was in voge in the UStates and Great Britain in 1800 & 1801 with a high crown rather larger at the top than where it joins the brim, the brim narrow about 2 or 2½ inches.

Several families of those people usially reside together in the Same room; they appear to be the father mother with their Sons and their Sons wives and children; their provisions appears to be in common and the greatest harmoney appears to exist among them   the old man is not always respected as the head of the family that duty generally devolves on one of the young men   They have seldom more than one wife, yet plurality of wives are not denyed them by their Customs. those families when associated [form] bands of nations each acknowledgeing the authority of its own chieftains, who does not appear to be herititary, or has power to extend further than a mear repremand for any improper deportment of the indevidual;   the creation of a chief depends upon the upright conduct of the individual his abiltity and disposition to render Service to the comunity, and his authority and the defference paid him is in extent equilibrio with the popolarity or volintary esteem he has acquired among the individuals of his bands, or nation   Their Laws like all uncivilized Indians consist of a Set of customs which has grown out of their local Situations

Not being able to Speak their language we have not been able to inform ourselves of the existance of any peculiar customs among them.

[Lewis:]   *Tuesday (Monday) January 20th 1806*

Visited this morning by three Clatsops who remained with us all day ; the object of their visit is mearly to smoke the pipe on the morning of the eighteenth we issued 6 lb⁵ of jirked Elk p⁵ man, this evening the Serg⁵ reported that it was all exhausted; the six lb⁵ have therefore lasted two days and a half only   at this rate our seven Elk will last us only 3 days longer, yet no one seems much concerned about the state of the stores ; so much for habit.   we have latterly so frequently had our stock of provisions reduced to a minimum and sometimes taken a small touch of fasting that three days full allowance excites no concern.   In those cases our skill as hunters afford us some consolation, for if there is any game of any discription in our neighbourhood we can track it up and kill it   most of the party have become very expert with the rifle   The Indians who visited us today understood us sufficiently to inform us that the whites did not barter for the pounded fish ; that it was purchased and consumed by the Clatsops, Chinnooks, Cathlahmahs and Skillutes.   The native roots which furnish a considerable proportion of the subsistence of the indians in our neighbourhood are those of a species of Thistle, fern, and rush ; the Liquorice, and a small celindric root the top of which I have not yet seen, this last resembles the sweet pittatoe very much in it's flavor and consistency

[Clark:]   *Wednesday [Monday] 20th January 1806*

Visited this morning by three Clapsots who remained with us all day ; the object of their visit is mearly to Smoke the pipe on the morning of the 18 ins⁵ we issued 6⁵ of jurked Meat p⁵ man, this evening the Serj⁵ reports that is all exhosted ; the 6⁵ have therefore lasted 2 days and a half only   at this rate our Seven Elk will only last us 3 days longer, yet no one appears much concerned about the State of the Stores ; So much for habet   we have latterly so frequently had our Stock of provisions reduced to a Minimum and Sometimes taken a Small tuch of fasting that 3 days full allowance exites no concern   In those cases our Skill as hunters affords us some consolation, for if there is any game of any discription in our neighbourhood we can track it up and kill it.   Most of the party have become very expert with the rifle.   The Indians who visit us to day understood us sufficiently to inform us that the white[s] who visit them did not barter for the pounded fish ; that it was purchased and consumed by the Clatsops, Chinnooks, Cath lâh mâhs and Skil lutes, and Kil a mox.

The native roots which furnish a considerable proportion of the Subsistance of the indians in our neighbourhood are those of a Species of Thistle, fern, and rush ; the Licquorice, and a Small celindric root the top of which I have not yet Seen, this last resembles the Sweet potato verry Much in its flavour and Consistency.

END OF VOL. III

The Original Journals of the Lewis and Clark Expedition

8 Volume Set: Tradepaper ISBN: 158218-651-0   Hardcover ISBN: 1-58218-660-X

Individual Titles:

Volume I Parts 1 & 2
Tradepaper ISBN: 1-58218-652-9   Hardcover ISBN: 1-58218-661-8
Part 1 - Journals and Orderly Book of Lewis and Clark, from River Dubois to the Vermilion River Jan. 30, 1804 - Aug. 24, 1804.
Part 2 - Journals and Order Book of Lewis and Clark, from the Vermilion River to Two-Thousand-Mile Creek Aug. 25, 1804 - May 5, 1805.

Volume II Parts 1 & 2
Tradepaper ISBN: 1-58218-653-7   Hardcover ISBN: 1-58218-662-6
Part 1 - Journals and Orderly Book of Lewis and Clark, from Two -Thousand-Mile Creek to the Great Falls of the Missouri May 6 - June 20, 1805.
Part 2 - Journals and Orderly Book of Lewis and Clark, from the Great Falls of the Missouri to the Shoshoni Camp on Lembi River June 21 - August 20, 1805.

Volume III Parts 1 & 2
Tradepaper ISBN: 1-58218-654-5   Hardcover ISBN: 1-58218-663-4
Part 1 - Journals and Orderly Book of Lewis and Clark, from the Shoshoni Camp on Lembi River to the Encampment on the Columbia River near the Mouth of the Umatilla River.
August 21, 1805 - October 20, 1805.
Part 2 - Journals and Orderly Book of Lewis and Clark, from the Encampment on the Columbia River near the Mouth of the Umatilla River to Fort Clatsop October 21, 1805 - January 20, 1806.

Volume IV Parts 1 & 2
Tradepaper ISBN: 1-58218-655-3   Hardcover ISBN: 1-58218-664-2
Part 1 - Journals and Orderly Book of Lewis and Clark, from Fort Clatsop (preparation for the start home) to Fort Clatsop, January 21 - May 17, 1806.
Part 2 - Journals and Orderly Book of Lewis and Clark, from Fort Clatsop (preparation for the start home) to Musquetoe Creek March 18 - May 7, 1806.

Volume V Parts 1 & 2
Tradepaper ISBN 1-58218-656-1   Hardcover ISBN: 1-58218-665-0
Part 1 - Journals of Lewis and Clark, from Musquetoe Creek to Travellers Rest.
May 8 - July 2, 1806.
Part 2 - Journals of Lewis and Clark, from Travellers Rest to St. Louis.
July 3 - September 26, 1806.

Volume VI Parts 1 & 2
Tradepaper ISBN: 1-58218-657-X   Hardcover ISBN: 1-58218-666-9
Part 1 - Scientific Data accompanying the Journals of Lewis and Clark; Geography, Ethnology, Zoology.
Part 2 - Botany, Mineralogy, Meteorology, Astronomy, and Miscellaneous Memoranda.

Volume VII Parts 1 & 2
Tradepaper ISBN: 1-58218-658-8   Hardcover ISBN: 1-58218-667-7
Part 1 - Journals of Charles Floyd and Joseph Whitehouse; Appendix.
Part 2 - Appendix; Index.

Atlas -Tradepaper ISBN: 1-58218-659-6   Hardcover ISBN: 1-58218-668-5

Printed in the United States
19651LVS00002B/355-360